CLOSE CONNECTIONS

Caroline Gordon at Benfolly. *(Ward Dorrance)*

CLOSE CONNECTIONS

CAROLINE GORDON AND THE SOUTHERN RENAISSANCE

BY ANN WALDRON

THE UNIVERSITY OF TENNESSEE PRESS

KNOXVILLE

First published in paperback in 1989
by The University of Tennessee Press
Knoxville, Tennessee 37996-0325

The paper in this book meets the minimum requirements
of the American National Standard for Permanence of Paper
for Printed Library Materials.
∞
The binding materials have been chosen for strength
and durability.

Library of Congress Cataloging in Publication Data

Waldron, Ann.
    Close connections : Caroline Gordon and the Southern
renaissance / by Ann Waldron.
        p.   cm.
    Bibliography: p.
    Includes index.
    ISBN 0-87049-594-1 (pbk. : alk. paper)
    1. Gordon, Caroline, 1895–1981—Biography.   2. Novelists,
American—20th century—Biography.   3. Southern States—
Intellectual life—1865– 4. Authors, American—Southern States
—Biography.   5. Southern States—Biography.   I. Title.
PS3513.O5765Z97 1987b
813′.52—dc 19
[B]   88-20706   CIP

To John Luskin

CONTENTS

Contents

No themes are so human as those that reflect for us, out of the confusion of life, the close connexion of bliss and bale, of the things that help with the things that hurt, so dangling before us for ever that bright hard medal, of so strange an alloy, one face of which is somebody's right and ease and the other somebody's pain and wrong.

—HENRY JAMES,
Preface, *What Maisie Knew*

CLOSE CONNECTIONS

1

Benfolly, the Summer of 1937

When Caroline Gordon and Allen Tate drove up to Benfolly on April 25, 1937, after a two-year absence, their hill overlooking the Cumberland River in Tennessee was greener than Caroline had ever seen it. She did not have time, however, to admire the flourishing grass, the blossoming wisteria and locust, or the pale blue iris. She had to get Benfolly—"the most inconvenient of all houses," with its white columns, high ceilings, three stories, basement kitchen, fireplaces in every room, and all the space in the wrong places—ready for the arrival on May 1 of Ford Madox Ford and his wife, Janice Biala, and Janice's sister-in-law, Wally Tworkov, who were coming to spend the summer.

Ford had been half in love with Caroline when she had worked as his secretary in New York ten years before. He had helped her write her first novel and then, reviewing it, had placed her among the best writers in America. Allen was not as fond of Ford as Caroline was, but he tolerated him for Caroline's sake, and some people said he encouraged Ford's attentions to Caroline, hoping for a clear field for himself and his flirtations with other women. Nobody in the world except Allen would ever dream that Caroline would succumb to advances from Ford or anybody else; Caroline was a relentlessly chaste wife—and a jealous one.

She was forty-one years old that summer of 1937, small and slight with black eyes and one eyebrow higher than the other. She had a sharp wit and a quick temper that could flare suddenly and implacably. She did not, as the local phrase went, "fix herself up much," and that summer she wound her long dark hair in a braid around her head and usually wore whatever came to hand, mostly dresses she had made herself. She had two obsessions: the writing of fiction and Allen Tate, and these consumed her, pushing her own appearance far down on her list of priorities. Allen, four years younger than Caroline, was described invariably as "charming" and "courtly." He had a large head—someone called it a bombé forehead—on a small frame, but any oddity in his appearance was more than compensated for by this charm. He was called "brilliant" almost as frequently as he was called charming, and he was in 1937 the best known of the Fugitives, the Southern poets who had come together at Vanderbilt University fifteen years before. In fact, T. S. Eliot had pronounced Allen and Phelps Putnam the best poets in America. Caroline and Allen were very much a part of that amorphous literary phenomenon, the Southern renaissance that began in 1929 with the publication of Thomas Wolfe's *Look Homeward, Angel* and William Faulkner's *The Sound and the Fury* and lasted until about 1955.

Caroline's problems of household management at the moment were enormous. That summer each adult would need not only a place to sleep but a place to work. Caroline's third novel, *None Shall Look Back*, had been published earlier that year and she was trying to finish another, *The Garden of Adonis*, which Scribner's wanted for fall publication. Allen, poet, critic, and biographer, was a third of the way through his first and only novel, *The Fathers*. Ford would be writing his history of world literature, and Janice, a painter, would require a studio. Wally Tworkov, who was to act as Ford's secretary, would need a place to type. (Janice had been born Janice Tworkov, but she adopted the name Biala from her native town in Poland. Her brother, Jack Tworkov, was a painter in New York.)

And then there was Nancy. From the time she was born, the Tates' eleven-year-old daughter had spent a great deal of her life with Caroline's mother and had just passed a year in Chattanooga with Pidie, Caroline's Aunt Margaret Campbell, while her parents lived with Andrew Lytle in his family's summer home, a log cabin at Monteagle, Tennessee, near Sewanee. Nancy was tired of being farmed out with relatives and furthermore she wanted a room of her own. Caroline had promised her "in a moment of maternal abandon" that she could have her own room "even if Mr. Ford and Janice came," but that was before she found out about Janice's sister-in-law. Well, thought

Caroline, as she bustled about Benfolly, the sister-in-law would have to share a room with Nancy after all—Nancy would like having Wally for a roommate. "She loves to hang around grown up ladies," Caroline wrote Janice. "I'm sorry we can't offer Wally more private quarters but Nancy is a very good inoffensive child and won't be much bother."

Then Nancy wrote her mother to say she hoped the Fords wouldn't stay long because she knew she couldn't have company while they were there, and there was a little girl she wanted to have visit her. "You will like her," Nancy wrote. "Her mama is a clubwoman, but she liked your book better than *Gone With the Wind.*" Caroline, touched, promised Nancy she could have her company, "Fords or no Fords."

But now where would the sister-in-law stay? wondered Caroline. Well, Benfolly was elastic. She would put Ford and Janice in the bedroom on the middle floor and she and Allen could sleep on the top floor. Nancy's room was on the top floor too. Caroline could turn the parlor over to either Ford or Janice for work and the dining room to the other, and she could work in the garage—Andrew Lytle always worked *en plein air.* Or should Janice have the garage for a studio? No, the light wasn't right. There wasn't a decent north light in the place, as a matter of fact. The dining room would probably be a better room for Janice than the parlor but she and Ford could decide that between themselves. Caroline had used both of these rooms for a study and found them really quite private in the summertime since nobody ever went in the parlor but gathered on the upper gallery. The main thing seemed to be to provide everyone with good working quarters. The bedrooms wouldn't be luxurious, but they would be better than a New York apartment.

She had told the Fords they could stay two months and promised them "very indifferent cuisine, fairly comfortable sleeping quarters and one large and private room apiece to work in," and had agreed to let them pay part of the grocery bill, although she hoped they would not be as hard up as they were the last time Ford was at Benfolly. Her own book had sold over 5,000 copies and if it did as well in England they would have enough to live on for a year—that would be luxury, she said.

Ford liked the South and admired Benfolly. The Tates' balcony seemed "an earthly near-paradise," he had written in *The Great Trade Route* after his earlier visit. That spacious balcony ran across the back of the tall, narrow, white brick house and overlooked the river. Caroline had tried hard to grow flowers at Benfolly, bringing pussy willow and creeper and ferns from the woods and planting jonquil bulbs every fall, only to be living somewhere else when they bloomed in the spring. "A perfect climate, a magnificently fertile soil . . . It is peaceful and lovely and hospitable and kind," Ford had rhapsodized.

The Tates always welcomed company and were seldom alone in any house for very long. Ever since they bought Benfolly in 1930 with a $10,000 interest-free loan from Allen's rich brother, Ben—hence the name—they had entertained a stream of visitors who journeyed down from the New York literary world to observe the Tates and their life in the Deep South, stay a while, and return, most of them, to write about the experience. And, of course, all the brethren came to Benfolly—to play charades on Saturday nights and drink mint juleps on Sunday afternoons. "Brethren" was a rubric for Fugitives and/or Agrarians like John Crowe Ransom, Robert Penn Warren, Lyle Lanier, and Andrew Lytle, men who had been at Vanderbilt with Allen and helped produce *I'll Take My Stand,* the Agrarian manifesto that protested the industrialization of the South and called for a return to the past traditions of the region. The Tates were used to sharing houses too. They had lived with Hart Crane for a whole winter in Patterson, New York, with Andrew Lytle in Memphis and Monteagle, and with Ford Madox Ford at Cap Brun in France and in New York.

While she and Allen were still getting the house ready for the onslaught of Fords, they entertained what Caroline called the "strangest visitation we ever had." They were standing in the circular driveway admiring the two lemon lilies that were blooming when a car drove up to the gate and a young man got out. He stopped by the mailbox and "answered a call of nature," as Caroline put it. She and Allen refrained from shouting, *"Défense d'uriner,"* and waited until he came up and began to talk about Ford Madox Ford.

"Something made us treat him more gently and ask him into the house," Caroline wrote to her friend Sally Wood. "He is a young man named Lowell from Massachusetts who heard Ford lecture in Boston and as he wasn't getting on well at Harvard decided to come South to learn how to write. We kept him overnight and sent him on to Nashville to learn further about writing. . . . He does have a queer eye on him but is very well behaved and affable, but imagine a Lowell (yes, the poor boy's mother is a Cabot)—imagine one coming all the way from Boston to sit at Southern feet."

The young man was, of course, Robert Lowell, and he was desperate. His parents objected to his girlfriend and, during an argument about her, he had knocked his father down. His Boston psychiatrist was Merrill Moore, a Vanderbilt man, a former Fugitive, and a prolific writer of sonnets, who suggested that he leave home for a while. Perhaps he could go down to Tennessee and apprentice himself to Ford Madox Ford who was then in Boston but would be staying with Moore's old friend Allen Tate. It would be good for Lowell, Moore said, to meet "a real writer." A cocktail party for Ford had been arranged at the home of Lowell's girlfriend. Ford behaved badly at the party, refusing for a while to speak anything but French, but somehow, Lowell impressed Ford, who declared him the most intelligent person he had met in Boston. Lowell said later that this indicated Ford's low opinion of Boston rather than a high opinion of him. At any rate, Ford told Lowell to go to the South to learn about poetry and agreed to recommend to his parents the kind of apprenticeship Moore had in mind. Lowell set out south, reading the Fugitive poets on the way and deciding that Allen Tate was a very good poet indeed.

Years later Lowell wrote with condescension about this first sight of the Tates, labeling them "stately yet bohemian," sneering at the "peeling, pillared house" and at the "schoolboy's loaded twenty-two rifle . . . under the Confederate flag over the fireplace, a reproduced sketch of Leonardo's *Virgin of the Rocks*, . . . an engraving of Stonewall Jackson." After he listened to the Tates' Southern stories and Greenwich Village reminiscences, he began to realize that he, too, was part of a legend. "I was Northern, disembodied, a Platonist, a puritan, an abolitionist." Tate quoted a stanza from Oliver Wendell Holmes's *Chambered Nautilus* and said it was rather beyond Lowell's renowned great-uncle. Lowell realized "that the old deadweight of poor J. R. Lowell was now an asset. Here, like the battered Confederacy, he still lived and was history."

Lowell was impressed that Tate knew all the English classics, some of the Greek and Latin writers, could recite key lines, and dismissed droves of modern poets from the Untermeyer anthologies. Lowell left Benfolly the next day and went to Nashville to see about studying at Vanderbilt under John Crowe Ransom, who had been mentor to Tate, Warren, and Lytle.

In the garden, the peas were in bloom, and young lettuces were ready to eat. Caroline visited neighboring farms and went to her grandmother's place, Merry Mont, a few miles away in Kentucky, to stock the pantry.

Caroline's mother was a Meriwether, and since the early nineteenth century the Meriwethers had been big landowners in the blackpatch tobacco region that straddled the border between Kentucky and Tennessee. The dust jacket of *None Shall Look Back* stated that Benfolly was on land that had been in Caroline's family for generations. "This is a recurrent shock to the descendants of the Greens who once entertained Lafayette in this house," Caroline wrote Katherine Anne Porter, her editor at Scribner's. "It is also a great shock to the Meriwethers who wouldn't be caught dead owning that poor land. You remember my grandmother once sent one of her negroes over to Benfolly and when he got back he said he certainly hated to see Little Miss Carrie living on that poor land. He never looked at the house which was all fine in new paint."

At any rate, now Caroline was able to garner supplies of fresh lamb and country-smoked hams, cream, milk, and eggs to supplement the Benfolly garden, and began to show Ida, the new cook she had found, how to cook. "I have discovered after forty years of dealing with negroes that you can never tell them anything but they can always imitate motions," she wrote to Sally Wood. Ida often went upstairs when she meant to go downstairs and said the house baffled her. Caroline told her it had baffled her for years.

After a triumphant course of interviews and lectures and ballyhoo in Chicago, the Ford party arrived at Benfolly on May 10; they carried their belongings in duffel bags, which looked very strange in Tennessee in 1937. Wally Tworkov turned out to be "a pretty, modest child [with] one of those half dozen typical Jewish faces you see so often in New York." She asked Caroline shyly how wise it would be to have *The Daily Worker* sent to her there. "She apparently thought she might be ridden off of Benfolly on a rail if caught with a copy of the *Worker*," Caroline wrote to Sally Wood. Wally, in turn, was startled to find that the talk at dinner was not about the Spanish Civil War but about the American Civil War. Janice and Wally were sometimes appalled at the Tates' dicta about the old Southern aristocracy and their tendency to make statements like "Communism is just a ruse to maintain the New York supremacy."

Ford was sixty-three that summer and had already published more than seventy books. The grandson of Ford Madox Brown, the Pre-Raphaelite painter, he had collaborated with Joseph Conrad, edited *the transatlantic review,* and known nearly every writer in England and America for the past fifty years. He was, in his own words, "an old man mad about writing." He also liked country life. He had farmed in Kent himself and had attended lectures in agriculture at the Sorbonne, and had in common with Caroline a more practical interest in agricultural matters than any of the Agrarians. He was happy to be back at Benfolly, but he was more difficult that summer than he had ever been—"notiony," as one of the visitors to Benfolly put it.

Nancy and her friend Elizabeth Jones came on the train from Chattanooga. Caroline was busy—already slim, she lost five pounds running the ménage. And the crowd grew. Robert Lowell returned and asked if he could stay. When the Tates told him that the house was so full that any other guest would have to pitch a tent in the yard, he went to Sears, Roebuck in Nashville, purchased an olive-green umbrella tent, and came back and put it up under a locust tree, which he called a lotus tree.

"The grandnephew of James Russell Lowell lives in an umbrella tent on the lawn," Caroline wrote to Sally. "He's such a nice boy. Drives me out to Merry Mont to haul in buttermilk, etc., flits the dining room—the handiest boy I ever knew, in fact. When he isn't doing errands he retires to his tent whence a low bumble emerges—Robert reading Andrew Marvell aloud to get the scansion."

Ford, irrationally annoyed with Lowell for taking him seriously and following him to Benfolly, refused to speak to him, even at meals. Usually so helpful to young writers, Ford was for some reason afraid of what Lowell might write about him someday. Caroline remonstrated with Ford, who then took to addressing Lowell as "young man." One could have only a certain number of guests not speaking to each other, said Caroline.

Nancy hated having the Fords at Benfolly. She felt they took up the whole house and made her mother cross. As consolation, Caroline saw to it that Nancy acquired a pony that summer, and Ford sent to England for a riding crop for her. Bessie the pony bit Nancy, leading Caroline's Uncle Rob, who came over nearly every day, to say, "She can't learn to ride on a horse she's afraid of," and give her his own horse. "Brownie will teach you how to ride," he told Nancy. "He's taught lots of people to ride."

Life inside the house crackled and hummed. Everybody worked every morning. One could hear the typewriters clicking away and Ford dictating his thousand words a day to Mrs. Tworkov and see the stacks of manuscripts grow taller.

"I moaned and groaned about working hard last year but I know now that was just child's play," Caroline wrote to Anne Winslow, a friend in Memphis. "I've had to develop a brand new technique for writing—one hand on the kitchen stove and one on the typewriter. It works to my surprise—I do my five or six pages most days. Rotten they are, too." She managed to finish *The Garden of Adonis*, which deals with two contemporary Kentucky families, one of them landowners and the other tenant farmers. She had started it years before, right after *Penhally*, her first novel, was published, and then abandoned it to write *Aleck Maury*.

She also managed to set a good table on a shoestring—no one had much money. When Janice ventured a faint criticism of the food, Caroline "slapped her paws." Caroline had knocked off work at ten in the morning to cook dinner herself—dinner was in the middle of the day, as was the custom of the country. She prepared spring lamb, home-grown strawberries, new potatoes, and cauliflower with hollandaise sauce.

"If you'd only told me in time," Janice said, "we could have had cauliflower polonaise."

"No, we couldn't," said Caroline. "We prefer it hollandaise."

Allen, even less enthusiastic about Janice than he was about Ford, predicted that Ford was about to get rid of Janice and might even go away and leave her with them. Caroline said if he did she would drop Janice in the river with less compunction than if she were a puppy or a kitten. This was not much of a threat, since Caroline Gordon never drowned a puppy or kitten in her life. Whatever house the Tates lived in teemed with animals. One pastime at Benfolly was waiting to see how long it would take the hogs to knock down their pen.

"I won't have hogs again," Tate said.

"Oh, but think of the romance," said Ford.

In the afternoon there was swimming in the river, where the Tates had installed a big floating raft mounted on empty gasoline drums, or in nearby creeks, where the water was cooler. There was good fishing for bass, crappie, and pickerel in the creeks and ponds in the neighborhood.

At night the Tates and their guests sat on the upstairs back gallery and looked at the lights of Clarksville. Frequent guests that summer were Frances and Brainard Cheney—Fannie and Lon to everyone. Fannie was a reference librarian at Vanderbilt and Lon was a reporter on the *Nashville Banner* but wanted to write fiction. He had written several chapters of a novel, and in the midst of running the house and writing her own novel Caroline found time that summer to go over Lon's novel sentence by sentence with him. "I never published that novel," Cheney recalled many years later. "It was "Worlds Beyond Worlds"—the title was the best part of it. I brought it into the best shape I could and Caroline sent it to her agent, who said, 'Come in with a bigger turn of wood.' It was a little lightweight."

The heat bothered everyone. They couldn't close doors because of the heat; there was very little privacy and no quiet at all. "This is one of the noisiest spots in the world," Ford said, "what with children and chickens and birds and cows and steamboats and Tennessean voices and doors slamming in the wind." Probably longing to retract what he'd written about "the perfect climate" and the "peace" of Benfolly, he said that consorting with the Tates was like living with intellectual desperadoes in the Sargasso Sea.

The cistern ran dry, and rebellion raged over Allen's tight control over what water there was. Tate blamed the Ford party for flushing the toilets too much. Ford volunteered to build a Sussex dew pond, and sank an old washtub in the meadow and filled it with twigs. He was astonished when it failed to fill with water.

And Ford did not care for Ida's cooking; he failed to understand why she did not produce Provençal dishes. Allen asked Ford what he would have done in France if the Tates had demanded hot biscuits and sorghum molasses. Allen said he had never realized before how indignant it makes you to have people disapprove of your food. It was insulting to have biscuits called fritters, not once but many times. "The household groaned with the fatigued valor of Southern hospitality," Robert Lowell wrote. "Ida . . . grew squint-eyed and aboriginal from the confusion of labors, the clash of cultures."

Ford had insomnia, gout, and indigestion and was confined to the middle floor a good deal of the time, but he worked away on his history of the world's literature and spent his mornings translating Propertius and Tibullus. Caroline confessed she was eating every unkind word she'd ever said about Janice, who was an immense help, waiting on Ford hand and foot.

That year John Crowe Ransom was invited to join the faculty of Kenyon College in Gambier, Ohio. The offer included a better salary than Vanderbilt was paying him, a rent-free house, and a lighter teaching load. Allen thought Vanderbilt should try to keep Ransom, and, loving intrigue and machinations, and happy to be diverted from working on his novel, he seized the chance to get away from Benfolly. So he could devote all his time to a campaign to pressure Vanderbilt into keeping Mr. Ransom in Nashville, Allen moved to Nashville and, with Andrew Lytle, stayed at Lon and Fannie Cheney's apartment. He wrote an open letter to the Vanderbilt chancellor, James H. Kirkland, with a copy to the Nashville *Tennesseean,* protesting that Vanderbilt's decision to permit its most significant man of letters to go to a small college in the Midwest was another example of the region's lack of interest in the "notable revival of letters" in the South. "John Crowe Ransom profoundly influences, through his teaching and writing, the course of modern literature." Tate cited the fact that the "Lowell family of Boston and Harvard University has just sent one of its sons to Nashville to study poetry with Mr. Ransom."

Kirkland, who had once remarked about the Fugitives and the Agrarians that he wanted Vanderbilt to turn out businessmen, not poets and farmers, replied to Allen's letter in the pages of the *Tennesseean.* The wire services picked up the story and *Time* sent a correspondent to Nashville. There are those who have said that Allen's activity insured Ransom's departure, since the publicity made it impossible for Vanderbilt to negotiate with him.

Vanderbilt did offer Ransom a small raise. "Vanderbilt made little effort to keep him—none till Allen stirred things up," Caroline wrote. "And they offered a five hundred [dollar] raise if he would edit the college catalogue—that's their idea of a literary man."

Tate and Lytle organized a dinner in Nashville for Ransom in honor of his service to Southern literature, to be held whether he accepted the Kenyon offer or not. Tate called Robert Penn Warren, the editor of *The Southern Review,* who was spending the summer in California writing a novel, and got his support. Ford got on to Morton D. Zabel of *Poetry* and persuaded him to come down for the dinner. Randall Jarrell and Peter Taylor whipped up feeling among Vanderbilt undergraduates. Allen was interviewed in *The Chattanooga Times.* He and Andrew wrote letters to the trustees, the alumni association, and administrators at Vanderbilt. They rallied the troops in the New York literary world to write letters and send telegrams. Allen even returned his Vanderbilt diploma to Chancellor Kirkland. Unmoved, the trustees took no further action on meeting the Kenyon offer.

Andrew and Allen worked hard at planning and promoting the testimonial dinner at Hettie Ray's Dinner Club on Nine-Mile Hill. Andrew gave Hettie Ray a steady stream of instructions: the corn, for instance, must be really fresh and picked in the field no earlier than noon that day.

The dinner was well attended. Caroline drove Ford, who was to be master of ceremonies, from Benfolly to Nashville, stopping at an old-fashioned dry goods store in downtown Nashville so Ford could buy a pair of white duck trousers. He wore them with an ancient dinner jacket and espadrilles. Caroline said he "called everybody by their right name to our surprise."

"I was perhaps the first person in Europe to recognize what is taking place here," Ford said in his speech.

"We have just concluded an attack *en masse* upon the University of Vanderbilt," he wrote to a friend, "ending in a glorious victory for the forces of intellect. Nevertheless, I write my daily thousand words with the regularity of a grandfather's clock."

Ransom went to Kenyon College that fall, taking with him, like a Pied Piper, Robert Lowell, Peter Taylor, and Randall Jarrell.

In July, Allen, Caroline, Nancy, the Fords, and Robert Lowell set off for a writers' conference at Olivet College in Michigan. After one day on the road in the Tates' car, Ford and Janice got out and took the train. At Olivet they discovered the conference needed another creative writing teacher, and the Tates suggested Katherine Anne Porter.

After the conference, the Tates and Katherine Anne drove back to Benfolly through the Virginias—visiting Bethany College in Bethany,

West Virginia (where Caroline had gone to school), and Fairfax Court-house, Mount Vernon, and Kenmore (which had once belonged to Allen's family) in Virginia and spending "three days in sweet Alexandria," as Katherine Anne put it. Alexandria is the scene of much of the action in *The Fathers,* Allen's novel. They also visited Harpers Ferry and the Civil War battlefields at Antietam and Appomattox.

Caroline, exhausted from the summer's activities, was, as she put it, "flat" by the time they got back to Benfolly. "By taking two naps a day for several weeks and reading many detective stories I managed to recover my moral health" by late September, she said.

Katherine Anne stayed six weeks at Benfolly, which was nicer than she had expected, she wrote to novelist Josephine Herbst. A "big, ample, shining place." And the lawns were in good order, with a hundred-acre wood with a spring in it. There were so many animals, she said, "and I love feeding them and playing with them—living day to day is so pleasant I forget the future."

Katherine Anne did no writing at Benfolly—life was too distracting. She made mint liqueur, five gallons of elderberry wine, four quarts of apple butter, and brandied peaches, and almost wept when Caroline would not provide her with more peaches and with grapes to make more wine. Caroline believed that Katherine Anne had a natural passion for domestic activity but indulged it to get out of writing.

When Albert Russel Erskine, Jr., twenty-six years old, a graduate student at Louisiana State University and the business manager of *The Southern Review,* came for a visit, he and Katherine Anne, who was forty-seven, sat up most of the night talking on the porch in the light of a full moon, clearly enjoying each other's company. (The Tates were horrified when Katherine Anne and Albert Erskine were married the next April. It was to be a disastrous—and brief—marriage.)

After Katherine Anne left Benfolly she wrote from New Orleans, "You are a kind of saint, Caroline—one of the more turbulent ones."

In the summer of 1937 the Tates appeared onstage at Benfolly at the high point of their lives. All the earmarks of their complicated personalities and the elements of what they considered most important—hospitality, a commitment to literature and to young writers, good fun and good food, a classical kind of agrarianism, the knack for living on little money—stand out in brilliant relief. Their lives would never be dull, but they would never be quite so theatrical again.

THE FUGITIVES—AND ONE OF THEIR REVIEWERS, 1921–1924

In November 1921 an English teacher at Vanderbilt University in Nashville invited Allen Tate, the most brilliant and most arrogant student on campus, to attend a discussion group that met on alternate Saturday nights at the home of James Frank.

The eight or ten members of the group were either on the faculty at Vanderbilt or recent graduates, except for the host and his brother-in-law, Sidney Mttron Hirsch, a dilettante autodidact interested in Eastern religions who had written plays produced at civic festivals in Nashville and other cities. More than any other person, Hirsch was responsible for starting the discussions. Since 1915 the men had been getting together (except for a forced hiatus from 1917 to 1919, when most of them went overseas in World War I) to talk about philosophical questions. Lately, their attention had turned to poetry, and some of them had been bringing their own poems to read out loud so the group could discuss them.

Allen, the first undergraduate anyone ever invited to the gathering, was president of the Calumet Club, the campus literary society, and had published a poem in the college humor magazine. The professor who invited Allen was Donald Davidson, and another professor there that night was John Crowe Ransom, a Rhodes scholar who had published a book of poetry, *Poems About God*. A couple of other faculty members were present, as were several young businessmen who were interested in philosophy and wrote poetry or fiction as an avocation.

The group, which had no name at the time, invited Allen to become a permanent member, and he attended regularly, dazzling the older men with his criticism, his untraditional poems, and his familiarity with Baudelaire, Mallarmé, and de Gourmont. Tate, Ransom, and Davidson formed a small group within the group, and they would remain friends and maintain a literary correspondence for years. These three, along with Robert Penn Warren, then a tall, gangly, red-haired sixteen-year-old freshman at Vanderbilt who would not be invited to attend meetings until the next year, would become the most famous of the group.

In the spring of 1922 the members had accumulated a store of unpublished poetry among them, and Sidney Hirsch suggested that they start their own magazine. Little magazines had sprung up in other Southern cities—*The Lyric* in Norfolk, *The Double-Dealer* in New Orleans, and *The Reviewer* in Richmond, and it seemed the thing to do. The Nashville poets named their journal *The Fugitive*, referring to the poet as a lonely wanderer, the outcast who possesses secret wisdom. They were in flight, too, they said, from the sentimentality and conventions of current "Southern literature." "The Fugitive flees from nothing faster than from the high-caste Brahmins of the Old South," they wrote.

They voted on the poems to appear in that first issue, took the winners down to a black printer, and got their magazine. *The Fugitive* went on sale in Nashville on April 12, 1922, and copies were mailed to newspapers in Nashville, New York, and Paris, and to universities, editors, and authors around the world. In all, nineteen issues would appear, the last in December 1925.

After *The Fugitive* appeared, several other students joined the group—among them Ridley Wills, who had written a novel called *Hoax*, and Merrill Moore, who would write 55,000 sonnets and become Robert Lowell's psychiatrist.

The Fugitives were a tightly bound group—they called one another "Brother"—and their attendance at their frequent meetings was phenomenally faithful. There were just as many poets at other universities, but the Vanderbilt poets were unique because they were organized and met regularly. They took themselves and "literature" seriously, and some of them thought of themselves as, or expected to become, "men of letters."

Before the second issue of *The Fugitive* appeared, Allen left Vanderbilt, fearing he had tuberculosis. He went to Valle Crucis, in the North

Carolina mountains, where the climate was thought to be salubrious. In November 1922, when the tuberculosis scare was over, he left North Carolina and worked for his brother Benjamin in his coal business in Ashland, Kentucky. Here Allen proved he was no good at business— he lost the company $600 in one day—and felt keenly his isolation from the literary ferment of Nashville. He longed to talk about cubists, futurists, imagists, and dadaists, but to him Ashland was a "dirty little town" and there wasn't a congenial soul around. "I am marooned," he said. He had already sold poems to other magazines besides *The Fugitive*—to *American Poetry Magazine, The Reviewer,* and *The Double-Dealer*—and he knew that he wanted to become a writer, a "man of letters." *The New York Times,* discussing the writers in *The Double-Dealer,* had mentioned him as "a new personality, from whose pen interesting things may be expected." *The Dial* and Gorham Munson at *Secession* asked to see his work. On January 3, 1923, a young editor at *Vanity Fair,* Edmund Wilson, returned some poems Allen had submitted, but added in his letter that he "expected great things of him." Everybody did.

Ben Tate, nine years Allen's senior, was extremely good at business and had been supporting the family for several years. Their father, John Orley Tate, had suffered two blows—he had failed miserably in running the business his father-in-law had started, and he had been involved in a scandal (Caroline told her friends that he had shot a black waiter) at his club and was forced to resign. After that, he lived virtually in seclusion—except to carry on a series of extramarital love affairs—until he died. The family had "lived off capital," selling pieces of real estate, since 1912. Like all Southern women, Allen's mother, Eleanor Parke Custis Varnell, felt she'd married beneath her—she was a descendant of the Bogans of Pleasant Hill in Fairfax County, Virginia, whose house was burned by Yankee mercenary forces during the Civil War. An unstable, puritanical, domineering woman, preoccupied with religious questions although she was not much of a churchgoer, she had raised Allen, her third son, almost single-handedly, dressing him like Little Lord Fauntleroy and making him play the violin. The two of them moved from town to town and, in the summer, from one Southern resort to another. He was born in Winchester, Kentucky, on November 19, 1899, but he thought for years he had been born in Virginia—this misapprehension was fostered by his mother, who felt he should have been born in Virginia. Allen went to public schools and private schools here, there, and everywhere—Georgetown Prep, in Washington, D.C., the Cross School in Louisville, the Tarbox School in Nashville, high schools in Evanston, Indiana; Ashland, Kentucky;

and Cincinnati. At all of them he was good at Latin and music, poor in science and math.

At any rate, Ben was paying Allen's tuition at Vanderbilt. Allen returned to Nashville for the spring term of 1923, still arrogant, still an irritant, still brilliant. Allen himself said later that his conceit at this time must have been intolerable. "Had not the editors of the *Double-Dealer* written me a letter saying that they saw in me the White Hope of the South?" Had he not learned from the French poets an "easy lesson in shocking the bourgeoisie"? He was, he said, "a twenty-two year old prig as disagreeable as you could conjure up."

Prig he might have been, but he was welcomed back by the Fugitives. He roomed in Wesley Hall with Robert Penn Warren, by this time a sophomore, and Ridley Wills. On the walls of their room, Warren drew pictures of scenes from *The Waste Land,* which had just appeared in *The Dial.* A young poet named Hart Crane in Cleveland had seen one of Allen's poems in *The Double-Dealer* and had written to praise his work, commenting that he could tell that Allen had read T. S. Eliot. Allen had not, but he did so at once. When *The Waste Land* came out, he read it aloud to his fraternity brothers, who were not impressed. (Neither did John Crowe Ransom share the enthusiasm for Eliot.) Warren became Allen's disciple, and Allen his champion.

The Fugitive continued to appear and began to attract contributions from outside. When John Gould Fletcher, an expatriate Arkansas poet, lectured on American poets at Oxford, he was castigated by two Fugitives in exile, William Elliott and William Frierson, both Rhodes scholars, for failing to mention John Crowe Ransom. Fletcher looked up Ransom's work and then contributed to *The Fugitive* himself. Witter Bynner, president of the Poetry Society of America, contributed to the magazine, as did Robert Graves, William Alexander Percy, and Hart Crane. *The Fugitive* staged poetry contests that attracted hundreds of entries. Several women published poems in the magazine, but only one was admitted to membership in the Fugitives—Laura Riding Gottschalk, a strange, troubled woman who sent in poetry by the bale from her home in Louisville. Born Laura Reichenthal, she changed her name to Riding and married a professor named Louis Gottschalk. When she won a prize in a *Fugitive* poetry contest, to everyone's astonishment came down from Louisville to claim the prize in person. She then proposed herself as secretary to the editors, but there was, of course, no money to pay a secretary. The waves *The Fugitive* made splashed on distant shores, and in England Robert Graves and his wife saw Laura's poem and wrote to her, asking her to come and visit them.

Critics like H. L. Mencken, Christopher Morley, and Louis Unter-meyer commented favorably on the little magazine, and a laudatory article by "Carolyn Gordon" (Caroline Gordon spelled her name "Caro-lyn" until she was past thirty years old) appeared on the book page of the Chattanooga *News* under the headline "U.S. Best Poets Here in Tennessee." The Fugitives loved the article, as well they might, and asked each other if they knew Carolyn Gordon. John Crowe Ransom thought she was related to some of his relations. (Actually, his father had been the pastor of the little Hazelwood Methodist Church, in Tennessee, near where Carolyn's Ferguson cousins lived at Summer-trees. She had met Johnny Ransom when she was visiting the Fergusons as a child.) Prophetically, the *News* article listed Allen Tate as "the most radical member of the group."

Allen Tate, cum laude and Phi Beta Kappa, left Vanderbilt in January 1924 to teach Latin and English in a high school in West Virginia, where he once more yearned for Nashville and "the brothers." That spring, Robert Penn Warren made an unsuccessful attempt at suicide—he wrote a note saying that he was going to take his life because he wasn't a poet, and put a chloroform-soaked cloth over his face—but he was discovered by Donald Davidson, who called a doctor who took him to the hospital. Warren's parents came down and took him back to Guthrie, Kentucky, where Red Warren recovered quickly and wrote to Allen several times, urging him to come and visit that summer. They could swim and play tennis, he said, ride horses and walk in the country, read and write. They might also get jobs doing manual labor, and Warren promised Allen that for company there would be an heiress and a "female" who had moved there from Clarksville. War-ren's mother wrote to Allen, too, seconding the invitation to spend at least a month with her son.

When school was out, Allen went to Washington to visit his mother and then on to New York to meet Hart Crane, who was "a peach . . . a 160-pounder, strong as an ox, looks like an automobile sales-man"; Crane treated Allen "royally" and took him to 30 Jones Street, where Susan Jenkins, an editor of *Telling Tales*, a pulp magazine, had a huge apartment. There he met a classmate of Susan's from Peabody High School in Pittsburgh, Malcolm Cowley, a freelance reviewer, poet, and translator. Allen was neatly dressed in a dark suit, carried a walking stick, and wore his Phi Beta Kappa key, but still, for once he felt at a disadvantage—Cowley had been to France and knew the dadaists. Cow-ley told him, "We no longer wear our Phi Beta Kappa keys," and picked up an old stick from somewhere and carried it with him the entire evening, which ended when Crane, Cowley, and Allen walked over the Brooklyn Bridge. Tate thought Cowley looked like a truck driver and acted like a snob but was "a very keen and refreshingly unpretentious person withal," and he went to the Bronx Zoo with him. Crane introduced him to E. E. Cummings, who had already published two books, one of them poetry, but was, to Allen's regret, "opposed on principle to Poetic Theories." He met William Slater Brown, who had been with Cummings in the ambulance corps in France during World War I; the two were imprisoned in a French concentration camp, suspected of being spies. Cummings had written about the experience in his book *The Enormous Room,* in which Brown figured as B. Allen met Mark Van Doren, who taught English at Columbia and published his first book of poems that year. He also met Gorham Munson, who had started the little magazine *Secession* in 1922, and Matthew Josephson, who founded *Broom.* It was a heady experience for Allen, the would-be man of letters, and he arrived at the Warrens' home in Guthrie a messenger from a larger world.

One day not long after he arrived, Mrs. Warren received a telephone call from her neighbor, Mrs. Gordon, the wife of Brother Gordon, a Campbellite preacher. Mrs. Gordon told Mrs. Warren that she understood there were two young men who were writers visiting in the Warren house; Caroline, her daughter, wanted to be a writer and would like to meet them.

Mrs. Warren immediately invited Caroline over, but when she told her son and his guest about the phone call, Warren and Tate decided to walk over to the Gordons' house to meet Caroline at once. (Perhaps the "heiress" and the "female" from Clarksville were not available.)

"I saw her in the driveway," Allen Tate was to say years later. "She was the prettiest girl I ever saw and I pissed in my pants."

Warren remembers that the three of them spent the whole afternoon walking in the woods and that the conversation was "generally bookish." Caroline had not heard of some of the poets Allen talked about and "expressed her joy at being so instructed." After that, Warren said, he didn't see much of his houseguest. There was no more horseback riding or hiking. Allen began to stay out later and later at night.

Caroline Gordon was overwhelmed by the attentions of this glittering young man, the published poet who had been to New York and knew real writers, who was a real writer himself. She was twenty-eight to Allen's twenty-four, she had been a newspaper reporter in Chattanooga for four years, and she was working on a novel. But she had lacked the support of a group like the Fugitives—or any literary friends at all—and she was enchanted, literally spellbound by Allen Tate.

He was the first man, by all accounts, to take a romantic interest in her. Caroline was not like her cousin, Little May, about whom they said you could always tell at which house she was staying by the number of horses her beaux hitched up outside. Allen had no trouble seducing Caroline. They first made love, Allen told his friends, in the churchyard at Guthrie. Since they both wanted to be writers, they decided they must go to New York and agreed to meet there in the fall. Caroline would go to Rochester, to visit her cousin, Little May, whose husband, Sherman Morse, a former city editor of the *New York World,* had retired to raise apples on the shores of Lake Canandaigua, and from there to New York City. Allen gave Caroline his mother's address in Washington and went down to Nashville, where he bought a secondhand tuxedo and sold all his books to Bill Bandy, a Vanderbilt student, to pay his railroad fare, and set out himself for Washington and New York. It was November, however, before he could get away from his mother in Washington and head for New York.

3

CAROLINE AND THE MERIWETHERS, 1895–1924

It was characteristic of Caroline Gordon to go from Kentucky to New York City by way of a cousin's home in Rochester. The family, the Connection, as its members called the vast web of Meriwethers, Barkers, and Fergusons, was the most important thing in the world to the members of Caroline's family—or, to be more precise, Caroline's mother's family, the Meriwethers. Caroline's grandmother, Caroline Ferguson, whose mother was a Meriwether, married Douglas Meriwether. Her oldest daughter, Loulie, married another Meriwether, and old Mrs. Meriwether was fond of saying that the Meriwethers had no problems until they started marrying outside the family. But that kind of thing cuts two ways. "We're all crazy now, all run down," a member of the Connection said years later. "That's what you get for being snooty."

The first Meriwether to come over the mountains from Virginia to Kentucky in 1809 looking for fresh land on which to grow tobacco claimed 10,000 acres for a dollar an acre in southern Kentucky and built a house called Meriville. His son (Caroline Gordon's great-great-grandfather) built a much finer brick house called Woodstock. (The name came from the title of a book by Sir Walter Scott, whose novels the antebellum South adored.) Woodstock, the largest and most elegant of all the Meriwether houses, had a deer park and a racetrack. During the Civil War two Confederate generals and many another officer rode on Woodstock horses. Caroline's grandmother grew up at Woodstock with her grandparents and inherited land nearby. After the Civil War she married a cousin, Douglas Meriwether, who had "ridden with Forrest," the legendary Confederate Cavalry commander, Nathan Bedford Forrest. Caroline and Douglas built a tall, narrow house and named it Merry Mont for the setting of a Hawthorne short story.

The Meriwethers divided themselves into two groups, Kinky Heads and Anyhows. The Kinky Heads took up causes like abolition and spiritualism and did good works. They went to church. Caroline's grandfather Douglas Meriwether was a Kinky Head, but the Woodstock Meriwethers were Anyhows and did "any how they pleased." Anyhows gave their children family names, but the Kinky Heads named their offspring after heroes like Robert Emmet, Charles James Fox, and Robert Dale Owen.

Douglas Meriwether was always thin and undernourished from his years in the Confederate army when he had to forage for his food, but what he regretted most was that the war had made him miss out on an education. Blue-eyed and with a short brown beard, he would sit in a cane-bottomed chair under a sugar maple in front of the house at Merry Mont through long summer afternoons, reading Locke and Ingersoll and Paine, his chair tilted back against the tree trunk. When Caroline was a child, he died a suicide from an overdose of his headache medicine, crying, "If I only knew! If I only knew!"

Kentucky was one of the last states to establish a system of public education, and before his death Meriwether hired a tutor for his four children: a young Virginian, James Maury Morris Gordon, who had attended the University of Virginia, left it mysteriously, and worked "out West." He came from a good but suitably eccentric family in Louisa County, Virginia—his grandfather had been a general in the War of 1812 and a congressman, and his father, trained as a lawyer, retired early to take up poetry, recited Shakespeare at the dinner table, and spent the last year of his life rendering Sir Walter Scott's *Bride of Lammermoor* into blank verse.

Gordon's salary was small but Meriwether furnished him a horse. At first he taught only the Merry Mont children, Robert, Loulie, Nancy, and their little sister Margaret, but other families in the Connection wanted to send their children to his classes. They built a log schoolhouse on the Eupedon farm, another Meriwether property, at the intersection of Peacher's Mill Road and Trenton Road. Gordon, on his horse, led a caravan of pupils on horseback to the schoolhouse every morning.

When she was seventeen, pretty Nancy Meriwether, thoroughly grounded in Latin and Greek and able to read French and German, married the schoolmaster. (Like Allen's mother, she would feel she'd married beneath her.) The young couple lived at Merry Mont in the Old Place, which had been the overseer's house, and Caroline Ferguson Gordon, named for her grandmother, was born there, the second of three children, on October 6, 1895. Her brother Morris was five years older than she, her brother Bill four years younger.

Caroline's first years were spent at Merry Mont in the midst of Confederate veterans, former slaves, impoverished landowners, and accomplished storytellers. There was neither electricity nor running water at archaic Merry Mont. Tobacco was raised for a cash crop and most of the food on the table grew on the place. Though there was little cash, there were plenty of servants. Caroline learned the names of trees and plants and, more important, the look of leaves and bare branches with the light coming through them; she felt at home in the woods and stored up images of light and shade and leaf and bough. Merry Mont was an Arcadian incubator that nourished her love of the natural world and her liking for eccentrics and provided her with the characters and themes of several books. It was always the Lost Paradise for her, a garden into which barbarians had come and destroyed the good, the beautiful, the true.

Caroline's mother was always something of an enigma to her. She turned to her grandmother and appreciated that her grandmother accepted her as she was from the very beginning, while her mother seemed to have expected something different. Miss Carrie was always busy—making cookies, overseeing the "putting up" of vegetables, fruits, and jellies, working among her flowers, tending to the milk and butter, or driving her buggy along the red clay roads that led through the Old Neighborhood to the farms and houses with names like Eupedon, Woodstock, Meriville, Cloverlands, West End, and Summertrees, owned by various Meriwether, Barker, and Ferguson cousins. Miss Carrie had definite ideas: for instance, she refused to have screens at the windows—she did not believe, she said, in "sifted air."

Caroline, a little girl with a slightly crooked nose and one eyebrow higher than the other, and great, limpid, dark eyes, was probably the favorite grandchild; she stayed with Miss Carrie at Merry Mont after her father moved away to teach school in Tullahoma, Tennessee, and Hopkinsville, Kentucky, taking his wife and sons with him. (Nancy Gordon taught school, too, in Hopkinsville, a most unusual move for a married woman with children in 1902.) When Gordon opened a classical preparatory school in Clarksville, Tennessee, Mrs. Gordon taught there, and Caroline was a pupil. Caroline always said that her mother, who became something of a recluse and a religious fanatic, rejected her totally. It was her grandmother who "saved" her.

Gordon tired of teaching school and became a Church of Christ preacher. In 1908 he took his family, including Caroline, to Wilmington, Ohio, where he was pastor of the Central Church of Christ; Caroline went to high school for two years there. From Wilmington they went to Lynchburg, Virginia, for a year, where Mr. Gordon was "state evangelist" and also tried, unsuccessfully, to farm. No matter where the Gordons moved, Mrs. Gordon always brought the children back to Merry Mont for the summer to swim in the icy water of Spring Creek, ride horseback, and play with innumerable cousins who also came back to the Old Neighborhood. In spite of all the moving around, Caroline managed to get in four years of Latin and two years of Greek and to graduate from the Princeton Collegiate Institute in Princeton, Kentucky, in 1912. She went off to Bethany College, a Church of Christ school in Bethany, West Virginia, where she had more Latin and more Greek, joined Alpha Xi Delta sorority and a literary society, and attended compulsory chapel every day. She graduated in 1916.

By then her father had a church in Poplar Bluff, Missouri, and Caroline went there to teach. The Gordons were very poor, and in 1917 Mrs. Gordon wrote her mother to thank her for a ham she had sent, saying that they would have gone hungry at Christmas if it had not been for the food the members of their church brought them.

In 1918, Gordon went back to Guthrie, Kentucky, where he preached at several churches in surrounding towns. Caroline moved with her parents and taught high school in Clarksville, Tennessee. She always said that Pidie, her Aunt Margaret, saved her life. Perhaps she did, for Caroline got a job on the Chattanooga *News* and lived with Pidie and her family: her second husband, Paul Campbell, her daughter by an earlier marriage, Catherine Wilds, and Moggie and little Paul Campbell, all of whom called Caroline "Kidy." Every morning Caroline left the Campbells' house on Missionary Ridge and rode the streetcar to work. She liked her job on the paper, made friends with other young people, and began setting the alarm clock early so she could get up to work on her novel before she went to work. She wrote without encouragement, without the help of writers' conferences or creative writing courses.

Most of her newspaper work consisted of editing society news and the magazine section that came out on Fridays. The signed story she did on the Fugitives for the book page of February 10, 1923, was unusual.

About a year after that story, in hopes of doing more writing, she left the *News* to go to work for the *Times*. She and Jane Snodgrass, another reporter, arranged for two women wearing lampshades for hats to come into the Palace, an ice cream parlor and luncheonette where *tout* Chattanooga gathered for lunch. The lampshade wearers were supposed to be protesting the high price of hats, and Caroline and Jane planned to write a story about it for the *Times*. The publisher found out about the fabricated story and fired Caroline.

Years later, in 1954, Caroline would recall the nervous breakdown she had at that time and the "unobtrusive kindness and firmness" with which Pidie and Paul "saw me through that illness. I don't know how I'd have got through without it."

She went home to Guthrie in the summer of 1924—and met Allen Tate.

Caroline carried out her plan to visit Little May and Sherman Morse in Rochester, where she was entertained at luncheons and teas. The Rochester young people were enchanted with Caroline and her "slightly crooked but very attractive face, dark eyes, the 'magnolia' complexion of Southern women so different from our tanned and freckled faces, and her very pretty hat, a Panama brim sloping slightly toward her left eye with a ravishing rose on the brim and a velvet ribbon." She was considered not beautiful but very attractive. At one of these parties she met Mary Maxfield, a young girl who also wanted to go to New York and, although Mary was not interested in writing—or anything but men—they decided to room together. One day, while canoeing on Lake Canandaigua with a young man named Remsen Wood, Caroline told him she wanted to be a writer. His sister Sally wanted to be a writer and lived in New York City. "Look her up when you get there," he said.

Soon Caroline appeared at Sally Wood's door and introduced herself, thus beginning a lifelong friendship between a Wellesley graduate who had trained as a nurse during World War I and a Bethany girl who had worked on a Chattanooga newspaper.

Johnson Features, a new newspaper syndicate run by Burton Rascoe, hired Caroline for its Sunday magazine supplement to interview celebrities of the day. One of them was Texas Guinan, a flamboyant blonde of the Roaring Twenties; a silent movie star and nightclub owner and hostess, she greeted her customers with "Hello, sucker." One of Caroline's cousins, Elizabeth Meriwether Gilmer, wrote a syndicated column under the name Dorothy Dix. Other people in the Connection asked Mrs. Gordon "if Carrie was going to be as good a writer as Cousin Lizzie." The answer, Caroline said, was always no. Caroline and Mary Maxfield lived on Washington Square, then at 20 West Eighth Street, and later on Waverly Place, with a third roommate. Caroline's mother wrote that she worried about three girls getting along together, but her father congratulated her and said it was a good idea for girls to team up. Now better-off, with four churches paying him a small stipend, he wrote, "We'll back you to the limit and don't think of paying us back until you have some money in hand." Caroline's mother told her to look at the dress on the back cover of the Dollie Gray catalog, the one labeled: "So slim, so tall, so sweet withal." If Caroline would like it in seal-brown satin crepe, she'd make it for her, or would she like an ensemble suit? She wanted to make her something green, and a cloak.

Caroline saw Allen Tate, who was in New York by early November, working at the Climax Publishing Company, which published *Telling Tales*, where Susan Jenkins had gotten him a job. Allen lived first with Hart Crane, then near him in Brooklyn, then on Grove Street, and later on Morton Street.

New York in the fall of 1924 was teeming with excitement for people like Allen and Caroline; new magazines, new theaters, new galleries were springing up all around Greenwich Village. The Village, where they both lived, was full of young people, all of whom wanted to throw off the shackles of their respectable upbringing and live for art and love.

Allen relished what he called the "physique" of the city, especially the subway, and he liked the fact that he could dine for seventy cents. He was enjoying life tremendously and had never felt better, he wrote Donald Davidson in Nashville. "There's nothing like being happy. . . . I'm not getting so much writing done; very little, in fact. But I'm making valuable friends, and that, as I've found, is very important in New York. . . . I can never forget you all. But really I shall never return to Nashville."

Allen made friends with the young men he considered to be the most talented in New York, and there was a mutual regard. Matthew Josephson wrote that they were all impressed with Allen, "a wispy, blond young man with an enormous cranium and diminutive and delicate features," who was even then terribly well informed about contemporary literary movements in France and England, as well as in the United States. Josephson noted that Allen used to ridicule the pretensions of Southerners to culture, holding that all they did was second-rate, and tried to suppress his Southern accent.

Allen wrote reviews for *The Nation* and the *New York Herald Tribune* and kept on writing poetry. Harold Vinal asked him to be a contributing editor of *Voices*. He refused to review for *Saturday Review of Literature*—he thought Henry Seidel Canby, the editor, a fool and dishonest to boot. He also refused offers from *The Bookman*. (This was high-minded, indeed, for a young man trying to make his way by his wits in New York.) He was making new friends constantly: Edmund Wilson, who had left *Vanity Fair* and was working as a freelance journalist and poet; John Dos Passos, who had already published several books and was working on *Manhattan Transfer;* John Hall Wheelock, a prolific poet who was working at Scribner's bookstore. (Wheelock would rise to be editor in chief at Scribner's, and would write poetry until his death at ninety-one.) Through Susan Jenkins and Malcolm Cowley, he met still another alumnus of Peabody High in Pittsburgh, Kenneth Burke, a future literary theoretician then working at any job that came to hand. Allen saw his friends at Squarcialupi's in the Village, where they read their poetry and caroused. (Crane played the piano while everyone else sang, always ending up with the Peabody alma mater.) These young men, all about the same age, came from various parts of the country, but were held together by one consuming interest—writing. They were conscious of being men of letters, sharply aware that they were part of a new literary generation, and they lived for nothing else.

Caroline did not attend the sessions at Squarcialupi's and barely met Allen's friends. "She wasn't 'one of us,' " Malcolm Cowley wrote. " 'We' were mostly poets and intellectuals and men. Caroline was a newspaperwoman from Chattanooga. Allen was Sue Jenkins' assistant and Sue, by exception, *was* one of us. She liked Caroline. Caroline was writing unpublished novels that 'we' didn't read. Later she felt—and rightly, in part—that she was a victim of sexual discrimination."

Caroline and Allen saw each other for two months until they quarreled at Christmastime in 1924. That was when—although they didn't know it—their only child was conceived. They did not see each other for months.

A Wedding—and Hart Crane,
1925–1926

It was a dreary little wedding at City Hall on May 15, 1925. Allen was a reluctant bridegroom and Caroline was five months pregnant, deadly serious, and determined to make the baby legitimate.

After the argument at Christmas, Allen had begun to go out with other women, including two of his cousins who were up from the South. Caroline complained to her friends of nausea; after visiting several doctors who found nothing wrong, she finally went to an osteopath, who told her she was pregnant.

Years later, Allen told his daughter that when Caroline appeared at his "Greenwich Village hovel," visibly pregnant, he said, "Now you'll have to marry me!" The truth was, however, that he was extremely reluctant to marry and agreed only after Caroline promised to divorce him as soon as the baby was born.

Sue Jenkins, alone among Allen's new friends, supported Caroline throughout the crisis. (Sue would soon move in with and later marry William Slater Brown, a friend of Allen's.) Caroline could scarcely have considered an abortion at that stage in her life. Since Sue thought the baby should have a name, she urged Caroline and Allen to get married, helped Caroline arrange the wedding, and then persuaded Brown to join her in standing up with Allen and Caroline.

When the date was finally set, Caroline called Sally Wood, who had planned a dinner party to introduce Caroline to an attractive young man, and said, "I can't come to dinner tonight—I'm marrying Allen this afternoon," and she warned Sally not to tell Mary Maxfield.

Sue and Slater went with Allen to serve as witnesses at the ringless ceremony at City Hall. Caroline wanted desperately for people to believe that they had been married for months, but one of the New York newspapers at that time published the names of every couple who applied for a marriage license. Allen was indifferent, but Caroline went to the City Hall pressroom and found the young woman who sent in the marriage announcements and asked her as a fellow newspaperwoman not to put their names in the paper. "Why not?" asked the reporter. Caroline threw open her cloak; the reporter understood and agreed to cooperate.

Afterward, Sue and Slater went with the newlyweds for a grim dinner at an Italian restaurant. The wedding was like the funeral of Caroline's grandfather at Meriville in 1899—no flowers, no music.

Caroline showed great courage—she was a young Southern woman, a minister's daughter, alone in New York, away from relatives for the first time in her life, and five months pregnant. In 1925 a woman in her situation was considered "fallen" or "in trouble." She breathed deep the heady air of New York, held her chin up, and carried it off. She continued to work after she was married, and she told her co-workers at the Johnson Syndicate that she had been secretly married for months, explaining that she was a Lucy Stoner and believed married women should retain their maiden names. She had worked as Caroline Gordon so far and she would continue to be known as Caroline Gordon. She worked almost until the time the baby was born. Not then nor at any time was there a breath of scandal.

Caroline and Allen sent the news of their marriage to the South, and Allen's friends at Vanderbilt and Caroline's relatives, like her co-workers, believed she had been married for some time when she wrote home about the expected baby. Mrs. Gordon's letters to Caroline that summer were affectionate and chatty, full of details about the dresses she was making for Caroline and the baby. She was reading all the works of Ibsen, she said, and she thought it might be a good idea to have a Meriwether family sanitorium—"We are all a little queer and apt to go off at any moment." In July Mr. and Mrs. Gordon realized that Caroline was still using her maiden name and stopped addressing her letters to Mrs. Allen Tate.

Caroline and Allen continued to make new friends in the city. One day Malcolm and Peggy Cowley took them to Staten Island to meet their friend Dorothy Day who was living in a small beach cottage with

Forster Batterham, referred to in those days as her common-law husband. A radical journalist who had worked for *The Masses* and *The Liberator* and author of a novel, *The Eleventh Virgin*, Dorothy Day was known as a communist and a freethinker. Caroline liked Dorothy immediately and they all stayed there in the cottage until after midnight. Dorothy kept looking at Caroline's stomach, and saying, "Oh, I hope I'm pregnant!" (She was.)

Sue and Slater Brown came into some money in the summer of 1925 and bought a dilapidated pre-Revolutionary farmhouse with a hundred acres of land in Putnam County, New York, near the Connecticut border. Old-timers called the place Tory Valley or Robber Rocks because a band of Tories had used a nearby cave as a base from which to rob the carts rolling down the nearby turnpike to supply Washington's army camped in the neighborhood. Sue resigned from *Telling Tales*, leaving Allen in charge, and Hart Crane quit his job at *Sweet's Architectural Catalog* and went out to help Sue and Slater paint the house.

The Cowleys bought a place nearby, just over the Connecticut border in Sherman, and Allen told several friends that he was thinking of getting a country place in the Berkshires since Brown, Crane, and Cowley were all there. A house on twenty or thirty acres a couple of hours from New York City would be Elysium—and all very cheap, too, he said. He urged Kenneth Burke to sell his place in New Jersey and move up with them.

On the Fourth of July all the Browns' friends from New York, including Allen and Caroline, flocked to Tory Valley for their big party. Charlie Jennings, who had sold Sue and Slater their house, told them about a small house in the neighborhood that a local house painter had bought for about a hundred dollars in unpaid taxes. Jennings thought he would sell it for five hundred. Caroline and Allen looked at it—it was in good shape, but they couldn't buy it. "We can't even buy a Woolworth plate," mourned Caroline, who longed to live in the country even more than Allen.

Guests at the party drank gin and jugs of hard cider from neighboring farms and sang and danced and played games. Caroline spent the afternoon sitting under a tree, at one point the only sober person there, and watched Hart Crane, his face and body painted like an Indian's, put a record on the Victrola and pour salt on it "to make it work better." While he gazed at a young cedar tree, he recited the line, "Where the cedar leaf divides the sky," the first line of his poem "Passage," a line that Caroline often repeated throughout her life.

In September, when Caroline went into labor, she called her friend

Sally Wood, who was vacationing at the Jersey shore. Sally, a trained nurse, hurried back and sat with Caroline in the labor room at Sloan Lying-In Hospital. Caroline, white-faced, talked between contractions about the novel she was trying to write. At one point Allen broke away from some friends who had taken him to a speakeasy and came by the hospital, carrying his cane. After the baby was born, Allen went back to the speakeasy. They named the baby Nancy after Caroline's mother, great-grandmother, and great-great-great-grandmother.

Allen wrote to Caroline's parents to tell them about the baby, and to Donald Davidson to say that he was delighted with the "stupendous novelty" of fatherhood. "The damned nurses will hardly let me near her," he told Davidson. "But I did see her today and I rejoiced to observe the absence of her original very wicked and angry expression, which I took to be a protest against the hard riot of unrequested sensation from an extremely undesired world. She has fine blue eyes, a perfect chin, and amazingly prehensile fingers. What more could one wish?"

Sally Wood had to hurry off to France to see about her brother, and it was Laura Riding Gottschalk, the Fugitive, who helped Allen clean the apartment before Caroline came back from the hospital and then carried Nancy home. Allen wrote Davidson how good it was to have Laura there. He was impressed with her poetry—he said he thought she and Hart Crane were the two whose work would live on—and he was impressed with the praise her poetry had received in England. "Laura is great company and we've had a fine time since she arrived," he wrote. "She is a constant visitor to the Tates, and Carolyn finds her very charming, if strenuous." (Caroline always referred to her as "Laura Riding Roughshod.")

To Laura, Caroline "was brave, she did not shirk suffering, had impatiences and irritabilities, faced obligations. I do not think that the nervous strain she exhibited in that period was caused by her pregnancy and the trials of new motherhood in cramped domestic surroundings. She seemed set against sparing herself full consciousness of her predicaments and bent on accepting them without feigned ease. . . . She *was* grumpy in her acceptance of my services, but, it seemed to me, healthily and honestly so." (Allen, Laura said, "bound himself to minor scruples as if he had satisfied all the major ones.")

When Laura Riding left New York, she went to England at the invitation of Robert Graves, who had admired her poetry in *The Fugitive*. She lived for some time with Graves and his wife and four children, writing the Tates that Mrs. Graves was dressing her in white muslin with blue sashes and, later, that Mrs. Graves was "nervous" and did they know of a cottage in America where Mrs. Graves could live? Graves left his wife and children and went to live with Laura for years on Mallorca.

There was no hint of scandal even in Guthrie and the Old Neighborhood around Merry Mont about Nancy's arrival. The Tates always gave November 2, 1924, as the date of their marriage (except when Allen forgot and gave the correct date, to Caroline's fury.) The fact that Caroline was four years older than Allen caused a little talk in Guthrie, but that was all.

Caroline's mother arrived in New York shortly after Nancy was born. She had nothing to eat on the train and when she arrived at the apartment found there was no food in the house. No food in the house! Mrs. Gordon went out and bought some groceries, and when she left a few weeks later, she took Nancy back to Kentucky with her. They had to turn the baby over to Mrs. Gordon, Caroline told Nancy later, "so you wouldn't freeze to death as well as starve to death."

Caroline was ambivalent about Nancy's departure. Nancy was the "darlingest baby," but Caroline was desperate for time to write. Considering the circumstances of their marriage, she must have felt her hold on Allen was insecure; to send Nancy away might strengthen that hold. And Mrs. Gordon really wanted to take Nancy. She did not think that New York City was the proper place to raise a child. She had been put off by some of Caroline's wild friends, Dorothy Day and Peggy Cowley among them. Allen did not appear to be eager to earn a living to support a wife and child. Caroline wrote to Sally Wood that she was "afraid Allen would break down trying to work day and night." It struck everybody as a "sensible" thing for Mrs. Gordon to take Nancy with her. Caroline sometimes said that she missed her baby and she agonized about the decision in letters to Sally Wood, but she never expressed any real regret or guilt. She herself had stayed with her grandmother for long periods when she was a child, sometimes over her mother's protests. ("I'll never name another child after my mother," Mrs. Gordon had written to a friend, when "Carrie" had been at Merry Mont for months and Mrs. Gordon was in Hopkinsville, where she and her husband were both teaching.) It solved many problems for Nancy to stay with the Gordons for a while.

In one way, it was the best thing that ever happened to Nancy Tate. Mrs. Gordon had no use for what were then the "modern" rules about not picking up a baby, no matter how hard she cried, until time for a scheduled feeding. She could hardly put Nancy down. (Caroline shuddered at her attitude.) And wonder of wonders, Brother Gordon, the man who never accepted a call to a church unless there was good fishing nearby, the man who loved to hunt and fish better than anything else in the world, went fishing only once the first year Nancy was with them. Nancy, thriving under enormous amounts of affection and care from her grandparents, was a happy, robust child, able to survive all sorts of vicissitudes when she rejoined her parents two years later.

In "The Only Poem," written many years later, Robert Penn Warren tells about the afternoon his mother took him over to Mrs. Gordon's to see Nancy.

But the facts: that day she took me to see the new daughter

My friends stashed with Grandma while they went East for careers.
So for friendship I warily handled the sweet-smelling squaw-fruit,
All golden and pink, kissed the fingers, blew in the ears.
Then suddenly was at a loss. So my mother seized it,

And I knew, all at once, that she would have waited all day,
Sitting there on the floor, with her feet drawn up like a girl,
Till half-laughing, half-crying, arms stretched, she could swing up her prey
That shrieked with joy at the giddy swoop and swirl. . . .

After Mrs. Gordon and Nancy left, Allen corrected the grammar in a memorandum written by his boss at *Telling Tales*—and the angry boss fired him. Caroline, tired of the hectic life in New York, persuaded Allen that it would be a good thing to give up their apartment and find a place in Tory Valley near Sue and Slater Brown. Mrs. Addie Turner rented them half her house that was just half a mile through the woods from Sue and Slater Brown for eight dollars a month. They invited Hart Crane, who was broke and not working, to live with them at Mrs. Turner's, and he happily agreed to join them later.

The Tates moved in early December, leaving Allen's city clothes behind in Dorothy Day's apartment. (When they later heard Dorothy had moved again, Allen worried about his good clothes.) Slater Brown met their train in Patterson in the old Model-T he had bought for twenty-five dollars and drove them over muddy, rutted roads through the pouring rain to Mrs. Turner's house. There was no electricity, no indoor plumbing, and they had to cut wood to heat the house. There was, however, a pump on the porch—more than Sue and Slater had at their house. This was the way Caroline had lived at Merry Mont and it held no terrors for her, and although Allen was not a country-man, they were excited about their situation. They were ecstatic, in fact, and told everybody they planned to stay indefinitely. Allen ordered new boots and a shotgun from Sears, Roebuck and then almost chopped a hole in one of the boots. He had a few things to learn, he said. Caroline learned to saw wood, and Allen gained weight and boasted that his right arm was as hard as a hickory log from all that woodcutting. Living was cheap, Caroline exulted, and there was nothing to do but keep the fires going, cook, and write. They saw Sue and Slater when the four of them gathered at one house or the other every afternoon for tea, and when the moon was full they had a cider party, although Allen said it was hard to get drunk on Slater's cider since it tasted so bad. Friends came out from New York City on the weekends, and Southern friends found their way to Patterson, even in two feet of snow.

Caroline's parents sent frequent letters with full reports about Nancy's health and progress, her food, her bowels, her smiles, her chuckles, often sending along Kodak pictures. They thought Nancy was the most wonderful baby who ever lived and they said so in every letter. Caroline said merely that she hoped Nancy could visit her and Allen in the spring.

The Tates set aside the two best upstairs rooms for Hart, including the one that held Mrs. Turner's antique sleigh bed. He arrived a week later than he was expected and he was no longer broke. He had appealed to Otto Kahn, financier and philanthropist, who had given him $2,000 in cash so he could finish his poem *The Bridge*. He brought with him a sculpture by Lachaise, plenty of liquor, and everything else he owned. He hung his pictures and put away his books, and retrieved from storage at the Browns' a little drop-leaf desk for the room he used as a study. He put quilts, blankets, and comforters from home in his bedroom and hung his grandmother's knitted shawl on the wall where everyone could admire it.

For a while all went well at Mrs. Turner's. Hart washed dishes, and Allen cooked breakfast. With his shotgun, "The White Powder Wonder," Allen spent a great deal of time "ranging over the hills shooting at sparrows." There were pheasants and partridge and deer in the woods, and he had high hopes of bagging them. He did shoot rabbits and squirrels, with which Caroline made stew. Hart helped Caroline fix Christmas dinner—he made the cranberry sauce and the sauce for the plum pudding—and there was a party at the Browns' with much drink and talk. New Year's Eve was quiet. Allen went to Washington to visit his mother and stopped to see Edmund Wilson in New York on the way back. He and Wilson conceived a plan to publish a series of new poets including Allen, Edmund, Laura Riding, Phelps Putnam (a young Yale graduate admired by Allen and Wilson), Malcolm Cowley, Hart Crane, and John Peale Bishop (a friend and Princeton classmate of Wilson's). Allen felt all these were fine poets who had little chance of publication under the Louis Untermeyer dictatorship. Tate and Wilson talked of starting their own press in the country since Slater Brown knew something about printing.

Allen did reviews for *The Nation* and *The New Republic*. He reconsidered his opinion of Mr. Canby of *Saturday Review* and wrote some essays for him. He reviewed T. S. Eliot for *The New Republic*, which then asked him to do an essay on Eliot. Meanwhile, Eliot himself wrote that he was considering publishing some of Allen's poems in *The Criterion* and asked Allen to write an essay on the writings of Paul Elmer More, leader of the New Humanist movement. Allen also reviewed Oswald Spengler's *Decline of the West* for *The New Republic*.

Caroline started a new novel and worked on it when Allen was not using his typewriter. After Hart Crane bought a new typewriter, he gave Caroline his old one. At this point, she lived in Allen's shadow. She was a journalist and was not taken seriously by the young "men of letters" who were interested only in poetry and criticism—not even fiction. Katherine Anne Porter once described Caroline in those early years as "a little ole brown thing," and at that time she certainly played a subordinate role—almost a walk-on part—in the drama of their lives. She, too, wanted to be a writer, a woman of letters, but for now she was a housewife who gardened and cooked and tried to write a novel on the kitchen table.

Caroline's brother Morris paid her way to Washington for a visit, and Allen, missing her, said he was living on cornmeal and rice and would probably have scurvy if Caroline stayed away very long. (The Tates had introduced the Browns to the wonders of hoecakes and batter bread made from water-ground white cornmeal imported by mail from the Pawmunkey Mills in Kentucky.) When Caroline came back from Washington, Allen met her in New York City, where they reveled in the luxury of the Albert Hotel and took hot baths. "Of course we drank a little and saw a few people," she wrote Sally, "but the hot baths were the brightest lights."

Hart Crane worked on his poem. The trouble was that he didn't work with the dogged perseverance that the Tates did, and he annoyed them. He had more money than they did and spent it freely on art and liquor. He drank more than they did. But the worst thing he did was interrupt them when they worked. When he rushed in to talk to Caroline while she was writing, Caroline did not ask him to leave, but he could feel her coolness. Hart started to spend a lot of time talking to Mrs. Turner, who was in her sixties, not very bright, but had a "moderately kind heart." People called her a widow, but her husband, Blind Jim, had been in the insane asylum for five years. He fancied he was a girl and wore beads around his neck and flirted with a fan. Caroline told everybody that Mrs. Turner fell violently in love with Hart, and called it a "Eugene O'Neill situation" in which the older woman was in love with a young homosexual. At any rate, Mrs. Turner was very fond of Crane and they spent a great deal of time together.

It was an unusually cold winter, and Hart bought expensive snow-shoes and prayed for storms. The storms came, and at Mrs. Turner's they were snowed in. Sometimes Hart alone went a mile on snowshoes to the nearest farm on the main road to get the mail, and sometimes they all went, "skipping right over seven-foot drifts" on snowshoes, as Caroline said with delight.

Hart complained it was dull. Everybody had stiff fingers and chilblains—and they all soaked their chilblained feet in a common tub of steaming water. He began to wear his grandmother's shawl and a toboggan cap night and day. He complained that Mrs. Turner's cats kept him awake at night tramping up and down the stairs. As he became even more irritated with the Tates, he started taking most of his meals with Mrs. Turner.

The Tates in turn were more annoyed by Hart. He hunted Allen down to show him elaborate diagrams of how subjective and objective imagery operated. It seemed to Caroline he burst in on her every time she spread her manuscript out on the kitchen table, so she put a lock on the door. Hart moved his soap, razor, washcloth, and towel and installed them in Mrs. Turner's kitchen. If he met either Allen or Caroline in the yard or on the road, Hart didn't speak but turned away.

The feud climaxed on a cold Friday morning in April after some of the snow had melted. The Tates were in bed and through the bedroom window they could hear Hart and Mrs. Turner talking about the mess in the yard on "their" side of the house and how they'd have to clean it up.

The mess consisted of wood chips left over from Allen's sawing and chopping of firewood. Hart did not like to chop wood—he told Malcolm Cowley that chopping "constricted his imagination"—and so Allen had to cut all the wood to keep them warm that winter. When he heard Hart talking about the chips of wood and how dirty the yard was, he was furious, and while Caroline snuggled back in the warm bed, he threw the covers off and stormed through the icy house to accost Hart. Caroline decided to follow Allen downstairs.

"If you've got a criticism of my work to make, I'd appreciate it if you would speak to me first!" he said to Hart. Hart wrote his mother that he and Mrs. Turner stared at each other in "perfect amazement." They hadn't mentioned Allen "or anything that concerned him." Hart felt himself losing all control, but he managed to talk to the Tates "without breaking anything." He wrote his mother that Tate finally admitted he was all wrong.

That night, neither Allen nor Caroline could sleep. They each got out of bed at a different time, typed a letter to Hart, and slipped it under Hart's door. The gist of each letter was that they had invited him to live with them when he was penniless, but he arrived temporarily well-off and spread out all over the house, invading every corner.

Hart wrote his mother that he would have to leave Mrs. Turner's. "While I could bury my pride and become reconciled, they really wouldn't you know, and Mrs. Tate especially. I couldn't get any work done in such an atmosphere." He went to New York City and found a place to live and then returned to Patterson and packed up his belongings. From New York he wrote to a friend: "And my poem was progressing so beautifully until Mrs. Tate took it into her head to be so destructive!"

After Hart left, the Tates had more space, and Caroline had a study, "a darling little white room upstairs." She had now written 10,000 words on her novel, in which "a young gentleman is in love with somebody else's wife. The mood of the book is a slowly increasing madness." She wanted to introduce reality into this unreal scene and chose an adulterous love affair as the "most poignant example."

Allen was in a "fecund period," as Caroline put it, and it was almost indecent the way he produced poems. Any minute he was likely to be seized with labor pains. One publishing company told Allen they might publish his poems if he would also write a novel for them. ("I wish I could offer mine in lieu of his!" said Caroline.) Allen tried to outline a novel. He had no interest in writing a novel, but he wanted his poems published. Caroline thought that if he could write a novel his "thoughts would have turned that way long ago." Allen went into New York, and Caroline was annoyed that he brought no news of Dorothy Day's baby except to report its weight and sex.

Caroline wrote Peggy and Malcolm Cowley that they hung on "from one freelance check to another," and kept an order to Sears or Macy's all made up, ready to send the minute a check came. They needed shoes and garden seed, for instance. It was quite a blow when Irita Van Doren at the *Herald Tribune* offered Allen fifty dollars to write an article and then refused the article, paying nothing. Caroline wrote a potboiler and made forty dollars, her first contribution to the family larder in a long time, and she gamely tried, without success for a while, to write another.

When the weather turned warmer, life was more pleasant. Caroline waded in the brook every day, picked cowslip greens, dandelion, and dock, and cooked them. She planted a garden and went into "a perfect frenzy over the clods." She had lettuces in a cold frame by early May. Allen, she realized, would never make a gardener, although she tried to get a few rows' worth of work out of him every day. Then they quarreled violently over the garden. "But now we understand each other's limitations better," Caroline wrote to Sally Wood. "He realizes I must finger the soil and I see that he will never really enjoy hoeing. So I don't try to drive him into the garden and he doesn't try to drive me out of it." A little later Allen took over the dishwashing, and Caroline continued to do the gardening.

They were eating better. When the wild strawberries ripened, Caroline made strawberry shortcake for all their visitors, and they had vegetables from the garden, apples from the orchard, wild berries, and always cheap milk and eggs. As the weather grew warmer, they seemed to spend a great deal more time entertaining guests, lying on the grass, swimming, or just talking.

Caroline's parents continued to send pictures of Nancy, and Mrs. Gordon agreed to bring her up for a visit later in the summer. Mr. Gordon wrote that Caroline must realize that when Mrs. Gordon brought the baby, it would be only for a visit, that she and Allen were not prepared to take care of Nancy, and that the Gordons did not propose to jeopardize the progress she had made.

"This is the most explicit statement I've had yet of an attitude I've been aware of all along," Caroline wrote Sally. "I can't blame them. I want to have a talk with Dad somehow before I do anything decisive. I'm really afraid Mother will go all to pieces if Nancy is taken away from her. We think we may work out some system of dividing the year between the two households. Nancy, in that case, would have a more varied experience than most children."

Caroline redoubled her efforts to write potboilers for the money to pay for Mrs. Gordon's railroad fare. In a letter to Sally she commented:

> Mother, who is as wily and designing a female as ever lived, has us. She has spent so much on us that I can't urge her to make the trip up here unless I can furnish the money, and it's so damn hard to get hold of. She writes now urbanely that she will have to defer her visit until August because my aunt Margaret who has been planning to go to see the baby can't leave home until the middle of July. Of course it will be too hot to travel in August. All I can do is to point out that it is a little more important for us to see Nancy than for her to be inspected by her aunt, and to observe also that I know exactly what she is up to. Of course this is a minor irritation when I think of how wonderfully Mother has cared for Nancy. She really seems to be the model baby.

When Mrs. Gordon arrived with Nancy, everyone marveled that Nancy wasn't afraid of her parents, but Caroline, unused to caring for a baby, could only thank God that Nancy took two naps a day. Caroline could appreciate Nancy's good looks (she had the Meriwether blue eyes and blond hair) and good humor (she giggled all day and occasionally broke into a guffaw). Allen, who had never known a baby intimately before, was in a state of constant amazement. Caroline reflected on the situation to Sally:

> However we have our troubles in spite of all her loveliness. I think it would kill Mother if we took her away from her, yet I can't let Nancy be brought up the way she will be brought up if she remains with Mother. It is no worse than I foresaw when I let Nancy go—in fact I painted the picture for Allen at the time. He says he thought I was exaggerating and that my fears were all due to my nervous condition—but admits now that it is all exactly as I prophesied. Mother is—indescribable. She is mediaeval in spirit. Her ratiocinative processes are those of the schoolmen of the middle ages. Imagine such methods applied to every day life in this century! The result is appalling. She has no mental life outside this system, which her whole being is constantly defending. Fortunately, or unfortunately, she still has her natural affections—this is what complicates relations with her so much. And of course she is simply mad about Nancy. In the rearing of Nancy she hopes to correct all the errors she made with me! Poor Allen is frequently embarrassed when she says to him quite naively, "And you see how Carolyn turned out." He realizes he is the bad end to which I have come, in Mother's opinion, but he doesn't think he should be called upon to cry out on my ruin. We have decided to leave Nancy with Mother another winter, then snatch her away at any cost. When it comes to a choice between Mother and Nancy I am quite capable of being ruthless. But just now I honestly don't know whether it's best for Nancy to risk our uncertain fortunes. It is fiendishly cold here in the winter. Then, too, there are times when we simply don't eat.

Mrs. Gordon and Nancy stayed six weeks. Mrs. Gordon had arrived with a low opinion of Northern men and told her daughter she was astounded that Slater Brown removed his hat when he talked to her. She was pleased with the country life, though, and picked blueberries. When she and Nancy left, Caroline was relieved. The visit had been "harried" and "hectic," and they "couldn't enjoy Nancy much because Mother wouldn't let us." Nancy was a darling, but Caroline wanted to get on with her writing. It was to be almost two years before she saw Nancy again.

Right after her mother and Nancy left, Caroline wrote to Sally:

I suppose I try to put the situation as regards Nancy rationally because it seems so hopelessly involved emotionally. I don't know what to do. Mother is the sort of person with whom no one can have a satisfactory relationship. She uses theology—the theology of the first century church—as her weapon of offense and defense—in the affairs of every day life. She is enormously learned in this lore—before Nancy came she gave all her time to it for five years. Unless you have seen it in operation you cannot imagine what an effective weapon it is. After a week of Mother's society I begin to think the fathers of the church were men of superhuman intelligence. The system really takes care of every human foible, if as Mother piously avers, you can just "lay down your mind and take up the mind of God." I, who want to keep what little mind I have, can't agree with her there, so nothing I say has any weight with her, coming as it does from "the carnal mind." She has a great scorn for the modern, who confuses Christianity with humanitarianism. She sees that "the mind of God" is capable of cruelty, and she uses cruelty to gain her own ends, always of course within the strict letter of the system. As she is very careful to make her actions consonant with the system she remains always virtuous. I think she came heartily to dislike Allen for he made her uncomfortable—she has always disliked me. Nancy is to become all things I have failed to be!!!! You can imagine how that prospect pleases us. I can of course take Nancy away from her—Allen was on the verge of doing it half a dozen times while Mother was here, but that is a very hard thing to do. Mother, in spite of having taken up the mind of Christ, still retains her natural affections. She is a person of strong passions, and she has set her heart on Nancy. I really think she would collapse if we took her away. Then I feel some responsibility towards my father. She always makes him suffer for any disappointment that comes to her. He and I have had a sort of gentlemen's agreement ever since I was fifteen or sixteen, to help each other out when we can.

My disapproval of Mother, my indignation against her—and Allen's—is all on moral grounds. And she feels great disapproval of us too, so we're completely antagonistic. At the same time she insists on stressing family affection. We're going to let her have Nancy another year anyhow. After that I don't know what we'll do. Nancy will probably decide the matter for herself eventually, though; so there's no use in bothering. Meanwhile, I'm trying to finish this novel before I do anything else.

Caroline gathered elderberries and started some wine. She would be happy, she said, to stay there the rest of her life. She was making money doing hack work, and Allen was making a little more each month. She was afraid that as they made more money they would move back to town. "Allen has the strangest attitude toward the country—the same appreciation you'd have for a good seat in the theatre," she wrote Sally. "I think Allen feels toward Nature as I do toward mathematics—respectful indifference. He walks about the garden hailing each tomato and melon with amazement—and never sees any connection between planting seeds and eating fruit. Allen, by the way, has changed a lot in the last year. He's certainly a more integrated personality."

NEW YORK, 1926–1928

Allen said he could not face another New England winter without steam heat, and abandoning their plans to stay in Tory Valley the rest of their lives, the Tates went back to New York City in the fall of 1926. They were offered the basement apartment at 27 Bank Street rent-free in return for simple janitorial duties; Allen stoked the furnace while Caroline, responsible for the stairs and hallways, hired black women from the neighborhood.

Matthew Josephson, dadaist poet and former editor of *Broom* who had temporarily deserted literature for Wall Street, tipped off a newspaper reporter about the poet-janitor of Bank Street. When the reporter appeared, Allen, outraged, refused to be interviewed and sent him away. Allen remained furious with Josephson for the rest of his life. In vain did Josephson protest that he had hoped a sympathetic reader might offer to subsidize Tate's writing just as Otto Kahn had subsidized Hart Crane, and then say it was just a dadaist prank. Allen was proud, he was a poet, and he had made a deliberate choice to be a poet, not a coal man, he said, and he was willing to put up with near starvation to reach that goal.

When Donald Davidson sent him the manuscript for a volume of verse from *The Fugitive,* Allen was astonished all over again at how good the Fugitives were. He was sure no other group of poets in the country could offer such a show. He took it to several publishers and finally Harcourt, Brace accepted it in the fall of 1927; *Fugitives: An Anthology of Verse* appeared the following autumn.

Caroline had various jobs. She did some proofreading and worked briefly as a typist for the American Society for Cultural Relations with Russia, a Communist-front organization. Eventually she worked as a secretary to Ford Madox Ford, who spent some time each year in New York. She was lucky to meet Ford when she needed him most. He built up her confidence and inspired her when she was scrambling to keep on with her writing in the midst of the brilliant young poets. Ford was fifty-three, a renowned novelist, author of sixty-five books. In his childhood he had heard William Morris arguing with Friedrich Engels in his own grandfather's house and had met Algernon Charles Swinburne, William Holman Hunt, and John Everett Millais. His aunt was married to William Michael Rossetti, brother to Dante Gabriel and Christina. When he was eighteen he published his first book, a fairy story called *The Brown Owl,* illustrated by his grandfather. He had absorbed Ford Madox Brown's rule: "Art is all important and . . . beggar yourself rather than refuse assistance to anyone whose genius you think shows promise."

Ford knew personally Henry James, Ezra Pound, T. S. Eliot, H. G. Wells, John Galsworthy, Arnold Bennett, Wyndham Lewis, D. H. Lawrence, and Norman Douglas. As editor of *the transatlantic review,* he published the work of Djuna Barnes, Glenway Wescott, Man Ray, William Carlos Williams, John Dos Passos, Havelock Ellis, and James Joyce.

He had written books of poetry, biography, criticism, and travel, as well as suffragette pamphlets, Allied propaganda, and dozens of novels, the best known of which were *The Young Lovell, The Good Soldier, No More Parades,* and *Some Do Not.* He was trilingual. None of his books ever made much money, but he continued with relentless optimism to write them. He was fat and he wheezed from being gassed at Armentières during World War I, but he was full of life. Ford was, as someone said, "a man and a half." Even his love life was outsize: he married when he was a teenager, left his wife to live with Violet Hunt, and left her for Stella Bowen, an Australian painter.

At the moment, he was enjoying a triumphant success. The *Herald Tribune* in New York had said that *No More Parades* was "far and away the finest book of the year," and the *Transcript* in Boston called him a genius. He was writing for *Harper's Magazine, Vanity Fair, The Bookman,* and *The Yale Review.* He made friends with E. A. Robinson, Theodore Dreiser, Padraic Colum, and with Burton Rascoe, Caroline's old employer at the Johnson Syndicate, who was now editor of *The Bookman.*

Harold Loeb, of *Broom*, took him up to Tory Valley to one of the Browns' Fourth of July parties.

Caroline Gordon of Merry Mont and Ford Madox Ford, international literary figure, took to each other. Ford was living in one of those "rambling, old, gloomy apartments on West Sixteenth Street" with a lot of "rather rude, very early Colonial furniture and some fine prints of birds and flowers." Terribly fat, Ford wore only his underwear while he dictated to her the novel that was to be *The Last Post*. The place was overheated, and he sweated profusely.

But Ford was awfully nice, Caroline wrote to Sally Wood, "and I love to see him take his sentences by the tail and uncurl them—in a perfectly elegant manner. I don't believe there's anybody writing now who can do it so elegantly. At times he almost weeps over my lapses into Americanisms. 'My deah child, *do* you spell "honour" without a *u?*'" All her life after that, Caroline would spell words the English way—*honour, colour,* and *splendour.*

After Caroline had been working for him for three months, Ford decided he wanted to have a large tea party. When he had served tea before to one or two guests, Caroline had made it on a gas ring in one of the two parlors. This time, though, he wanted to have fifty or sixty people, and sent Caroline to ask the janitor for an electric kettle or spirit lamp. The janitor said, "Why doesn't Mr. Ford use his kitchen?" Only then did they discover that a hallway Ford had never explored led to a kitchen.

"Imagine a man who is in an apartment six months and doesn't know he has a kitchen!" said Caroline.

"Imagine a young lady who makes tea every day for three months on a gas ring in a parlour and does not know she is in command of a perfectly appointed kitchen!" said Ford.

Ford was impressed with the Tates—Allen was "a nice fellow and a good poet" and Caroline was "extraordinarily well educated and quite a lady—from the South." Ford soon moved to the second-floor apartment of the Bank Street building and took his meals with the Tates, and there he met the stream of Southern poets who came to stay with them.

Andrew Lytle, who had gone to Vanderbilt after Allen left and had published one poem in *The Fugitive*, was studying playwriting at Yale that year; Davidson and Ransom had told him to look up the Tates. Andrew was a tall, handsome, blond young man who wore steel-rimmed spectacles and loved to square dance; he was what in the South used to be called an unreconstructed rebel, a true believer in the Old Confederacy. He was for years like a younger brother in the Tate household. Robert Penn Warren, tall, gangly, and red-headed, who had earned his master's degree at the University of California in Berkeley and was working toward a Ph.D. at Yale, was often in New York with the Tates. Ford liked these Southerners and, in fact, encouraged the Tates and their friends to value and use their Southern heritage instead of suppressing it, ignoring it, or belittling it.

Josephine Herbst wrote that she would stop in on her way home from the pulp magazine where she worked and stand in the doorway, listen idly to the conversation that went on, and wonder just which war was being discussed. Then she would hear a name and know it was the Civil War. She came in once on a poker game; Allen, "for luck," was wearing a wide-brimmed black hat that made him look like a Kentucky colonel. Hart Crane might be there, or Malcolm Cowley, and Caroline, usually in the kitchen. Josie considered the Southerners in New York to be the real expatriates; they had, she said, a bloom of other lands more remote than modern France. If you looked at Allen, he could have been an exiled dauphin of France. Caroline sweeping by, full of energy, made her think of some "grandmother who had once had her hands full with a thousand supervisory chores and had stood looking out over plowed acres with the authority of a commander." There was nearly always some newly arrived ambassador from the South. Ford's voice whistled and wheezed, Josie said, but he sat stoutly erect.

Allen tried desperately to get his poems published. A publisher to whom Caroline took them with Ford's recommendation was, she said, "rather snooty." Ford, who thought Allen's poems were more English than American, sent them to English publishers. Finally Allen agreed to write a biography of Confederate general Thomas Jonathan "Stonewall" Jackson for Minton, Balch; the company would then publish his poetry. He signed a contract and plunged happily into Southern history, reading nine hours a day, plowing through war memoirs, campaign histories, and official records. He was soon convinced that if Jackson had been in command of the Confederate forces from the beginning the South would now be a separate nation, and everybody would be much better off. If Jackson hadn't been killed in 1863, Allen maintained, the Battle of Gettysburg would have been won.

They were getting quite unreconstructed, Caroline said.

The Tates thought of going back to Tory Valley for the summer, or of camping on the property of James Rorty, a radical newspaperman, in Easton, Connecticut. But Caroline decided not to give up her job, and as Allen was having trouble with the battle accounts—he had never seen a battlefield—he and Caroline rattled down to Virginia in an old Ford to look at Manassas, Fredericksburg, and Chancellorsville. Allen's grandfather had fought at Manassas, while his great-grandfather, four miles away on his farm, listened to the roar of the battle. Caroline and Allen took camping equipment and slept outdoors, but "mostly in tourist camps because we were too lazy to hunt for water at night," according to Caroline. Allen was "putting powder, blood, dirt, stink, and sweat" into his book. He aimed to organize it like a novel, telling it all from Jackson's point of view. They wanted to camp at Oakleigh, the house that had been built on the site of Pleasant Hill, the house that Allen's Bogan ancestors had owned and seen burned by Yankee mercenaries, but for some reason did not.

Although they had not seen Nancy for a year, Caroline and Allen did not go to Kentucky on this trip. Almost two, Nancy flourished, visiting Caroline's grandmother at Merry Mont and making friends with Miss Carrie's spotted pony, Dixie. Caroline's father and mother wrote often, reporting on the baby's progress. She took her first outdoor walk in little overshoes given by a parishioner, she was a "little princess of the aryan race." . . . A visitor admired Nancy and said "she would make two of his youngest who was twenty months old." . . . She called Mrs. Gordon "Ninny Baby" and Brother Gordon "Diddy Daddy" and referred to a copy of Briton Riviere's painting of Daniel in the lions' den as "Dander and the dogs." . . . Nancy had Caroline's old doll bed and about ten dolls. . . . "I know you are counting the days until you see her," Brother Gordon wrote his daughter. (Was she? She never said so.) "She is full of original sin and deceitful. . . . If she gets any smarter, I fear we can't raise her. Isn't it strange two such commonplace beings as you and Allen should produce such a wonderful child! She must be a throwback to some unknown ancestor!"

Mrs. Gordon made dresses and blouses for Caroline and sent them to her. She offered to send Caroline a new spring coat, if Caroline would send her old green one to Guthrie—it would be new enough for her there, Mrs. Gordon said. The Gordons sent small checks to help the Tates, some of which Caroline returned.

By the summer of 1927, the summer of the Sacco and Vanzetti executions, and the excitement and demonstrations surrounding them, Allen and Caroline had moved to a cold-water flat in what Caroline described as a "fine pre-Revolutionary tenement house at 561 Hudson Street known as The Cabinet of Dr. Caligari." Katherine Anne Porter, a tiny woman with gray hair and a soft, low, husky voice, lived in the same building, while Dorothy Day, Forster Batterham, and Dorothy's sister, Della Day, lived across the street. Just as Ford had persuaded the Tates not to deprecate their Southern heritage, the Tates passed on the lesson to Katherine Anne.

Katherine Anne actively protested the Sacco and Vanzetti sentence, as did other writers the Tates knew, like Dorothy Day, John Dos Passos, and Edna St. Vincent Millay. The story has been told often of the visitor who came to the Hudson Street apartment building looking for Katherine Anne Porter. Allen bowed and told him courteously and gravely, "The ladies of the house are at the riot in Union Square."

Robert Penn Warren brought his fiancée, "Cinina Elena Anna Clotilda Maria Borgia Venia Gasparini Brescia," to meet the Tates, and Caroline said they stayed six weeks. Warren had met Cinina, daughter of the conductor of the San Francisco Symphony, when he was at Berkeley. Nobody else could ever stand her. "She felt she must live up to her descent from the Borgias and raised as much hell as she possibly could all the time," Caroline wrote Sally. "I would have thrown her out of the window the first week but for my deep affection for Red."

As Caroline told Sally, she "elbowed them all out of the way" once or twice that summer and wrote her first short story, "in two sittings." Never published, it was about old Mrs. Llewellyn, who loved Mayfield, her grandfather's home, better than anything—husband, children, or grandchildren—but couldn't live there and lived instead at the Old Place. The plot, as outlined by Caroline, matches the facts of her grandmother's life.

While Allen was finishing up his book on Stonewall Jackson, word came from Kentucky that Caroline must come and get Nancy. Mrs. Gordon had been operated on that fall for breast cancer and Caroline's Aunt Margaret from Chattanooga had kept Nancy for a while, but now the Gordons regretfully realized they would have to give Nancy up for good.

Caroline went down on the train to pick her up. Her father met her at the station and told her Nancy was "the worst spoiled child in the United States"; he didn't know how Caroline would ever manage her.

"We did manage, however, to establish a routine for her in the course of several weeks, but it was certainly hell while it lasted," Caroline said. "She was used to being rocked to sleep and all that sort of thing."

"I was afraid if you and Allen did not have the care of her you would not love her as you ought," Brother Gordon wrote after Nancy was in New York. Allen finished the Jackson book and agreed to do a book about Jefferson Davis before his Civil War fever cooled. At first he planned to write not a full biography, but a study beginning in 1860 and ending with Davis's arrest by Union troops in 1865.

The Tates were "happy, happy to breathe without orders," Katherine Anne wrote Josie Herbst. "They set out to the country to visit the newly wedded Jim Rorty, with Nancy between them, all three beaming and fresh and free, a pretty sight if ever I did see one."

Nancy was the pet of a large company of surrogate uncles—mostly young Southern poets—who enjoyed her observations. At three, she urged her father on to greater efforts. "Go on, Daddy, and make me a living," she would say. A "living" was any piece of typewritten paper. She picked up several from Allen's desk one day and said, "Is this my living, Daddy?" and when he said it was she said, "It's mighty thin, Daddy."

A *Fugitive* anthology appeared, and shortly thereafter *Stonewall Jackson, the Good Soldier,* subtitled in homage to Ford. Allen sent twenty-six copies to his relatives; they were sure, he said, to think it was good because of the subject matter. At his publication party, Katherine Anne Porter said, "everybody was drunk with everybody putting his tongue out at everybody else: You know the charming atmosphere of goodwill and good manners that animates the artistic life of this vast cultural metropolis." Reviews were favorable, and the book appeared to be selling. Then came a double dose of happy news—in one day, Allen learned that he had won one of the new Guggenheim Fellowships and Earle Balch agreed to publish a book of his poetry, to be called *Mr. Pope and Other Poems.* Allen exulted that "Old Jack" had done it all.

When Allen had applied for the Guggenheim in late 1927, he proposed to use the grant to write a long ten-part poem dealing with the "cultural situation of an American in the industrial age," for which he needed detachment from the American scene. He had told the committee that his ultimate purposes were the writing of poetry, the criticism of modern poetry, and occasional monographs on past writers. He said he wanted to be considered "a man of letters." In the space for his employment history, Allen typed in across the ruled columns: "The applicant has never been employed by an institution; he has made his living, since leaving college, as a free lance writer."

The Tates were excited about going to Europe—the Guggenheim Foundation then required its fellows to travel abroad—and Allen's book sold 3,000 copies the first three weeks. Caroline could hardly believe that by fall they would have enough money on hand to live on for two years. It didn't seem possible, she told Sally. They had not known where the next package of cigarettes was coming from these last two years.

She was, however, discouraged about her own work and felt she had little to show for the two or three years she had spent writing: an unfinished novel and two stories. All those young poets from the South sapped her time and energy—they called up as soon as they hit Pennsylvania Station and stayed anywhere from a week to a month. "I have gotten a bit bitter about it," she said.

Before the Tates left for Europe they made another, more extensive camping trip to the Southern battlefields. This time they took Nancy along, as well as Andrew Lytle, and they dropped Katherine Anne off at Josie Herbst's house in Erwinna, Pennsylvania, where they all drank mint juleps around the pump. They stopped in Philadelphia to visit Caroline's Radford cousins, and then headed south. They camped outside Richmond for several weeks in their six-by-nine tent, fighting off flies and ants, while Allen worked in the state library on Jefferson Davis. One day they all got dressed up and went into town to spend the night with Virginia Tunstall, a poet who had contributed to *The Fugitive,* and her husband, Robert, and enjoyed the luxury of sleeping in beds and taking baths.

They stopped at Monteagle, Tennessee, where Andrew's mother had a summer home, and as they drove down one of the little dirt streets in that summer resort, Allen turned pale and cried, "My God! There's Mama." His mother, a stout woman all in black, sat on one of the front porches, formidable, indomitable, unsmiling. It was the only time Caroline ever saw Mrs. Tate, and the visit was not a comfortable one. Allen kept saying, "Mama, we got to go now." They visited Civil War battlefields in Tennessee, stopped in Nashville to see Allen's old friends, and went to Guthrie to see Caroline's parents.

Back in New York, they dithered about when to leave for Europe, or whether to go at all. Although Caroline hated to leave the country when her mother was not expected to live very long, they bought tickets to sail on September 28.

Meanwhile, Allen's book of poetry, *Mr. Pope and Other Poems,* appeared. Allen was annoyed that the *Tribune* announced it as by the author of *Stonewall Jackson.* Caroline said she was waiting for the *Times* to come out with "The author of Stonewall Jackson tries his hand at verse." That would quite finish Allen, she said, but the idea amused her.

While getting ready to sail, Caroline was still trying to write. She lamented when she had a cold and couldn't work, but she used the time to read Virginia Woolf, whom she thought "marvelous!"

Caroline had had no new clothes for four years and yearned for some. When someone gave her a gold cloth evening cape, she used it to make "the loveliest gown" she had had in years, with a dark brown velvet basque waist and long scalloped skirt. "I don't see how I did it," she said. "I have been sewing madly on this garment for two days, crouched in a welter of young men from Vanderbilt. This is the time of the annual irruption. I have never seen anything like the way they come—some I never even heard of before appeared yesterday. There will be about two more weeks before they flutter south."

Caroline could not make up her mind whether or not to visit her mother, now being cared for by Caroline's brother Bill and his wife, Hallie, in Louisville, before they left. "I am sort of suspended," she wrote Sally, "waiting to know whether I'll go home or not. I think now maybe I won't go. I imagine Dad's decided that it's best after all for me not to come, but I can't take up anything else or finish anything till I know, for after all, one going into my home needs all her resources, mental and moral." In the end, she decided not to go back to Kentucky. Her mother concurred. "We can write better than we can talk," Mrs. Gordon wrote.

The Tates held to the September 28 sailing date, but planned to come back within the year and use the money Allen would make on *Stonewall Jackson* to buy a place in Pennsylvania. "We already know the place. You drive along through the woods by a brook, and suddenly there is an old stone bridge and you look across this vista at a beautiful old stone house. It is one of the most beautiful places I've ever seen. A little above the house is a gorgeous rock-lined pool, so baths will never be any problem."

6

EUROPE, 1928–1929

With a last-minute flurry of preparations, the Tates embarked. Hurrying up the gangplank of the SS *America*, Allen carried two large calf-bound volumes of *The Rise and Fall of the Confederate Government* and his grandfather's gold-headed cane. Caroline followed, holding Nancy by one hand and a big baby doll by the other. Nancy shrieked, "Where's the captain? He's got to see my ears!" Desperate to get Nancy spick-and-span for the journey, Caroline had told her the captain examined each passenger's ears to see if they were clean.

Although they paid for third class, there were so few passengers on board that they had first-class cabins and excellent food. The other passengers, Caroline said, included "mostly dark, wistful-looking Jews" and forty Rhodes scholars—"really quite terrible creatures," especially the Tennesseean who referred to her as "the wife." A storm raged for four days so that it looked, Allen said, as though the whole range of the Blue Ridge Mountains were descending upon them. The Tates were never seasick, but they got "quite morbid," as Caroline put it. Allen refused to take off his clothes at night, vowing never to cross the Atlantic again under any circumstances. Just before they arrived at Southampton, Caroline was asked to sign a letter praising the captain who had stayed on the bridge three days and nights and, like Allen, never changed his clothes. She was surprised to find that this eulogy had been written by Allen—surely, she said, the most florid piece of writing he'd ever done.

Caroline, full of what she called Celtic prejudice, hated England. She was disappointed that, because of the libraries, Allen wanted to stay there until the first of the year. He rented lodgings near Kensington Gardens, and Caroline mourned. "I could afford a nurse for Nancy in France, but not in England," she wrote Sally Wood. "Six weeks, with no interruption, would enable me to finish this novel I've been working on now for three years—but I see little chance of getting the six weeks."

Since Allen was going about London meeting T. S. Eliot, whom he admired a great deal, and Herbert Read and other literary people, he liked London. Caroline did not. "I always knew that London would be hellish," she wrote Andrew Lytle. "It has rained every single damn day since we have been here. We are told, however, that this is an exceptionally beautiful October. The sun shines a few minutes every day, and then our fellow lodgers look at each other and say, 'A lovely day, isn't it?' Sometimes they go about panting and exclaiming, 'How hawt it is! I can hardly get my breath!' "

She was scornful of English food, but she said she would gladly eat curried rice and rice pudding every day of her life as long as somebody else did the cooking. Allen adored the glutinous food, she said. Fresh from Prohibition-bound America, they were delighted to have good liquor to drink.

In London they saw other Guggenheim fellows—Ford K. Brown (whose wife was the mystery writer Leslie Ford) and Léonie Adams, a lovely young poet Allen had known in New York. Léonie had graduated from Barnard, where she had roomed with Margaret Mead, and for the past six years had worked at various teaching and editing jobs. She had published a book of verse in 1925, *Those Not Elect*. Léonie was so homesick she was thinking of giving up her fellowship and returning, but instead she joined forces with the Tates and proved wonderful at helping Caroline with Nancy.

They were all busy writing. "Caroline had thought of herself as a writer from the time she was born," Léonie said. "I wouldn't have been able to be deeply friendly with anyone who wasn't interested in writing. To us the life of the writer was the life to lead."

A few days after they arrived in London, Allen wrote to the Guggenheim Foundation for permission to earn some money by writing two articles before January 1. Getting to London and getting settled, he said, had cost exactly twice as much as he had expected, but the money from the articles would keep them afloat until the next payment from the foundation. The foundation gave its permission.

They went to Oxford to see Red Warren, there on a Rhodes scholarship. A friend of Warren's in Merton College gave them tea in his chambers, which Caroline thought very monastic, overlooking what she said was the oldest and certainly the ugliest college quadrangle. Red's college, New College, had at least one advantage over Merton: all the fines for being out later than nine-thirty were paid by an old gentleman who established a fund for that purpose after his son died of heart failure trying to make the gate.

Allen felt he could work in Oxford, so the Tates left London for a six weeks' stay in lodgings Warren found for them there. Oxford was "a grand place to work," Caroline said, and she "worked like hell" on her novel, rewriting half of it, before they decided to go on to Paris, where Ford Madox Ford was expecting them.

Allen, carrying his two volumes of *The Rise and Fall of the Confederate Government,* the gold-headed cane, and a small toilet kit, went ahead to buy their boat tickets. Caroline had just washed her hair and lain down to take a nap, when a telegram arrived from Allen telling her to take a train that left in fifteen minutes. In addition to the twelve suitcases and ten dolls that they had to bring with them to Paris, there were twenty-nine large calf-bound volumes to be returned to one of the college libraries. Caroline, Léonie, and Nancy got in a cab and had the maid pile the books on top of them and the luggage. They drove madly to the station and found that there was no such train. They then went to Red Warren's lodgings in New College, where Red, "always an angel," dug them out of the pile of volumes, sorted each woman's legs and arms, and took them up to his rooms for tea.

Eventually Caroline, Léonie, and Nancy were reunited with Allen at Newhaven and took the boat to Dieppe; it was the longest and cheapest crossing to France. When they reached the hotel near the Luxembourg Gardens recommended to them by Sally Wood, they found a note from Ford Madox Ford.

The Tates had thought they might go to Vence or Montpellier, but Ford persuaded them to stay in Paris. Besides, as Caroline said, the railroad fare to Vence or any other place was quite an item, so they settled down in Paris.

In Paris they sat outside the Closerie des Lilas and the Deux Magots and went to those three landmarks of the American colony at the corner of boulevard Montparnasse and boulevard Raspail: the Dôme, the Rotonde, and the Sélect. Caroline wrote to Sally that "the Dôme and Rotonde are really quite terrible . . . a sort of super–Greenwich Village. They actually appall." They discovered a restaurant run by a former chef to the king of Italy, where the food was superb and very cheap. They loved the good, cheap liquor, still a glorious novelty to them. It was much easier to live in Europe, Caroline said. She gained fifteen pounds and for the first time worried about her figure, but by all accounts Caroline looked wonderful in Paris. She had "a handsome face, a Southern face, like she should wear a sunbonnet," said a man who knew her then, "and eyes like brown velvet."

Sally Wood had written Caroline a list of names of people she might look up, but Caroline was not interested in "people who make a cult of drink"; they bored her. "I know they are amusing at times . . . but my experience has been that you have to wade through such dreary wastes for those few moments, that it's hardly worth while." For example, she regarded E. E. Cummings as one of the greatest bores who ever lived. "He will sit for hours gearing himself up to make some brilliant stroke—when it comes out it is usually something like 'Fuckaduck.' "

Aware that her mother was ill, Caroline tried to write to her every other day with detailed information about Nancy. Before Christmas she wrote that they had bought a doll and the smallest carriage they could find, but it was still big enough for a real baby. She made a little white quilt and a little flannel robe for the carriage and Léonie contributed a little pillow, "so it will look very fine."

Caroline also wrote her mother a long report about a visit to the Louvre. She did not like the Mona Lisa as much as she liked another Leonardo, *St. Anne and the Virgin*. There was a Velasquez portrait of a girl with a nose that looked like her cousin Catherine Wilds's nose. Nothing in the French gallery interested her much except *The Gleaners*. "Although you have seen it reproduced so often it seems perfectly fresh to you. I think it is one of the most marvellous pictures I have ever seen." She found the Winged Victory to be "one of those things that can't be photographed, much more beautiful than I ever imagined it would be, and more thrilling."

In her letters Caroline also offered to buy face powder for her female relatives. She needed to know whether they used *naturelle* or rachel, or they might send a sample of what they used in an envelope. "You can get the powders we pay two and three dollars for at home for forty or fifty cents here," she told them. She reported to Josephine Herbst that clothes were much cheaper in Paris. She paid eighty francs for a knitted sweater-suit that would have cost fifteen dollars in New York. Eighty francs was three dollars and twenty cents, wasn't it? she asked.

Allen had put the Jefferson Davis biography aside in the fall in order to write an essay on the humanists for *The Criterion*. He wrote to the Guggenheim Foundation in January 1929 that he had had to stop work on the book because he had been ill for three weeks and because the magazine articles he had done to help with finances had delayed him. He wanted, he said, to leave the book in abeyance for some time and work on his long poem. But his publisher, eager to have the book for late spring publication, had called the foundation and insisted that Allen finish the book. Allen realized that if he finished the biography he would not finish the poem before September 1, when his fellowship expired. He applied for a six-month extension of the fellowship, and this was granted.

The book on Jefferson Davis was tough going, he said, and difficult to write in Paris when he should have been in Montgomery or Richmond. One day at the American Library, where he was rooting around in the Civil War shelves checking dates, he met another American writer interested in the South—John Peale Bishop. Bishop and Allen had actually been introduced by Kenneth Burke in a New York speakeasy the night that Nancy was born, but Allen had forgotten it. This time they talked about their Southern backgrounds, discovered mutual cousins, and became friends. Bishop was from West Virginia and had gone to Princeton, where F. Scott Fitzgerald had been so impressed with his aristocratic air that he used him as a model for Thomas Parker D'Invilliers in *This Side of Paradise*. Bishop lived with his wife and children in a château, Tressancourt, in Orgeval, near Paris; he enjoyed going to the capital to do research and talk to other writers. He liked Allen a great deal but found Caroline, at first, "too southern." Margaret Bishop disliked Caroline, and Caroline, as did most people, disliked Margaret.

Bishop introduced Allen to Fitzgerald, who immediately asked him if he enjoyed sleeping with his wife. "It's none of your damn business," Allen said huffily to Fitzgerald. Bishop told Allen not to be upset, that Fitzgerald asked the same question of everyone he met. Caroline liked Zelda and said once she thought her a victim of Fitzgerald's delusions of grandeur in a top hat.

On January 22, 1929, Caroline's mother died. "We were all glad that she did not have to suffer any longer," Caroline wrote to Josie Herbst.

Early in 1929, when Ford went to the United States, the Tates and Léonie moved into his apartment at 32 rue de Vaugirard. Caroline loved the apartment with its view of Saint Sulpice. Ford would take no rent, but Caroline had gotten a 500-page manuscript in shape for him after a French typist had typed it and made every *e* an *a* and all inanimate objects either male or female. Allen and Caroline slept in the *petit salon* on a sofa that turned into a bed. The small bedroom went to Nancy, and there was a narrow closet just big enough for Léonie. A *femme de ménage* did the work and took Nancy for walks in the Luxembourg Gardens for twenty francs a month. Nancy began to play there with French children, and her French was far superior to her parents'. She even talked to her imaginary family, the Keder-Jenkinses, in French. Caroline said she wished she did have some French, but she couldn't be bothered to learn it then. "It upsets me to even think about it when I'm trying to write. Of course, I pick up necessary phrases from the concierge, waiters, our *femme de ménage*, etc." She thought it might even be time to take Nancy home. Nancy would look at her favorite book, *Battles and Leaders of the Civil War*, and say, "There's Monsieur Stonewall Jackson."

Caroline wrote Josephine Herbst about the novel she had been working on for ten years. "I've been nibbling around the edges of it—the novel I've been working on recently is a part of it—but I've got the whole thing in hand now, and hope to get a good part of it done before we come back." She went on to describe it as the history of a Southern family for three or four generations, from 1800 to the beginnings of industrialization in the South. She thought she had the perfect title, "The Making of Americans," until she realized that Gertrude Stein had used it.

It was to be a Meriwether book, called *Penhally*. Caroline's grandmother's grandfather, Charles Nicholas Meriwether, who came "over the mountains" on the Wilderness Trail from Virginia with his father looking for land, is the prototype for Nicholas Llewellyn. John Llewellyn is a portrait of Caroline's grandfather, the Robert Ingersoll–reading dreamer, and her grandmother, who would countermand her husband's orders in the field in front of the farmhands, is the model for John's wife, Lucy. Other Meriwethers provide the basic outlines of other characters, and anyone who has read about Caroline's family can spot anecdotes from the family's history. Meriville was the model for Penhally, the eponymous house, and Nicholas's style was Meriwether style—sometimes, for that matter, Tate style. One passage tells how one Jessie Blair came out to Penhally from Virginia forty years before and had stayed to keep house, "but during all those years she and Nicholas had never sat down once alone to dinner. There had always been company in the house."

The Tates and Léonie had all had flu—three bad attacks that winter, with lesser attacks in between. In fact, Nancy's earliest memory is having her ear lanced by a French doctor in pin-striped trousers. The winter,

Caroline said, was a combination of rum and aspirin. She would sit by Ford's one fireplace and get up every few minutes to put drops in her nose, Léonie on the other side of the fireplace would do the same, and Nancy in bed in the corner would wait for drops to be put in her ears. They had hundreds of bottles and droppers for those little drops. They never moved without their droppers. Allen was in such a state that when pear blossoms fluttered down in the courtyard he looked up and said, "Great God, it's snowing now!"

Caroline still wanted to go south to Antibes or Cannes, where it might be cheaper and where they could all get some sun, but they had a free apartment in Paris and train fares would be high.

Hart Crane, who had finally received his legacy from his grandmother, arrived in Paris, and nobody referred to the quarrel in Tory Valley. He lifted their spirits, telling them about what Caroline called "his goings on at the Coupole . . . how Kiki (I cannot call her Mrs. Man Ray) slipped her left breast out of her décolletage and wagged it at him by way of greeting." From the terrace of the Closerie des Lilas, the Tates and Crane sent an affectionate postcard to Mrs. Turner in Patterson.

Crane said that everyone was tired of Allen because he was always going on about the importance of the War Between the States. Allen replied that for years he had tried to suppress his views and feelings, but he could no longer pretend to believe anything but what he did believe. If this was snobbishness, he would stand by it, he said. Allen decided Crane was as irresponsible as Nancy, who greeted a visitor with "This is the man we don't like."

Crane once found himself at the Sélect with no money, unable to pay his bill. The proprietress called the police, and he slugged it out, decking several waiters and then two gendarmes who came to arrest him. He was taken to La Santé and kept in jail for several days. Afterward all his friends, including the Tates, boycotted the Sélect.

Stella Bowen, Ford's wife, painted a portrait of the Tates: "*en famille*— Allen and I held together in space by Nancy, as it were." (Stella Bowen was known as Ford's wife, but she was not actually his wife, since Ford had never gotten a divorce from Elsie Martindale, whom he had married when they were very young.) Pavlich Tchelitchew, a Russian-born "neoromantic" painter in Paris, remarked that "Nancy's head was quite *moyen age,* what ever that means."

To meet the publisher's deadline, Caroline and Allen both worked on the Jefferson Davis book that summer. Caroline wrote her cousin Little May that she "pitched in and helped him (if there's anything you'd like to know about the foreign relations of the Confederacy just call on me). Well, anyhow, working day and night for several months we finally got Jefferson Davis laid to rest—on the Fourth of July."

The Tates and Léonie went on vacation to Concarneau in Brittany, a port famous for its fishing boats with red sails. "They are really almost too beautiful," Caroline said. The town was full of English and American painters. The Tates stayed at a hotel on the waterfront, but Léonie wandered farther afield where she met Leon Edel, a young Canadian-bred writer. Edel had come to Concarneau on a friend's recommendation, rented a bicycle, explored the neighborhood, and found a quiet pension out of town, on the coast. The pension was full of French families, but Edel liked the food and the Breton cider. At lunch he noticed what looked like a young American girl, "a slip of a thing," in the corner; "she wore an off-the-face hat, as young things were taught to do then." The landlady told him she was indeed a *jeune americaine*. "I began to talk to her and found that she was Léonie Adams, a poet I had been reading in the left bank magazine *This Quarter*," Edel said. "I had never met a published American poet. Since I was then filled with the reading of James Joyce and Henry James, I chattered literature. Léonie was kind and amusing and witty." She mentioned her friends, the Allen Tates, who were staying at the first-class hotel about half a mile away, and I had a friend there with whom I played tennis. She mentioned that she was on a Guggenheim and Allen was too. Edel asked her if Tate wasn't a black poet? Léonie roared with laughter—Edel had mixed Tate up with some black poets in Montparnasse—and said, "I'll take you down there and introduce you to him. He's written a life of Stonewall Jackson." Edel, although American-born, grew up in Canada and knew little about American history, less about the Civil War.

Léonie did take Edel along to the Hôtel des Sables Blancs where the Tates were staying. "Allen was young and lithe, and his wife seemed just out of college," Edel said. "I babbled out of my college English, although I had read lots of Yeats and Joyce and was now absorbed in Henry James. Caroline danced with me and said she was writing a novel. Caroline and Léonie agreed that I must meet Ford if I was working on Henry James and promised to introduce me to him." Edel remembers Caroline as good-looking, lively, and attractive, with bobbed hair and dark eyes. "I was a bit overawed to be in such high literary company," recalled Edel.

While the Tates were in Concarneau, Allen answered letters from his Nashville friends about the "Southern movement" and a "Southern book" they wanted to publish. They had been talking about "doing something about the South" since 1926, when press coverage of the Scopes trial in Tennessee had enraged at least three of the old Fugitive group—Ransom, Tate, and Davidson. They perceived a contemptuous attitude toward the South, a region the rest of the country seemed to view as a kind of Third World—poor, undeveloped, ignorant, and faintly exotic. The South's economy was in disarray, and Ransom and the others resented the economic exploitation of the South and yet felt that the spread of industrialism was a threat to everything that was good about the region. From Brittany, Allen sent Davidson a possible outline for the book. Allen was also thinking a great deal about religion and wrote to Davidson that he was heading more and more toward Catholicism. It was either Catholicism or naturalism, he wrote, and he could never give in to naturalism.

When the cable came saying that Allen's mother had died suddenly in Monteagle, he wanted to go home, but it was impossible. "It seems strange that both our mothers should die while we are over here," Caroline said.

After Brittany, the Tates intended to go to London, where Allen could start on a third biography, this one of Robert E. Lee, but they couldn't tear themselves away from Paris. They settled at the Hôtel de la Place de l'Odéon. Léonie was across the street at the Corneille. "The Café Voltaire across the *place* has the coldest best beer," Caroline wrote Katherine Anne. "The Café de l'Odéon is where we sat to idle away summer afternoons, and Lavigne's (Au Negre de Toulouse) has the best dinner for the least money."

Jefferson Davis, His Rise and Fall: A Biographical Narrative was published in New York on September 20, 1929, but the Tates did not see a copy until Ford received one in the mail much later.

Now Caroline had her own first success. In Palo Alto, California, Yvor Winters and his wife, novelist Janet Lewis, had started a little magazine called *Gyroscope*. Winters, who admired Allen's poetry and criticism, had written to him for suggestions about contributors and Allen had recommended Caroline's stories. *Gyroscope* published "Summer Dust" in the Fall 1929 issue—her first publication—and asked to publish "The Long Day" in March 1930. "Summer Dust" had been turned down by every magazine in America, but it was still the best writing she had ever done, she wrote Sally Wood.

Told from the viewpoint of a little girl, Sally Ellis, "Summer Dust" foreshadows many of the themes that would thread through Caroline's work the rest of her life. "She walked on a dusty country road," it begins. "The dust was hot; it lay so thick on the road her feet went out of sight each time they sank into it, and each foot went down with a little plop, the dust rose, sometimes as high as her chin, never as high as her head. . . ."

Sally is going with a black servant and two of the servant's children to pick some peaches at the Old Place, part of her family's property now rented out to "poor white folks." The tenant's wife protests at their picking the peaches, and says, "I wisht I'd picked 'em yestiddy. I was just lettin' 'em sun one more day. . . ." Sally picks none of the peaches. There are three more incidents in the story, each one taking place in the Old Neighborhood. In one, Sally and her brothers go to Ellengowan, a place like Woodstock, and have to greet Aunt Silvy, an ancient black servant, who is identical to Aunt Emily at Woodstock, whom Caroline described in many a letter. Her brothers told her that Aunt Emily ate black babies and drank blood, and these appetites are given to Aunt Silvy. One story about Aunt Emily that does not appear in "Summer Dust" is that of Caroline's five-year-old cousin Richard protesting that he wants to chew his own food, he's tired of Aunt Emily doing it for him.

In "Summer Dust" Caroline early on demonstrated her gift for describing the natural world. Flannery O'Connor often pointed to the passage where Sally is riding the Black Horse. "They moved forward, through sunshine. It fell on his mane, turning some of the hairs red, then slid along his neck, past his shoulders, and on over her leg. She turned in the saddle and watched it slide off his rump. They were in the wood." "That is real masterly doing," said Flannery O'Connor. "Nobody does it any better than Caroline."

As Sally moves through the story, she slips back and forth from the real world into the world of the *Green Fairy Book*, where an old woman lives in a house made of peach stones in the middle of a wood and a king catches little fish out of the brook with a golden hairpin tied to the end of a queen's girdle. The story shows Sally's loss of innocence as she becomes aware of the unfairness of life.

Most Americans left Paris in the fall of 1929, called home by the crash of the stock market and the loss of income. But the Tates stayed on to be with Ford, who was disconsolate over his health and his breakup with Stella Bowen.

Howard Baker, a young writer from California who had helped found *Gyroscope*, arrived in Paris with a letter of introduction to Allen from Winters. He lived near the Tates, and he and Allen generally had lunch together while Caroline worked. Ford, the Tates, and Baker, with one or two others, ate dinner together. They went to small restaurants like the Michaud, where Allen always ordered tournedos and a *compote de fruit,* or to the Cochon au Lait, across from the Odéon, where suckling pigs were roasted on spits, or to Lipp, where they ate the famous sauerkraut. They spent the rest of the evening talking or playing auction bridge on the terrace of the Deux Magots. Ford liked to talk and talked a lot, about Henry James, for instance, his life and art. Caroline and Léonie did make sure that Leon Edel met Ford, but Edel later recalled, "I was with him for an hour or so and he wheezed and made whale-sounds . . . and told me his myths about Henry James: I knew they were myths because I used to ask questions, the answers to which I knew from my researches, to test the credibility of my informants. An old biographical trick I learned early. But Ford was amusing, and generous, and the afternoon was brightened for me by the arrival of Glenway Wescott who came with an enormous bouquet of roses for Ford."

Caroline, "at her happiest," according to Howard Baker, worked on her novel at a little table in the main room of their suite, while Allen worked in the bedroom. An elderly French woman named Madame Gau looked after Nancy. Nancy had found Madame Gau herself: playing in the Luxembourg Gardens with a little English girl she'd met in Concarneau, she saw an old lady watching her and went over and said, "Come home with me." "Voici Madame Gau," she said to her parents, and Madame Gau took care of Nancy from ten in the morning until seven at night, taking her to the Bois du Boulogne, to the Tuileries, and to a funeral every day. They went to Notre Dame to see a cardinal lying in state, and one day she had Nancy baptized. Caroline said they missed Nancy terribly, but she was getting in some marvelous long stretches at her novel.

Every Saturday Ford gathered a small group of friends in his apartment to try their hand at writing sonnets. Ford, who had played the *bouts-rimés* parlor game in London in the 1890s, revived the pastime that fall. He prepared in advance a number of sheets of paper on which he typed the rhyme words in a vertical column. Each person was given one of the sheets, on which he or she was to complete the lines leading up to the rhymes. The best sonnets won prizes. The first prize was always the same three-layer cake with white frosting and the runner-up received a wooden spoon, but the prizes were never actually awarded. The winners wrote their names on labels which were then attached to the cake or the spoon.

At the meeting on October 27, William Bandy, a Vanderbilt graduate who was in Paris writing his dissertation on Baudelaire, announced that he and Alice Burghardt were to be married in Saint Luke's Chapel on November 4. His best man was to be Allen Tate, and Bandy invited everyone at the session to come to the wedding.

At the next meeting, on Saturday, November 3, Ford selected rhyme words that were associated with marriage, the last of them being *wedding*. The sonnets were read in order of their completion, and Ford, as always, finished his first.

Bandy received the greatest number of first-place votes and Alice, who wrote only the last line—"I cannot write of anything but wedding"—still was declared the runner-up. Bandy's first prize, of course, was the same cake that had been around for weeks, but it was decided that this was the time to cut it and eat it. All the labels with the names of past first-place winners were removed, and Ford tried to cut the cake. It was so stale he had to get a heavy wooden mallet to pound with until he penetrated the icing. Strangely, the interior of the cake was moist and delicious—or so it seemed to the guests.

Sylvia Beach, proprietor of the famous bookstore, Shakespeare & Co., introduced Allen to Ernest Hemingway that fall, and the two of them walked up to the place de l'Odéon and had an apéritif at the Café Voltaire. "Ford's a friend of yours," Hemingway said to Allen. "You know he's impotent, don't you?" Allen said that didn't concern him, even if it were true, since he wasn't a woman. Allen soon learned that Ford had been one of the first to help Hemingway, and Hemingway could not bear being grateful to anyone.

Hemingway and his wife, Pauline, and their baby were living in the rue Férou near the Hôtel de l'Odéon, and the Tates saw them constantly that fall. Allen and Hemingway went to the bicycle races every Sunday. "He is trying to persuade us to settle in Arkansas—Pauline's people have a lot of wild land down there," Caroline wrote to Josie Herbst. "It sounds fine for hunting and fishing; I know that country. We lived in Poplar Bluff once and did what they say you can't do—eat quail for a month. And wild ducks. My God, those duck dinners! But my father spending all his time on the river got frightful malaria and would have died if we'd stayed there."

Caroline and Allen still hoped to get "a place in the country out of Jeff Davis." They were planning for her father to live with them, and he wanted them to move to Virginia, "not that he has any great love for Virginia, but those streams in the foothills of the Blue Ridge are great for fishing." Caroline favored Pennsylvania herself, if they could find a good fishing stream.

Allen was in bed with the flu when Hemingway brought him one of the first copies of *A Farewell to Arms* he had just received from New York. He came to the door of the room and asked Caroline to hand Allen the book so he wouldn't be exposed to germs. Allen began to read as soon as Hemingway left and did not stop until he'd finished the book. Hemingway asked him later what he thought of it, and Allen said truthfully that he thought it was a masterpiece. Caroline agreed. John Bishop told Allen that the only novelist Hemingway liked was Scott Fitzgerald, who was full of hero worship. Hemingway had no use for other novelists but chose his writing friends from among the poets.

Hemingway came to the Hôtel de l'Odéon one morning, climbed the four flights of stairs, and asked them to go with him that night to Gertrude Stein's apartment on the rue de Fleurus. This was the historic occasion when Miss Stein took Hemingway back in favor. The Fitzgeralds, the Bishops, and Ford went along too. Zelda, Margaret, Pauline, and Caroline were taken in tow by Alice B. Toklas, while the men sat at Gertrude Stein's feet in the salon. Caroline thought Miss Stein ludicrous, and Miss Stein never liked Caroline. When she saw a mutual friend of the Tates years later, she spoke fondly of Allen and asked, "Is he still married to that girl?" That night in the fall of 1929 Gertrude gave them a lecture on American literature, from Emerson to Stein, the pure genius of abstraction. After the lecture, the visitors left and went to the Closerie des Lilas.

The Tates had Thanksgiving dinner with the Hemingways that year, complete with cranberry sauce and sweet potatoes. "We ate and drank steadily till round four o'clock," Caroline wrote Katherine Anne Porter. "Then we drove around the Bois, jolted it all down and started in again on a sort of community dinner . . . finishing the serious eating about twelve o'clock."

Katherine Anne Porter told someone at Harcourt, Brace in New York that Caroline had a "swell" novel ready for publication, and Harcourt, Brace wrote to Caroline in Paris. The novel was far from ready; she was working on the Civil War section. Coward-McCann wrote expressing interest in a book of short stories that Yvor Winters told them Caroline had ready for publication. Caroline said she didn't have a book of short stories, but proposed, instead, a biography of Meriwether Lewis. (Nothing came of this proposal, but at the time of her death, Caroline was working on a biography of Meriwether Lewis.)

As Christmas came near, Caroline "caroused" by night and worked on her novel by day, while Nancy now stayed night and day with Madame Gau. Nancy had acquired, Caroline said, a habit of waking at five o'clock in the morning and singing French songs in a piercingly sweet voice.

Ford knew that Caroline was working on a novel, but he had never seen any of it, although he had asked to see it several times over the years she had known him. She had shown him some short things that she rather liked herself, some better done than the novel, she thought, and he had mumbled in his mustache about "beautiful writing, but I don't know what it is all about." Caroline didn't think the novel was ready to show to anybody and she was afraid Ford wouldn't like it. But at last, just three weeks before the Tates were to sail back to the States, she showed him what she had done so far.

Ford flew into a great rage and accused her of concealing it from him until there was no time to do anything. He made her sit down in his apartment every morning at eleven o'clock and dictate a total of 5,000 words to him. If she complained that it was hard to work with everything so hurried and with Christmas presents to buy, he observed, "You have no passion for your art. It is unfortunate." He said it in such a sinister way that she reeled off sentences in panic. Ford told Caroline that she had an unparalleled command over words and the prose paragraphs of which effective narratives are made.

She left the manuscript with him; he was going to try to get her a contract and an advance on it. It was hard to do anything with a half-finished manuscript, she knew, and she had no great hopes.

Ford's approval and praise must have intoxicated Caroline. She had worked alone and without encouragement for ten years before she sold a single short story, although she had lived in the midst of writers for the past five years. As she had written Josephine Herbst earlier, "You are right about Allen and his attitude toward the novel. He really has no interest whatever in the modern novel; I never even think of showing him anything I write unless he hounds me into it." Ford must have seemed the Messiah.

Ford was very fond of Caroline. He wrote poems to her and letters that are very tender. Two of the poems and a few letters he wrote to her right after she left Paris are all that have survived. (Caroline burned his other letters years later "to protect his reputation." She threw them in the fire and sat outside looking up at the chimney. "The smoke," she said, "was very black.") In one letter he told her he lived for nothing but the time when he would see her next and in another he said he planned to settle down near her in America, but he couldn't do that for years and wouldn't last for years. But this was just talk. He was very soon to form an alliance with the painter Janice Biala. He was always fond of the Tates, but the evidence against his having had an affair with Caroline is very strong indeed. Nobody who knew them both can believe that it was remotely possible.

The Tates booked passage on the *George Washington* for December 28, 1929. Caroline was torn between Paris, on which she "doted," and her native land. "I could stay in Paris forever," she said.

The last week there was hectic. Polly Chase Boyden, described by Caroline as a rich lady from Chicago bent on literary fame, gave them a fine, large farewell party. When Caroline asked what she could do to help with the party, Mrs. Boyden said, "Bring a lot of unattached young men, but they are no good to me unless they are fresh." Red Warren brought four that Caroline thought were pretty fresh from Oxford, only two of them homosexual. Ford brewed the punch after his grandfather's recipe, double strength. By ten o'clock he had his hat and coat on and was saying that he had to get Nancy to the boat train and therefore must leave, as he saw that Allen and Caroline were going to get very drunk. "Come and let us have a farewell talk," Ford said to Caroline. He was about to sit down on a divan when Caroline perceived a slight movement under somebody's coat lying on the divan and uncovered Helen Crowe, a friend of Dorothy Day's from the Village, completely overcome by the punch. The party lasted until four in the morning, but the Tates made the boat.

"I hated leaving Paris. God, how I hated leaving Paris. . . . It was all so nice and easy," Caroline said. But she and Allen planned to buy a place in the country once they got to the United States, and a place in the country was what they both wanted.

Since they spent time in Europe exclusively with Americans and Ford, they might as well have spent the time, as Allen said, in Harlem or Minneapolis as Paris. Still, they had both had time to write, and Caroline had made her real beginning as a professional writer. She had published a short story and was well on her way with a novel in which Ford Madox Ford and two publishers were interested.

7

BENFOLLY, 1930–1932

Caroline thought grief at leaving Paris made her seasick during the trip home and once on land she felt bombarded by the rattle and roar of New York. "I didn't want to come, I didn't want to come," she said, and wished she were walking home from the Closerie des Lilas along the rue d'Assas. In New York, the Tates stayed at the Carteret Hotel, where Allen wanted to settle down in a suite at ninety dollars a month.

"You can't finish your novel unless you have a comfortable place to work," he said.

"I'll be damned if I'll do it," said Caroline, who always preferred household help to fancy quarters. She found a "two by four furnished" apartment at 364 West Twenty-sixth Street, where they slept, ate, and worked in the living room, cooked in Nancy's bedroom, and washed dishes in the bathroom. "But it isn't as bad as it sounds," Caroline said. "We have a beautiful colored creature who comes every morning and stays till one o'clock. That seems too good to be true." She worked on her novel every morning and vowed to finish it that year "or come very near dying trying." A letter from Ford spurred her on. "I have *never* in all the course of my literary experience had such a shock as that which attended my reading the first chapter of 'Penhally,'" he wrote. "Such a shock of real delight at the beauty of the writing and the handling of the material. That may have been partly because I have known you a long time without your ever telling me that you wrote at all." He was certain he had never read a first novel he liked better.

While Caroline worked on her novel, Allen bustled around New York and got a contract from Harper's for the Agrarian anthology that he, Donald Davidson, and John Crowe Ransom had planned. They wanted to publish a group of essays by themselves and other Southerners that would set forth the Agrarian argument that industrialism would ruin the South, which needed to return to the traditions of the Old South and become a region of small, independent farms. They hoped their "symposium" would alert the South and the world to the danger posed by industry to all the good things about the Old South—the strong family, the hierarchal society, and the carefully structured world. Davidson had lined up several contributors, including Stark Young, a Mississippi-bred novelist and reviewer for *The New Republic*. In New York, Allen corralled John Gould Fletcher, the Arkansas poet.

Caroline wove some of these Agrarian themes into *Penhally*. Just as the Civil War is breaking out, old Nicholas Llewellyn reflects: "But everything was breaking up nowadays. The country was in the hands of the New England manufacturers—men who gave no thought to its true interests. The tariff of abominations, as they called it, made it almost impossible to feed and clothe your negroes." He muses that the men who were leading the South to war were "irresponsible, these new-fangled politicians, landless men, with nothing to lose and everything to win." The land, primogeniture, the stable society of past times—these are the things that the "good" characters value. The villains move to town and go into trade. Farming, even if done poorly, is better than business.

Caroline showed part of the novel to one publisher who refused to give her an advance. "If you don't bring the whole book off, I'd be left with nothing but some fine writing on my hands," he told her. The poet Louise Bogan came to dinner one night and urged her to show it to Maxwell Perkins, at Scribner's. Caroline dashed over without the manuscript of her novel. "I took two stories and told him that was the way I wrote, only different. He is grand, though—the only publishing person I ever met whom you could talk to like a human being. Louise said he was like that, but I couldn't believe it." She later sent Perkins seventy pages of her novel.

About the first of March, the Tates, ready to leave New York to look for a place in the country, gave a farewell party for themselves.

One guest was hit in the head and passed out for several minutes, and another passed out for good at twelve o'clock. One of the guests kept saying, "The trouble with you Southerners is you won't marry Negroes." The last guests left at four-thirty in the morning. Malcolm Cowley got Louise Bogan down a long hall, down a flight of steps, and out on the sidewalk with four long shoves, reiterating with each shove, "What a splendid woman you are. How I admire your poetry."

The Tates left town in a new Model-A Ford and went to Merry Mont—beautiful with the plum trees in bloom and the sugar trees just coming out. The farmhands were burning plant beds for tobacco and there was a fringe of smoke around all the woods. Caroline and Nancy picked jonquils all one afternoon, and Caroline dreamed of taking jonquils, hyacinths, althea roots, roses, irises, lilacs, mock orange, and crimson rambler roots to plant wherever they settled.

Caroline saw many members of the Connection for the first time in years. Cousin Kitty Meriwether had lost her memory, but, as Caroline said, this did not detract from her peculiar charm. The Tates spent one night with Cousin Lucy Hunter, who gave them advice in ringing tones. When Caroline said Allen would have to drive her home the next morning so she could work on her book, Cousin Lucy said, "Why, pray, can you not think on one hill as well as another?"

Caroline's father, widowed and retired from preaching, arrived carrying his fishing rods on the train—he told Allen he could use his fourth-best rod since he was his son-in-law—and the three of them drove around the countryside looking for a suitable place to live. Prospects narrowed to two. One was a bargain, a charming eleven-room brick house, an "angel of a house," on the Cumberland River, a few miles from Merry Mont. Allen had seen it from across the river and said, "That's the house where I want to live." It had several outbuildings, including a cottage that Caroline thought would be perfect for Katherine Anne, and ninety-seven acres of land, for $6,000. Allen went off to Cincinnati to see if his brother Ben, the coal dealer, would help them buy it. Caroline had little hope. Rich people were always hard-pressed for money. If they didn't get the brick house, they planned to build a rough cabin on the banks of the Little West Fork of the Red River.

On March 10, while Allen was in Cincinnati, Caroline was listening to her father, the avid fisherman, talk about the habits of bream. The telephone rang; it was a telegram from Perkins at Scribner's offering her an advance of $500 on her novel and $200 for "The Long Day," one of the short stories that had appeared in *Gyroscope*, for *Scribner's Magazine*. (Perkins had had a hard time finding her, she found out later.)

Very soon, Caroline got word that Edward J. O'Brien was using "Summer Dust," the other *Gyroscope* story, in his *Best Short Stories of* 1930 and, furthermore, wanted to dedicate the book to Caroline. Caroline thought it was amusing that she had never really been "in print" before—*Gyroscope* was mimeographed.

On top of this good news, Ben came through and "lent" the Tates $10,000, interest-free, to buy and renovate the tall, narrow brick house on the banks of the Cumberland River. Caroline's father called it Ben's Folly, and its name became Benfolly. Industrialism, which Allen fought, had made Ben's fortune and financed their return to lead an Agrarian life in the South.

Benfolly was an hour from Nashville and three miles from Clarksville, beyond the pale of the Old Neighborhood, but possessed of a wonderful view of the river, which was fine for fishing and swimming. "Our hill— probably the most beautiful hill in the world," said Caroline, ". . . is shaped just like a crouching lion. The lion's head and shoulders front the river and the house sits on, say, his forehead. One drives up his spinal column, right to the front door; the ascent is gradual and you do not realize till you get out on the big porch how high up you are. It is swell, at night, when the lights in the town come out." The house was in dreadful condition—porches sagging dangerously and hens roosting in the downstairs bathroom—so the Tates stayed on at Merry Mont while carpenters and plasterers went to work. Nancy played with black children and slipped from English to French and back again— when a load of coal was delivered, she said, "Here comes the *charbonnier*." Allen did some of the interior painting in the new house, but Caroline went out and hoed the vegetable garden. Corn, beans, carrots, and beets were up, and she set out five dozen tomato plants and fifty-two cabbage slips in one day. The garden was "nothing special," she wrote Josie Herbst, what with her writing on her book and staying at Merry Mont for weeks.

By the last of April, still at Merry Mont, Caroline wrote to Perkins at Scribner's to ask about a letter he was supposed to have sent. "We send a little Negro a mile for the mail," she said, "and I always feel he may have scattered the letters over the fields." Two days later, she asked for an additional $250. Perkins sent $100.

Caroline became very interested in the whole Cumberland Valley— the river was supposedly named after the Duke of Cumberland because he was so crooked—and planned to write a long short story on the adventures of a party of settlers that came through the area. She tried to verify the persistent local legend that the Marquis de Lafayette had been a visitor at Benfolly. Several Clarksville people claimed to own cups from the silver service from which he had drunk tea when he went there, but the house wasn't built until 1831, long after Lafayette had visited Tennessee. Caroline decided he might have stayed in an earlier house on the property. (A local historian discovered fifty years later that in 1825 Lafayette came up the Cumberland River from Nashville, went ashore at Clarksville for half an hour, but got no farther than the wharf.)

Caroline thought it was funny that they were absolutely broke, "even broker than usual," yet about to move into a house with two bathrooms that seemed magnificent after all those cold-water flats where they had slept on sofa beds in living rooms. At first there was no water for the bathrooms, but there was a huge cistern in which to store rainwater that would later provide running water. Although there was no electricity yet, Ben Tate was trying to work what Caroline called razzle-dazzle on the local power company.

The Tates worried about where they would get furniture for the house. Stark Young suggested they buy it at a secondhand store in Clarksville or order from Sears, Roebuck. Then Allen fell heir to all his mother's large, old, heavy furniture. Moving took two weeks, Caroline wrote Léonie, and put her in bed with a temperature of 103. "The doctor, in his ignorance, called my malady malaria." She doubted his diagnosis, but she approved of his treatment—quinine—and recommended it for years as a cure for chills and fever. Still she felt the fever was simply the result of contemplating the many thousands of objects collected by Allen's mother in her lifetime—four large truckloads of objects that ranged from ninety-nine empty boxes to the luster pitcher that belonged to George Washington's sister. Everything was carefully wrapped with quantities of string, and they were able to fill a hole in the yard, once the excavation for a house, with the boxes and paper. "Some of the objects were lovely—whatnots and quantities of old silver and daguerreotypes, but the sum total was too much for me. I developed along with the fever neuralgia of the heart. I do not think I am long for this world. I was never meant to live with so many objects. We have quantities stored in the attic. The remainder furnish the house most nobly. The whatnot in particular has melted into just the right corner where it seems to have sat for years. The house is really perfect. I do not believe I have ever seen a house I liked better. The back gallery, the one that fronts on the river, is a heavenly place on hot nights."

When Allen and Caroline moved in, Miss Carrie would not relinquish Nancy, who spent most of her time at Merry Mont and even suggested one day, "Let's go visit the Tates."

They acquired a wonderful cook, who could make batter cakes and chess pies, for ten dollars a month. They began early to collect a menagerie—cats with names like Hind Tit and Oedipus, and one named Violet Emma Cinina Elena Anna Roma Clotilda Borgia in honor of Red Warren's fiancée (later renamed Uncle Penn when the cat's sex became more apparent), and a German shepherd dog, Freda. Caroline said she tried to keep the number of animals down, "with one eye on going to New York some time," but they multiplied. A hen stepped out of the deep weeds one morning with a stolen flock of little chickens. A kitten dropped on her from the top boughs of the cedar tree. "I swear that is how we got that kitten," she said. They found another kitten, Hind Tit II, sitting in the middle of the state highway, purring and with paws folded, while automobiles whizzed over her. Someone dropped a foxhound pup off the river bridge and they rescued it and adopted it. Relatives even sent dogs to stay; Ben Tate's chauffeur drove down with a dog named Whiskers that belonged to a friend of Ben's in Cincinnati.

The temperature went up to 104 degrees and Caroline's garden dried on the vine. "My lovely tomatoes, cucumbers, squashes—everything!" she mourned. There were other country crises. The Tates had a cow, Daisy Miller, who would not drink from the pond, so Caroline and Nancy had to go to the spring in the woods to get water in buckets to fill Daisy's trough. Caroline would usually be diverted by the woods and not get back to the house for hours. There was always something going on to distract them from writing. "Mr. Perry's two mules dash over the lawn, dragging wagon loads of dirt," Caroline wrote to Sally. "They are followed by our colored henchman Jim, Allen, Nancy, Freda the shepherd dog, and all the chickens. There is a great deal of shrieking and shouting and clucking. They're making a circular drive and gravelling it and God knows what else. It is all going to be very grand."

And the company! Guests came in floods . . . old friends . . . new friends . . . relatives . . . New York writers who had never been to the South before . . . Southern Agrarians who mistrusted the North. Robert Penn Warren came as soon as he got home from Oxford, and they all went swimming in the river and drank homemade beer that the washerwoman had taught them how to make. Stark Young sent a recipe for making claret that called for raisins and cherries; if they used more raisins, he said, they would get port instead of claret.

Malcolm Cowley, by this time an editor of *The New Republic*, came in the fall of 1930 on his way north, bearing gifts from Katherine Anne Porter, who had scampered down to Mexico to write. Mark Van Doren, who came by train, said that the Tates had found "the one piece of ground intended for them." They started out with Van Doren one day after lunch and drove him around the whole Meriwether block of land, and did not return home until seven o'clock. "We saluted such of the kin as we met along the way with a new respect, marvelling that those dull and loutish people had managed to stay put when most of us are so hurled about the world," Caroline said. Josephine Herbst came that fall and wrote to Katherine Anne Porter that the place was wonderful, "the most nearly ideal of any I ever saw. The house is perfect, I can't talk without raving. A fireplace in every room and Allen ensconced in a jewel of a room looking over the river like in the cabin of a ship with his little fire going in his grate and surrounded by his books and family photos and old generals steeped in sun. Caroline is in a big room on the ground floor with a huge fireplace and plants and Allen's mother's dining room furniture which is kind of awful but they hope to better same before long. Outside the river rolls way down below them for they are on a high hill and hills roll away behind them to lovely soft valleys, about like golden velvet now with all the golden dead leaves neatly covering the ground and the sun coming down and the clean beech trees rearing up. . . ." Katherine Anne replied that "everyone who pops in at the Tates' goes away sending rapturous accounts but yours was the best," and said that she was trying to find enough money to build a cabin there.

In October, Sue Jenkins Brown, Harold Loeb, and Ford Madox Ford drove down with Loeb's girlfriend, Marjorie. Caroline thought Loeb (the model for Robert Cohn in *The Sun Also Rises*) "a very nice person." It was still warm enough to swim and they drank corn liquor and talked. Ford made Caroline go over every inch of her manuscript with him and that prevented her from taking him to Meriville to see the Meriwether cemetery.

Red Warren, now teaching at Southwestern in Memphis for the academic year 1930–1931, came again with Cinina, followed by Bill Bandy and his wife. Sally Wood arrived with a portable Victrola and a collection of French music-hall songs and was impressed with the Tates' Agrarian friends, who sat around the dining room table, each one reciting a sonnet of Shakespeare. "It was harder the second time around when the more popular ones had been used," she said. There were other amusements at Benfolly. Sometimes there was dancing in the parlor, and sometimes there was "fiddlin'" with country people invited in. The local fiddler said that Allen, who had taken years of violin lessons as a child, was a "fairly good fiddler if he didn't use them Eyetalian strings."

The most popular amusement was the Tates' own form of charades, and Benfolly charades were of a high order. Once Nancy was allowed to stay up to participate, and she played the part of the infant Ford Madox Ford at the bier of his Aunt Rossetti and the infant Alexander Pope being taken to call upon John Dryden at a tavern. The first part of "Rossetti" Caroline considered very good: Hemingway in a high hat calling upon Gertrude Stein who explained to him that "rose is a rose is a rose." Somebody else played the part of a "mad ox" very creditably. Allen acted as Ford himself, wearing a battered gray hat with a pillow stuffed in his front and walking with a slight limp. On another occasion, Nancy was Lady Godiva and Red Warren her horse. John Crowe Ransom got himself up as the archbishop of Canterbury and Andrew Lytle once played Dante.

Years later, in her novel *The Strange Children*, Caroline would describe, from the point of view of the ten-year-old Lucy, the charades at a country house in Tennessee. "The person who thought of the word would repeat it over and over, shaking with laughter. Sometimes they would laugh so hard that they would have to put their arms about each other's shoulders in order to stand up. For days afterward they might go off into gales of laughter at the mere mention of that word. Visitors did not understand how important the selection of the word was and were always suggesting words of their own. But the father and mother hardly ever listened to them." In fact, *The Strange Children* would capture very well the tone of life at Benfolly. An English reviewer, Anthony Curtis, writing in the *New Statesman and Nation*, commented on how the pattern of the grownups' lives emerged—"the lack of money, the incessant drinking, the rich meals, the conversational tearing to pieces of their friends."

Andrew Lytle settled down at Benfolly in the fall of 1930, spent the winter, and wrote his first book, a biography of General Nathan Bedford Forrest, the slave trader who became a Confederate general. "We were becoming artists," Lytle said many years later, describing life at Benfolly as pastoral-agrarian, reflecting the Garden of Eden. "We had a very fine accidental community. We had a common background and inheritance; we understood things the same way." While Andrew worked on Forrest and Allen tried to get started on Lee, Caroline was writing about a character who rode with Morgan's Raiders. (General John H. Morgan, one of the Confederacy's cavalry commanders, had tormented the Yankees with spectacular raids on railroads, bridges, and supply depots.) Before another winter went by, Caroline said, they would have to do something to break up the old-soldiers'-home atmosphere that was slowly settling down about the place. They sat around the fire at night talking about battles until Caroline said they should be wagging long gray beards. Caroline and Andrew both worked for a time in the dining room, but it made Caroline sick to look at Andrew's "damned old manuscript, obese, disgustingly obese," while hers always seemed the same size it was three weeks before.

The newly married Warrens and Andrew spent Thanksgiving at

Benfolly, and Christmas brought more company. Caroline wasn't able to sit down at her typewriter for two weeks.

Evelyn Scott, whose Civil War novel *The Wave* was published in 1929, visited Clarksville, her old hometown, in 1930 and came to Benfolly to see the Tates. "None of the townsfolk called on Evelyn Scott when she was here—we cannot decide whether it was because of what they call 'her colorful life,' or because they simply don't know she's a best-seller," Caroline said.

Edmund Wilson arrived, followed closely by Louise Bogan and her husband, Raymond Holden, who was then in book publishing and would later work for *The New Yorker, Fortune,* and *Newsweek.* Andrew Lytle remembers working on the last chapter of his book while Edmund and Allen talked across the hall. The Holdens, the Tates, and Wilson all sat around the fire at Benfolly drinking for a day or two, and Beatrice, the cook, started the ball rolling by getting dead drunk. Caroline told her a hot toddy would help her cold, and Beatrice drank one that knocked her out. They all had hot toddies and made a pilgrimage to the Hermitage, the Nashville home of Andrew Jackson, where Caroline said she had sworn never to go. They sat under Jackson's trees and passed the bottle around and then went downtown to the Andrew Jackson Hotel and played murder until far into the night. "A fine game," said Caroline. The Tates left the Holdens and Wilson and got back to Benfolly, where Andrew met them with the complete Forrest manuscript. Andrew insisted on celebrating, so they set out again, this time for Monteagle, stopping in Murfreesboro while Andrew stole a quart of whiskey from his grandmother. At Monteagle, the opening of a new hotel was being celebrated, and, Caroline wrote the Warrens, "We all expressed ourselves as highly pleased and drank some more and danced and so on. Andrew got gloriously tight. He brought up to us once a shrinking youth. 'My cousin,' says he, 'hasn't he a fine face?'" When they finished Andrew's grandmother's liquor, they went to bed. "A football player . . . went berserk and tried to get in the girls' rooms and hung himself out of the window and so on till three o'clock in the morning when a sheriff and his aide came and carried him off to the lockup," Caroline wrote. "The tourists who had driven up to the fine old Southern inn earlier in the evening all got up and left, saying that it was too much. I got back to Benfolly somehow but Allen seems to be in Nashville." To Katherine Anne, she added a sorrowful note, "These debauches are very weakening to us rustics, though. That was last Saturday, and today, Thursday, is the first time I've been able to write a word."

The Tates had developed a sightseeing circuit for visitors that included Fort Donelson, site of a siege during the Civil War; Merry

Mont, where the visitors were introduced to Miss Carrie and Caroline's Uncle Rob; and Summertrees, where they met Cousin John Ferguson. Cousin John's daughter served the visitors fruitcake and wine, and Cousin John showed them the schoolhouse where he had taught the neighborhood children the classics and French and told them anecdotes about Woodrow Wilson's father, who had once been the preacher at a church in the neighborhood. Cousin John thought the Depression was a good thing because it would send people back to the land and make the government get rid of the high tariff. Like Allen and the other Agrarians, he thought the growth of the cities was the cause of evil.

Edmund Wilson wrote about his visit in *The New Republic,* describing the tenant sharecropper and his wife in their little log cabin, the willow trees, coal fires burning in cold bedrooms, cornbread, chicken gravy on waffles, sorghum, the tall, dark tobacco barns, and Caroline's relatives. Cousin John had, Wilson wrote, "a passion for the classics," and disputed Origen and Josephus.

There were other houseguests, among them "Cousin" George Wilds, a Confederate veteran and father of the first husband of Caroline's Aunt Margaret. (Frank Wilds had died when he was struck by lightning while sitting underneath a silver maple tree on a cloudless day, or so went the family story.) Caroline had a rule never to mail to any visitors, except Confederate veterans, anything they left at Benfolly, and then not anything but false teeth. Cousin George Wilds had two sets of teeth, one for dessert and one for solid food, but he had to be reminded to bring his false teeth to the table for meals—it was Nancy's job to stand at the foot of the stairs at mealtime and shout, *"Teeth!"*

Herbert Warwick, another Confederate veteran known as Uncle Doc, had lived at Caroline's Aunt Loulie's boarding house in Nashville. Then, as Caroline said, Loulie, "who several years ago, nursed me through a nervous collapse of two months during which I lay in bed unable to walk, fell ill herself and cast Uncle Doc on me." Afraid to stay at Benfolly by herself, Caroline was glad to bring him back after the Monteagle excursion. "He is an oldfashioned drunkard, the thorough kind," she wrote the Warrens. "We have been told never under any circumstances to give him a drink. The country air is filling him with ambition, though. He has been telling me this evening how to make raisin jack. I said I would like a little good beer. 'I never paid much attention to beer,' says he. . . . I told him I was certainly glad to have him here with me. 'Miss Carrie,' he said, 'you might just as well be alone.'"

In June, Howard Baker and his bride, Dorothy, who would write

Young Man with a Horn, stopped by on their way from Paris to California, reporting that Ford's new wife, Janice Biala, was very much in love with him. Phelps Putnam, a thirty-seven-year-old New Englander educated at Exeter and Yale and by now the author of two volumes of poems, arrived at Benfolly in the summer of 1931 on his way to New Mexico for his asthma. Accompanied by an invisible bodyservant, he would call out, "Pompey! You black rascal!" He quickly acquired a thick Southern accent, referred to himself forever afterward as Old Marse Phelps, and loved to read his poems, especially, "Hasbrouck and the Rose," out loud with his newfound accent.

Stark Young appeared on his way to Texas, and amused Caroline with his gift for mimicry and his marvelous way with old ladies. "He patted my fierce grandmother on the hand and said, 'You are a dear old thing.' Allen and I looked on aghast, expecting to see her take his head off any minute." The next day Miss Carrie said, "Such a pleasant gentleman." Stark was just back from Italy, where he had been decorated by the king, and had his ribbons in a satin-lined box to show his aunts in Texas. Caroline made him wear them one afternoon to go calling on her Cousin May and Cousin Mag at Woodstock. John Gould Fletcher (whom Nancy called "John Goof Fletcher") paid them a visit on his way to Arkansas. Fletcher had a habit of taking a hot biscuit when Beatrice passed them, then holding it as he gestured and talked while it cooled in his hand. Beatrice used to take the cold biscuit and replace it with a hot one. Fletcher never noticed.

Allen's family even had a kind of reunion at Benfolly—his father, his brothers, Ben and Varnell, Ben's twelve-year-old son, and Varnell's wife. "It was very strenuous, but came off very well," Caroline reported to Sally. The family meeting caused the Tates to miss an old-fashioned hoedown at Uncle Rob's house, attended by everyone else in the neighborhood. "They had to go out and bring in the leader of the chain gang to call the figures," Caroline said with regret at not being there.

They blended guests from mixed backgrounds—Caroline's cousin from Rochester, Little May Morse, was there at the same time as Phelps Putnam, and they all had a picnic on a new raft in the river. On the hottest days of summer, they deserted the river for Spring Creek, where the members of the Connection gathered every summer; the creek was spring-fed and the water so cold it turned people blue in a very few minutes.

With all these guests, Caroline ran tirelessly up and down the stairs (somebody said the back steps at Benfolly were so steep you'd almost fall down backward when you tried to go up), did much of the cooking, devising inexpensive dishes out of eggs and vegetables, supervised the housekeeping—and managed to write. Company, she insisted, did not interfere with her work. "We go straight to our typewriters in the morning, but in the afternoon we are free," she said.

They went, sometimes with their houseguests, to dances at Dunbar Cave, where name bands came to play. Danforth Ross, a younger cousin of Caroline's, remembers seeing her, black-eyed and black-haired, dancing there in a long black dress. The cave was the scene of many local revels besides dances—ladies used to gather to play cards at the mouth of the cave, where it was always cool, even on hot summer afternoons.

Occasionally the Tates dined at the houses of people in Clarksville or members of the Meriwether-Barker connection. Once, at the home of a Dr. Ross and his wife, Mrs. Ross asked Allen something about one of his poems. Allen replied that he had written that poem for specialized readers and he liked to talk about other things at parties. Mrs. Ross, indignant, never forgave him.

WRITING, 1930–1932

"I am glad you are wallowing in family after years of exile," Caroline wrote to Katherine Anne Porter. "It should be particularly valuable to your kind of writer. I, of course, get right down among mine, pick up the gems—and gems do fall from their lips—as said gems fall. I am really a sort of reporter of my family."

When Josephine Herbst, who wanted to write a novel with a Reconstruction background, wrote to ask advice, Caroline suggested she go to Atlanta and talk to some old people there. "I know now, from experience, that you can get things this way that you can't get any other way," she told Josie. "You don't really get much stuff, but your imagination picks up, unbeknownst to you, all sorts of things. I was writing my book out of ten-year-old memories of long monologues of my grandmother's that I hardly listened to at the time. This spring, sitting on the porch, in the evenings, I have gotten the detail that I needed—what they wore and drank and so on. I picked up material for one chapter which I know will be the best in my book from a chance remark of my uncle's."

Living at Benfolly certainly gave Caroline a chance to refuel her imagination, to stockpile local legends and myths, and to reabsorb the language and folkways of the country; she made good use of the opportunity. While writing her first novel, Caroline also wrote short stories, some of her finest. One of them, "Mr. Powers," was, she said, the life and works of Mr. Suiter, a friend of the Tates' new tenant farmer, Mr. Norman; she hoped Suiter didn't sue her for libel or take after her with an axe. In the story, a young couple from the city let Mr. Powers work at their country place and then find out that he has attacked his wife with an axe and accidentally killed his son instead of his wife. *Scribner's Magazine* bought it for $200. Caroline commented that *Scribner's* took only her stories "dealing with murder, sudden death and the like, which is not as inconvenient as it sounds, my mind running as it does." Caroline's early stories were indeed laced with violence.

In "The Long Day," a chilling story that appeared in *Scribner's* in August 1930, Henry, a little boy, spends the day digging worms, eating sandwiches, and playing around the cabin of his family's black servant, Joe, unaware that Joe has mortally wounded his wife. In a shocking ending, he catches a glimpse of her bloody corpse inside the cabin— and runs.

Scribner's, however, did not take "The Ice House," which Caroline wrote a little later. Maxwell Perkins returned it saying that they had too many "tragic and gruesome" stories. In "The Ice House," set in 1866, two boys in Virginia are hired by a Yankee to dig the skeletons of Yankee soldiers out of the pit of an old icehouse and load them into coffins, which their employer hauls off. The two realize that the man is spreading the skeletons out over more coffins to get more money. "Thar ain't a whole man in ary one of them boxes," says one of the young men. "If that ain't a Yankee fer ye!" says the other in the closing line of the story.

"I'm sure Perkins couldn't swallow that," Caroline wrote Warren. "Also one of them says handling a dead Yankee ain't no more to him than handling a dead hawg." Apparently, Sally Wood, a native of Rochester, New York, read it in manuscript and protested the last line of the story, for Caroline wrote her she "was quite off," and went on to say:

When I say "If that ain't a Yankee fer ye!" I am not expressing a judgment on Yankees. I am merely recording the attitude, deplorable as it is, of two Virginia urchins in 1866 or whenever it was. I *know,* from observation, from history, from family tradition and so on that such would have been the attitude of these urchins. The phrase, however, is sort of makeshift. I wanted to end the story on "Thar ain't a whole man in ary one of them boxes," but neither Allen or Andrew would admit that what had happened was clear with no more than that said, so I had to go a little further than I wanted to go. But enough of "The Ice House." It has had a little private circulation and is now laid away in the old desk that I got in from Merry Mont the other day.

The story did not stay in the desk, but appeared in *Hound and Horn*. Caroline thanked Lincoln Kirstein, the editor, for publishing it. "I am sure you are the only editor in the country who would have done it," she wrote. Kirstein told her it was "a beautifully conceived description of a national attitude that is both excellent criticism and distinguished writing." "You really cannot beat the Jews," Caroline said to Katherine Anne Porter. "He has kept his ear to the ground faithfully for some months and has now decided to take a chance on me and this story is fine for his purpose, will establish him as impartially discerning."

Even before she finished her first novel, Caroline had an idea for her second. The Tates acquired their first tenant farmer—Jesse Rye, black, aged eighteen, with a new bride the same age—and built him a log cabin in the hollow by the spring, "the loveliest spot and the cabin is beautiful, built of hewn logs, chinked with clay and lime in the old fashioned way. They even got the shingles from an oak tree on the place." Allen told Caroline that when he took Jesse to the second-hand store to buy furniture for the cabin, the new tenant kept demanding "all sorts of fancy things."

"Like what?" asked Caroline, thinking of a radio.

"Chairs," said Allen. "I told him there was nothing doing. 'Why, Jesse,' I said, 'you can sit on a box.'"

Caroline realized that it was an infringement of the system to give black tenants anything, but also that "they really don't have enough to eat." So Caroline said to herself, "Be damned with the system!" and called Jesse into the house to give him half a cake.

When company came from Nashville, Caroline planned to serve a country meal of turnip greens and poached eggs, but Beatrice said, "Aw, Miz Tate, we can't have no eggs. Jesse went through the kitchen just before supper." He had picked up two dozen eggs.

Another day Allen engaged Jesse to do a day's work in the yard when he and Caroline were going to Nashville. As soon as their car disappeared Jesse hitched up his horse, went to town, and charged a number of things on their grocery bill.

"If you're going to do things like that you'll have to hunt another home," Caroline told him.

"It don't make no difference what I do. I can come up here and have a fuss with you all every morning and you can't put me off this place," replied Jesse, who had consulted a lawyer.

He was right. The verbal contract between the landlord and tenant made it almost impossible for the landlord to evict a tenant farmer, even a thief or an incompetent. The landlord simply had to stand him until the year was up. "Then he can't put him off his place without written notice on the very day that the contract is up," Caroline said. "If he waits a day later the tenant has a right to live on that farm another year!"

The Tates got rid of Jesse at the first possible moment and acquired Mr. Norman, often called "the sanctified one" because he was a member of a charismatic fundamentalist religious sect whose members considered themselves sanctified by grace. Mr. Norman and his family were to be Benfolly fixtures for many years.

The relationship of tenant to landlord led Caroline to think of the novel she wanted to write next, even though having the next subject ready made her feel like a woman who knows she is going to have another baby before the one in her arms is weaned. "Two families, white and poor white, living on the same farm," she said. "The situation seen through the eyes of one and then of the other. Each regards the other as his natural enemy. I am sure that Jesse thinks it perfectly proper to steal from me. I *should* regard him as so much vermin. Little May's uncle, Morris Banker, was killed by one of his tenants. You can see how the situation piles up through the years. It is complicated, of course, by money; when the tenant comes out owing two or three hundred dollars each year the landlord will keep him on, hoping to get his money back."

Andrew Lytle's book came out, and Maxwell Perkins pressured Caroline to finish hers. She was glad when she finished the Civil War section. She wrote the Battle of Shiloh chapter with a raging toothache. "My progress is so slow," she wrote Perkins. "It is the invention, not the actual writing, that comes to me so slowly, and it is something I can't hurry." Her Uncle Rob remembered that the "Elegy Written in a Country Churchyard" took Thomas Gray seven years. Uncle Rob called every morning to see if she was through yet.

As she drew near the end, she told Sally Wood, she went to pieces. She was frightened when Allen told her plainly that the last chapter, "the climax that I had built up to so fondly, simply would not do. My hands got to shaking so I couldn't even hit the keys. Finally I told Allen he had to write it then if it didn't suit him. He wrote a few pages and I got interested trying to fix up what he had written—it seemed to me so impossible—that I worked out of the fit."

She finished the novel shortly after Confederate Memorial Day 1931.

"The stage has been swept of corpses," she wrote to Katherine Anne. "Two suicides, one fratricide and one man shot from ambush by the Yankees: these were all the killings I found in my novel when I reckoned them up this morning." She felt the first chapter in the third section was so bad that it might ruin the book, which otherwise might come off very well. The knowledge depressed her but she was so weary that she could think of nothing to do about it. All the young men who wandered in and out of Benfolly read it and wrinkled their brows and suggested things to do that would require from 2,000 to 5,000 words, and she wondered if she could squeeze out one more scene. The manuscript went off to Perkins. She felt shaky, wandering around like a man just out of the pen who thought he might perhaps be just as well-off behind bars. "I really don't know what to do with myself. Three years I've been working on that damn thing, ten I've been triggering with it one way or another. I can't believe it's off my chest."

Publishing production methods were different in those days—Perkins sent the manuscript to the typesetter without having it copyedited. Over the years Perkins spoke often to Caroline and to other people about how much he admired her writing.

"I hope nothing will divert you from going on with the writing," he wrote to her after he received the manuscript for *Penhally*. "Certainly you have every reason to believe in yourself on the basis of what you have done now. I only mention it because it is so much harder for women to write with all the details that they have to think about, than for men."

Caroline agreed: "It is certainly much harder for a woman to write than it is for a man. It is so much harder that I am in a panic half the time fearing that something will happen to prevent me from writing. But I am very firm about it, I assure you. And we have a wonderful servant who does everything she can to help me get on with my writing."

When she read the proofs of *Penhally*, they made her sick—"such rough writing, such barbarous punctuation, such incredible genealogical slips—I feel pretty depressed over the whole thing. Another month would have done wonders. And of course it ought to be longer to get the right effect." Marion Henry, a cousin who lived at her family's farm, Oakland, helped with the proofs and caught all sorts of little errors. Marion could be businesslike when she wanted to, Caroline said. Marion wanted a job, Caroline said, "but if you don't *have* to earn your own living, people aren't going to do much about it. Allen took her up to see a friend of his, a librarian at Nashville—her attitude and address weren't right, but that is mostly just being brought up in this out of the way part of the world where you have to keep saying something pleasant whether you feel like talking or not."

In August Caroline wrote Katherine Anne that she had a contract for another novel, but it hadn't begun to weigh upon her to any marked extent. She knew what the novel was to be about, she said, and it was shaping up in her mind. She found that sandpapering old furniture brought it out. She and Allen had happened to buy for five dollars "the sweetest chest of drawers, massive and just what I've been longing for, but terribly battered."

Caroline decided she had agoraphobia, which only severe claustration would cure, and moved into a smaller room to work. "Marion Sadler, the son of the druggist (a lovely boy with beautiful eyes who wants to be a professor of history and falls into a trance when Mr. Tate speaks), is upstairs copying excerpts from the letters of Robert E. Lee. Allen is in his room writing to T. S. Eliot, Nancy and little Paul Campbell (185 pounds) are wrestling in the hall, Beatrice is making beer in the kitchen and I really don't see how a person can work with the summer in such full swing. Besides that I was up until twelve o'clock last night—Manny [Caroline's cousin Marion Meriwether] is spending her vacation at the Red Creek Cabin and we had a creek party yesterday afternoon. And the night before Cousin Robin's folk were here and we all got very tight on beer—August is perfectly bewildering here. . . . I am going away next year if I have the money. Doug (Brother's son) has just brought his bride (Hildred Neuernschwander) home—another picnic is indicated. I suppose I will have made a thousand sandwiches before the week is over."

Penhally was published in September 1931. Its first sentences have been often quoted: "The shadows that laced the gravelled walk shifted and broke and flowed away beneath his boot soles like water. He plunged through them as a horse plunges through a shallow stream. Passing the big sugar tree he tapped it smartly with his cane." The novel traces the history of a farm, Penhally, through four generations of owners. In 1826 Nicholas Llewellyn quarrels irrevocably with his stepbrother because he believes in primogeniture, in keeping the land together at all costs. A bachelor, he leaves Penhally to his nephew John, a worn-out veteran of Morgan's Raiders in the Civil War. John's grandsons repeat the old quarrel of 1826—Nicholas, the oldest and therefore owner of Penhally, doesn't like to farm, but Chance, the younger brother, does. When Nicholas sells Penhally, Chance kills him.

A colorful, readable family saga, *Penhally* is nonetheless a tragedy and was conceived as a tragedy. In her first application for a Guggenheim, Caroline wrote that she wanted to write prose that was "personal and American and yet derived from the classical models. My study of creative writing began with the Greek tragedians. My ideas of art form have been influenced by their traditions and by the early English novelists."

Nashville bookstores displayed *Penhally* in their windows, and the Dixon-Sadler drugstore in Clarksville held an autograph party, much nicer, Caroline thought, than one held in Nashville. At a Nashville bookstore, Caroline sat on a small balcony at one end of the shop. A woman came and stood downstairs for a long time, staring up at the balcony, whence a steady stream of smoke ascended. "Is that the lady that wrote 'the book'?" she asked. "She must be mighty smart, but Lord, don't she smoke a lot!"

The Meriwether Connection gave mixed greetings to *Penhally*. Caroline was reprimanded by Cousin Gus Henry, Marion's father, for having a blasted sycamore in the book. "Don't you know that lightning never strikes a sycamore tree?" he said. Gus Williams of Peacher's Mill came to her rescue, testifying that in his lifetime he had known three sycamores to be struck. Cousin Armistead Gordon, a Virginia cousin who used to collaborate with Thomas Nelson Page, the author of *Two Little Confederates,* wrote to say he liked it, to Caroline's immense pleasure. Caroline's father read it twice, and said he read a little in it every day, finding it amusing because he knew all the people in it so well. He wanted to know what Miss Carrie thought of it. "My cows won't touch onions," he said, roaring with laughter, because Miss Carrie always declared that Merry Mont cows wouldn't eat onions and spoil the flavor of her milk, and Caroline used the expression in the book. Miss Carrie was, Caroline decided, conventionally proud of a granddaughter who could write a book.

Stark Young wrote to say he thought her photograph on the dust jacket with her hair brushed straight back above the ears was "sweet," but said her writing was "masculine," with its "steady mentality and purpose." He added that he was "glad I saw your Cumberland country and the people, it enabled me to see how accurate your picture is, quite astoundingly accurate without any fuss."

Caroline happily answered a congratulatory letter from Janet Lewis, and grappled with the criticisms from Janet's husband, Yvor Winters. Winters thought that *Penhally* was one of the five or six best novels of the past two decades but that it should have been written in an entirely different way. Caroline wrote to Janet: "I think of a novel, in a way, as a piece of sculpture, I feel that I am moulding the material—a novel written the way [Yvor] proposes . . . would be like painting, painting in—what is that stuff?—tempera."

A letter from Josie Herbst cheered her immensely because of something Josie had said about the sense of time in *Penhally*. "I was sitting here feeling pretty low about time when your letter came," Caroline replied. "I took a place for a subject but I wanted . . . to make time flow around it, and the book is too short, too compressed—I feel that very much, am pretty sick about it."

She told Lincoln Kirstein that he was a kindred soul. The focus of her feelings, she said, was regret for the lost cause. "It would have been better, I think, if our grandfathers had been carried off the field dead. The South that exists today has little of the Old South in it— we have sold out, certainly."

She told John Gould Fletcher that the Cousin Alfred of her book had just died. "He lived in the oldest house in the country. It was falling to pieces around his ears; when people asked him why he didn't build a new house for his son he said, 'Yes and I'd lay down and die and he'd fill it up with damn Yankees.' He wore jaybird's feathers in his hat and his invariable reply when approached by tractor salesmen was 'No, by God!' "

She wrote to Ford at length, apologizing for not dedicating the book to him. "God knows I would have if it had occurred to me that it would give you even a moment's pleasure." It was "indescribably stupid" of her not to have dedicated it to him. *Penhally* is dedicated "to the memory of Charles Nicholas Meriwether of Woodstock and to that one of his great grandsons who best exemplifies the ancient virtues Robert Emmet Meriwether," in other words, her Uncle Rob.

Caroline told Ford that in conversation with other writers, "and God knows I see too many of them," she tried to put into words what he had done for her, because it was amazing and exciting: "If I should ever amount to anything everybody will know that it is your doing."

She wrote Ford that originally she had written another ending for *Penhally*. "The young man went out on the porch and looked around and the land which he had known seemed to have been obliterated— I believe the last words were 'as if by a wave of the hand.' Thinking about it I became convinced that reflection wouldn't do, that there must be some symbol of the destruction of the house and only violent action would suffice for that. I may have been influenced by Allen; he thought that too. . . . A curious thing . . . Several years ago I wrote a novel which was really a section of this present book and it ended with one brother shooting another brother. Allen says I have a bad homicidal complex."

In a warm review in *The Bookman*, Ford called *Penhally* "a triumphant tragedy of a house and the vindication of a mode of life." He wrote that five writers of the day interested him—Ernest Hemingway, Glenway Wescott, George Davis, Elizabeth Madox Roberts, and Caroline Gordon. It was wonderful "to have golden opinions from the person whose judgment you most respect," Caroline wrote him.

She told Ford about her plans for the new novel about the two families, white and poor white, living on the same land. "It is hard to understand poor white people. . . . There are so many things that have to be comprehended and yet are hard to put into such a novel—

the terrible and swift deterioration of a whole people after the Civil War—you see it in architecture, my grandmother and her husband deserting a really beautiful house like the Old Place to live in an atrocity like the Merry Mont house. But it pervades the whole fabric of society—my grandmother says of two cousins who turned Republican that 'they grew up after the Civil War when people had no principles.' "

Caroline was touched that Sally Wood's mother was going to give a talk about *Penhally* in Rochester, and flattered that she referred to Caroline as a young girl. "I am thirty-seven years old, not a young girl, alas," she wrote Sally. "And as for the war, in a sense I was there. Really, I've been through it so many times in 'Battles and Leaders' I have to stop and remind myself that I was neither at Shiloh, Antietam, Malvern Hill, nor Bull Run—nor sang within the bloody wood."

Caroline finished up a long short story, "The Captive," based on a true narrative of Jinny Wiley, a white woman captured by the Indians and kept for years. "I feel sorry about the Indians," she wrote Léonie Adams. "I have gotten quite a feeling for them, having been worrying with them now for some time—I have a pioneer lady out in the woods living more or less happily with the Indians after having all her children brained and her house burned and so on. I am imitating the style of Davy Crockett and if you don't think that's hard, try it some time. . . . Nancy was fussing about her food the other day and I caught myself telling her that little Indian children are never allowed to eat anything hot for fear of getting soft. Really, though, people don't appreciate the Cherokee as they ought to."

She sent the story to Maxwell Perkins for possible publication in *Scribner's* and also for entry in the magazine's long short story contest. When the Tates were desperate for money, she wired Perkins for a decision on the story. Perkins wired back that the magazine was turning it down because it lacked story interest. Caroline was outraged. "It is the story of what actually happened to a pioneer woman, told as simply as possible. The story starts with the burning of a cabin and proceeds through the tomahawking of a few children, the dashing out the brains of another, and torture at the stake to a sensational escape across a river in full flood." She had flattered herself that there was not a dull moment in it, what with murder, rapine, and constant fear of death. She was so furious, she said, that she couldn't use her mother tongue. Perkins wrote her that in the beginning the story was too much like a chronicle. Caroline replied: "My treatment of this story is the best writing I can do, and I am willing to stake my reputation as a writer on it. . . . I am not a talented amateur; I am as mature as I will ever be; and I see no reason why my publisher should let me starve until he can catch up with my work." She added that the letters about *Penhally* pointed out without exception "the maturity of the craftsmanship and the possession of a genuine subject matter."

Then she sat down and used Perkins's criticism to rewrite the story's first pages, trying to make Jinny a character sooner.

"The Captive" was published in *Hound and Horn,* led off her first short story collection, and became one of her best-known works.

9

AGRARIANS AND THE AGRARIAN LIFE,
1930–1932

Allen spent a great deal of time with the Agrarians, planning their book and talking about future projects. He also spent a great deal of time worrying about but not writing the biography of Robert E. Lee. Lee soon became the family's very own albatross.

A close group, the Agrarians sometimes met at John Crowe Ransom's house in Nashville but more often at Benfolly, where they brought their wives and children. Their book, which appeared in the fall of 1930, was called *I'll Take My Stand.* Tate and Warren disapproved of the title, but Harper's, the publisher, loved it. Ransom wrote the introduction. Allen wrote a very dense essay on religion, urging Southerners by an act of will to reestablish a "private, self-contained, and essentially spiritual life." He believed poetry suffered from a "malady of disbelief," and he saw a need for myth and tradition, stability and order. As many of his friends in the North—Edmund Wilson, Kenneth Burke, Matthew Josephson, and Malcolm Cowley—leaned toward the Communist party, Allen became ever more conservative. Donald Davidson wrote on a climate for the creative arts. Robert Penn Warren had sent the chapter on race from Oxford. Although Warren called only for fair treatment for blacks and not for an end to segregation, Davidson thought it was much too extreme. Andrew Lytle wrote the liveliest chapter, "The Hind Tit," in which he lamented, among other things, the passing of ice cream socials and Sacred Harp hymn singing. His title comes from the last phrases in his essay, where he mourns that industrialism has turned the farmer into "the runt pig in the sow's litter . . . forced to take the hind tit for nourishment." Other contributors to the anthology included Stark Young, John Gould Fletcher, Lyle Lanier, a professor of psychology at Vanderbilt, Herman Nixon, who taught economics at Tulane, and Frank Owsley, a Vanderbilt historian.

All the Agrarians, except Allen and Andrew Lytle, lived and earned their livings in cities. None of them, except Lytle, knew anything about farming. Caroline, who had lived on a farm and knew all about farming, never attended any of the meetings. Allen *talked* Agrarian, but Caroline *was* Agrarian. Not that Tate, Ransom, and Davidson were not sincere in what they said; they were. They thought an Agrarian South was absolutely necessary for many reasons, one of the most important being their belief that great literature, although universal, needed a rich and stable regional background. It was a time when regionalism was often talked about and Midwesterners, especially, sought to legitimize regional art. The Agrarians wanted to protect their region in order to protect their literature.

I'll Take My Stand met ridicule and scorn, even from Southerners. *The New York Times* said the Agrarians were twelve Canutes trying to hold back the sea of change. Allen's friend Yvor Winters wrote to Katherine Anne Porter that he liked Allen's essay, though it seemed weak and inflated and ended with a passage that was "wholly obscure. I haven't the vaguest idea whether he is recommending a new Civil War, an evangelical campaign, or act of the will. I do wish Tate had not rushed into an agrarian manifesto, though, before getting his first crop of tobacco planted." This was not quite fair. Benfolly produced a crop of pea hay—grown by the tenant farmer—that year, from which the Tates' share was expected to be five tons of hay or $200. They also had what Caroline called "a fine turnip sallet patch on the side of the hill." What more appropriate crop for Southern Agrarians than turnip greens?

The Agrarians were seen as foolish romantics by progressive Southerners, who believed that industrialization was essential if the South was to achieve any kind of prosperity. The Agrarians thought the progressives were traitors to the South.

A Chattanooga newspaper editor suggested a debate between the Agrarians and a pro-progress group. Several debates actually took place, the first in Richmond on November 14, 1930, with John Crowe Ransom speaking for the Agrarians and Stringfellow Barr, native Virginian, Rhodes scholar, professor of history at the University of Virginia, and editor of *The Virginia Quarterly Review*, speaking for the progressives. Ransom, Lytle, and Tate drove to Richmond for the debate while Caroline stayed home: she could farm Nancy out easily enough, but Freda was expecting puppies and Caroline didn't want to leave her at a time like that. Thirty-five hundred people came to the Richmond City Auditorium for the debate, including the governor of Virginia, Ellen Glasgow, Norman Thomas, and H. L. Mencken. Sherwood Anderson, who was living in Troutdale, Virginia, presided. Somebody commented that Stringfellow Barr had a small garden, but Ransom had never raised a pea. Allen said that Barr lost the debate because he was an Agrarian at heart.

There were other debates in Atlanta and New Orleans and one in Columbia, Tennessee, pitting Davidson against W. S. Knickerbocker, editor of *The Sewanee Review*. The Tates, the Ransoms, and the Lyle Laniers went in a group to this one, stopping in Franklin, Tennessee, for a picnic before the debate, in which, said Caroline, Davidson made mincemeat out of Knickerbocker.

The book on Robert E. Lee kept the Tates from visiting the Warrens in Memphis. "God knows when we'll get down there," Caroline wrote. "Allen has to write Lee now. I don't believe we can come till he's through with it. Hasn't even started yet!" Caroline was criticizing Red Warren's first attempts at fiction, telling him that she liked one story "quite as well as 'Prime Leaf.' . . . "I got from it a feeling of genius, like Keats', that illuminates everything it touches," she wrote him. She went on to make quite specific suggestions. "I am sorry to report, Mr. Warren, that it doesn't get over where one lady calls the other a bitch. . . . Perhaps you are trying to handle too many ideas in one sentence. . . . An important fact would have to be said in one sentence and stand alone long enough to reverberate."

By the time the summer of 1931 rolled around, Caroline was sick of her relatives and longing for good company. There was not one congenial person in Clarksville, she said. All the Agrarians went away— even Andrew Lytle was in Southampton, Long Island, working with the Hampton Players. He went into New York City to explain to Allen's publisher why Allen was taking so long to write the Lee biography. Caroline said she actually looked forward to the Saturday-night poker games at Chink and Lyle Lanier's house in Nashville that winter. At least the Warrens would be in Nashville for the school year. Red Warren would be teaching at Vanderbilt the 1931–1932 academic year, taking John Crowe Ransom's place while Ransom was on a Guggenheim in Great Britain. "I can't hand Cinina much but I adore Red, and he is a sweet creature to have around if you have any time at all to play." No one, not one of the brethren or their wives, liked Cinina Warren or could say a good word for her. Angered once at Benfolly, she started waving a knife. (The Tates' cook always referred to it as "the night Mrs. Warren got loose.") Cinina said that no one liked her and no one took her writing seriously. "We don't like you because you're bad to Red," Caroline told her. Everyone liked Red Warren so much that they put up with Cinina as best they could. Warren taught, wrote reviews, and tried, "poor devil," said Caroline, to write a novel. Cinina was taking a class at Vanderbilt, and Warren typed her papers for her. She was frail and had to stay in bed until noon. She had a perfectly competent maid, but Warren did the housework. "He doesn't have the guts to deal with such a situation," said Caroline.

Casting around for amusement, Caroline discovered the writing of one of her relatives, Uncle Jimmy Ross, who reportedly "never saw his feet after he was grown" and whose motto was: "Never stand up when you can sit down, never sit down when you can lie down, never do today what you can put off till tomorrow." She had always heard him spoken of with gentle contempt, but she and Allen decided he was one of the finest prose stylists who ever lived. When he was an old man he wrote a book about his grandfather, Elder Reuben Ross, a Baptist preacher. Caroline particularly admired two short pieces in the book, about the trip that Uncle Jimmy made when he was a child of six, crossing the mountains from Virginia; she considered his first sentence a "knockout":

"On the sixth of May, 1807, according to appointment, all bade adieu to their friends and relatives, the scenes of their early life, the graves of their fathers, and many objects besides around which memory loves to linger and turned their faces toward the setting sun."

Caroline said she wouldn't care if she never saw her feet again if she could turn a sentence like that.

She reread *Ivanhoe* and thought it "the most gorgeous thing—the whole feudal pageant passing before you and all very cleverly put together." She went on to read *Kenilworth* and found it "magnificent," the way "the whole Elizabethan countryside streamed towards Kenilworth on every road." In the first two years at Benfolly, she reread all of Scott and Dickens and started on Trollope.

Allen suffered the tortures of the damned over Lee, she said. "God knows when he'll get through with it. Day before yesterday and the day before that he burst forth with eleven poems. Yes ma'am, eleven in three, or four days. Eight of them are a sonnet sequence, and fine, too. 'Sonnets of the Blood,' he calls them." "Emblems," a group of three lyric poems, reflects Allen's bemusement with life at Benfolly, as the first and last stanzas of the first of the three poems show:

Maryland, Virginia, Caroline
Pent images in sleep
Clay valleys rocky hills old fields of pine
Unspeakable and deep

Far from their woe fled to its thither side
To a river in Tennessee
In an alien house I will stay
Yet find their breath to be
All that my stars betide—
There some time to abide
Took wife and child with me.

Scribner's had agreed to publish his poems, with no bargaining, no biographies to write, Caroline said, adding, "Perkins really is nice. I continue to dote on him."

The Tates needed money, but they kept thinking everything would be fine when Allen finished the Lee biography, for which Earle Balch continued to hound him. "It's just Mr. Balch," Beatrice would say when the telephone rang. If only Allen could finish Lee, Caroline wrote Sally, he could get a sizable advance for his next book.

At the end of October 1931, Allen and Caroline drove to Charlottesville, Virginia, to attend a conference of Southern writers, called "The Southern Author and His Public." Ellen Glasgow, who was then fifty-seven and had published a dozen or more novels, suggested the conference to James Southall Wilson, one of the editors of *The Virginia Quarterly Review*. The South had more good writers than any other region, she felt, and they never had a chance to get together; the University of Virginia agreed to be the host. Besides Caroline and Allen, those present included William Faulkner, thirty-four and already firmly established with *The Sound and the Fury, As I Lay Dying,* and *Sanctuary* behind him; Alice Hegan Rice (*Mrs. Wiggs of the Cabbage Patch*); James Branch Cabell (*Jurgen*); Mary Johnston (*To Have and to Hold*); DuBose Heyward (*Porgy*); Archibald Henderson (*Relativity: A Romance of Science*); Paul Green (*In Abraham's Bosom*); James Boyd (*Drums*); Struthers Burt (*The Interpreter's House*); and Sherwood Anderson, who though born in Ohio was living in Virginia. Invited but not present were Roark Bradford, Thomas Wolfe, Elizabeth Madox Roberts, Stark Young, Julia Peterkin, Irvin S. Cobb, and Burton Rascoe.

It was not much like writers' conferences of today. The invited guests had been screened by a committee; reports of the conference use the words "house party" and "gracious"; and the leisurely schedule included lunch for the whole group at Wilson's home, dinner at the Farmington Country Club, tea at the Colonnade Club House on the west lawn of the university, and lunch at the home of the lawyer who had successfully defended Cabell's *Jurgen* case in court in 1922. The writers were driven to Castle Hill, home of Amélie Rives, the Princess Troubetzkoy, and also the first Meriwether place in America. Caroline thought Amélie Rives "a sort of Southern Ouida—at eighty she still has the golden hair and the enormous violet eyes that set the country-side agog." The prince and princess gave the conferees the only decent liquor they had the whole time, Caroline said, and she hoped the university paid them for it. The Troubetzkoys were so poor they charged fifty cents to go through the grounds. The boxwood was won-derful, Caroline said, taller than the trees, and was worth $200,000.

Ellen Glasgow made the introductory address, which was followed by open discussion during which the two subjects most often brought up were the dearth of book reviews in the South and the question of Progress versus Stability.

Caroline thought the conference a very funny affair and peculiarly Southern. "It was really like a gathering of second cousins who hadn't ever seen each other before but had to admit the tie of blood," she wrote Ford Madox Ford. "Paul Green got up and said we were all going to God in a machine, which incensed us agrarians, but we were pretty polite about that even."

Faulkner was the man who most interested everyone there. Caroline, who admired his work tremendously, deplored his behavior, especially when he spat a drink on a new dress that she had made herself. "He was trying to say 'Yes ma'am,' and the drink he had just taken went the wrong way and there was a geyser in which I was engulfed. John Bishop was standing there holding my hand and making his farewells. I must pay a tribute to his expatriate breeding. Not a muscle of his face stirred. I fear one of the off muscles of my mouth quivered a bit. Faulkner reeled off into a corner with a handkerchief. The poor devil felt pretty bad about it. I heard him muttering something about his bad manners . . . and I went over and said everything pleasant I could think of to him but he just sat there staring at me like a dejected coon and finally I couldn't stand it and went off. Thank God it wasn't my white satin dress," she wrote Léonie. Even among hard-drinking Southerners it was felt he drank too much. When someone asked, "What do you think, Mr. Faulkner?" he replied, "I think I'll shorely get a little drink in three, four minutes."

Allen had written to Donald Davidson in 1929 that Ellen Glasgow had an abominable prose style, that she was one of the worst novelists in the world, and that it was time they repudiated people like her and Cabell. Furthermore she was an incredible old snob. But when he met her at the conference he changed his tune and decided she was "just like a worldly old French woman of the 18th century." Caroline felt that "everybody there was engaged in trying to conceal the fact that they knew that Ellen Glasgow lacked intellectual subtlety," but still, "she sprang valiantly into the breach with her ear trumpet and really did very well, a grand old girl she is."

Back home, the Tates had to face their money problems. Caroline longed to go to New York for a visit, but money "gets scarcer and scarcer," she wrote Léonie. "Allen has just gone off to Nashville to try to borrow some money. This town, full as it is of dark-fired tobacco, is getting un-agrarian. The merchants are wanting their bills paid every month or so. . . . If they are doing that there is no hope." Still, they managed to give a weekend house party for "dozens" of people. Everybody drank beer steadily for two days, Caroline wrote Sally, but it must have been pretty good beer because nobody had a hangover. The amount of alcohol consumed at Benfolly was astounding. Caroline's cousin Carrie Ferguson was once at Merry Mont and asked Nancy, "What kind of party was it that Carrie and Allen went to in Nashville— a bridge party or a dancing party?" Nancy replied that it wasn't either one, it was a drinking party.

Allen, avoiding the Lee biography, wrote more poetry and began a novel. Caroline made school dresses for Nancy, who started first grade at the Catholic school in Clarksville that fall. Nancy decided the nuns didn't marry because it was too much trouble to cook for men, leading Caroline to say she hoped Nancy didn't get that idea from her. "She knows already there is something a little queer about Allen and me and distrusts our judgment," Caroline added. Someone told Nancy that she could, like Mama, write a book when she was grown. "Don't mention no books to me," Nancy replied. "Mama has nearly drove me crazy locking herself up every morning." Allen was distressed by Nancy's use of the double negative, but Caroline assured him that it was in the best Agrarian tradition.

Caroline was reading seriously about early Tennessee with a view to writing a book of related stories. She was aware that Scribner's was not enthusiastic, but she was going to do it anyway. "Such tales! Such gore!" she wrote Katherine Anne Porter. "One advantage you have in writing about those times—you start off in an atmosphere of tremendous excitement. The exploits of some of those pioneer women are things that occur usually on battlefields."

Caroline was torn. She wanted to live in the country where she could walk in the woods and plant a garden and where she found the sources of her work, but she liked to be surrounded by intelligent, amusing people all the time. She needed time to devote to her writing, but she never turned her back on a chance for uproarious celebration.

She wanted Nancy to have a happy childhood, but she resented the time that a child took from her writing, and she never let Nancy's existence interfere with a party. She loved Allen possessively, adoringly, passionately, almost to the point of monomania, but Allen dithered about Lee, wrote little or nothing, and brought in very little money. She wanted to spend more time on everything she wrote, but they needed money so badly she felt compelled to hurry and finish each book and each story as fast as she could in order to get more money.

How would they get through the winter with no money? she wondered. Allen could get nothing done on the Lee book, and their debts in Clarksville mounted. "We have been so busy trying to borrow money at from any sum to 15 percent. Finally got it of course from the poorest member of the family, darling Loulie—that we haven't realized until this week that Christmas was on the way," Caroline wrote to Cinina and Red Warren. Loulie had abandoned her Nashville boarding house and come to live with her mother at Merry Mont. Eighty-three years old, Miss Carrie sighed and said of living alone in a dilapidated country house, "I knew I had too good a thing to last."

Red Warren's mother was ill in November, and while she lay at the point of death for more than a week, Allen and Caroline stayed at the hospital with the Warrens, sitting up several nights. After Mrs. Warren died, Allen went to Guthrie, but Caroline stretched out to read *Pickwick Papers,* grateful for a bed after several nights of sleeping in chairs.

In late November Caroline asked Maxwell Perkins for more money. Allen had bogged down on Lee, she said, and wasn't doing any reviewing at the moment. Perkins replied that *Penhally* had not sold more than its advance and asked her if she had any short stories she could sell.

Her cousin Manny Meriwether came for Christmas and Caroline invited Red and Cinina and Red's father and brother to have Christmas dinner with the Tates at Benfolly. She began busily sewing on some white satin scraps—it was fun after writing so long about Jinny Wiley in "The Captive" sewing on deerskin leggings with porcupine quills. She made Beatrice a set of boudoir pillows, satin and lace and pink rosebuds, even though they might tempt her to "much sinning." She also made a satin quilt ornamented with pink rosebuds for the "big baby doll" Santa was to bring Nancy. And then she dressed three dolls for the "sanctified children" of the Normans.

The Christmas turkey, raised painstakingly by her grandmother, was penned up behind the lattice under the porch. Andrew Lytle was coming from Alabama, bringing a brace of guineas, some of the bounty from a freshly killed hog, and a gallon of sorghum. He would be a most welcome guest, she told Ford, what with all those people coming and nothing to feed them with. "At this moment we haven't even money to buy a stamp for this letter but God doubtless will provide," she said.

They cut a cedar tree in the woods that year and put it up in the dining room with real candles on it. Red, Cinina, and Andrew spent a week at Christmas with them, and Bernard Bandler, an editor of *Hound and Horn,* appeared on Christmas day and spent a week. "We diverted ourselves shooting craps and playing charades and drinking Hopkinsville liquor," Caroline wrote to Malcolm Cowley. After the others left, she and Bandler went for long walks, leaving Allen, who wouldn't go on walks unless he had an objective, along the bluffs over the river. Caroline found Bandler "very intelligent."

The new year brought more money problems. They were living on black-eyed peas. Would Mr. Kimbrough at the bank take the car that week or next? Should she fire the cook? "But I owe her three weeks' back wages, and besides I need her to borrow money from," Caroline said. "Oh well," as Mr. Norman, the sanctified tenant, said, "if I'm going to starve, let me starve on a farm."

In an effort to make money quickly, Caroline wrote a fairy story and tested it on Nancy, who suggested she take some parts out of *The Wizard of Oz.* Allen tried to read it, but couldn't, and though she thought it dull herself, Caroline sent it on to Perkins. If she could write a juvenile a year, she could keep them from starvation. Scribner's children's department turned it down. Perkins told her "The Captive," still unsold at this point, would be a fine story to lead the collection he would publish after her second novel came out. How could she write a second novel when she could not take her mind off money? And it was hard to write about poor white people. There was one distinguishing characteristic, though, and that was constant understatement. They said, for instance, "There ain't nothing to murder," and of a murderer, they said, "There ain't a thing to him."

She started raising chickens and had seven frying-size ones. They would do better, she said, if Allen would keep his damn coal out of her chicken house. Allen's second book of poems, *Poems: 1928–1931,* came out and was reviewed scathingly by Louise Bogan, a recent houseguest at Benfolly, who called the Fugitives "parochial" and said that Allen's genuine talent was too often crippled by "determined incoherence, perverse ostentation, and sterile vocabulary." The Tates were furious.

Then it looked as though Caroline would get a Guggenheim Fellowship; at least the foundation asked her to prepare a budget of her financial needs should she be awarded one. Caroline sent the foundation a letter about anticipated expenses that marvelously illustrated her concept of financial planning. She asked for a stipend of $3,000 for the year, although she calculated they would need $3,450; she and Allen would furnish the rest out of their combined incomes. What she wanted to do, though, was pay $900 from the first installment of the stipend on their debts. Their creditors, she said, understood their financial schedule, but "they would not understand the Fellowship or understand how people who can go to Europe might need to postpone their debts." Their joint income, she said, would see them through in Europe.

The foundation offered her $2,000 for the year and refused to allow her to spend any of it on paying debts at home. She accepted, privately complaining of the foundation's attitude, in view of "the millions of bills we have to settle before we go." Then she added with her customary resilience, "Now when Mr. Norman says, 'I always tell 'em if I'm going to starve to death let me starve on the farm,' I can say I feel that way about Paris."

Both she and Allen had the flu that winter, and it lingered on until they felt rundown and spiritless. Everything was so awful that Caroline didn't see how it could be worse, and when you felt that way, she said, the next thing—if you are female—is to discover that you are pregnant. In February she had an abortion in Clarksville. "I had several, in fact, the first two not seeming to come off right," she wrote to Katherine Anne. The doctor said Caroline was the meanest patient he ever had. "In the midst of the last affair I had an acute attack of appendicitis. The doctor I was having said it was quite all right for me to have a temperature of 106. Our family doctor whom we called in the middle of the night requested that he be called formally at once for consultation but as the other old fool wouldn't call him he went back to bed round three o'clock not expecting to see me again. He thought I had a bad infection and I suppose he thought there was no use in getting mixed up in it. Anyhow, I wangled out of it."

Allen then had a relapse and stayed in bed three weeks, became anemic, and had to stuff himself on raw eggs, iron pills, spinach, and raw cabbage. Beatrice walked off while they were both in bed. "I was never so shocked in my life," Caroline said. "I can't understand it. She had made some horrible soup for dinner and I asked her what in the world she put in it but aside from that all was harmonious between us, except that she had let all the work slide and left the house perfectly filthy. She simply pranced off in the middle of the afternoon. I wouldn't take her back now for anything," Caroline wrote Cinina. She was delighted when Andrew arrived to do the shopping and even help her with the dishes, and even more delighted when her father sent a check and the Tates were able to pay the Warrens twenty dollars they owed them.

10

Europe Again, 1932–1933

Caroline wrote to Ford that they were coming to Europe in July. They would stay in Paris a few weeks, but did he know a cheap place where they could settle down and do some work? Would he and Janice still be in Toulon? Would that be a good place? She could not live through another winter in Paris. His advice would be good, she thought, since he was broke too, and would be able to see things from their point of view.

She wrote to Sally Wood and urged her to join them for the trip. Sally was not as enthusiastic about Ford as Caroline was; she always thought Allen a model of restraint to put up with Ford—he did it, Sally said, because he knew Ford helped Caroline.

Caroline told Sally she really liked being in Ford's vicinity. "To have even one person sort of planning things so you can get your work done helps a lot. And his mild tyrannies will be exerted over Janice this time. . . . Really, he never did any thing worse than demand that we spend all our evenings with him at a period when he was undergoing all sorts of terrific troubles."

Caroline vowed to "work like hell" in Toulon. "If the circle proves so distracting that Allen doesn't work I'm going to move off and leave you all. I'm fed up on starving." She was sure her second novel would be easier to write, since it was all in the present. "I feel it winding up inside me slowly and am counting on France to act as mid-wife," she said. "Such a relief to have only two characters."

They rented Benfolly—completely furnished down to the apparatus for making beer, and with labor to produce a garden—for thirty-five dollars a month, to a German tobacconist who was about to be married. He wanted possession in the spring, so the Tates decided to move over to Merry Mont with Caroline's grandmother until they left for Europe in July. Caroline came down with a second attack of appendicitis just as she started to pack at Benfolly. She had a frightful pain in her stomach, which Allen thought was caused by a large dill pickle she had eaten. "The family doctor having condescended to give me a curettage by that time had his mind clear to recognize appendicitis—it was the third time I'd had an attack and called him in—the first time he said it was too much Thanksgiving dinner!" He told her if the pain got better she could wait a week for the operation and finish packing up Benfolly.

After they finished the packing, Caroline was almost reluctant to leave Benfolly now that it was getting its lush green look and the dogwood was in bloom in the woods. She hated to think of the tobacconist's bride lolling about on her porch. Once they unloaded at Merry Mont in late April, Caroline went to the hospital again. Sally Wood sent some money, which Allen wanted to refuse, but Caroline accepted "with heartfelt thanks" and treated herself to extra days in the hospital.

Out of the hospital, she stayed in bed several weeks at Merry Mont, rejoicing to be where she did not have to keep house. She had always liked Merry Mont in spring, when the fields were "unbelievably green" and there was "a light veil of dogwood bloom all through the woods." By May 3 she was back at the typewriter, though still spending a part of each day in bed.

Her father came to Merry Mont; Loulie and Pidie were already there. They all sat on the porch all day long, she said, and stared at the green fields, wondered if her grandmother was still in a good humor, went in and ate enormous meals of country-butchered mutton, and went back and sat on the porch some more while the shadows lengthened. By evening, when they did more porch-sitting in the dark, "the tide of reminiscence has risen until we have called to mind most of the old time characters of these parts—Cousin Owen who walked from the house of one relative to another and carried his teeth in a basket and said, 'Kisses for girls and switches for boys,' and Uncle Thomas Watson and Uncle Joe Morris each of whom kept in the side-board at Brackets a black bottle labelled 'Thomas Watson, His Bottle' and 'Joe Morris, His Bottle.' They too sat on the porch all day long and when they saw a man approaching they speculated on which one of them he was nearer kin to and whose bottle he would get a drink out of. A nice way, it seems to me, of passing the time—just the right amount of intellectual interest," Caroline wrote. She was not wasting her time as she sat on the porch with her relatives—she already had an idea for a short story from some of the talk.

Caroline's father and Allen went fishing every afternoon, and the women could not get them to go to Molly Ferguson's funeral. Allen would have gone, Caroline said, but her father instilled the spirit of rebellion in him by announcing grandly: "Cousin Molly Ferguson is no more kin to me than a catfish. Why should I go to her funeral? I don't have many more years to live and I have already preached four thousand funerals and some of them were the very devil." Caroline wanted Allen to go even if her father did not, but Mr. Gordon pled for Allen's company. "We hold high concourse on that pond," he said. "I am starved for intellectual companionship." Gordon marveled when Allen received a hundred-dollar check in the mail, the year's prize from the Poetry Society of South Carolina. He took Allen's book in his hands and said he couldn't write a poem if he was going to be hung for it, but he recited "Hail to the Chief Who in Triumph Advances" in full.

Allen, commissioned to write a poem for the last Confederate veterans' reunion in Richmond, turned out "To the Lacedemonians," and then made some minor repairs at Merry Mont, winning Miss Carrie's gratitude. Miss Carrie looked at Caroline and remarked that it was strange how anybody with good blood could keep a room so dirty. Caroline said she herself had always marveled at how dirty she could keep a room.

She went with her grandmother and aunts to Cousin Kitty Meriwether's eighty-ninth birthday party. "The honoree, who looks like a little brown witch, could not reconcile herself to the fact that she was eighty-nine and had all those grandchildren. . . . She bore up well during the onslaught of the first eight grandchildren but when seven more appeared she said, 'Now whose children are these? Sweet little things, aren't they?'" She sidled up to Caroline and said, "If somebody would just give me the name of my oldest son I could say the names of all my children." Caroline started her off with "Robert Tutwiler Meriwether," and sure enough, she did. "It must be rather a happy state," Caroline mused, "no memory, no regrets and it's rather reassuring to think that four sons and two daughters and all their progeny can slip off the mind so easily."

Pidie was trying to persuade Caroline to leave Nancy with her in Chattanooga for the year. It was a mighty wide ocean between them,

Caroline said, but on the other hand if it were just she and Allen they could live in a room somewhere and she wouldn't have to run a ménage. It would be much easier for her to work if Nancy stayed with Pidie, and Pidie's house would be a more normal atmosphere for a little girl; the problems of school, proper food, and suitable friends would all be solved there. Caroline couldn't make up her mind what to do, but she began making Nancy some school dresses in case she stayed behind.

They learned of Hart Crane's suicide from the newspaper. "Hart Crane . . . jumped off the SS *Orizaba* en route from Vera Cruz to New York about a month and a half ago and was drowned," Caroline wrote to Katherine Anne. "It was premeditated suicide. He and Peggy Cowley (who were living together!) were coming up to NY together and Peggy had been trying to stay with him all the time, fearing he would do something desperate. (He had just been informed that his father's estate was bankrupt.) Peggy burned her hand badly . . . and had to spend a good deal of time getting it dressed. She had just got back to her cabin from one of these times when Hart burst in, told her goodbye and dashed off. He stalked through the smoking rooms, lounges and so on, clad in pajamas and bathrobe, climbed to the stern of the vessel and dived off. One version has it that passengers threw him a life preserver, that he came up, waved his hand to the vessel and swam away from the life saver. The *Orizaba* stopped and they searched for his body but never found it. The captain thinks a shark got him. It's horrible, isn't it? I can't keep from thinking about it. Later advices from Bill Brown contain other details, all pretty sad and mad. Bill says some sailors had beaten him up the night before—in spite of his great reformation. It seems, though, that he and Peggy intended to be married—he had made a flamboyant will, leaving her, I believe, his non-existent income. . . . I suppose Hart's death is a logical end to his life. It will probably add enormously to his reputation. Allen has been very busy writing two articles, one of them very good, the other not so hot, for the H and H [*Hound and Horn*] and *Poetry*."

Allen said that he felt Crane had already done the best work he would have done, but that the poetry he had written would be a land-mark in American literature.

The size of the party going to Europe grew. Chink and Lyle Lanier and their little boy were going and planned to stay until September; a young cousin of Caroline's, Dorothy Ann Ross, who was going to school in Switzerland, would go to Paris with them; and Caroline's cousin Manny was going for a short stay. Sally Wood would meet them in New York. They all booked passage tourist, third-class, on the *Stuttgart*, sailing from New York on July 21—two cabins for the whole group of eight, with each person paying only $164 for the round trip.

Caroline was ready to leave the country. The economic situation was so bad she said she would be glad to get to France; if the French were suffering she didn't understand the language very well and couldn't suffer with them. Besides, there would be no one she was kin to in Toulon, no one to call her cousin.

The departure was complicated. The Tates planned to drive their Ford to New York and take it to France with them, but first they left Merry Mont and drove to Chattanooga so Caroline could visit Pidie. Allen went to Kentucky to see his father and brother. He went back to Chattanooga to meet Phelps Putnam and drive him to Alabama to visit Andrew Lytle's father at his farm near Huntsville.

Caroline decided, finally, to leave six-year-old Nancy with Pidie while they were in Europe. Nancy was ambivalent. She wanted to go, but she sensed her mother would like to leave her behind. Pidie wanted her to stay and said, "Kidie can't look after a child," using her children's nickname for Caroline. And so Nancy said, "I don't want to go to that stupid old France." It was settled.

In New York, Caroline got to visit Maxwell Perkins briefly, and she and Allen both saw many of their old friends at a party that Bernard Bandler gave for them.

In Paris, where they stayed in Ford's apartment, the first thing they did was to go to the Closerie des Lilas—and there was Bernard Bandler, ready to continue the conversation started at the party in New York. When Caroline went into the Brasserie de l'Odéon, the proprietor came over at once and demanded to know the whereabouts of *la petite fille*. "Nancy was delighted to be left in Chattanooga and I know it was best for her. Poor Larry [the Laniers' son] has to be dragged about up till all hours." Caroline said that she was afraid to stick her head out the door for fear she would run into Madame Gau, who would be furious that Caroline had left Nancy behind.

Allen went to Orgeval to see the John Peale Bishops, who were beginning to feel the effects of the stock market crash. Margaret Bishop's father thought stocks could go no lower and bought on and on—ruining the whole family, Caroline said. Dorothy Ann Ross was sent to Switzerland, and the Laniers went off on their own. Sally Wood and Manny went shopping a great deal and Caroline stayed in the hotel to write, partly because it was hard to go out when she had to go up and down six flights of stairs and her side still hurt from the appendectomy.

They stayed in Paris two weeks while Allen wrote two pieces for *The New Republic* and drove, with Sally, down to Toulon, where they

stayed first at Ford's Villa Paul. Villa Paul was doubtless the most uncomfortable villa on the Riviera, said Caroline, but it had an unparalleled view of the Mediterranean. Half a dozen terraces sloped down
to the sea, and halfway down was a pool with roses growing all around
and two fat frogs, Willy Seabrook and Henry James. On quiet evenings,
Ford looked up and said, "Ah, that clear bell-like note. Henry James."

Caroline met Ford's new wife, Janice Biala, for the first time. "She
is a Russian Jew," Caroline wrote to Léonie. "More Russian than Jew.
Slavic eye and Slavic melancholy and a Jewish way of making herself
unpopular. She is a fine gal, though, and sticks to Ford through thick
and thin. Dotes on him, in fact. We distressed her often by our lack
of reverence. She has the most beautiful eyes and doesn't take baths."

The Fords were starved for companionship, Caroline felt, and
wanted the Tates to stay with them a month. There was really not
room enough for them all, and with some effort Caroline got the
Tates and Sally out of Villa Paul and into a pension at La Garonne,
which Caroline described as a "tiny *plage* between Toulon and Carquei-
ranne," where they waited for the nearby Villa les Hortensias to become available on September 25.

Caroline loved the Villa les Hortensias, which, she said, was "embowered in mulberries and roses." Their landlady was "properly respectful
to a poet." Every morning she brought Allen a small gift—a cluster
of red roses, or a bunch of grapes from the garden. *"Pour Monsieur
Tate,"* she would say, and then produce a slightly worm-eaten offering
for Madame Tate. "I'm afraid she thought I didn't know my place,"
Caroline said. "Once when she was there for tea I sent Allen out to
the kitchen and she said reproachfully, 'Madame, Monsieur is a poet!' "

The landlady had one cat she called *le chat de la maison* and several
others, *chats perdus*. She called them *Ma suite* as they followed her about
the garden. "Poor Allen," said Caroline, "he always seems to land in
a nest of catwomen."

Caroline began, with the help of the *femme de ménage*, Gisette, to
plant a winter garden—"cauliflower and celery growing and carrots,
navets, epinards, and salade planted and this afternoon Allen will get
the ground ready for the petit pois or I'll know the reason why," she
wrote to Katherine Anne.

Every night they had dinner with the Fords, at one villa or the
other, or in a restaurant in Toulon. The talk was constantly about
fiction writing—no wonder that Allen, already profoundly ambivalent
about Robert E. Lee, turned and wrote his first short story, "The Im-
mortal Woman." Allen had come to feel that Lee was not a hero at
all, but a cynical man who had no will to win. Avoiding the biography,
he turned halfheartedly to a novel, "Ancestors in Exile," which he

planned to base on his own family history from the seventeenth century to the twentieth, exploring the Scotch-Irish on one side and Virginia planters on the other. He never finished it, but it was a kind of training exercise for his one published novel, *The Fathers*. Ford was writing a volume of memoirs, *It Was the Nightingale*, and Sally Wood was writing a novel.

Caroline outlined all the chapters of her novel "so that it should click into place like something by Mr. Faulkner," she announced on the day one year after she had written the first two paragraphs of the novel—and never written another line since. She finished a short story, "Tom Rivers," which she'd begun that summer when her Uncle Rob told her a tale about his adventures in the West. In it she used some of the summer's porch conversation verbatim, including real names, as the family in the story reminisces: "Cousin Owen, who walked from house to house, carrying his teeth in a basket; Cousin Ella, who was forced to play cards all her younger days to entertain the old folks, and so bore three sons who were gamblers; Cousin Henry Hord, who was deafened by cannonading in the Civil War and lost all his property by ill-advised investments and had to live with any of the kin who would put him up." In nearly every story that Caroline wrote there is a description of light and shade, and this story's example is memorable. "There is a curious thing I have observed. If you sit day after day, summer after summer, in a chair under the same tree, you will notice how the light falls under and through the boughs to strike always in the same pattern," the narrator muses. She sent it to Perkins, and when he turned it down, sold it to *The Yale Review*.

Ford took them all to visit a British painter, Sir Francis Rose, in a village above Cagnes-sur-Mer. A special guest that evening was a Bourbon and his wife a Hapsburg. Allen, with his Southern courtesy and charm in full sway, bowed and said, "Madame, your relative, the Comte de Paris, was right about the Battle of Gettysburg," and went on to explain that he agreed with Louis Philippe Albert d'Orleans, Comte de Paris, who wrote a multivolume history of the Civil War soon after it was over. The count said that the Confederates lost at Gettysburg because of the death of "the great Jackson" and because Jeb Stuart and his cavalry arrived late, allowing Union forces to pick the battle site. The count, like Allen, blamed Lee for extending his line too far and General James Longstreet for beginning his attack too late and not supporting Pickett's charge. The Hapsburg lady's heart was won.

One day the Tates went on a picnic with some Parisian friends of Ford's who had a summer house at Cassis. It was perfect to the last detail, if ever a party was, Caroline said. They drove through the romantic, beautiful countryside to Cassis, a small port about twenty miles from Toulon, where they met the other guests and the fisherman and the chef who were the *"personnages"* of the affair. Marius, the fisherman, was small, bronze, compact, a man of few words. The chef was large, with bovine eyes and all the airs of a tenor. They went in Marius's boat to a *calanque,* like a small fjord, on the coast, a place almost too beautiful. The guests swam while the chef cooked and they then sat down at the table. There were about twenty people, including the wives and children of Marius and the chef. An old peasant had walked from Cassis, fifteen miles through the mountains, to meet them; he brought a hamper with at least six different vintages, his own wines. The dinner began with bouillabaisse and went on for six or eight courses to a marvelous goat's cheese—they put sugar on it and then poured *marc* over that. Caroline was pleased that the French host, the bon vivant, was the first to take the count. He fell down on the ground and said from time to time, "It is irrational to move." The chef and some of the young people sang old songs. In a song about Mary and Joseph, one person took the part of Joseph, one the inn-keeper, and so on. Then there was another boat ride, during which the chef sang a solo from *Manon.* The party went on, but the Tates and Ford had to leave at six o'clock to water Ford's chickens. On the way back to Cassis, Ford remarked that the refugees from Troy must have stopped in coves like that. A day or two later Allen found a copy of *The Aeneid* in a bookstall in Toulon and read it for the first time since his prep school days. The result was a poem, originally called "Picnic at Cassis," that became "The Mediterranean." "Where we went in the boat was a long bay / A sling-shot wide walled in by towering stone" were the first two lines.

In November, Caroline wrote to ask the Guggenheim Foundation for more money and an extension. She believed she would have her book ready for fall publication if she could only be free from pressing money worries for a few months. She was very anxious, she said, to get the book done this year so she could begin her third project. The two books, with *Penhally,* would form a trilogy.

Happy as Caroline was at Villa les Hortensias, Allen said he had to be near a library. They set off for Paris by way of Arles, Tarascon, and Avignon. Caroline became more depressed as they drove north from Avignon, plodding through fog at ten miles an hour, and into Paris with its grim November weather. They settled in a studio on the ground floor of a back court at 37 rue Denfert-Rochereau; there was no running water, and a coal stove provided heat. Caroline got water from the courtyard, where one faucet was labeled "Eau Buvable" and the other "Eau de la Seine." But it was really very pleasant, Caroline said, and impressive with its good light. They had a big bed in the studio, a little bed in the balcony bedroom, and a little kitchen with a little gas stove. One could take baths on the balcony—all the heat rose up there, Caroline pointed out. Allen fell in love with it at 500 francs a month and said he was sure he could work there. The last tenant had left a huge mural—"You get used to it in time," Caroline said—and other canvases, which they stepped around. "We are both working like hell, have settled down into one of those routines in which people do produce books. It's funny. God—or the devil somehow creates these islands about once a year for us, the only time you seem to get anything done."

There was not one soul in Paris Caroline had a passing interest in, she said, and it was marvelous. They worked in the morning. They had lunch. She went to the market, came home, slept until two o'clock, got up and went at it again until five. Then she walked briskly around the court eight or ten times, and came inside to get supper. After supper they worked more and so to bed.

Caroline managed to get an advance on her letter of credit, and she was able to pay the Fords some money she owed them and to send some money, long overdue, to Nancy. She and Allen stayed in the studio only a month and then moved into the Hotel Fleurus. "Thank God," Caroline said. They had a large, light room and paid only sixty-five francs a day for everything for the two of them. Caroline felt she couldn't run an apartment that cheaply, and it was a relief for her to get out of the housework. She was delighted when she found out Katherine Anne Porter and her new husband, Gene Pressly, just arrived from Basel, were paying much more for demi-pension and "horrid dark little rooms" at the Malherbe than the Tates paid for full pension at the Fleurus.

Caroline and Allen were taking a turn in the Luxembourg Gardens one day and Caroline was transfixed by the sight of an oversize white French poodle and a tiny Mexican chihuahua. "It's Gertrude Stein," said Allen, who paid more attention to women than he did to dogs. Miss Stein stopped for a chat and Caroline learned that the toy terrier's name was Lord Byron and that he was a brother of Sir Francis Rose's Squeak. Miss Stein was surprised to hear that it was Caroline, not Allen, who had the Guggenheim. "You?" she said. "And what can you do?" "I'm trying to write a novel," Caroline said meekly. Miss Stein and Miss Toklas were reading Faulkner, as Caroline wrote to Janice Biala: "Miss Toklas says she is just too excited over the story of *Sanctuary* which she hears is very interesting."

Caroline arranged for Nancy's Christmas presents, and she and Allen treated themselves to Christmas Eve dinner at the Cochon au Lait with Katherine Anne, Gene, and Helen Crowe. They then went to the Walter Lowenfels' to help trim the tree, and from there to eat onion soup, she wasn't sure where. Christmas was pretty fuzzy to Caroline, not because she drank much, but because everywhere they went she would pick out a soft spot and go to sleep. Allen would haul her up and set her on her feet when the time came to move. Finally she broke down and spent a day in bed, and after that, she said, she had a better idea of what was going on. Janice gave Caroline her painting *The Castle of the Good King René* for Christmas, and Stella Bowen gave the Tates the family portrait she'd done two years before. "I certainly have been lucky in the way of art," Caroline said, "not having a cent to buy a picture with."

She wrote Maxwell Perkins that they were settled in Paris, but that they missed the Fitzgeralds and the Hemingways and other people who were there four years before. She heard that Zelda Fitzgerald had written a novel. How do people have the time to write novels? she wondered.

In January, the Fords came up from Toulon and took over the studio the Tates had vacated. The Tates and Katherine Anne got up early to meet the Fords' train, and Katherine Anne kept saying that if Ford was difficult or in a complaining mood, she intended to see very little of them. Allen concurred heartily. Even Caroline was wondering how much she would stand for. Fortunately, the Fords arrived in good spirits, and they all went to lunch at the Pâté d'Or and got very tight and then went to the Fleurus for dinner. A *petit cercle* was once more formed.

Sylvia Beach and her housemate, Adrienne Monnier, gave a dinner party for the Tates, and Adrienne said, "Monsieur Tate is so conservative that he's almost radical!"

Grippe knocked Caroline out of her working rhythm, but Allen managed to escape the illness. In fact, she found that "Allen turns out to be a splendid nurse—to my surprise. He never had a chance to nurse me before; he always got sick first. He gives me splendid inhalations and pours hot grogs down me at night." After the flu was over, she would wake up, drink her tea, and then simply turn her head over on the pillow. It wasn't natural for her to be so lazy, she said. When she confided her problem to John Peale Bishop at the Deux Magots, he said, "You mean this is the first time this has happened to you? In Paris, in January?" Caroline took ammoniated quinine, the Southerner's cure-all, and went through the motions of work until she felt like really working. It was maddening to lose so much time.

She learned that Nancy, ill with the grippe in Chattanooga, had been in bed nine days with a fever. "I don't know how I'd have done any work if I'd had her along but I am never going to put the ocean between us again, work or no work," she wrote Sally Wood in Vence. "It's been better for her but it's hell on me."

Andrew wrote that there was a "lack of cohesion among the brothers in Nashville," and attributed it to the fact that "they lack the Tates as a nucleus to rally in, and Benfolly to meet at."

It turned bitter cold and Caroline thought the cold would kill the grippe germs. She and Allen had a roaring fire in their room and typed away. She wrote "Old Red," which she referred to as her "story about Allen and Dad," and said it was not one of her best, just a kind of trick. She wove into the story scenes from the past summer—her father visiting his "white-haired, shrunken mother-in-law, his tall sister-in-law who had the proud carriage of the head, the aquiline nose, but not the spirit of his dead wife; his lean, blond new son-in-law; his black-eyed daughter who, but that she was thin, looked so much like him." In the story Mr. Maury and his daughter and son-in-law eat hot batter bread and "Merry Point" ham, dishes that were the core of Merry Mont cuisine. Mr. Maury looks at Stephen, his son-in-law, "infected already with the fatal germ, the *cacoethes scribendi*," which he thinks skips every other generation. "His own father had had it badly all his life. He could see him now sitting at the head of the table spouting his own poetry—or Shakespeare's." There is even the funeral of a relative, just as there had been Cousin Molly Ferguson's funeral that summer, and Maury refuses to go and demands the company of his son-in-law. Maury plans to escape from the women and hide out in Estill Springs. In a marvelous analogy, he imagines the way Old Red, the much-hunted fox of his childhood in Virginia, escaped the hounds. He "ran slowly, past the big boulder, past the blasted pine to where the shadow of the Pinnacle Rock was black across the path. He ran on and the shadow swayed and rose to meet him. Its cool touch was on his hot tongue, his heaving flanks. He had slipped under it. He was sinking down, panting, in black dark, on moist earth while the hounds' baying filled the valley and reverberated from the mountainside."

Sally, Allen, Ford, and John Bishop all thought there wasn't enough action in the story. "I was really more interested in rendering the character of the man than I was in the action of the story and that always betrays you," she said. "Old Red" was sold to *The Criterion* in England, appeared in *Scribner's* with a different ending, and in her first short story collection, *Forest of the South*, with the *Criterion* ending restored. It was the title story in her second short story collection and won second prize in the *O. Henry Memorial Award Prize Stories of 1934*.

She wrote Sally that she was holding her breath, that Allen seemed to be actually started on his novel at last. "He wrote five pages this morning, his best day's work so far, and he has the whole book pretty well plotted by this time. It's a fiendish thing to write, half a dozen people telling their life histories and the problem of varying the style comes up of course. If he can just get this book written maybe we can get out from under this cloud that has hung over us for three years now."

Caroline was troubled with earache, insomnia, and lassitude. She was debating with Allen what kind of tonic to buy—he preferred copper and iron pills and she wanted to try Biondonimine, when a package of "fine, red-blooded ampoules" arrived from Sally. "I like a *dark* tonic," she wrote to Sally, "makes you feel there's strength in it. Swamp Root, Black Draught etc." Sally had diagnosed her ailment—*"anaemie banale,"* and Caroline was grateful for her diagnosis; now she could tell people what was wrong with her.

Caroline had not heard from the Guggenheim Foundation and she realized she did not want an extension. Allen needed to look at some family letters in the Library of Congress, and she supposed they should concentrate on getting his book done.

The mail brought news that the plumbing in the upstairs bathroom at Benfolly had burst because of the tenant's carelessness in not turning the water off. Jess Staton, the county trustee, wrote to say that he was suing the Tates for property taxes. Caroline thought Allen had paid the taxes before they left, and Allen said he thought they had until June 1 to pay them.

Even though they had been in France only about seven months, they decided to pack up and go home to deal with these matters. Caroline wanted to get there in time to set some hens and raise a garden against what was surely going to be another hard winter. Benfolly was rented until June, but they would stay at Merry Mont, where she could raise a much better garden anyway.

"The Tates came," Katherine Anne wrote to Janet Winters from Paris, "seemed not to be very happy, went again shortly."

They sailed on the Baltimore Mail line, spent four days with Phelps Putnam in Maryland, went to Chattanooga to see Nancy and decided to leave her there for the rest of the school year, and then went to Merry Mont.

11

THE SUMMER OF 1933

The Tates reached Merry Mont around the first of March, right after the hogs were killed. "You missed the strangest sight," Cath Wilds, Pidie's daughter by her first marriage, told them. "Every tree on the lawn had an enormous pink carcass hanging from it in the bright moonlight."

Caroline immediately wrote to Perkins that they needed money badly. "We decided suddenly to return . . . for financial reasons. . . . Two hundred dollars would be like manna." Perkins obligingly sent her the money—$150 for "Old Red" for *Scribner's Magazine* and another $50 as part of an advance.

Next she appealed to *The Yale Review* to pay her for "Tom Rivers." When the money came, she wrote, "Thank you very much for your prompt response to my cry. It was a godsend," she wrote, and seized the opportunity to recommend in glowing terms a story by Robert Penn Warren. It "impresses me more than any story I have read in some years. . . . I have urged him to send it to you as the *Yale Review* seems to me a proper place in which to publish such a story."

Then, to her astonishment, the Guggenheim Foundation sent her another $250. "I nearly fainted," Caroline said, and wrote the foundation that she was "grateful indeed" for what she again termed a godsend. "This sum has done me more good, I believe, as far as my work is concerned than any of the other fellowship money. . . . Two hundred and fifty dollars goes as far at Merry Mont as a thousand in Paris."

Like the Tates, the whole nation was facing a financial crisis. The bank moratorium, when it came, was really a great convenience for the Tates, "except for not having cash for small expenses," Caroline wrote Janice Biala. "The bank had to admit sadly that they couldn't hound us about our note for awhile yet and one or two other little things we've staved off. In the meantime, we can live indefinitely without cash as long as we stay here."

"Red Warren says he feels like he's been treading water for years and the flood has just gone down to his ankles," Caroline wrote to Muriel Cowley, Malcolm's second wife. But that was in the country. When they had stopped in Chattanooga, Caroline noticed that one person was kept busy going to the door to deal with people who were asking for food in exchange for work. Caroline's father worried about the insurance company in which he had an annuity. "I'm saving every cent I can to buy fishing tackle when the crash comes," he said.

They were lucky to be at Merry Mont. "This place produces almost automatically, it seems, hams, milk, chickens, eggs, Negroes—almost all the necessities of life except gasoline. My grandmother refers to any article . . . that isn't produced on the place as a 'luxury.' It is a relief to be where one can come very near living without money," Caroline wrote Perkins.

They didn't even have to buy gasoline, she exulted, after they rounded up enough riding horses. They started out in the car one day, visiting kinfolks they thought might have horses to lend, and acquired two, saddled and bridled. While Allen drove home, Caroline and Cath Wilds rode home by moonlight. "It was grand," she said. "I'd forgotten how much I love to ride." Caroline, Cath, and Allen were saddling up the horses one afternoon to ride to Guthrie and greet Red and Cinina Warren. Uncle Doc, Loulie's old boarder from Nashville who landed at various houses in the Connection from time to time, said he wished he could go too. They saddled up the old gray mare out in the pasture and off the four of them went. "We were a strange sight," Caroline wrote to Sally, "affording the whole countryside much diversion. Niggers came rushing out from cabins all the way to look at us." It was fourteen miles to Guthrie, and they rested the horses all afternoon and came home by moonlight. Uncle Doc sang, "I come from Alabama with a banjo on my knee."

The cook at Merry Mont, who was paid three dollars a month, asked Caroline if she could come in the room and watch her typewrite some-day. Having been warned not to spoil the cook, Caroline said she'd have to think about it. Caroline wrote to Perkins that she worked very well at Merry Mont. She didn't know whether it was the view from the upstairs window or the feeling that the plastering might fall on her at any minute.

There were, however, distractions. She stopped writing a letter to Josephine Herbst when she realized the strawberries were ripe; she ended up making twenty-one pints of jam. "Then I had to poison the potato plants and the beans so I just took two or three days off from work and spent it on the garden. We have a marvelous garden for the first time in our lives—I am determined to raise enough stuff to carry us through what will probably be a hard winter. It is so much easier to raise it here at Merry Mont where the ground is rich than on the rock slopes of Benfolly."

Nancy arrived from Chattanooga, twenty pounds overweight and destined to be called the Fat Girl by her parents for the next six years. She could read books by herself, which pleased Allen and Caroline, but she horrified them by saying "okay" and "hot dog" and singing songs with lyrics like "You go home and pack your panties and I'll go home and pack my scanties, and . . . we'll shuffle off to Buffalo."

Allen settled down to work before Caroline did. "Allen is still following the plan you suggested to him for his book," she wrote Ford. "He has written the foreword and a magnificent long first chapter, the best piece of prose he has ever done, I believe. But it is a tremendous task he's set himself, almost like writing six novels in one and he is handicapped all along by never having quite enough documentary material at hand."

Allen and the Agrarians were soon involved with Seward Collins. Collins, a Princeton graduate, described in the yearbook as "the bookiest member" of the class of 1921, bought *The Bookman* in March, changed its name to *The American Review,* and announced it would be a "radical conservative" publication, the voice of the Agrarians as well as other traditionalists like the humanists, the neo-Thomists, and the distributists. When Collins came down to Tennessee the Agrarians and their wives readied themselves for a round of parties in his honor. They managed to get hold of some good liquor, but discovered that Collins did not drink. The women dressed up for a formal dinner, only to learn that he had brought no dinner clothes. They had to hunt up little jackets to wear over their formals. The brethren took him to Cornsilk, Andrew Lytle's father's plantation near Guntersville, Alabama, for an informal meeting. Mr. Lytle prepared an old-fashioned Southern breakfast with eggs, grits, biscuits, and three or four kinds of meat; when he found out that Collins took only weak tea for breakfast, he was utterly baffled. "He would have said, 'Certainly, just a minute,' if he'd been asked for a roasted ox, but tea was too much for him. They finally found a package of jasmine tea left by Andrew's aunts in a remote cupboard," Caroline said.

The Agrarians were delighted to have a national outlet. When Allen considered taking a job on *The American Review*, Stark Young reminded him of the "waste and ruin of New York" and warned it might get in the way of his poetry. Allen did not take the job, but he and the other Agrarians supplied advice and articles for several years.

Malcolm Cowley wanted a quiet place to work on a book and said he was thinking of coming down to Tennessee or perhaps North Carolina. Both Caroline and Allen wrote, urging him to come to Tennessee. He shouldn't go to North Carolina, Caroline said, the scenery was too spectacular, and "he would be gaping around all the time and do little work." She urged him to come to Tennessee and board at Cloverlands, the next farm to Merry Mont, for twenty-five dollars a month. It would be quite private, with a private bath, in the east wing, she said. There would be no diversion except for a beautiful lake full of bass at the foot of the lawn, swimming in the creek, and a healthful half-mile walk through the woods to Merry Mont. He would get a lot of work done.

Cloverlands was the home of Henry and Clyde Meriwether and their two little boys, whom Clyde was teaching at home. Clyde was from Florida and had done graduate work at Radcliffe, and Caroline told Malcolm that since she was not from the Old Neighborhood, she "expected niggers to work in the afternoon." Henry, the son of Charles and Cousin Kitty Tutwiler Meriwether (the one who had celebrated her eighty-ninth birthday the year before), had taught Greek in a boys' school for years and was still "in a pleasant daze" about being back on his own land. They had a garden, plenty to eat, and a good cook who was not apt to leave because the Meriwethers bailed her bootlegger husband out of jail all the time. The chief drawbacks were the heat and the dullness, Caroline wrote to Malcolm. "It gets hot as the devil here in summer. . . . But the blighting heat doesn't come until August and then only when there's a drought. . . . Cloverlands is one of the coolest places in the country. It's on an elevation and the house has enormously thick walls. . . . Oh, the dullness. Well, we'd do what we could to alleviate that. There's nothing to do but swim in the afternoons. We usually immerse ourselves three or four hours in the creek. There is beer too now, thank God. Guthrie, sacred as the birthplace of Red Warren, has good beer and good food to go with it. It's a nice drive from here. We go right by Cloverlands gate whenever we go out in the car and could always pick you up. . . . We could spend the evenings together."

She wished Malcolm were coming now, she said. The country was heavenly. The fruit trees were all in bloom and the woods white with dogwood. The maple tree by her window was in full leaf now. "We're planning a big picnic, the Nashville crowd—we got hold of some good liquor (I'm trying hard not to drink it all up). If you're likely to come around May 1 we'll hold off the picnic until then."

Allen told Malcolm that Caroline had exaggerated the heat, and added that he and Mr. Gordon had caught seven to fifteen bream and big-mouth bass every day last year in the pond in front of Cloverlands. There were eight fine ponds within two miles of Cloverlands—full of crappie, pond perch, bass, bream. Allen told Malcolm to bring a fly rod and a short, four-foot bait casting rod for pond fishing.

When Malcolm came, Henry and Clyde Meriwether found him so pleasant and so good with the boys that they said they wouldn't dream of taking money from him for his board and his two rooms and a bath. Clyde belonged to two book clubs, one in Clarksville and one in Guthrie, and Cowley obligingly talked to both of the clubs.

Cowley wrote about his summer at Cloverlands in *The Dream of the Golden Mountains,* calling the "gentle and cultivated land *un pays doux*" with "undulations like those of a coverlet spread over sleeping children." He wrote of "the sheep meadows like immense playgrounds worn bare in patches . . . wheatfields already turned a paler green . . . cornfields pin-striped with the first bright-green shoots . . . tobacco fields ready for planting." He heard the stories of the Meriwether Connection and decided that they had forgotten about slavery and perceived the Civil War as having been fought between agrarianism and industrialism. He listened as tobacco farmers explained that the 1930 tariff had made the Italian monopoly stop buying dark-fired leaf and how this made prices fall disastrously. Farms were mortgaged and few homes had telephones. He saw a typed list with the name of every person in the county who had paid income tax for 1932 posted on the bulletin board of the post office in Trenton, Kentucky. There were only three names on the list and Cowley decided they were lawyers, not landlords. Tenant farmers were trying to survive on cash incomes of less than fifty dollars a year.

Malcolm liked Henry and Clyde and admired their life at Cloverlands, an eighteenth-century brick house. "They had no money, but they lived on the fat of the land," he wrote. "We had everything as it came in from the garden—asparagus and strawberries, peaches, then snap beans in an avalanche, tomatoes, pitchers of cream and platters of hot biscuits and cornbread. Meats were fresh-killed lamb, country hams, milk-fed chickens, and bass from the pond." He worked on his book *Exile's Return* every morning, and in the afternoons the Tates took him around the countryside.

They saw Caroline's cousin Marion Henry every afternoon. Marion, about twenty-seven years old, was "very dark and very nervous and quite attractive," and "the hysterical type," Nancy remembered later. Marion sang in the Episcopal church choir, but she had never had a job until her father, Gustavus Adolphus Henry, died. Then she began running Oakland, the thousand-acre Henry farm. One afternoon when the group was swimming in the creek at Oakland, a creek with a wonderful waterfall where they loved to go for picnics, she told Malcolm that she wanted all the land that had belonged to her grandfather— 2,500 acres. That was all she wanted in her life, she told him.

Marion went with Cowley and the Tates to Fort Donelson on the Cumberland, but she refused to go into the Union cemetery. "But they're all *dead* Yankees," Caroline said. They drove to the Confederate monument, where Allen and Malcolm were photographed shaking hands: the Blue and the Gray, reconciled.

As the summer grew hotter, Cowley quit work earlier and earlier; he and Caroline went swimming together every afternoon. Nancy still remembers those afternoons. "Mama would show him the Old Neighborhood—Eupedon and all that. But we always found a place to swim. I was in the backseat. Malcolm drove. Ma sang. I knew he and Mama were having a perfectly marvelous time. Daddo never went. I think Mama was a little bit in love with him, but she would never have an affair with him."

"Caroline didn't confide in me," Malcolm remembered later. "We'd go swimming every afternoon. You'd think Caroline and I would start an affair. No. Caroline was the most chaste woman I ever met. I never even kissed her."

Something was going on that neither Cowley nor Nancy nor—for a while—Caroline knew. Allen was having an affair with Marion Henry. He left Merry Mont about the first of July, simply disappeared—with the Tates' car. The afternoon rides with Malcolm and Nancy had to stop, but Caroline made no explanation of Allen's absence. Clyde Meriwether, another one who was not aware of what was going on, sometimes drove Caroline where she had to go.

Caroline could easily walk to Cloverlands. "She always made it plain she was coming to see Mr. Cowley," Clyde said. "Sometimes she spent the days and nights, but I didn't mind. We had plenty of beds and plenty of food—a deep-freeze twelve feet long—and not much else. Caroline knew we had plenty of room and she never hesitated to come.

One day she brought Nancy with her and left her behind when she went away. Nancy had no clothes. I put her in one of my boy's pajamas and washed and ironed her clothes and Caroline didn't come the next day and I let Nancy wear the boys' clothes. Nancy didn't mind sleeping anywhere. She was no trouble."

Clyde recalled fifty years later that Caroline had shocked her that summer when she went swimming without any clothes on. Not that it was where anybody could see her. It was around the bend in the creek from where the children were swimming. "I did think, I wish I could get rid of these stockings," said Clyde Meriwether.

Miss Carrie once put her foot down when Caroline and Malcolm were about to go to Guthrie for supper. "You go out too much with married men," she said. Caroline meekly said, "Well, all right, Ma, we won't go."

Finally Allen returned. He told Malcolm, "I've been in love with Marion Henry." When Marion told him the affair was over, Allen was so distraught he disappeared for days, to Nashville, Malcolm thought. "There was a scene, but I was never told about it," Malcolm Cowley said years later. "Allen returned, very much subdued. We saw no more of Marion Henry."

The affair with Marion Henry, all agree, was a turning point in the lives of Allen and Caroline. Allen always said it was his first infidelity.

Caroline was wounded beyond recovery by the affair. Obsessed by two passions—the writing of fiction and Allen Tate—she was incapable of taking an extramarital affair lightly. It did not help that all her unmarried cousins seemed to regard the charming and accomplished Allen as a kind of family property. Caroline was humiliated that Allen would deceive her with someone in the Connection.

Caroline never forgot the affair, never forgave it, and Allen could not forgive her lack of forgiveness. Twenty-five years later, the two of them would still be writing letters to each other about the summer of 1933, Allen admitting the infidelity, but maintaining that Caroline drove him to it. That summer, he said, she became so caught up in the Meriwether mystique, so obsessed with her Uncle Rob, that he could stand it no longer and reacted with violence in an effort to humiliate her.

Caroline did have a strong affection for her Uncle Rob, an open-handed man who would lend anything he had, although he borrowed more than he lent. He was a lackadaisical farmer and often didn't get his tobacco out before the Fourth of July, to the horror of the banker who lent him money for the crop. Danforth Ross, a cousin of Caroline's who knew all the Meriwethers when he was a child, said he never saw Rob Meriwether when he wasn't followed by a dog. Rob was won-derful with children and horses, but he owned a mule that had kicked a man to death. He did not live at Merry Mont after he was married but commuted there every day on horseback and ran the farm for Miss Carrie. After his father's death, he was always the only man among a multitude of women. How Caroline could see him as the great-grand-son of old Charles Nicholas Meriwether "who best exemplifies the an-cient virtues" is hard to understand, but none of the Meriwethers was rational about the other Meriwethers.

When Caroline mailed a letter to Sally Wood from the Lytles' farm in Alabama later in the summer, it skirted the whole matter of Allen and Marion's affair. She had had a "nervous collapse for some weeks" but was feeling almost herself again.

> It's that wretched back of mine. I will confess to you what I concealed from the family so far. I hurt the damn thing pulling up some enormous weeds in the garden. The ache lurked about for a while then transferred itself to my knee just as it did the time I had that three months' breakdown in Chattanooga. But my nervous system is evidently in much better condi-tion now than it was then for it didn't really get involved. I coddled myself very seriously for a good while and have got over it. But I just haven't been able to write letters or rather to mail them. I have written you many.
>
> Going to Merry Mont was a mistake, I reckon. It is just too hectic and the place has a very bad influence on me and through me on Allen. The family responsibilities kept getting heavier and heavier. It is not only rou-tine, niggers to get out of jail, turkeys to run in, and all that. It is the moral pressure that my uncle constantly exerts on me to take care of my grandmother in her declining years. She is failing fast now, almost blind and fell down three times the other day. Of course he keeps wishing Allen and I'd stay there till she dies but I have told him I won't do it. We get Benfolly August 15, thank God.
>
> Pidie, the aunt who kept Nancy for me, arrived from Chat. the other day, took a look at me and said, "You need a vacation." I knew I did and with her help Allen and I got off to spend the next three weeks in Alabama with Andrew. We packed in two seconds, the family, all except Pidie, in full pursuit, saying finally, "Well, you won't leave before dinner." "Yes," I said through my teeth. "I am leaving this very minute." And leave we did.

Although Caroline did not mention Allen's affair in her letters, she certainly did not dismiss it. One hesitates to speculate about what Allen and Caroline said to each other on the way to the Lytle farm in what were probably the first hours they had been alone since they got off the Baltimore Mail boat. They reached some sort of temporary rapprochement, and Cornsilk, the Lytles' place, was a wonderful refuge to flee to.

The house was an old frame cabin with a dog run in the middle, fixed up just enough to make it livable, as Caroline said. It was a house run by men. The cook was assisted by several henchwomen "who are humble because they don't know the mysteries of cooking." Everybody went barefoot, including the cook, though he put on a white coat to serve dinner. Mr. Lytle had shut himself in the kitchen and made chess pies to welcome Allen and Caroline. "He also makes something he calls 'Charlotte Roosh,'" Caroline said. The Tates, Andrew, and Mr. Lytle had a sherry aperitif before lunch and raw corn liquor before dinner. Caroline, Allen, and Andrew went swimming in a lake or in the river and occasionally went out with Mr. Lytle to look at the crops on his 3,000-acre plantation.

Caroline abandoned the novel about landowners and tenant farmers, admitting later that "a crisis" made her put it aside. "I am in no shape now for very difficult work," she told Sally. She decided instead on a different book, one that would be both a relaxation and a labor of love. She was going to call it "Green Springs and White Oak." "It will be written in collaboration with Dad if I can ever get hold of him long enough [for me] to take two or three weeks dictation. I think the germ of the idea came to me from something you said once, that [his] stories were evidently works of art for him. It will be more like Siegfried Sassoon's 'Memoirs of a Fox Hunting Man' than anything I can think of, though no doubt people will find resemblances to Hemingway's bull fighting book in it. Anyhow it is to be a history of a life dominated by a passion for fishing. It will at any rate be an interesting experiment in prose writing for me. I hope to make the action very rapid. The first chapter will be called 'The Green Springs,' then there will be other place names for headings and a lot of detailed information in it. One chapter will be 'Game Fish Are Ground Nesters.' Another: 'The Spell Is on 'Em.' The action of the book will be chopped off arbitrarily at some place like White Oak, some place that he hopes is the perfect spot so long sought for. I noticed when he was here the other day that he often in conversation starts off a chapter, thus: 'Sometimes the Black Bass strikes from natural pugnacity.'"

12

ALECK MAURY AND ROBERT E. LEE, 1933–1934

The Tates were back at Benfolly by the first of September, and Nancy went to public school in Clarksville that year. Uncle Doc was established in the garage, and Loulie kept house for them. Caroline did not think Loulie would last long. Loulie had always been poor but never in the "hand to mouth, meal to meal" kind of poverty that the Tates survived, and it made her rather nervous, Caroline said. A young cousin and would-be poet, Manson Radford, and his wife, Rose, a painter, were living in the cabin, which had been moved to the locust grove. Daisy Miller was giving three gallons of milk a day and scattering the lawn with manure, which Caroline scooped up in a dustpan and put on her petunias. Caroline turned the old brick smokehouse into a hen-house, and canned dozens of quarts of beans and corn against that hard winter she knew was coming.

Hoping to repay Sally Wood the fifty dollars she owed her, Caroline wrote stories for a Methodist Sunday school periodical—she received six or seven dollars for each story.

She rushed off to get information for the book from her father, who was staying at the Hillside Inn at Caney Fork. "We worked all morning then Dad fished till four o'clock, then we worked till dinner time then we worked from dinner till bed time. Dad complained that it upset his mind. In the night he was heard to yell out: 'Take this down.' I shall model the book on the autobiography of Davy Crockett."

"I wrote the book in a rather funny way," she later wrote Katherine Anne Porter. "I set him down in a very large chair with a tin cup to spit in and said, 'Now, talk.' He would say, 'My Uncle James Morris had the finest pack of hounds in Eastern Virginia' and soon I'd have a chapter. I took seventy pages of notes the first whack, then went back to visit him one other time and did the whole book from those notes—a sort of mosaic, it is."

When she got home, the cook was gone and Uncle Doc had sold the cream to buy liquor. "He is, however, penitent this morning and we're all pulling ourselves together," she wrote to Sally Wood. "I shall go out to Merry Mont this afternoon and pick up another cook if I can and hope to be back at work tomorrow."

She and Allen jointly reached a momentous decision. Caroline realized that it was virtually impossible for Allen to write a biography of Robert E. Lee. They were living at Benfolly, sixty miles from the nearest library. Furthermore, Allen had come to the conclusion that Lee was, in large part, responsible for the South's losing the Civil War because of his "Virginia First" mindset. It seemed to Caroline that every time Allen tried to work on the book he got sick. She offered him what she said was the only professional advice she ever gave him: Give it up. Allen leaped at the suggestion. They would do something—they didn't know what—about the advance from Earle Balch.

"It seems to me that there is a chance of us throwing off the shackles that have bound us now for three years," Caroline wrote to Sally. "It had got to the point where neither of us could stand it any longer, the nervous strain, aside from the unpleasantness of slowly starving to death while Allen tried to write a book he never wanted to write. He has been tied up for three years now by this book and has made less money than he did before. He has offers all the time for magazine work he hasn't time to do—I believe he can make more writing articles than he will on this book."

Time would say that Allen had "written most of a long-planned life of Robert E. Lee, [when] Douglas Southall Freeman's four-volume definitive *Robert E. Lee* made completion pointless." It simply was not true. He had written only fifty pages since he started and his decision was made before Freeman's first two volumes were reviewed.

The decision to abandon Lee heartened them both, and while Caroline pushed ahead on the book about her father, writing five pages a day, Allen began meeting with the Agrarians at Benfolly about another symposium. Minton, Balch agreed to publish Allen's novel, then entitled "Ancestors of Exile" and billed as a study of the disruptive forces in American life, in lieu of the Lee biography.

In the late fall Caroline wrote Ford that she was writing "my father's autobiography. I am calling it—it is in the guise of fiction—The Life and Passion of Alexander Maury and it tells about his humble origins and struggles from the time he really knew nothing much except Sir Izaak Walton's directions for scouring worms to the time when he became a great man, the morning, that is, on the Caney Fork river when he really felt there was nobody could cast any better than he did. It is pleasant work, rather like knitting. Still, having the story and the style . . . I am able to make some experiments in timing. I'm trying to make it read as fast as a novel. Scribner's haven't given me a contract on it yet but talk as though they may. Anyhow I had to do something."

She gloated to Ford about the twenty-three golden Buff Orpingtons she raised that summer. "You should see them," she said. She now had forty chickens, and was having coops built to raise more that spring.

Uncle Doc continued to get up and milk the cow early and secretly and sell the milk to the people at the nearby filling station. The Tates talked of getting up early to catch him milking, while Loulie suggested they just buy their milk from Uncle Doc. For a while, "our whole thoughts were bent on milk," Caroline said. One night all of them went out in the moonlight to bag the cow, she wrote Sally. "It was the cook's idea. We solemnly fastened a pillow case around that noble bag then secured it by tapes that ran up over her back, tied the knot in a way known only to Lucy [the cook] and there she was. I thought this was Lucy's brilliant invention but she says it is a common practice, a sort of chastity belt for cows. It was too much for poor Uncle Doc. He gave up. But he couldn't bear to live here without stealing milk so he went off."

Caroline threatened to write short stories or rob a bank; she ended up soliciting book review assignments. She reviewed Roark Bradford's *Let the Band Play Dixie* for *The Nation* and Carl Carmer's *Stars Fell on Alabama* for *The Yale Review*. "Reviewing isn't as hard as I thought it would be," she said. "I never thought I'd be able to do it."

Allen, also oppressed by their finances, said there would have to be a revolutionary change, but he didn't know what it would be. He began to look around for a teaching position.

That fall there was the usual procession of visitors—Sally Wood, John Gould Fletcher, Stark Young, and the Nashville group. The Tates made some homemade sherry they thought was pretty good. The Warrens and Cousin Manny were at Benfolly for the entire Christmas holiday, with Cinina Warren taking to her bed after three days. The Owsleys, Laniers, and Ransoms came out for a party and two couples were sent to sleep at the house of friends in Clarksville. "Allen and I slept in the bed with Manson and Rose [Radford], quite cosily. Anyhow everybody seemed to have a fairly good time, what with dice and poker and charades. The charade hit of that evening was Lyle Lanier stripped to his shorts as the human fly diving into the black mantilla—or perhaps Manson as the bull being worn down by Andrew as the toreador." Caroline said after it was over she felt as if she had been in a violent storm. "Loulie passed out New Year's day after two glasses of eggnog, not cold but rather limp—she, not the eggnog. She said it was from sitting too near the fire and the next day to show that she didn't have a hangover she got up, or rather started ringing bells at six o'clock."

After Caroline sent Scribner's five chapters of her "Life and Passion of Alexander Maury," Perkins wrote that he liked it, and urged her to get it finished for early publication. "I have got to get through with it before garden time," she wrote Katherine Anne. "It was that damn garden ruined me last year."

The January cold spell caused its usual havoc. The cook quit and Allen went to bed with the flu. Caroline hauled coal and even milked the cow. "I always thought it was like playing the piano," she said, "you either had to learn or have the gift but it seems if you just yank hard enough and rhythmically enough the milk flows. The only problem was keeping your hands warm enough—if it had lasted much longer I was going to drive her into the dining room for the operation. We lived through it, Loulie and I."

Life progressed. Nancy began taking violin lessons and rolled up her hair at night. Caroline read *The Wings of the Dove* and thought it a "lesson in construction for any aspiring writer." She alternated between *Pickwick Papers* and Spengler's *The Hour of Decision*. She and Allen decided Ellery Queen's *The Dutch Shoe Mystery* was the best detective story they had ever read.

She buckled down to work that spring and by early summer she was writing up to 5,000 words a day. Perkins wanted the book by July 1, and as the date neared, Benfolly became, as Caroline said, "a regular book factory."

Caroline, Cath Wilds, and Allen all went down to Caney Fork. "Fortunately, it was raining so Dad was able to give us his attention," Caroline wrote to Katherine Anne. "He read, exclaiming, 'What did you put that stuff in for?' (parts imagined by me) or 'Daughter, this is really magnificent' (verbatim quotations from himself). Cath meanwhile typed and I composed passages I hadn't yet been able to compose while Allen corrected."

To Andrew she wrote, "I think the inmates of the Hillside Inn thought we were crazy, shouting at each other, 'My God, you can't have that' and 'Don't you know you tie the fly on the hook, not on the pole' from Dad while Allen groaned over what he calls my boarding school style: 'I looked at her with something like surprise . . . I felt a little odd . . .' He says I must never use the word odd again under any circumstances. He cut out about five thousand odds in all, I think. After two days of this we came home and put in two gruelling days here, with Manson helping, then solaced ourselves with a little han't oil [corn liquor] last night."

She had promised the manuscript by the first of July and was eleven days late. "It could have been a really good book if I'd had another two weeks to revise it," Caroline said. She always felt that she had to relinquish a manuscript before she was ready.

Meanwhile, she was sorry that she was busy with the book when the wild-plum thickets bore that year for the first time in four years— "they make the most delicious jam and jelly—but I only got two quarts made being so tied down with that book. I was going blackberrying today, being free at last, but a steady rain is coming down, first in weeks."

"Scribner's salesmen have titled it Aleck Maury, Sportsman," she wrote Katherine Anne. "My own title I liked better: The Life and Passion of Alexander Maury. But Perkins said the personal support of the salesmen was too valuable to dispense with so I let them do what they liked. They seem to have hopes of selling the book and everybody there from Charles Scribner down, likes it, they tell me. They've been showing it around beforehand to people influential in the trade and that sort of thing. I have hopes, too, of publication in England. But God knows how it will turn out. I can't picture a book Aleck Maury, Sportsman hitting the popular fancy. It is, in a way, not bad: it is probably the best chance I'll ever have of a popular sale for the book has a sort of Cinderella motif, the man who manages to have sport all his life in spite of poverty, family troubles and everything. The man is my father, of course."

Fifty-five years after it was published, *Aleck Maury, Sportsman* has passionate devotees. Literary critics admire the language. Sportsmen marvel at the precision of detail about fishing. Local historians are impressed with the accuracy of geographical and biographical information in the book. The Meriwethers become the Fayerlees, and Clarksville becomes Gloversville. Mr. Gordon is portrayed accurately as schoolmaster and fisherman, but one whole aspect of his life is ignored—his preaching. It is perhaps the most popular of Caroline's novels, and certainly the easiest to read, the least tragic, the least violent.

In it Caroline Gordon's gift for writing about the natural world unfurls with splendor, and the Southern woods and streams and ponds are set before us as they have never been before or since. She easily captures, in Aleck Maury's voice, the sound of Southern conversation of an earlier time, the sonorous phrases, the grandiloquent tone of her father and Cousin John Ferguson.

Everything Caroline said and wrote about the book at the time she was writing it testifies that she thought it was a happy book, "a fairy tale," about a man who gets what he wants. Most people see it today, however, as the story of a desperate man who spent his time fishing to avoid paying the emotional price that relationships with people would demand.

Memphis, 1934

In the fall of 1934 Allen took the first regular job he had had since he and Caroline were married, and started teaching English at Southwestern, a Presbyterian college in Memphis. He said he took the job chiefly for the benefit of his creditors. Oppressed by debts, he could not write. At Southwestern he arranged to have $100 taken each month out of his $250 paycheck to apply to their debts. Even if they could not bear the life more than one year, they hoped to have their heads above water before spring. That fall, when Robert Penn Warren asked for a loan, the Tates had to tell him they had no money to send. They had been very broke when they took the job, Caroline wrote Warren, and a "damn car wreck" had eaten up the $200 in O. Henry prize money that her short story "Old Red" won, and they were still living "close to the knuckle."

The Tates left Benfolly in the care of the Normans and rented a bungalow at 2374 Forrest Avenue in Memphis; Allen called it the Hamburger House because of its strange brown lumpy brick and its strange brown lumpy roof. Caroline had mixed feelings about the move. Autumn at Benfolly was the nicest time of year and Memphis was dull. They felt cooped up in the two-bedroom, thirty-dollar-a-month bungalow after Benfolly, and Caroline hated to leave her chickens. To fellow Agrarian Ford Madox Ford she wrote that she had about thirty after eating fried chicken all summer; Manson Radford had given her his flock of very handsome black Minorcas when he left. On the other hand, the Memphis bungalow was all on one floor and seemed delightfully easy to manage after Benfolly, and she could plant jonquils and flags in the dingy backyard. She was glad they lived near a park with "acres and acres of just plain Tennessee woods," where she went for a walk every morning before she started to write. The park also had the "third largest free zoo in the world." Caroline found that the seals were the only animals she could watch with any pleasure—it might be nervousness that made them play all the time, but they did look happy. It was sad, she wrote Sally, to stand by the black panther and watch his eye light up as he gazed past you and saw a bird on a bough or a plump little boy.

Caroline found a cook, Rosy Jackson. Memphis had "the most wonderful niggers," she wrote Sally. "Cinina said you could just walk out in the street and hail the first one that passed and get a jewel and it's true."

Looking about her, she decided Memphis was different from Nashville, and cotton country different from tobacco country. The people on the street had a different walk. At football games the spectators were different from those at Vanderbilt games. "Not being able to understand the game," she said, "I concentrated on the crowd. The dialogue going on all around was pure Faulkner. I decided that he had a better ear than I had ever thought."

They settled down into provincial academia, making friends instantly, and joining a faculty play-reading group that met on Sunday nights. Sam Monk, a member of the English department, became a lifelong friend, and the chairman of the English department, a melancholy Dane, was awfully nice too, Caroline said. His wife was "so lonely and bored that she cries out with joy when you take her to a picture show or suggest a steak dinner downtown." They met a Mrs. Lake, "one of those peculiarly offensive, peculiarly Southern women filled with wind. Always talking about 'Uncle Andrew' (Jackson)." Allen said one might just as well say "Uncle George" (Washington) or "Uncle Napoleon."

Nancy, nine years old and fat and sassy, liked Memphis because she had a gang of friends on the block. Caroline started her in dancing class and thought she looked like an apple twirling on her toes. She took Nancy to her first art gallery, an exhibition of the original paintings for Mickey Mouse, made her a witch's costume, and decorated the house with black cats and orange moons for a Halloween party. She let Nancy have an angora guinea pig, although she had sworn to have no pets in Memphis. Then she seemed to forget about Nancy for the rest of year. "I went to Snowden School, a public school," said Nancy years later. "I flunked fourth grade and they never knew it—I didn't bring home a report card. I just never got connected."

They went back to Benfolly to sell the corn crop and to get Allen's winter hat and the electric iron, and Caroline said the shut-up house had "the chill of the grave." She could hardly stand to go in and jerk out the objects she needed. She decided to buy herself a winter coat— a good one—with the proceeds of the corn crop. "Let no one say the Tate family isn't consistently agrarian," she said.

Caroline acquired a writing pupil in Memphis, a woman who was working on a novel, and talked the 19th Century Club out of "honoring" the Tates with a tea. After Allen read Donald Davidson's "Lee on the Mountains" to a group of clubwomen, however, she was pestered ever after "with the chairmen of this and that ringing up and wanting him to read again." She decided Allen put entirely too much into his job. "But he says he can't teach anything unless he knows it thoroughly so he rereads Chaucer, Spenser, even Galsworthy," she said. "I don't really think we can stick it another year."

Then the company started coming. The John Peale Bishops came up from New Orleans, and Louis Untermeyer from New York. Nathan Asch, author of four novels, arrived with a bus ticket "two yards long on which he rides surveying the country." Although Nathan had turned communist, she said, he was not investigating things, but just wanted impressions so he could go on writing his impressionistic novels. She supposed he could be worse employed. The Tates took him to the home of Abe Waldauer, the assistant city attorney, where the men talked politics and paid no attention to Asch. "As we were leaving one of the ladies enquired if he were related to [Sholem] Asch and when they found he was his son they were pretty sick," Caroline wrote to Robert Penn Warren. Nathan Asch produced a very good nonfiction book about his trip. "I knew a poet in Memphis," he wrote, closing his chapter on Memphis, "who was one of the agrarians, believing that the sickness of the South could be cured by . . . going back to pre-industrial times, each man to till his own acres. . . . The poet took me to a pleasant home, and I met the editor of a newspaper, a city attorney, a reporter, a Southern novelist, and they talked of the past. . . . They were very liberal and used the word negro, instead of nigger or *nigra,* and very sophisticated . . . but they [believed] the South should be left to work out its own problems . . . and they kept on repeating: 'We love the negro, and we understand him; we know what's good for him.' "

John Gould Fletcher and Sally Wood were both houseguests the

night the faculty play-reading club met at the Tates'. After thirty minutes all the club members got up and left because they thought Fletcher
was talking down to them. Caroline felt this unjust, but she had to
admit Fletcher did not know they had gone. Caroline was very patient
with Fletcher, who was lonely living in Little Rock with his sister. When
he wrote that the Agrarians ought to be more aggressive about getting
a magazine of their own, she replied that not one of the Agrarians
had it in him to go after money. She thought that in the next year
the matter should be laid before at least six rich men of America.
"None of the others will listen to me, I being a mere woman and not
admitted to the councils and God knows I don't want to be in on
them," she said. Book publishers should help fund a journal. "It's no
accident that the best writers, and I mean even the big shots in fiction,
today are Southern and the publishers must know it," she said. But
then, she reminded him, the Agrarians were artists, and very seldom
did a man have the capacity for both thought and action.

The Agrarians were trying very hard to get their magazine, and
Allen had talked to his brother Ben about financing it. At one point
it seemed likely that Ben would raise enough money to start a weekly
journal to be published in Cincinnati. (Caroline thought living in Cincinnati, under Ben's nose, would be a drawback.) Herbert Agar of
Louisville, who wrote a syndicated column called "Time and Tide,"
had joined the Agrarians and tried to get a magazine started. Allen
had written Agar when he was London correspondent for *The Louisville
Courier-Journal*, asking him to contribute to *The American Review* because
Agar had become very interested in the distributists, who wanted to
break up large landholdings in England. Agar had earned his Ph.D.
at Princeton, writing his dissertation on Milton, but had become a
writer instead of a professor. He had written poetry and his book *The
People's Choice, from Washington to Harding* won the 1934 Pulitzer Prize
for American history. He and his wife, Eleanor Carroll Chilton, who
had published poetry and novels, were frequent visitors in Memphis,
as Allen and Agar began to talk of another symposium that would
have a broader appeal than *I'll Take My Stand*.

Aleck Maury, Sportsman came out in October. "My book is dedicated
to you," she wrote Ford Madox Ford. "I'm a little sorry now because
you will not enjoy reading it. It marches but is flimsy in spots and
you will see how I could have made a really good book out of it if I
hadn't been so harried. I wrote it in eight months, on five coca colas
a day. Wonderful the effect coca cola has on the imagination but alas
it is bad for the figure. I took on fifteen pounds in three months."
Katherine Anne Porter told her that *Aleck Maury* was magnificent

and that it read "as if a gentleman of the Old South who knows not only Latin and Greek but English had sat down and written his memoirs." She praised its "fine masculine prose." And why shouldn't it be, she asked, "you writing with the sound of your father's voice, all the voices of your fore-fathers in your ears?"

Howard Baker, whom they had known in Paris, wrote from California that Allen's short story "The Migration" was not as clear and charming as *Aleck Maury*, which was, he said, his favorite American novel. Like many people, he had been afraid that Caroline would not be able to handle the first person in writing about a man and a sportsman, but he said she wrote in a firmer and more powerful way than he had dreamed she could.

Red Warren suggested that her next book be "The Life and Passion of Caroline Gordon" by J. M. Gordon. Malcolm Cowley said he expected to see her the bearded contributor to a sporting column yet. Caroline replied that she thought of getting a large Cumberland River catfish and a false mustache and posing for a picture—the Hemingway of the Cumberland Valley.

Lovat Dickson wanted to publish *Aleck Maury* in England and promised a $200 advance and the usual ten-percent royalty up to 2,500 copies. "As I never seem to get above 2,500 I suppose the terms don't really matter," she said. She was dismayed that Dickson changed the title to *The Pastimes of Aleck Maury*, because, in her view, "the book was written, really, to prove that sport is not a pastime." Then Dickson advertised it as a book "full of clean thinking and healthful living." The only clipping she got from England commented, "Truly publishers are odd cards."

Reading Josie Herbst's latest novel led her to say she hoped the communist literary vogue was about over because she felt *Aleck Maury* suffered from it. "As it discussed no burning problem except how to have as good a time as possible it was dismissed as being very trifling," she wrote Léonie Adams. "I believe it has sold thirteen hundred copies." She thought seriously, while "smoking cigarettes, drinking Coca-Colas, and reading mysteries," of writing a real sporting book. She had met Nash Buckingham, "the best high duck wing shot" in the country when Scribner's had made her locate a Southern sportsman to go over *Aleck Maury*. Buckingham had introduced her to Uncle Jim Avent, an old man who knew, she told Warren, everything there was to know about bird dogs. She thought of writing his life "as a sort of literary spree." She told Warren she wished he could have seen Avent stepping out of his cabin, "seventy years old, booted, just on the point of going down into the bottoms to hunt deer. He has a fine beard, wonderful face and knows he's a great man. When I told him I wanted to write his life he said yes, there were a great many people who wanted to write his life. Mr. B. says that at field trials he always wears an old derby hat and shouts insults at the judges in a high, falsetto voice. . . . The names of some of the dogs he's trained would make fine chapter titles: 'The Coming of the Storm,' 'The Great Eugene M.' of whom they speak with bated breath. . . . We stood in front of his cabin and he gestured over the ravine: 'Gladstone has run over them fields,' as one would say, 'Charlemagne played here as a boy.' When I say Gladstone I do not refer to the premier by the way, but to the great dog."

Nothing came of her plan to write a book about Avent, although she actually proposed it to Perkins at Scribner's, but she did write a short story with Buckingham's help called "B from Bullsfoot." In it Falcon's Speed Boy by Speed Merchant out of Ensley's Flirt finds enough birds to win the National Field Trial stake, thus enabling his owner to lift the mortgage off the old home place and marry the girl. She had not planned to have a mortgage until she saw how shocked Buckingham was at the omission. "B from Bullsfoot" was turned down by *The Saturday Evening Post* and by *Collier's* and finally placed in *Scribner's*. Caroline was gratified that the young assistant editors of *Scribner's* said that it made them cry.

Before she settled down eventually to serious work, she wrote three first-rate short stories that fall, all about Aleck Maury. In "One More Time," an ardent fisherman, a friend of Maury's who is mortally ill, manages to drown himself at his favorite fishing place, and in "To Thy Chamber Window, Sweet," Maury avoids the advances of a widow. In "The Last Day in the Field," Maury goes hunting for what will probably be the last time. The route he takes out of Gloversville can be traced in present-day Clarksville: "We got in the buggy and started out, up Seventh Street, on over to the college, and out through Scufftown . . . on over the Red River bridge and out into the open country." Caroline's descriptions of the countryside are peerless: "It was rough, broken ground, scrub oak with a few gum trees and lots of buckberry bushes. One place a patch of corn ran clear up to the top of the ridge. As we passed along between the rows, I could see the frost glistening on the north side of every stalk. I knew it was going to be a good day." The last lines, after Maury shoots a bird, are memorable: "Up, up, up, over the rim of the hill and above the tallest hickories. I saw it there for a second, its wings black against the gold light, before, wings still spread, it came whirling down, like an autumn leaf, like the leaves that were everywhere about us, all over the ground."

Real inspiration came to Caroline. "I have just been sitting here day after day writing and getting pretty tired of it at times," she wrote to Ford. "But day before yesterday, I got the idea for my next novel, snap, like that, which is something to be thankful for. It's to be called 'The Cup of Fury.' Do you like that? Jeremiah, isn't it, something about wailing at the gates and a cup of fury being lifted up. And it's to be on a big scale, lots of people and generations. Do you think I can manage lots of people? It won't be much like *Penhally*. There I depended a lot on style for atmosphere; in this book the emphasis will be on characterization. I'm going to begin it right after Christmas, anyhow, sink or swim."

Caroline had written to Lincoln Kirstein the year before from Paris that she had cherished for years the idea of taking a soldier through four years of the Civil War. She decided it could not be done, at least not by a woman. Something made her change her mind. "It will be very long (that at least is fashionable)," she wrote to Léonie. "As Katherine Anne once said a time comes when one must sprawl a bit. I feel it has arrived for me."

She wrote to Warren that she had "plunged today into the Civil War" and it was "rather like getting home again." She had ambitious plans "for 'The Cup' which so far hasn't begun to brim. I rather want to have Forrest a character in the action, in somewhat the same way Napoleon is in *War and Peace*. And I plan to have a chapter of purely expository prose about the war—if I can write it. In fact, you may think I am Evelyn Scott herself before I get done." (Scott was the novelist from Clarksville who wrote a Civil War novel, *The Wave*, published in 1929.)

Scrawled on the bottom of this page of her letter to Warren was a note, "as far as I've got on writing 'The Cup of Fury,'" and a pencil drawing of a finger pointing to two typewritten lines reading: "It was the nineteenth of August, a day which Fanny Allard was all her life to think of as 'Grandpa's birthday.'"

On December 13, 1934, she wrote to Maxwell Perkins, outlining her plans for "The Cup of Fury." She said that Forrest was the archetype of the Old Southwest that could have saved the country if Virginia had given it a chance. The Old Southwest included Tennessee, Kentucky, Mississippi, and the other states "west of the mountains." The Agrarians felt strongly that Virginia had wielded too much power before and during the Civil War. "Lee lost the war because he wasn't committed," Caroline said, echoing Allen. "Forrest was replaced after every battle he won. . . . It would have been better for the South—and for the nation—if the South had won."

It is not surprising that Caroline had turned once again to the Civil War for subject matter. Her grandfather had fought in it. She had grown up on its legends and heard the Lost Cause endlessly glorified.

Once her grandmother had told her to run upstairs and fetch Uncle Ned's sword out of the closet. Mr. McEvoy, a tenant farmer, was dying and he wanted the sword over his bed. "I was in the Bloody Tinth," Mr. McEvoy kept saying. Five hundred men from the Texas Tenth went into the Battle of Chickamauga, and a hundred sixty survived. The crossroads at Graysville had been a picket post for Union troops, who had scoured the countryside for provisions and taken lard, meat, hay, and livestock. The guns at the siege of Fort Donelson could be heard at Woodstock. The children at Merry Mont sang, "Knock along, jog along, soldiers of the Jubilee . . . ," a song celebrating an exploit of General Forrest's. Caroline had toured the Civil War battlefields with Allen when he was working on his biographies of Stonewall Jackson and Jefferson Davis. Andrew Lytle was steeped in the history of the war and had written most of his biography of Forrest at Benfolly.

She said she had seen—and been bored by—many a Confederate veteran, but in Memphis she met Captain C. A. de Saussure, a Confederate veteran, whom she considered a gem. He called the Battle of Bunker Hill "a mere skirmish," and as for Paul Revere's ride, he said that "the fellow was scared and didn't know what he was doing." She read his memoirs and tried to sell them to various magazines. After *The Yale Review* editor said he might take them if they were cut and rearranged, de Saussure said that he didn't care to have his manuscript edited "by a man from that section of the country."

The Tates wanted to go to New Orleans at Christmastime to visit Manson and Rose Radford and then to Baton Rouge to see Red and Cinina Warren. It would be mad, though, to spend the money when debts pressed so hard, Caroline said, but Allen needed a change badly. They went. As soon as school was out they drove to Merry Mont. While Allen went on to Cincinnati to see his brother, Caroline and Nancy stayed at Merry Mont for Christmas. With "all the in-laws absent . . . all us *Maywethers* sat around the fire and said how nice it is there is nobody here to suffer from inconveniences." At Merry Mont, the Christmas celebration always included eggnog before breakfast. It knocked Caroline and her generation for a loop, but Caroline's aunts and grandmother stood up under it. Even Nick Dudley, Miss Carrie's invaluable black factotum, "made a fine oration on the subject of government and my grandmother," Caroline wrote Mark Van Doren.

When Allen came back, the Tates left, dropped Nancy off in Memphis, picked up Ted Johnson of the Southwestern English department and his wife, and headed for New Orleans. A great many people joined them: the Warrens, Andrew Lytle, and Caroline's cousin Manny Meriwether.

"Dry martinis and oysters are what I remember most clearly," Caroline wrote, describing what forever afterward was known as the Christmas Debauch. Some of the party stayed in hotels, but the Tates stayed with the Radfords on Dauphine Street, and their house reminded Caroline of Ford's place in Paris.

"We got up at nine o'clock in the morning and started the day with absinthe frappé," Andrew remembered years later. "I could eat two dozen oysters and Red could eat several dozen. One night we took over a bar and square danced. I saw Allen kissing Manny. Caroline's cousins were all avid for Allen."

Caroline felt fury at all of Allen's flirtations and did not hide it from him. For outsiders she managed to keep a good face on things for years, except for lapses when someone saw her white-faced and tight-lipped and would remember the intensity of her anger.

In Baton Rouge, it seemed to Caroline, the Warrens lived in Oriental splendor—"lovely cottage, beautifully furnished, camellias blooming in the front yard, liquor flowing, people inviting you somewhere every minute." Caroline told Warren that transferring the house party from New Orleans to Baton Rouge and from gin to whiskey without losing a member was really a feat that should go down in history.

When they got back to Memphis, they were a sorry crew. Andrew Lytle calculated they would have to pay three days of depression for every day of revel. "I drank so much liquor I began to pass blood," Lytle recalled. "We went through Arkansas at seventy miles an hour and we got to Memphis and got a doctor." The doctor prescribed a diuretic to get him back on the alkaline side, and he took it faithfully, although he complained it made his bones ache. After he had been taking it all day, the druggist came over and said he had given him the wrong prescription, one that should have gone to a middle-aged lady.

Caroline wrote Warren that she had vague ideas about work, and Allen occasionally mumbled that he intended to write some articles before spring. "But for the most part we have been perfectly sodden, just sitting before the fire meditating upon past deeds. The monotony has been broken several times by the postman who brings poems, long articles, etc. from the Warrens. I cannot tell you with what amazement we view these productions. How in the name of God do you do it? . . . I have not heard anything from the Radfords. I imagine—I like to imagine—that they are as sodden as we are. It was worth it. There are no regrets."

MEMPHIS, 1935–1936

The Tates recovered from the Christmas Debauch, and Benfolly jonquils bloomed in the grime of the backyard of the Hamburger House. Forsythia gilded the park, and plum blossoms showed white through the woods. The redbud was out and the willows were green, making them homesick for Benfolly.

When Caroline stopped at the zoo pavilion for her morning Coca-Cola, the man who worked there told her all the animal news. She mourned the death of the black panther, who got in a fight through the bars with the sick-looking puma.

Her writing was going poorly—or not going. "I am still trying to start my novel," she wrote to Andrew Lytle. "I have been trying ever since I got back from Baton Rouge. I have it all planned, but the words just won't come." It had been two years since Allen had written anything, and at this point Caroline was the better-known of the two. John Peale Bishop underlined this state of affairs when he wrote to Allen about his persistent writer's block: "I wonder if Caroline's success hasn't had something to do with your silence. I don't mean that you begrudge it to her, nor that she doesn't richly deserve it, and more. But the relation between a man and a woman is very complicated. Think this over. Sigmund F. Jr." Mark Van Doren wrote to a friend in March 1935, "I enjoyed hearing from you about the Tates. I have noticed the same curious reversal of positions on the part of Allen and Caroline—it is from the latter that I get the good long letters now. Indeed I have become very much attached to Caroline—as, of course, I have always been to Allen. I consider him at the moment to be under an eclipse."

Caroline wrote Katherine Anne that Allen's block cast quite a gloom on the household, but she thought he felt some stirrings again, so perhaps their spirits would pick up. Memphis was "horrible, awful—without doubt the dullest and at the same time the most vulgar city in these United States. I don't doubt but that there is an exciting life in Memphis—at catfish joints or say at a cafe on Beale street whose name fascinates me—'the Mississippi River Cafe for Colored People.' But for white folks, and white folks in academic circles—well as I say it's pretty dull."

Allen did write an essay on the profession of letters in the South and began revising his book of essays, which was published under the title *Reactionary Essays on Poetry and Ideas* in 1936. "Allen at last is working again!" she exulted to Sally. "If a paralytic had suddenly thrown away his crutch to take dance steps we couldn't be more pleased." But it was not a real or permanent break in the block.

That spring the Tates finally met "the poetess whom Allen had fought knowing." Anne Goodwin Winslow was a sixty-year-old widow who always wore a hat to lunch even at her home, Goodwinslow, a twenty-room Tuscan-style mansion outside Memphis, where peacocks strutted on the lawns under live oaks and wisteria festooned a beautiful well-kept garden. Caroline immediately thought Mrs. Winslow's daughter Mary would be perfect for Andrew Lytle since she had been to Vassar and could milk a cow.

Mrs. Winslow, proficient in ancient and modern Greek, Latin, French, Italian, Spanish, German, and Romansch, had educated herself in the book-lined tower at Goodwinslow. In 1925 she had published a collection of verse called *The Long Gallery* that included translations and adaptations from the Greek, Latin, French, and Italian, as well as her own work. Through an essay in *North American Review* that same year, she was one of the first to introduce Rainer Maria Rilke to English-speaking readers.

After the death of her husband, Eveleth Winslow, a general in the United States Army, she had settled down at Goodwinslow, publishing an occasional review or essay. The Tates accused her of dilettantism; in turn, Mrs. Winslow was shocked that Allen had never read Dante in the original, and so the two of them used to sit outside and read

Italian. (Caroline would go to sleep.) Allen and Mrs. Winslow collaborated on a dramatic version of Henry James's *The Turn of the Screw* that was finally produced in 1962 at the University of Minnesota. Mrs. Winslow published a number of books, including a book of personal essays and four novels, one of which was a best-seller.

The Tates made another excursion to Baton Rouge, this one for a writers' conference that Warren organized to announce the founding of *The Southern Review*. Stark Young wrote them that he wasn't going; he didn't like meeting "lesser literary people" and he never went to conferences. He was struck, he said, by their "sweetness and liberality about authors so much less good" than they.

John Gould Fletcher, who had several times told the Tates he was through with them and could never be their friend again because he disagreed with an article by Allen, wrote saying he would like a ride to Baton Rouge. Caroline wrote back that his place in the car was now filled by Ford. Fletcher said that Ford, an Englishman, had no right to be at the conference or to appear in the new magazine and that he'd fight him to the death. Caroline was going to suggest pistols and coffee for him and Ford under the dueling oaks, but Allen said to let him ride. When Fletcher arrived he was as "mild as milk and was particularly nice to Ford," according to Caroline. "I really think the man is mad."

The conference itself, by all accounts, was pretty dull. Caroline's description of it to Sally Wood is the liveliest: "It was divided quite neatly into two armed camps, the Agrarians and those who thought there were far too many Agrarians present. The Agrarians having the conference in a sack, as it were, through Red's being presiding officer, started out discussing the Southern tradition in relation to literature. Lyle Saxon and Roark Bradford, the only real big shots there, listened in puzzled silence. [Saxon had written several nonfiction books about Louisiana and New Orleans; Bradford was the author of books in Negro dialect, including *Ol' Man Adam an' His Chillun*, on which the play and the movie *Green Pastures* were based.] Finally, when they'd got to the point of whether it was a good thing to have all publishing come through New York Saxon gets up and says (looking very fat and well massaged) 'New York has treated some of us mighty well and I for one don't believe in biting the hand that's feeding you.' Bradford felt called upon to make a speech too then so he said that a good story was a good story anywhere and he didn't know what they were talking about anyhow. Mrs. Bradford in the rear could be heard audibly observing that she had worked in a publisher's office for five years and it was all a matter of making the right contacts. 'Just a talk over a cocktail in a speakeasy.' Any speakeasy (I swear this is what she said) would do. . . . The New Orleans *Times-Picayune* reported Allen looked like the Little Colonel."

In early 1935 the Southern Tenant Farmers Union tried to organize sharecroppers who had been turned off the land as a result of New Deal acreage reduction programs. The organizers, H. L. Mitchell and Clay East, inflamed white Southern sensibilities when they admitted black sharecroppers to the union. The centers of trouble were Marked Tree and Tyronza in Arkansas, both near Memphis. The Arkansas press refused to cover the story, and the coverage by the *Commercial Appeal* in Memphis was skimpy. *The New York Times* and other Eastern newspapers and magazines, however, sent correspondents down, and Caroline said the Northern journalists came to Memphis, spent an afternoon at Marked Tree, borrowed her typewriter, and sat down and wrote about it. When Dorothy Thompson, the syndicated columnist and wife of Sinclair Lewis, came down, the Tates were impressed because she spent an afternoon at Marked Tree, decided it was impossible to find out all about it so quickly, came back, spent a week, and said she still was not sure what she thought about it.

James Rorty, an old friend from New York days, came to Baton Rouge for the writers' conference and then to Memphis to write about Marked Tree for the *New York Post*. "I went out driving with James one night (while Allen was celebrating Easter in Nashville) and landed in what I never thought to be at, a meeting of black and white," Caroline wrote to Andrew Lytle. "James wanted to interview these people, all members of the tenants union, so we went to the cabin. They sent for the negro members who gave their stories. It was very strange— James got such a different impression from the whole affair from what I got. It was quite evident to me that not any of those people were real share croppers. They were all professional agitators, one a filling station operator, one a dry cleaner, and one the kind of negro who is bound to make trouble anywhere and was quite properly put off the plantation he'd been working on. After the white people had told their tales this negro came over to the table where James was sitting. He coughed pompously and said something to this effect: 'The proportion of protection of the ramifications of the divergent interests of the con- glomeration . . .' I swear it was just the ravings of a would-be preacher, inflamed with ego. James leans forward and blinks through his specta- cles and says, 'Yes, sir, I'm very glad to have met you.' And afterward he told me that this negro seemed to be a very good man. I saw then just how much sense he would make of the whole business."

Rorty himself told the story often of how Caroline had said, "He's a *baaad* niggah!" about a man he viewed as something of a hero.

Caroline and Rorty, with Allen this time, went back to Marked Tree. "Well, it was awful," she wrote Andrew. "We drove around and inspected a few share croppers' cabins. All very desolate, of course, but the people telling absolutely conflicting stories everywhere. Then we interviewed the district attorney and Spellings, the riding boss of the Chapman plantation. In a way I'm glad we went because of Spellings. It was a pleasure to see him work. The two of them had just got *The New York Times* with [F. Raymond] Daniell's articles and had just finished reading them and [the articles] burned them up. They would have liked to boil us in oil, of course. The d.a. was quite belligerent but Spellings was magnificent—James was a child in his hands. James questioned him for nearly an hour. He parried every thrust. He had every question covered beforehand—it was a marvelous exhibition. I got to thinking we weren't done for yet if the Southern rural sections could still produce such able men. Well, everything would have been all right if James had been content to leave it at that but on our way out he stopped the preacher, the Rev. [Abner] Sage, who is the spokesman for the planter crowd. Sage refused to be interviewed and when Rorty persisted threatened violence."

Rorty always said that it was that night that Allen undertook to address a gang of rednecks in the village square on how they should stop trying to lynch the local black radical leaders, and had to be hastily dragged off the stump in order not to be lynched himself.

Sage had telephoned Southwestern threatening to release a defamatory story about Allen to the Associated Press, and President Charles E. Diehl sent for Allen. The college was on the verge, as most colleges always are, of a fund drive, and Diehl was worried about repercussions. "He was awfully decent, of course, but very anxious to avoid any trouble," Caroline wrote Andrew. "The preacher who is the most horrible specimen I have ever seen just blackmailed us—there was nothing to do but shut him up at any cost."

The chief of police, who was named Robert E. Lee—for the steamboat, not the general—was present at the conference and said he had his eye on Allen because he was certain Allen was a communist. Caroline decided the chief of police couldn't read very well. When Allen first came to Memphis, he gave an interview saying he thought communism was a great menace. "I don't think the chief knows what a menace is," she said.

"Allen, of course, hardly spoke while he was over there, except once or twice to say he didn't share Rorty's views but the mere fact that he came there makes him a Red in their eyes," Caroline reported to Andrew.

James Rorty expressed contrition. He had filed a story that said he was "accompanied to Marked Tree by Allen Tate and Caroline Gordon who strongly disapprove of outside interference," but agreed to ask the *Post* not to run it after Allen said he would have to resign. Later he sent the Tates a hand-woven rug from Norris, Tennessee.

"Neither Allen nor I realized how bad things were over there or we'd never have taken James over," she wrote Sally. "He's really an awfully nice fellow—I like him very much. I just don't think you can trust a radical because where the revolution is concerned they can't have any personal loyalties. He is positively rabid on the subject that the Agrarians must develop a field technique eventually, which is certainly true. But adopting the present radical technique which is really what he demands of us won't get us anywhere and besides, as I have tried in vain to make him see, Allen and John Ransom and Don Davidson would make damn poor field workers. And I don't really think it's up to them—they've formulated the doctrine. Somebody else will have to put it into practice."

Caroline continued to follow the events at Marked Tree; the *Press-Scimitar* in Memphis had begun to carry the articles from *The New York Times*. "The poor white man who was president of the union has been deposed by that rascally negro," she said, "and the whole thing is just the sort of mess one would have expected. . . . This negro I imagine will sooner or later be lynched. He is really a little crazy on the subject of race equality. One day leading a parade he acted as traffic cop and held up cars containing white women on the street. That night, of course, his cabin was shot up—the union 'literature' has it by a mob of planters when of course it was those degraded white people who have nothing but race superiority left."

It is interesting to reflect that Caroline was working on *None Shall Look Back* during the Marked Tree affair. Writing imaginatively about the Civil War at the same time she was observing the real world of 1935, when black sharecroppers were just beginning to rouse themselves from torpor, it was easy for her, with her background, to view antebellum society—before the violence of war or social upheaval—as stable, rich, and beneficent for all.

After Rorty's visit, Caroline vowed not to provide housing for any more "communists" or "fellow travelers." When Dorothy Day, whom the Tates had known in Greenwich Village as a radical journalist, called up to say she was in town, Caroline suppressed her hospitable instincts and told Dorothy about her resolution. Dorothy laughed and said she was not a communist but a Catholic. In that case, Caroline said, she could come and stay.

They didn't talk about politics or religion but gossiped about old friends. "I think Dorothy began praying for me then," Caroline said years later. Allen was quite struck with Dorothy's newspaper, *The Catholic Worker*, which he considered remarkable. He wrote Donald Davidson that Dorothy had founded it three years before with a capital of exactly fifty dollars, and that now it had a paid circulation of 100,000. He admired her for her energy, her common sense, and her "fanatical devotion to the cause of the land."

The Tates fled Memphis as soon as Southwestern graduation was over and went to Benfolly, taking cook Rosy Jackson with them. (Rosy, the Memphis sophisticate, commented: "The niggers around Clarksville look like jackrabbits.") At Benfolly, they found the lower floor covered with green mold, the middle with coal soot, and the top with honest dust, Caroline wrote Andrew. Allen went on a painting binge and the house looked better than it ever had—just in time for Ford Madox Ford and Janice Biala, who arrived hard on the heels of a bunch of Caroline's relatives. Three Southwestern faculty members, John Davis, Sam Monk, and Ted Johnson, came by on their way from Memphis to the North, and they all played charades. Andrew Lytle's father had sent Caroline a ham, a boon with the house full of company. Ford and Allen took a truck to Merry Mont to get a new cow, which they named Valentine Wannop after the heroine of *Parade's End*. Ford puffed a great deal and offered sage advice.

By this time, Caroline had written three chapters of "The Cup of Fury." Although she did not feel it was very good, she plunged ahead.

As she wrote about the Civil War she drew once more on her family history. The protagonist of "Cup of Fury" was to be the Allard family of Brackets in Todd County, Kentucky, a family very much like the Meriwethers. In the book Fontaine Allard has a sixty-acre deer park and raises fine horses, which he shares with Confederate officers, just as the real Charles Nicholas Meriwether of Woodstock did. Lucy Churchill, an orphaned Allard granddaughter, marries Rives Allard, a young man from a far-flung branch of the family, just as Caroline's grandmother married Douglas Meriwether, a distant relative. Rives's mother, Susan Allard, is modeled on Caroline's grandmother's mother-in-law, Susan Meriwether, who was known as Mammy Horse because she rode horseback so much. Both Susans rode off to the battlefields to tend the wounded and the dying. A Miss Cally in the book converts the ballroom of the house into a small factory that turns out clothes and blankets for the Confederate army, just as a Miss Cally Meriwether set up sewing machines in the ballroom at Woodstock.

Caroline was not, however, simply setting down the facts of her family history. She would kill her hero Rives Allard although her grandfather Douglas Meriwether survived. In real life, Ned Meriwether died (killed when he and General Forrest outrode support forces), while the fictional Ned Allard would come home a permanent invalid. Woodstock survived the war, but Yankee soldiers would burn the fictional Brackets. ("Scum of the cities," says the Yankee officer apologetically to Mrs. Allard about the soldiers. "I can't control them. Nobody can.") Of course, Allen's family's home had been burned in Virginia during the war.

Planning to go to Olivet College in Michigan in July to teach at a writers' conference, Allen and Caroline sent Rosy back to Memphis, bought some clothes for Caroline ("that we could ill afford," she said), closed up Benfolly, and disposed of Nancy and all the animals. When they got to Louisville, a telegram caught up with them to tell them the writers' conference was canceled—not enough people had signed up. Since they were all packed and had forgotten to get Rosy's Memphis address, they went to Cornsilk.

The hospitality at Cornsilk was so generous that they felt a long visit was no imposition—Caroline had seen a grocery bill for seven people (including feed for 300 turkeys) and it was fifteen dollars a month.

She and Andrew's father liked each other enormously. Andrew watched them together and marveled at how Caroline "could come to the heart of a person's nature instantly. She saw my father walking up and down one row after another telling people what to do. She saw not that he was telling people what to do but that he was having such a good time."

Mr. Lytle made fancy desserts. He came in from the field around eleven o'clock attended by two field hands, shouted for a quart of whipped cream, and started in to make "something marvelous for dinner. We had Jesse Sparks' First Wife's Roman Punch for dinner the other night and all wished she could have been there to taste it. (Mr. L. rejects the second wife's recipes, says she was no housekeeper. He uses only a Murfreesboro cookbook.)"

The overseer, a white man named George, had a farm of his own but preferred to rent it out and live with Mr. Lytle because it was more fun at Cornsilk. One day when George and Caroline were alone, he kept coming back to the room where she was to tell her what a wonderful man Mr. Lytle was. Finally, emotionally, he told Caroline, "Why, that man, if he liked you he wouldn't think nothing of killing a calf for you!" Two nights later, when they had home-killed veal for supper, George looked triumphantly at Caroline.

There was no place like Cornsilk for work, she said. The first morning she walked purposefully toward a secluded corner of the dining room, cleared a spot by removing several bushels of peanuts, a medieval cuirass, and three or four demijohns of cherry bounce, set up a card table, and began to write steadily. She produced, she said, 15,000 words in one week—she would say 20,000 but she wanted to make a conservative estimate. She was almost through the first section of "The Cup of Fury." She hoped to start on the war part the next week and she thought it would be simple. She would use, she said, a style something like this: "Waving his bloody right hand high above his head he charged into the battle. 'My God, men,' he screamed, 'will you see them kill your general before your eyes?' " That was from Wyeth's *Life of Forrest*. "I am just lifting sentences like these from every place I find them." (She was joking, but after the book appeared, D. W. Hiltman, chairman of the board of D. Appleton-Century Company, wrote to Maxwell Perkins to complain that she had lifted passages from *Battles and Leaders of the Civil War*, a multivolume compilation of first-person accounts of battles by Confederate and Union officers and men that had first appeared in *Century* magazine. Perkins, who apparently never mentioned Hiltman's letter to Caroline, checked the allegations and replied that he saw nothing remotely suggesting plagiarism. "We see plainly," he wrote, "that the author has done what she should have done in going to the most authoritative source for a statement of what was happening at a certain time, and by re-presenting these facts more dramatically. Her quotations seem to be what were quotations in 'Battles and Leaders' as part of the record. Events cannot be copyrighted. All that can be copyrighted is the manner in which they are narrated. She has not taken anything but the events. Her whole method of presentation is different, and is her own except that she must depend upon the record for the facts.")

Perkins had hinted to Caroline that her book would be the leader on Scribner's list if she could get it in for spring publication. Caroline thought the reason was that "all of their big shots" had just published a book and Scribner's was actually looking around for a leader. It might never happen again, she said, and she intended to try to make the deadline.

Every day Andrew retired to the woods to write. They were neck and neck on their books and hoped to finish in time for a debauch in New Orleans at Christmas. Andrew's father saw that everything was done for the convenience of the resident writers. "It was a lovely, charmed time—we all had the feeling that it was one of those things that would never come again," Caroline wrote to Ford. In fact, the Lytles were in danger of losing the plantation. While the Tates were there, the sheriff served papers giving them six hours to get out. Mr. Lytle, with his high regard for the Muse, didn't even mention the matter to his guests. He told the sheriff he couldn't get his volumes of official records of the Civil War off the place in six hours, much less his team, tools, and other belongings and the sheriff would just have to let things go on a little longer. "It's a very melodramatic affair— a wicked brother-in-law who is determined to ruin Mr. Lytle and has managed to get his clutches on the plantation through Mr. Lytle's generosity," Caroline explained to Ford. (The Lytles managed to hang on to Cornsilk.)

The Cornsilk routine worked, she said. Even Allen wrote two pages one morning.

That fall the Tates went back to Memphis for a second year, renting another bungalow on the other side, "the leafy end," of Forrest Avenue. Allen called it the Gold Oaken Nest—it was full of golden oak, with a picture of George Washington over the fireplace in the living room. For the same money that they paid for the Hamburger House, there was more space—including a good workroom, a glassed-in sun parlor at the back of the house that both Allen and Caroline enjoyed, and five rosebushes and a fig tree in the backyard. Except for the garbage, the alley, said Caroline, who treasured anything bucolic, was like a country lane.

Nancy was enrolled in the Lausanne School, run by Emma Jett, Captain de Saussure's daughter; it had smaller classes than the public school. Nancy did well that year, although she complained that Mrs. Jett would say, "Now, Nancy, can't you recite one of your father's lovely poems?"

Caroline was lost in the Civil War. One day while writing a business letter she had to ask Allen the date—not the month or the day, but the year. "With me," she said, "it is September 18th, 19th, 20th, 1863— just starting on the battle of Chickamauga, having returned from a scout on Stone's river." She talked about the adventures of a Union woman who was a spy, prostitute, psalm singer, and possibly a nymphomaniac, who seemed to have the time of her life during the Civil War. And she discovered a Confederate Cranford—three old maiden ladies in South Carolina tyrannized by their servants. They had a butler so indolent that he burst into tears when they told him company was coming to tea. When Nancy and Allen complained about their dinner, it seemed unreasonable to Caroline, who had just been reading about men picking blackberries as they went into the line of battle. Once when she reported such a nugget to the family, Nancy said crossly, "Mama, I don't care what those Confederate soldiers ate."

Scribner's was holding out promises of big things if she could only finish it by December 1. It was an impossible deadline, but Caroline decided to try to meet it. She worked until ten and eleven every night. "I wrote *Aleck Maury* so fast I thought I couldn't force myself more than I was doing then," she wrote Josephine Herbst. "But now I find that was nothing. It is easier, too, in a way to keep steamed up for some months at a time. You don't have to go through those dreadful periods of working up to it."

One day Caroline felt so stale that she quit work and began to rake leaves in the backyard. In yielding to pressure from Scribner's, she decided she ran a chance of ruining the book. It would just have to take its chances in the fall of 1936, she decided. When Perkins took it off the spring list, she promptly asked him to publish a collection of her short stories and call it "Men That Ride Upon Horses" from Yeats's poem, "At Galway Races." "Such a title fits in with the whole trend of my work," she wrote Perkins. " 'Agrarian!' the communist critics will mutter, and rightly."

When Josephine Herbst wrote to ask the Tates to recommend her for a Guggenheim Fellowship, Allen replied that he could not because he did not like the propaganda in her books. He objected to using literature to further any cause, whether it was Buddhism, Methodism, or communism. (This was unlike Allen, who constantly recommended people to foundations, employers, and publishers. The Memphis police chief's accusation of communism must have still rankled.) Caroline, however, said she'd be glad to recommend Josie and apologized for enclosing Allen's letter. She added she was sorry to hear about the breakup of Josie's marriage. "It's strange the way these things happen. Successful male novelists always get rid of the partner of their lean days as soon as they hit the top. I suppose with female novelists it works just as inevitably only reversed. The unsuccessful partner can't stand the success."

The Tates went to Benfolly for Christmas in 1935 and it was, as Caroline said, a very confusing holiday. On Christmas Eve they went over to Merry Mont to keep Miss Carrie company. The Warrens, meanwhile, spent Christmas Eve at Benfolly, alone except for the Normans. "They had never written a word about it, but it seemed they expected to spend Christmas with us," Caroline said. "Cinina Warren was pretty mad." The Tates had, in fact, invited several people to Benfolly, but as the days went by and nobody telegraphed or wrote, they got tired of waiting and went off to Louisville so Allen and Herbert Agar could read proof for *Who Owns America?*, the second Agrarian symposium.

All the guests arrived while the Tates were gone. Some were annoyed. Andrew Lytle wandered around middle Tennessee for days with a twenty-five-pound turkey. The Tates finally got together with their guests, including the turkey, at James Waller's in Nashville. Waller, a Nashville investment banker who had known Allen at Vanderbilt, wrote an article entitled "American and Foreign Trade" for *Who Owns America?* He later earned a Ph.D. in economics and taught for the rest of his life.

"My idea of a good Christmas, really," said Caroline, "is staying in bed and reading an omnibus of crime."

Andrew was halfway through his novel, but when he got to the Civil War part he said he felt cold to it. Everyone agreed that if Andrew was cold to the Civil War something had to be done. "It seemed a good plan for us all to spend a few months together and try to whoop each other on," Caroline said. Andrew taught history at Southwestern during the spring semester and he and Polly, his sister, lived with the Tates. Caroline thought Andrew was easy to live with. He got up at five, cooked his own breakfast—he ate fried apples every single day—wrote on his novel for two or three hours, and taught all morning. Caroline was not so easy to live with that spring. Andrew could see strains in the Tates' marriage, but he paid no attention to what he called her "passions." They were caused, he said, because Allen was around all those young girls at Southwestern.

"It is certainly splendid to have Andrew and Polly here," Caroline wrote to Warren. "Andrew is working on Shiloh, I on Chickamauga. We compare symptoms and it helps a lot." She went on to tell him that she had written a horror story. "I always did want to write one. It is very lurid, about a man whose enemy is about to be hanged. The enemy (colored) tells the man to give him ten minutes after the hanging and he'll be with him. When the ten minutes has elapsed the man cuts his throat and goes forth to meet the ghost on his own ground." It was a neat idea, wasn't it, she asked Warren, and she told him she sent it to *Esquire* with Allen's name on it. The story is, of course, "The Enemies," published first in *The Southern Review* and awarded the second prize in the *O. Henry Memorial Award Prize Stories of 1938*.

The Tates acquired from Dr. Herbert Sanborn, Allen's old philosophy professor at Vanderbilt, a dachshund named Herr Baron Vili von Isarthal. They bought Vili for Nancy, but Vili could bear no one but Caroline and growled whenever Allen came into the room. Caroline began to talk for Vili, a practice she was to continue with the other dogs who succeeded Vili, for years. With Caroline as ventriloquist, Vili—and his successors—usually said nasty things. "He is like Abraham

Lincoln. He says that all he is or hopes to be he owes to his sainted mother," Caroline said. When she went away, Vili moped and would not eat, but could always be lured into a room if someone would type rapidly. "He spoke only German when we got him but now he speaks the vernacular mostly," Caroline said.

In April the Tates went to Nashville for the publication of *Who Owns America?* and took part in a marathon celebration involving the Warrens, Ransoms, Davidsons, Owsleys, Waller, Agars, George Marion O'Donnell, a young poet who taught at Vanderbilt, and Andrew Lytle. Events began with a party given by the bookstore, went on to an autographing session at the bookstore, then to a party at the Wallers' house where everyone, including John Ransom, reeled with drink. The next day they all had lunch at Petrone's in downtown Nashville, went out to the Ransoms' house, then to a cocktail party given by the publisher, and on to a party at the Davidsons' house. The next day they met again for lunch at Petrone's; Ransom left to meet his one-o'clock class, dismissed it, and hurried back to Petrone's.

That spring Allen had Peter Taylor for a pupil. Taylor, just out of high school, had refused to go to college and was working for the *Commercial Appeal.* He heard about Allen and went to Southwestern and enrolled in the freshman composition course Allen taught. For the class Peter wrote a story about his grandfather Robert Taylor, a Tennessee politician who had run for governor against his own brother, Alf Taylor. The two slept in the same bed at night and campaigned against each other during the day. Allen liked what Peter wrote, including a quote from one of his grandfather's speeches, "Speak not to me of the New South; there is only the Old South, risen, with the print of the nails on her hands," and invited Taylor home for dinner. The Tates encouraged him in his writing, as they had done and would do for scores, possibly hundreds, of young writers during their lives. No matter what projects of their own cried out for their attention, Allen and Caroline would always take time to work with anybody they thought had talent. Allen and Taylor read Chaucer together that spring and summer and Taylor took Tate's course in the Victorian novel. "I had had a very conventional life," Taylor, whose father was a wealthy Memphis lawyer, recalled fifty years later. "I had never met a writer. I thought Caroline would be a dried up professor's wife. She was plump then and didn't fix herself up but she was full of laughter and fierce. It was wonderful for me to meet the Tates, to find someone who made me feel that what I was writing was important and serious, that it was not just local color."

Tate encouraged Taylor to send his stories off to magazines and persuaded him to enroll at Vanderbilt that fall. "When I went to Vanderbilt, it happened that I was assigned to Donald Davidson for registration," said Taylor. "I told him I wanted to study under John Crowe Ransom and he said, 'Come on, I'll take you over and introduce you.' We went over to where Mr. Ransom was registering students and Davidson said, 'John, here's a boy Allen has sent us.' That was the way things used to be done."

The school year ended with good news. Mark Van Doren arranged for Allen to give five lectures at Columbia for a fee of $400. They would earn $300 from the writers' conference at Olivet College. Caroline got another $150 out of Scribner's, and Allen another advance from Earle Balch for his novel. Allen resigned his teaching position. They would go to New York for the first time in years and come back and live by their wits again, on money from Caroline's novels and short stories and Allen's essays and poetry.

Sam Monk wrote a few verses to mark the end of Allen's stay at Southwestern:

> Allen Tate, Confederate bred,
> "Dull critter of enormous head,"
> Came to live with the professors
> To raise some money for the tax assessors. . . .
>
> Now at the end of nine months' time
> He's given birth to not one rhyme.
> Nothing remains of poet Tate
> Save the confirmed Confederate.

MONTEAGLE AND *NONE SHALL LOOK BACK,*
1936–1937

Caroline finished "The Cup of Fury," and sent it off. Then she learned that Scribner's had postponed publication until January for two reasons—the 1936 presidential election and *Gone With the Wind.* The book was selling so well that Perkins did not want "The Cup of Fury" to run into it head-on. *Gone With the Wind,* said Caroline, was "a Civil War Becky Sharp, and Lord how they're gobbling it up!"

Excited about their summer plans, the Tates left Memphis, stopped briefly at Benfolly, lodged Nancy with relatives, and drove to Olivet, Michigan, which they found to be a "very pleasant elm-shaded village." The Midwesterners were lovely, kind people, but they were so enthusiastic that they drained the energies of the hardworking writers' conference faculty. Alfred Kreymborg got up in the morning and said, "Don't come near me. I've stored up some vitality and I can't waste it on you." Carl Sandburg told stories, sang, and played the banjo; he and Caroline tried to go off and talk about the Civil War when they could. Sandburg was puzzled sometimes by the Oxford accent of Joseph Brewer, the president of Olivet. When Brewer mentioned publishers' inventories during a talk, Sandburg roused from a dream of the Civil War to ask, "What infantry was that?"

In New York they had the use of the Van Dorens' Bleecker Street

Douglas Meriwether,
Caroline's grandfather.
(Nelson Sudderth)

Caroline Champlain Ferguson Meriwether,
Caroline's grandmother.
(Nelson Sudderth)

James Morris Gordon,
Caroline's father.
(Princeton University Library)

Nancy Meriwether Gordon,
Caroline's mother.
(Nancy Tate Wood)

Children's Day at Hazelwood Church. In photographs, Caroline is nearly always on the edge of the group, often standing a little apart from the others. Here, she is on the right, with Polly Gordon, her cousin and future sister-in-law, closest to her, and Polly's brother and older sister to the left. *(Polly Gordon)*

"Miss Carrie" Meriwether, Caroline's grandmother, in center. Standing behind her, left to right, are Marion (Manny) Meriwether, Mildred Meriwether, and Caroline. Anna Wilds, Caroline's cousin, is in front of the unidentified young man. *(Nelson Sudderth)*

Caroline with her Alpha Xi Delta sorority sisters at Bethany College. Caroline is at far left. Manny Meriwether is in the center of the front row, third from left. Mildred Meriwether, Manny's sister, is seated in the back row, fourth from right.
(Nelson Sudderth)

At Dudley's Switch, Uncle Rob Meriwether's farm, 1918. Left to right, Caroline, her mother, Bill Gordon, Polly Ferguson Gordon, and Morris Gordon.
(Polly Gordon)

Caroline in college. *(Nelson Sudderth)*

The privy at Mrs. Turner's house at Tory Valley. *(Ann Waldron)*

Robber Rocks at Tory Valley, the place Sue and William Slater Brown bought in Putnam County, New York, in 1925. *(Ann Waldron)*

Portrait of Allen, Nancy, and Caroline painted in Paris in 1929 by Stella Bowen, one of Ford Madox Ford's wives. *(Vanderbilt Libraries)*

Wedding breakfast for Bill and Alice Bandy in Paris, 1929. Left to right, standing, Horatio Krans, Lee Hersch, Ford Madox Ford, Paul Snodgrass, Bill Bandy, host E. W. Titus, Allen Tate; seated, Caroline, a clerk from Titus's bookshop, Mrs. Horatio Krans, an unidentified woman added because Ford would not sit at a table of thirteen, Virginia Hersch, Alice Bandy, Zonota Snodgrass. Photograph by S. Londynski, Paris. *(Vanderbilt Libraries)*

Benfolly from the river. *(Polly Gordon)*

Caroline Gordon, from the jacket of *Penhally*.
(Princeton University Library)

apartment, complete with garden and plashing fountain. Allen thought his lectures at Columbia went over very well and he was interested to note he had two "very respectable old colored women in gold rimmed spectacles in his audience." Caroline found New York much nicer, more like Paris, than it had been when they left in 1928. Sidewalk cafés and more trees had made the difference, she decided. They "ate too much, drank too much," and rushed around to see people, most of whom Caroline felt had remained static. Nathan Asch was still broke and living in the country, making plans to get his wife and child to town—"just what he was doing six years ago, different wife, of course," Caroline said. They went out to Tory Valley to visit Bill and Sue Brown and saw them "sitting in the same attitudes we left them in many years ago. I believe they have been separated and reunited a dozen times since I saw them." Caroline talked to Maxwell Perkins, who felt the Depression was over, but worried now about the European war that he was sure would come. He thought "The Cup of Fury" needed a little more rounding out—some of the minor characters were not accounted for—and complained that she killed off too many young men. Caroline took the manuscript for rewriting.

They went up to Cornwall, Connecticut, to see the Van Dorens; Mark and Allen were judges in a *Southern Review* poetry contest and needed to confer. The winner was "Orestes," by Randall Jarrell, a student at Vanderbilt. Caroline was fascinated with the countryside and the architectural beauty of the houses, and decided she would like a chance to poke around New England for a bit. "It fascinates me. My theory is that they were done for long before we were (and knew it) and then seeing us all swelled up with vigor they had to come down and put us out of business," she said.

On their way back to Benfolly, they stopped off at Monteagle to see Andrew Lytle and decided to stay with him a few weeks. They hurried to Benfolly, stopped "only long enough to say hello to the cow and the Normans," then went through Nashville, where they visited the Ransoms and Caroline picked up "a small Civil War library from the Vanderbilt library." Nancy was with Pidie, Caroline's aunt in Chattanooga. "They begged to have her," Caroline wrote Ford, "and it is much better for her there. Allen would have had to drive her twenty-five miles a day getting her back and forth to school."

Then they settled down at the Lytles' log cabin in Monteagle. Monteagle was an old-fashioned summer resort on the Cumberland Plateau, about six miles from Sewanee and the University of the South and about forty from Chattanooga. There were, Caroline told Dorothy Van Doren, "quite hideous cottages tucked around among the trees" with many little old ladies rocking on porches. Monteagle was founded in 1882 by the evangelical denominations (Presbyterian, Methodist, Lutherans, and Campbellites) and the Episcopalians as a campground and chautauqua for summertime lectures and concerts. The village, with its bus station and Western Union office, was a ten-minute walk from the log cabin. "The dominant dowagers all have bishops or Confederate generals for fathers; sometimes they have a father that is both," Caroline wrote Ford. She and Allen went to movies and weekly poetry readings in Sewanee. When Allen read "Ode to the Confederate Dead" there, Vili accompanied him with a low growl throughout the poem. "It was quite effective," Caroline wrote to Andrew's father, who had sent her a caramel cake he had made.

The log cabin had huge rooms and corridors that ran back to front and side to side and crossed in the middle. A gallery ran around all four sides of the outside of the house. Caroline, Andrew, and Allen each set up a typewriter table on the veranda and worked all morning. Andrew's grandmother, his Great-aunt America, his Aunt Mary, his sister Polly, Polly's friend Henrietta, and somebody's uncle's divorced wife were all there, too, but they were all expected to leave soon, and they would have the mountain to themselves, Caroline said.

The roof did leak, Caroline told Ford, but only in the halls and "one only passes through the halls." The rooms where they lived and worked were tight and could be made very warm.

Mr. Lytle sent up a cook from the Alabama plantation and came up every Saturday with a truck loaded with chickens, vegetables, eggs, and butter.

Since Polly Lytle did the cooking, Caroline had no excuse not to work, she told Ford, but she was tired of working. "I do not expect to have much pleasure for some time to come. Going back into the Civil War after you thought you were through with it is really almost too much."

A letter to Sally Wood written September 10, 1936, is unusually tense and frenetic:

> I was just getting ready to get drunk in preparation to calling on Mrs. Waller, an old lady here on the mountain—desperate situation this call. Have to go. Will kill us to do it. Polly and I decided it was better to go drunk than not at all—well, I will write you a brief note before hitting the bottle. . . . We have been here two weeks during which two weeks I have mastered details of life in Camp Chase, Douglas, Johnson's Island and Fort Lafayette [Union prison camps]. I have also written nine thousand words. I have twenty more thousand to write, including the Battle of Brice's Cross Roads, the technical details of the strategy of which I have not yet studied out. When I get these thirty thousand words done I shall

be through with my Civil war novel, entitled "The Cup of Fury"—and hasn't it been one? One reason I haven't written to you or anybody else has been that until the middle of June I was working all day and all night on said novel. I am nearly dead. However, I am usually nearly dead so let that pass. Where was I? Oh, at Andrew's cabin. Well, we came up here because we like to live with Andrew and also because we can live here so much more cheaply than at Benfolly. We will probably never open Benfolly again till one of us writes a best seller. . . .

I am now going out to get that drink. . . . I wasn't writing today because I was too exhausted, after knocking out two thousand words yesterday before lunch. . . . I am going to have to stick to it every minute in order to get through by the eighth of October, which is the last day that Scribner allows me on revision.

Although Perkins had complained that she killed too many young men, she killed another one, gave one chronic diarrhea and another a gangrenous foot. "I can't help it," she wrote Perkins. "All the good people in the South were killed off by the war, one way or another." In the same letter, she pointed out that Bobbs-Merrill seemed to have put over *The Long Night,* Andrew Lytle's novel with a Civil War setting, in spite of *Gone With the Wind.* (Andrew didn't think his book did so well: "I got the reviews and Margaret Mitchell got the jack.")

Winter came on, but cold weather did not drive the Tates and Andrew away. They curtained off one end of one of the halls and ceiled it with "handsome Cimabuean blue builders' paper" to make a living room. It had a fireplace and was comfortable "except in the most severe weather, and tolerable then."

The Tates went to Nashville for a week and heard W. T. Couch, of the University of North Carolina at Chapel Hill, deliver a paper, "The Agrarian Romance." According to Caroline, it "enraged the brethren so that they kept a united front and mighty blows were delivered. I don't think any of them have had so good a time in months."

By this time, the Agrarians were being attacked on all sides, ridiculed by the Southern Historical Association, the Southern Regional Committee of the Social Research Council, and the Southern Policy Association on one hand, and attacked as fascists by Northerners. Allen and Donald Davidson considered drawing up a statement of principles, pointing out their fundamental opposition to fascism. Ransom and the others were losing interest, and Allen himself was thinking of other projects.

Right after Thanksgiving—spent with Nancy in Chattanooga—came a blow to Caroline. Perkins telegraphed her on November 27 that the title *The Cup of Fury* had been used for a 1919 novel by Rupert Hughes. Hastily, Caroline and Allen thumbed through the Bible and

Yeats looking for a new title. The possibilities she sent Perkins included "The Great Invasion," "All the Merry Hearted," "None Shall Look Back," "Under the Sun," and "Men That Ride Upon Horses."

Perkins rejected "The Great Invasion"—as Caroline had been sure he would—and suggested "Terrible Swift Sword" or "Grapes of Wrath." Caroline said she could not swallow a title from "The Battle Hymn of the Republic." They finally settled on "None Shall Look Back," from Nahum 2:8, " 'Stand, stand,' shall they cry, yet none shall look back."

Mrs. Winslow in Memphis helped her read the proofs for the book. "Don't worry your head over my mistakes in grammar, punctuation, etc.," Caroline wrote her. "Scribner's proof readers are really very learned in that line and catch me up on all those things. They also try to catch me up on things they don't know anything about. They cannot believe there is a game called 'setback' or such a thing as a back log. Logs with them are all 'black.' We also quarrel a good deal over horses. I maintain that you can't own a horse and ride it and feed it and call it 'It,' but they allow horses no sex whatever."

Caroline continued to revise proofs until a week before Christmas. She took Nancy to do her Christmas shopping, leaping straight from Forrest's capture at Murfreesboro into the Christmas frenzy. Toward the end of the afternoon Nancy whispered: "Mama, don't tell them your mind is going. They know it, anyhow."

They spent Christmas in Chattanooga with Nancy and went to Merry Mont to see Caroline's grandmother and Loulie. "My grandmother is in high feather," Caroline wrote Sally Wood. "She and Loulie wage continual war. Ma: 'If I didn't have any better memory than you have I'd offer myself to an institution.' Loulie: 'I would if I weren't already the head of one.' "

Loulie always attracted lame ducks; she had Cousin Mag and Cousin Kitty under her wing at Merry Mont. Cousin Mag thought she was a pea that might roll into a crack in the floor but she was quite sound otherwise. Cousin Kitty wrung her hands and paced all day, muttering, "Lord have mercy on me. . . . I told Loulie not to do that. . . . Lord have mercy on me." Allen confided to Caroline that he was not afraid of Cousin Mag, but he was frightened of Cousin Kitty, and put a chair against the door of their bedroom.

It was "all pretty grisly yet they managed to have quite a little Christmas spirit with eggnog before breakfast and all the other ritual observances. . . . Yes, I'm going to write a novel about them. It will be pretty Russian. I think I'll call it 'The Women on the Porch.' The two lunatics will furnish the chorus."

From Merry Mont, the Tates went to visit friends in Nashville, then on to Richmond for a meeting of the Modern Language Association. It seemed to Caroline that everybody on the program was a Fugitive except Mark Van Doren, who came down from New York. Ellen Glasgow gave an eggnog party for the MLA at her home, and Caroline said she "got through nicely by collaring the first man I saw and saying bring me a whiskey and soda." Miss Glasgow was supposed to address the meeting but an attack of laryngitis made her ask Allen to read her paper on the relationship of the scholar as elder brother to the creative artist.

"It was just the kind of time you have at such places, mostly talk and drinking in hotel bedrooms," Caroline wrote to Dorothy Van Doren. "I went, intending to have a fling and I think I must have flung far and wide. My very last recollection of Mark is when we were all having supper at the Rueger. I must have got his oysters for I do remember him saying plaintively, 'Are you sure those are the oysters you want, Caroline?' and I also remember assuring him that they suited me exactly when doubtless he had ordered raw and I steamed, or vice versa. Tell him if I did eat his oysters (and the oysters there were grand) I didn't really intend to be piggish."

Caroline met Thomas Wolfe at the MLA meeting and told Sally that he was "drunk and dumb and extremely amiable." He told Caroline, "Mrs. Gordon, Max Perkins thinks you're wonderful." "He is so dumb," wrote Caroline, "that he can hardly follow a conversation. We were talking about the wonderful whorehouse scene in *Sanctuary*. Wolfe assured us solemnly that he had intimate acquaintance with whorehouses in many places and that whorehouse wasn't true to life."

Seward Collins and his wife, Dorothea Brande, who wrote the best-seller *Wake Up and Live,* went down to Richmond to drive the Tates back to Washington, where the Tates stayed with Mrs. Winslow's son, John, and his wife, Marcella. (The Collinses stayed at the Willard, where Brande's new mink coat was stolen. "And it had plenty of minks in it," commented Marcella, "as she weighs two hundred pounds.") One night they all ate quantities of waffles and sausage and played ghost at the Winslows'. "Allen is one of the most simpatico men I have ever met in my life," Marcella wrote her mother-in-law. "The combination of mind, manners, charm, and simplicity is rare indeed."

Finally, the Tates were back at Monteagle. "Next year—if I have the cash—I am going into a hospital two weeks before Christmas and emerge only when it is safely over. I believe I hate it worse every year. Nancy, however, had a grand time," Caroline wrote Sally Wood.

The day after they reached Monteagle, Allen abandoned "Ancestors of Exile" and started a new novel. He seldom missed a day's work on it that spring. "He fought hard—for five years—against writing a novel but it certainly has taken him hard. He mutters to himself and gets up in the middle of the night to jot down incidents he's just thought of, keeps a permanently glazed eye—in short, a genuine seizure," Caroline wrote to Dorothy Van Doren. "What amazes me is the relentlessness with which he goes forward, once he does get started. All his sufferings seem to come before he starts whereas I suffer—and groan—every inch of the way."

George Haight, one of Andrew Lytle's friends from his New York days, was working in Hollywood, and Andrew decided to visit him. Allen and Caroline felt there was no sense in his going to Hollywood, pointing out that Andrew himself had said, "I have no heart for it but I am too restless to stay at home." They did not want to see him become a screenwriter or get tied up with a contract since, as Caroline wrote Katherine Anne, he had "another novel to write as soon as he had the moral courage to tackle it. He finished 'The Long Night' last May and has been at a loose end ever since."

Caroline used the same high moral note—writing a novel was the most important thing in the world—when she wrote journalist Lon Cheney long letters of criticism and encouragement. She urged him to read and study *Madame Bovary* and *Tess of the D'Urbervilles*, "and it wouldn't do you any harm to study Hemingway for his beautiful sense of form and for his dialogue."

Caroline was doing all the housework at Monteagle but found it easier than running Benfolly with one servant. She couldn't face the stove in the dirt-floored kitchen in a "cave" under the house, so she cooked on an electric grill and over the fireplace in the hall. It was surprising how much one could cook on a wood fire after getting the hang of it, she decided. She was especially proud of one meal that included pork chops, broccoli, potatoes, and banana fritters. One guest was reminded of one of George Washington's maxims of conduct: "Do not spit in the fire, especially if victuals be cooking."

None Shall Look Back came out in February. Caroline had wanted to write a big book, a magnum opus, and this was a big book. The presence of historical figures like Forrest and Grant and Buckner and Pillow and other commanders from both sides gives it an epic quality. It is not a happy book. Any joy people feel in love or sex is muffled (Caroline hated it when reviewers used the word "muted," but it leaps inevitably to mind) by the cloud of doom, defeat, and loss apparent from the very beginning. As soon as the scene is set at Brackets, seventeen-year-old Ned Allard brings his cousins George Rowan and Rives Allard, of the Georgia branch of the Allards, home from school. They are about to join Forrest's rangers. Almost immediately, from the garden, we see Ned's orphaned niece, Lucy Churchill, inside the candlelit parlor, singing, with obvious symbolism, "Let thy loveliness fade as it will."

Lucy loves Rives Allard, but she marries him partly because she feels there is no room for her in the small house to which the Kentucky Allards move after Brackets is burned. Aunt Cally, arming herself with an axe at the prospect of a "servitors' uprising," turns on Lucy and says, "You don't know how to do anything. . . . There's nobody. Nobody but me!" When later that evening Lucy sees Rives, who is briefly hiding out at Brackets, she cries out to him, "They don't want me. . . . I haven't anywhere to go. . . . They don't want me." Rives says, "I want you, more than anything in the world," and adds they will ride to Hopkinsville to get married. And they do.

Through all the novel run the themes that were important to Caroline and to the Agrarians: Land, the most important thing in the world, must be cared for. Lucy's grandfather Fontaine Allard even quotes Edmund Ruffin, a Virginia agronomist much admired by the Agrarians, who developed methods for restoring soil fertility. (Ruffin had the distinction of firing the first shot of the Civil War at Fort Sumter and is said to have killed himself when it was clear the Confederacy was defeated.) Shopkeeping is infinitely inferior to farming. Jim Allard, Ned's older brother, married Belle Bradley, whose father has a store in Clarksville. "Old Joe Bradley was conspicuous in Clarksville as being a 'sharp' man to deal with. Allard actually winced at the thought of the word being applied to any connection of his." But Fontaine Allard himself is not above a little sharp trading in slaves with his neighbor, Colonel Miles. Allard believes in treating slaves well, and he acts quickly to get rid of a white overseer at Cabin Row, a plantation Lucy has inherited from her mother, when the overseer beats a female slave. But he never questions whether the system is right or wrong. (Fontaine's cousin Tom Allard, Rives's father, a "peculiar" man, did not believe in slavery and freed his slaves, whereupon most of them went to Liberia.) Allard, doting on his granddaughter, finds only one fault with her: her lack of interest in the management of Cabin Row. "Boy, what do you think of a farmer who won't go out to look at her crops?" he asks. Lucy, however, as the war goes on, is clearly capable of doing hard outdoor and indoor work when she must. She manages the poultry at Brackets until it is burned. She goes to cut and haul cane to feed the remaining animals. When she stays with Rives's family in north Georgia, she works hard to learn to spin. She has the stamina and the spirit to work alongside her mother-in-law to tend the wounded soldiers in awful circumstances. ("The odor [from a wound] was living evil. It crouched above the bed on angry feet, made forays into the room. Rives thought: nothing like this on the battlefield.")

The legendary Nathan Forrest is a very large figure in the novel, and his prominence in the book reflects the conviction of both Andrew Lytle and Allen Tate that he was the best of the Confederate generals and that if he had been in charge the South would have won the war. Rives, in fact, is so lost in Forrest's thrall that he becomes single-minded in his service, almost unconscious of wife, family, or anything else. (Caroline wrote to Lon Cheney after it appeared that "I wanted Forrest to be like a god," but added that there were dangers in this method, the chief one "that it is difficult to get katharsis at the end when one of the heroes is a demi-god." She feared the book wasn't "human" enough. She brushed over Forrest's past as a slave trader and his lack of control over his troops and, of course, ignored his later role as the founder of the Ku Klux Klan.) Heroism in war is entirely proper in this novel, and the schoolmaster, aroused by Ned, Rives, and George when they leave to join the rangers, says, *"Dulce et decorum est . . .";* the phrase seems to echo through the pages as the young men ride forward almost seeking death.

Caroline used the scheme of the omniscient narrator, going inside the minds of nearly every character, male or female, high or low, important or not important. This dilutes the book's strength and energy, but academic critics admire her technical skill in using a shifting point of view.

Caroline creates vivid characters and demonstrates pitilessly how they act in times of high excitement, extreme dangers, and desolate defeat. She sketches in the background with a sure hand, using a stand of silver poplars, a clump of sumac, Virginia creeper on the walls, the enthusiastic cries of ladies admiring a yellow rose, a red clay gully and dark pine woods, the condition of a starving horse, to set a scene and create a mood.

Reviews were mixed and many reviewers compared it, inevitably, to *Gone With the Wind.* Katherine Anne Porter wrote a glowing piece, "Dulce et Decorum Est," in *The New Republic* in which she said Caroline was as "all-seeing as an ancient chronicler, creating a panorama of a society engaged in battle for its life," and compared it favorably to Stark Young's *So Red the Rose.*

Caroline went to the Sewanee library to see the review and wrote at length to thank Katherine Anne. "It is not a review, really, but a tribute . . . to the Confederacy. . . . In fact, reading it, I found myself thinking, 'She ought to have treated the subject rather than me.' The phrase 'the pride of Lucifer' is illuminating. It is exactly what I was trying to show. And people have written and told me that this book shows the horror and futility of war! One dear old general at Sewanee praised the book but said as a professional militarist he would have to take exception to that. I told him my theme was 'Dulce et decorum est . . .' wish now I'd put it as a motto somewhere. He replied that he'd been kicked around so much by pacifists that he was like a cur dog who snarled before he was kicked. . . . What you said about men born to die for a cause was so fine and so much a point I wanted made. I am reminded of a conversation I once had with Malcolm. It was really the inspiration for this book. Malcolm was talking about trends of the times—or something, but the gist of it was that certain ideas took possession of men every so often. . . . I had as near a mystical experience as I will ever have. I suddenly seemed to understand the nature of war, of righteous war. I understood how men could be glad and proud to die, could thirst for death in order that ideas that they hated should not prevail. I felt that I myself would be glad to die against the idea Malcolm stands for. This feeling was so strong, so immediate that all through the book I was merely trying to report it. I was never just trying to imagine how men would feel."

A letter from John Crowe Ransom must have meant more than the reviews: "It feels strange and a little harsh; has no pretty passages in it; has no episodes or complete little stories in it; is a single unit, stricter than anything I know in novels offhand. It's an artistic revolutionary wonder for these exclusions. You took a vastly moving subject matter and decided it needed no sentimentalizing; you just proceeded to put it through a severe, denying form; and there it is. It is a terrific experience; real tragedy. It is not half as big as *Gone With the Wind*, I guess, and covers almost precisely the same subject matter, and is many times as powerful—I call you a Great Artist."

The Tates had a houseful of company over Easter, including Sam Monk and his new bride, who was, Caroline said, "tall, dark, and efficient as hell." Caroline wrote a short story with a Monteagle setting, "The Brilliant Leaves," which she told Red Warren would be her last. The reason Ford was able to keep producing the way he did, she said, was that he realized long ago that he couldn't write short stories. "I am quite seriously determined never to try my hand at another," she said. "I can face a lifetime of incessant toil writing novels but each short story takes as much out of you—me, anyhow, as a novel and then you have to start all over again."

For a brief time, it looked as though *None Shall Look Back* was going to be a commercial success. Caroline wrote Ford that Scribner's was really pushing the book and there was some talk of a movie sale.

She decided to go back to "A Morning's Favour," the novel about landowners and tenant farmers she had begun in 1931 but abandoned. "It went dead on me," she told Fannie Cheney, "but suddenly revived itself." She asked Perkins for an advance, and he sent $150. She toyed with ideas for other books—she told Perkins that next she wanted to write a horror story about the old ladies who ran a girls' finishing school in Murfreesboro while they polished off all their relatives for insurance. She also invented an Agrarian detective who lived in the office in the yard at his sister's house and solved all problems with his knowledge of the history and pedigree of every man, woman, child, and horse in the county. He had a colored Watson, who when consulted said something like "White folks is mighty peculiar."

These weren't serious ideas, and she kept at "A Morning's Favour." By April, she had changed the title to "The Gardens of Adonis." It became, eventually, *The Garden of Adonis*. "Three illicit love affairs, an elopement, an illegitimate baby and a murder ought to keep things moving," she exulted to Dorothy Van Doren. "I fear, however, that when I get through with these events reviewers will be saying the book has a muted charm or something like that."

She was very conscious of being part of the Southern renaissance in writing. "Thank God for being a Southern writer," she wrote Dorothy. "I do feel at times that in comparison with the rest of you we are sitting in at a game where the cards are already stacked. Or rather to shift the metaphor our stuff due to the upheaval of '64 is lying around loose for any fool who has a big tow sack to pick it up. . . . If you are from other parts of the country it seems these days that you have to use much more skill to strike a vein of the real stuff and get it out."

The japonica and jonquils were in bloom already, she said, but the big show would come in April when the laurel blossomed. Why didn't the Van Dorens come down? She and Allen had gone to a place called Blue Bell Island in the Elk River and it was "absolutely blue where it wasn't yellow with dog tooth violets." Caroline said she never saw a more spectacular sight, but Allen remarked when he got home that he was surfeited with Nature. It took, said Caroline, very little Nature to surfeit Allen.

They planned to stay at the log cabin forever, they announced. They invited Ford Madox Ford and Janice Biala to visit them there that summer. "We are going to stay right here until Allen finishes his book," Caroline wrote Dorothy. "It's the best place to work I ever struck."

But they had to leave Monteagle in April. "The Nelson ladies," relatives of Andrew's mother, were coming to the cabin, and there would not be enough room for the Tates and the Ford entourage. So Caroline and Allen hurried to open Benfolly, find a cook, and get organized before Ford, Janice, and Janice's sister-in-law arrived.

16

BENFOLLY AND GREENSBORO, 1937–1938

It was hard, after the productive year at Monteagle, for Allen and Caroline to make a mad dash to open Benfolly. That summer—with Robert Lowell camped in a tent in the front yard, the Fords all over the place, the campaign to keep John Crowe Ransom at Vanderbilt, and the visit of Katherine Anne Porter—was the last summer they ever spent at Benfolly. That summer of 1937 was a kind of apogee of their joint trajectory, after which they seemed to spin off in separate directions. That legendary summer was, too, a kind of microcosm of their life at its best, with interesting people of great talent under their roof, literary politics occupying immense amounts of Allen's time, good food and swimming in the river, crises that made them shriek with laughter, and writing somehow getting done.

At the end of that summer, an unaccustomed quiet fell on Benfolly.

Caroline did more canning, but after Katherine Anne left it was not as much fun. She worked in the garden every morning, and one day she realized she felt really rested. It was "a sort of super feeling, like, I imagine a cat that has just been thoroughly wormed." She had been so tired for four years that it had been like "mild insanity."

Caroline took her grandmother to Eupedon to call on mad Cousin Kitty, aged ninety-four, and then drove her to Summertrees, the only antebellum house left in the Old Neighborhood, to see Cousin John Ferguson and his daughter Susie. They sat on the long back porch, and it seemed that the trees and the light looked exactly as they had when she was a child. Cousin John glued himself to her side and gave her a detailed account of the adolescence of Nero from his first triumphs to the time the Senate pulled the walls of the city down for him—all working up to the climax that Nero, like Roosevelt, was a "histrionic pervert." She drove her Uncle Rob to Elkton to engage in a lawsuit "with those Hutchinsons who insist on driving through the place and stealing the hogs." Mister Rob was jubilant; he loved court-houses.

The Frank Owsleys came out with their "demon child," Larry, to spend the day. Several hours after they left, Caroline started rounding up the cats and couldn't find one of them, Angelique. Someone remembered that Larry, as he was leaving, had run back and looked in the old trunk on the back porch. They found the cat in the trunk, as well as a chicken.

Caroline thought about writing a book about Merry Mont, with a daughter who hated her mother and characters like her Uncle Rob and Loulie, or a historical novel about Indians. Maxwell Perkins wrote to her urging her to write the historical novel "for practical reasons," since she had established her reputation as a writer of historical fiction. Caroline agreed, and told him that A. V. Goodpasture, an authority on Tennessee history and Indians, lived ten miles away, had a wonderful library, and would lend her books. She got new glasses to prepare for all the reading.

Allen worked steadily but slowly on *The Fathers,* hoping for a few bursts of speed so he could finish it by Christmas. He had one particularly unproductive day after a night of lost sleep when Daisy Miller, the cow, lowed all night because Uncle Andrew, her calf, had been taken away. "Really you have to struggle for everything you get in the country, even sleep," Caroline wrote to Katherine Anne. And then another cow caused trouble. "Mr. Norman took Minnie off to the bull but soon a call came for help. 'She's sulling,' he yelled. 'Git Mr. Tate to push her with the car.' Mr. Tate came with the car and pushed it right against Minnie's hind legs. She didn't budge. We whacked her with a stick. No motion. Suddenly a knowledgeable stranger leaped out of a passing truck and began twisting her tail. She leaped forward like a mountain goat till that twisting wore off when we all rushed forward and twisted the tail again, and so got her over the bridge."

Caroline read the proofs for *The Garden of Adonis,* and enjoyed the unnatural quiet of Benfolly. They began building fires in the evenings, and Allen remarked that the place was getting that cluttered winter look. The country was lovely now, she wrote to Sally, with "that October haze over everything, helped out a bit by the smoke from the tobacco barns curling up everywhere." She wrote another short story after her brother Bill came over for a visit and told them about Lee Jones, the confirmed drunkard who was a genius at firing tobacco. Lee took a fancy to Frankie, Bill's cook, and Frankie's husband objected strenuously. Bill had to choose between genius and Frankie. He took up a tobacco stick and told Lee he would make knots on his head if he didn't go on down the big road. Lee went off yelling, "You'll regret this. You don't know how to fire tobacco. You'll ruin your whole crop." She gave the story the title, "A Morning's Favour," a title she had had in mind for *The Garden of Adonis*.

It became apparent that *None Shall Look Back* was not going to be a best-seller. *Gone With the Wind* monopolized the sales for Civil War books. Caroline did not think much of Mitchell's book; she told Perkins it was "half a dozen of the best plots in the world wrapped up with the Civil War as cellophane." She heard it took Mitchell ten years to write it. Why couldn't it have taken her twelve?

Allen's brother Ben came down for Thanksgiving—his first visit in a number of years—and bought the Tates a brand-new Plymouth. When they took Ben to Nashville for a football game, Vili got loose, ran away, and was never found, although Caroline stayed for days, walking the streets and calling the dog's name.

Christmas was quiet because of the death by suicide of Caroline's cousin Catherine Wilds in New York. Cath, Pidie's daughter by her first husband, had gone to New York and fallen in love with a sculptor named Harold Cash, who did not want to marry her until he had possession of his child by an earlier marriage. Cath's funeral was at Meriville, where all Meriwethers wanted to be buried. "The death has cast a gloom over the whole connection," Caroline wrote to Anne Winslow, explaining that for Christmas they had had just a tree for Nancy and the Norman children "and not a visitor, for once." This was the third of Caroline's first cousins to kill herself. The first had been Mildred, Loulie's daughter who had been at Bethany with Caroline, in 1916, and the second was Cath's twelve-year-old sister, Anna, in 1917. These deaths, seldom mentioned by the Meriwethers, haunted Caroline even in her old age.

The Garden of Adonis appeared in late 1937, to generally bad reviews. (Adonis gardens in Athens were small pots of seeds that were forced to grow artificially; the plants faded rapidly, symbolizing, supposedly, the brevity of sexual pleasure.) Caroline was never very happy about the book, saying that she was unsure of herself when she wrote it and complaining that it was hard to write about poor whites. Her picture of Ote, the tenant farmer, is vivid and full of vitality, but he disappears for the entire middle of the book while Jim Carter, an essentially uninteresting fallen aristocrat, takes over. Unable to go to college—he was the youngest son of a poor widow—Jim gave up training dogs to take a job in St. Louis, but he returns to his hometown to work for the Camps, Yankee industrialists who have moved there from New Jersey. (In fact, Caroline wrote to Max Perkins that Allen "doesn't think it humanly possible for a man to be as dumb as Jim Carter.") Caroline uses the Camps and their factory to repeat the Agrarian themes, returning—too late—to the real tension in the book, the tragic dilemma of Ben Allard, the landowner, and Ote, the tenant.

The two female characters in the book are the girl Ote loves, a tenant farmer's daughter out to get all she can from whomever she can, and Letty, the landowner's daughter. Letty is perhaps the most uninspiring young woman in modern literature, interested in nothing. Even her suitor suggests she raise dogs, or find something to engage her interest. She is totally unaware of what goes on on her father's farm, knows neither the names of the tenants nor whether they're dropping tobacco plants or setting them. Academic critics have remarked on the passivity and silence of Caroline's heroines; Letty, although more an ingenue than a heroine, is the most passive of them all.

Ben Allard, the landowner, is modeled loosely on Caroline's Uncle Rob and other Meriwether men who were unsuccessful farmers, but he has none of their humor. Caroline was a woman who loved to laugh at the people in the Meriwether Connection; she always regaled dinner parties with tales of her kinfolk; her letters about them never fail to amuse. None of this sense of the absurd in Southern life ever entered her books.

Maxwell Perkins wrote her that by Christmastime *The Garden of Adonis* had sold only 2,800 copies. The trade, he said, was "all against books about sharecroppers or poor whites." Caroline had little interest in the book after it was finished and scarcely mentioned it in letters at the time.

That fall Allen and Caroline were approached about teaching at the Woman's College of the University of North Carolina in Greensboro. Caroline wired Perkins for money to make the trip for the interview. "It would be swell pay for little work," she wrote him. In Greensboro they stayed at the O. Henry Hotel, "the first literary hotel I ever struck," said Caroline. On the drive over, Caroline was impressed with the French Broad River, the Southern boundary between Indian and white territory for years. "It is one of the most romantic and beautiful rivers I've ever seen," she said.

They got the jobs, to start at the beginning of the 1938 spring term— each was to teach one course, at a joint salary of $4,800, and each would have the title of full professor. Caroline would rather be in North Carolina than anywhere else to work on the historical novel about Indians, she wrote Perkins. "The good stuff here [in Tennessee] is in the state library. But they have promised me all the resources of the Chapel Hill library." She asked for another advance so they could move, since they wouldn't get paid from North Carolina until March 1. Greensboro was "frightful," she said, but they would manage. "I hope nobody beats me to my subject this time."

They left Benfolly once more—just as her tulips were coming up, Caroline noted, and just when her hens were starting to lay—and settled down at 112 Arden Place in Greensboro: a nine-room house with three bathrooms, a good furnace, and dogwoods and hackberries in the front yard, all for only sixty dollars a month.

The period Caroline and Allen spent in Greensboro was to be the quietest time of their lives, when they had the least company and seemed rather bored with the people around them. Caroline met her class of ten students at eleven o'clock three days a week in a small room in the administration building. She had them read Stephen Crane, Chekhov, Joyce, Sherwood Anderson, Hemingway, Katherine Anne Porter, and Flaubert. Allen cut his class down to six pupils and scheduled it at two in the afternoon so he would have the mornings free for writing. "Allen's work is much easier than mine," Caroline wrote Andrew Lytle. "He doesn't let them write anything, but mine write short stories." There was always the danger, she said, that she and Allen would start thinking about teaching too much, but they were trying not to do that. They must work the racket, Allen said, as long as they could, or until one of them published a book. Although Caroline said she had never been overly fond of the young and com- plained occasionally of how stupid her students were—they didn't know Latin and they didn't know Greek and they stared at her with "haughty blankness"—she said she enjoyed the teaching. All it required, she said, was to lie in bed at night and read *Tom Jones*. Most of her students liked Caroline—and brought her bouquets of quince blossom, jasmine, and hyacinth, over which Caroline made a big fuss so they would continue to bring them—but some of them found her aloof and cold. They all admired her teaching and her dedication to the art of writing fiction and they appreciated the demands she placed on them, but one or two thought that she was too concerned with technique. Some of them considered her Agrarian ideas and her admiration for the society of the antebellum South ludicrous. One of the students whose work she praised the most was president of the YWCA, the social action group on campus at that time. These young women were troubled by segregation and realized that integration was necessary to achieve racial justice. Caroline was sarcastic about the YWCA and its attempts at social action. Although she was particularly impressed with a short story the YWCA president wrote that semester and said it was the best thing done in the class, Caroline gave her a C in the course. The student asked her about the poor grade after all the praise, and Caroline said she had not graded her on her ranking with her peers but on her potential. She disapproved of the student's spending so much time on the YWCA and its work instead of devoting herself totally to her writing.

While Caroline worked with twice as many students, plus several townspeople who sat in on her class and wanted to write, Allen, with his charm and his courtly manners, was the more popular figure on campus, the object of many a crush. It was his ironic smile that did it, one of the students said. Allen basked in their admiration, but said privately that while he liked to look at girls, he didn't like to teach them.

Caroline invited students to her house, and two of these would become lifetime friends of hers—Sheila Brantley and Eleanor Ross, who would also become a distinguished writer of poetry and fiction. One day Eleanor Ross gave Caroline two short stories written by her brother James, who was twelve years older than she. Ross had never finished college but, a victim of the Depression, worked at a political patronage job with the Internal Revenue Service in Greensboro. Caroline read his stories and sent for him. She told him that one story was not a story, but the other could be salvaged if he made some revision. When she found out that Ross, a tall, handsome young man, had played baseball in college and in a semipro league, she told him his trouble was that he wound up too long before he delivered the first pitch. After Ross revised the story, she prevailed on Allen to send it to *Partisan Review*, which published it. Ross later wrote a novel, *They Don't Dance Much;* it was published after the Tates left Greensboro and has been reissued several times.

Not only did Eleanor Ross publish books of poetry and prose and James Ross publish short stories and a novel but another brother, Fred, published a novel, *Jackson Mehaffey,* and their sister, Jean Ross Justice, was still publishing short stories fifty years later. The Rosses grew up on a farm in Norwood, North Carolina, children of parents who had never been to college. Searching for a reason for the extraordinary literary output of the four siblings, James Ross once said that his parents had gone to the Norwood high school, which held school six months a year instead of the four months customary at that time in North Carolina. "They had to pay tuition for the extra two months," he said.

Although the Tates occasionally saw Paul Green, the playwright who had won a Pulitzer Prize for *In Abraham's Bosom* in 1927 and who then taught at Chapel Hill, they had few visitors and made few friends. Green read his play *The Lost Colony* out loud at the Tates' house and Caroline said if she had five dollars for every time he said "American dream" she wouldn't have to teach school that year.

Caroline acquired Fossegrin von Isarthal, known as Bibi, a nephew of the lost Vili and a dachshund of equally distinguished lineage. Caroline thought Bibi had the family charm, but was a very different dog, a complete extrovert. "Everybody (except me) likes him so much better," she wrote Katherine Anne. "Allen is maudlin about him. 'I am afraid he will strain his heart,' Allen says when he is romping with the other dogs." Later she got a second dachshund, Heros von Borcke, called Bub.

While Allen worked steadily on his novel, Caroline hoped—although she had almost given up hope—that he would finish it this time. Flinging herself into research for her book about the pioneers, she went over to Old Watauga, the area near Kingsport, Tennessee, to locate the first home of her hero, Orion Outlaw. She had the good fortune to run into a young man in Kingsport who had worked out the location of all the forts and even knew where the cabins of the various settlers had been. "The Long Island was wonderful until Eastman Kodak built a plant there," she wrote to Max Perkins. (The Long Island in the South Fork River was where Daniel Boone's Wilderness Trail through the Cumberland Gap began and where a treaty with the Indians was signed.) It was curious, Caroline thought, how many industrial plants were on the old trading sites. She went down to Salisbury to locate the Trading Ford on the Yadkin, terminus of the Great Trading Path, and found a Duke Power turbine where settlers used to cross the river. The swans and waterfowl had disappeared, she found; the river was yellow and the banks looked "as though they had been skinned."

In Greensboro, she spent every day reading in the Woman's College library. Her notes on her reading, preserved among her papers at Princeton University, show that she ranged far and wide: reminiscences; the travel writings of the naturalist William Bartram; history books; letters; the diary of Morgan Brown, which described the first lot of settlers leaving Hillsborough; Tennessee Historical Society publications; Virginia State papers; and North Carolina colonial records.

She read so much about the Indians that she became quite fond of them, and the more she read, the less she admired the pioneers.

She always remembered the minute she found a firm grasp on old Dragging Canoe, the Indian chief in her book. After reading North Carolina records for weeks, she came on this sentence: "I saw the Canoe yesterday. He was sitting on a log in the woods and had his gun and a bundle with him." As soon as she saw the Canoe sitting there like that, she said, "I never had to bother, except to watch him."

She wrote letters asking for information and received long, helpful answers, including one from her Kingsport friend, who sent her pages of detailed information about the location of the landmarks of the eighteenth century—Watauga, Eaton's Station, Fort Patrick Henry, Moccasin Gap, foot trails, and the Great Rode, as it was spelled. A Chattanooga lawyer sent her a list of possible names for a young Indian man and offered to read her manuscript to catch "any Cherokee errors."

Her methods of recording information were primitive. Sometimes she typed out information from books, and sometimes she made handwritten notes, but she always covered several subjects on each sheet of paper. She did not bother with index cards. Her novel, she said, would be historically accurate, except that, for various reasons, she shifted the date of the convention of settlers of Watauga from 1772 to 1773. As every writer knows, research is ever so much more fun than writing, and she reveled in the search for information, enjoying even the facts she would never use. The knowledge that bears took a good dose of mountain laurel to purge their intestines before they went into hibernation was the fruit of one whole day's reading. She thought it worth the effort.

She set a goal to finish her research by June 1 because she and Allen had rented a house for the summer in West Cornwall, Connecticut, near the Mark Van Dorens and not too far from the Cowleys in Sherman and the Phelps Putnams in Pomfret. Allen struggled on with his novel, wrestling over which method to use in every scene but managing to write two pages a day with metronomelike regularity. Dorothy Van Doren read his manuscript and suggested he change the narration to the third person. He'd be surprised, she said, how little work it would take. Allen told Caroline that he was continually surprised at how much work a novel *did* take. Caroline was delighted when he said that until he started his own he had no idea what it took to write a novel. Caroline said she'd never realized before what it meant to be married to a novelist.

As he reflected on Dorothy's criticism, Allen said he was no Flaubert, who, he was sure, would have thrown it away and started again. He cared enough about his book to finish it, but not enough to rewrite it. As for Caroline, Allen told Mark, she was afraid he would take Dorothy's advice and do it over.

Allen decided they should leave early for summer vacation. He had run out of incidents for his novel but would think up some on the drive. While Caroline packed, they got the surprising news that Andrew Lytle, who was then thirty-five, was marrying beautiful Edna Barker, a twenty-three-year-old former student of Allen's at Southwestern, and they were going to Hollywood for their honeymoon. Andrew wrote that he was sorry they didn't agree with him about his marriage plans, that it was the first thing "we haven't seen eye to eye on." "I can't take it in," Caroline said. It was, in a sense, the beginning of the end of Andrew's role as a kind of younger brother in the Tates' household. The marriage astonished a number of people; Red Warren wrote from Italy that he would never recover from the shock.

CONNECTICUT AND GREENSBORO,
1938–1939

In June they left for Connecticut, by way of Merry Mont, with a brief glance at Benfolly. Benfolly, Caroline said, had never looked so nice; the earth *would* bring forth its fruits when they weren't going to be there.

The cottage in West Cornwall was just the kind of house they could work in, Caroline said. No bathroom, only one tap for water—in the kitchen sink—and no electricity. The bedrooms were the size of handkerchiefs and the house shook when they walked through it, but it was right next to a lake, which, Caroline said, made up for the lack of a bathroom.

They settled in with Deborah, a cook from New York, the dogs, Bibi and Bub, Nancy and a friend of Nancy's, Dot Arnett, a twelve-year-old daughter of a professor, who awed Allen because she bred white rats and discussed socialism. The Van Doren boys, Charlie and Johnnie, played with Nancy and Dot and were entranced one afternoon when Allen set up their blackboard on the lawn and diagrammed the Battle of Gettysburg, explaining every move the armies made. (That summer Dot was madly in love with Allen while Nancy was enamored of Mark Van Doren; both of them kept score of the times each man spoke to, kissed, or patted one of them.)

Allen began getting up at five o'clock and making his own coffee;

he did not want to see people that early for fear they would contaminate his thoughts. He wrote all day, sometimes until eleven at night, and finished his novel on July 21. It was scheduled for publication on September 23, Nancy's birthday. The whole family shared his exhilaration. This was "the first time we've been free of this old man of the sea contract with Balch in ten years," said Caroline. "It's a grand feeling." Earle Balch, who had bought Putnam's, came up from New York and reported that the advance sale was already 5,000. Everyone cheered, until they realized that the royalties from those sales would just cover the advances Allen had received over the years for what had started out as the Lee biography. "However, when you're in a hole, it's a comfort to get your head even with the earth," said Caroline; ever optimistic, she hoped that the next year would see them out of debt and with a little money ahead.

They swam, fished, and partied with Mark and Dorothy Van Doren and with Mark's brother, Carl, and his wife, Irita, who lived nearby. Léonie Adams and her husband, William Troy, came to visit, as did the Putnams, the Wilsons, John Peale Bishop, and Manson and Rose Radford.

Mark Van Doren asked the Tates if a young poet named John Berryman, who had been impressed with Allen's lectures at Columbia in 1936, could stay with them for a while that summer, and the Tates gladly took him in. Berryman was unable to find a job and was deeply depressed. Nancy and Dot thought he was the "most awful fink" they'd ever seen and would mimic his accent until John said, "I wish you wouldn't let Nancy eat with us." John had fits, which Allen and Caroline thought always came when he was not getting enough attention. John also took Deborah, the cook, out into the bushes.

One night when she was sitting by the fire with John, Caroline mentioned some lines from Ransom's "The Equilibrists" that she liked. Berryman recited the whole poem and followed it up with "Antique Harvesters" and "Captain Carpenter." Since the only books in the house were Abolitionist tracts and botanical works, she found a young man with a memory like that handy to have around.

The summer ended with a house party—Edmund Wilson and Mary McCarthy, and Una and Phelps Putnam, and Mark and Dorothy Van Doren joining them for the evening. "None of the guests cared much for each other," Caroline wrote to Katherine Anne Porter. "Bunny [Wilson] took a high moral attitude toward Phelps. When Phelps said he had to leave the next morning Bunny says, 'Why? You haven't any work to do, have you?' 'No, but I have hundreds of thirsty flowers waiting for me.' 'They're not as thirsty as you,' says Bunny with a hard laugh. One of the things everybody worried about all summer was why Phelps can't work. The reason, of course, is that he doesn't want to and also he is more interested in gardening right now than in poetry. Bunny has given Phelps up, hence the hard laugh but he worries about John Bishop whom I'd sooner give up than Phelps. John spends a great deal of time observing aquatic birds through a telescope, a pastime which Edmund finds somehow sinister."

The Tates went to Stamford to visit Wilson and McCarthy in what Caroline thought was their "large, expensive, gloomy, and dingily furnished" house. The Wilsons' cook had just walked out—Caroline wished she'd brought Deborah instead of putting her on the train to New York—but Mary cooked spaghetti, which they washed down with Chianti. "Edmund, who is no longer a Marxist but a great Russophile, read us Russian poetry (in Russian) till three o'clock in the morning. I had had enough to drink to be able to enjoy it rather but Allen took it pretty hard." In some ways, Caroline thought Edmund had made the transformation from his thirties to middle age more gracefully than most of their other old friends. Mary seemed very nice. Caroline was impressed that she got up the next morning and left the house in "incredible confusion" to make her daily visit to her psychoanalyst. She decided that New Yorkers went to psychoanalysts the way Southerners go to the dentist, but more regularly.

From Stamford they went into New York to meet the Warrens, who were returning from Italy. They had "a horrible evening" with Red and Cinina. "Red is more withdrawn than ever. The mask hardly ever slips now," Caroline wrote to the Putnams. "Cinina is as tiring as ever even though she behaved very nicely."

The Tates returned to Greensboro, where they settled farther out in the country in a new house, a six-room cottage they rented for only forty-five dollars a month; it had mimosa trees, pomegranate bushes, three fig trees, and dozens of roses. Caroline began writing the novel of pre-Revolutionary frontier life that was to be rich and full of energy and vitality. She was really working with two heroes. Rion Outlaw (whose real name is Orion, like the mighty hunter of mythology) is compelled to keep moving westward and goes with Daniel Boone to Kentucky. Rion loses his wife and children and his little brother—but westward he must go. His antagonist is Dragging Canoe, the Indian chief who refuses to give in to the encroaching white settlers and fights to the death. She was filling the book with violence and death, as she dealt with the fruit of her research into a period that has not been often used for historical novels.

When *The Fathers* appeared, Allen was irritated by the reviews, even the favorable ones. When reviewers said the novel was better than his poetry, he said it was because they were illiterate and did not know how to read poetry.

The Tates invited Ford, who was in New York, to come down to speak to their students in the spring of 1939. He came, wheezing more than ever, hardly able to get up and down stairs, and spoke. He was incomprehensible to most of the students, since he "swallowed three-fourths of every sentence," as Caroline remarked. Still, the dean said, "It was a good thing for them to look upon him, even if they couldn't hear him. In my youth I once looked upon Henry Grady," a famous Southern orator and journalist. After a public lecture, the president of the alumnae came up to Caroline and said, "After all, we don't need so many books. The Bible and the Sunday school commentaries are enough, don't you think?" "More than enough," Caroline said.

At Easter Caroline and Allen took five students down to Savannah for a writers' conference, where Caroline gave lectures entitled "The Southern Short Story Today" and "How a Story Is Written," both topics suggested by Allen. His lectures were "How a Novel Is Written" and "The Analysis of a Poem," and he obligingly offered to provide an extra lecture if another speaker fell through; Allen also made arrangements for their students to bunk four in a room at the YWCA (one of the students had a place to stay). Caroline, who enjoyed staying at Wormsloe Plantation, where camellias were blooming, complained bitterly that "the brutes" didn't pay the lecturers, just reimbursed travel expenses. "I didn't want to come in the first place," she said. George Stevens, the editor of *Saturday Review of Literature,* one of the speakers, told Allen that Warren's *Southern Review* was a good magazine but it was edited by a clique. "Clique!" said Allen, "Great God, how can you talk about a clique when those three old whores, Canby, Benét, and Morley have been slapping each other on the back for twenty years?" Still, said Stevens, *The Southern Review* was edited by a clique. The difference, said Allen, was that *The Southern Review*'s clique was a good clique. "Yours is a bad clique," he said. Andrew Lytle and John Peale Bishop were both at the conference. Bishop, who came down from Boston by boat, stayed over in Savannah several days to do some birdwatching.

Bishop was still hunting for a subject for a novel. "He feels that he has exhausted his native region," Caroline wrote to Katherine Anne. "Of course he has only tickled the surface with a golf stick—hasn't even taken a hoe to it yet. Still if he feels that way it's exhausted for him. He is now thinking of doing a little something about Gerald Murphy. Murphy was the first man to put a bar in his house—that still fascinates 'em. Of course Scott Fitzgerald has done him in 'Tender

Is the Night' but then as John says Scott's characters are always ninety per cent Scott so that leaves ninety per cent of Murphy intact."

In March, Caroline's grandmother died, at the age of ninety. "We are all rather bewildered. She kept us all hopping so long," Caroline wrote Katherine Anne. "I feel a little like Ben Tate who several years after his mother died used to stop on the street and say, 'Great God, Mama's dead!' . . . Oh, well, mothers are always trying. Nancy was reading *Penhally* the other day. She says, 'Mama just uses that time shift business in her novels because she never can get anything straight.' "

Almost out of the blue, Allen got an offer to teach at Princeton, which had a Carnegie Foundation grant for an experiment in the teaching of creative arts. They had already hired people to teach painting and composing. "The writer came last," Caroline said.

Dean Christian Gauss of Princeton came down to Greensboro to meet Allen, who had been recommended by Willard Thorp, a member of the English faculty who admired Allen's poetry and criticism. Caroline said that she and Allen felt they already knew Dean Gauss because they had heard Princeton alumni like Wilson, Fitzgerald, and Bishop talk about him for years. "He lives up to all they say," she wrote Katherine Anne. "A grand old fellow." The offer was not munificent—the job would pay only $5,000 and, since the program was experimental, only one year's employment would be guaranteed. The Tates asked for a leave of absence from the Woman's College, "not wanting to give up a permanent thing for what may be in the end only another Guggenheim fellowship."

Gauss promised that the first year's work would be light, that only twenty students would be allowed to take Allen's course. Later, he committed himself to almost guaranteeing two years' work for Allen. Since a leave for two years was out of the question, Allen resigned from the Woman's College. He felt he couldn't afford not to accept the Princeton offer, and besides, as he wrote Dean Gauss, he was looking forward to teaching men. A further reason, included in a letter to Frank Graham, president of the University of North Carolina, of which the Woman's College was a part, was that Caroline "has imperceptibly been drifting into full-time work, which she could ill-afford to do." The dean of women at the college told them they would expect the next writer they got to stay ten years. "As if writers could ever stay anywhere ten years!" said Caroline.

"And I just planted gourds on the fence," Caroline wrote to Katherine Anne. "For years I've wanted to plant gourds and got to it this year. It was the year I managed to get tulips planted at Benfolly that we got this offer here."

Years later, Caroline wrote to Allen's biographer that she thought the decision to go to Princeton unwise, "but I always left things like that to him. He told the Dean of the College that he was leaving so I could have time for my writing, then, carried away by his own fiction, began writing his friends the same version of the matter. The Dean was so mad at *me* that he wouldn't speak to me at a farewell party the department felt obliged to give us. It was years before it occurred to me that Allen had resigned my full professorship—always a hard thing for a woman to come by—without consulting me!"

This consideration did not enter her head at the time, since she was glad to get out of teaching. Her own writing had suffered while she was teaching. She had started her new novel in November and had written only twenty-seven words on it by the time they left Greensboro.

They made a hurried trip to Princeton. They stayed with the Gausses, whom they liked very much, and met the English faculty and members of the committee who had hired Allen. "Pretty stuffy, the lot of them," Caroline said. "Gauss is the livest man of the bunch. He said he wanted Allen to take the freshmen before the college ruined them!" The house Mrs. Gauss had found for them "apparently with a turn of the wrist" on Linden Lane was "a little like those darling little houses in Georgetown that I've always admired so much. . . . Seven big rooms and two small ones and two, thank God, baths. Also a sun porch and a nice little garden in the back. It belongs to a Frenchwoman (whose husband was a professor there). She has gone back to France and didn't want to sell her furniture and we didn't want to bring ours up from Benfolly. The dining table is long, thank God. We had just after years got ourselves the kind of dining table we want at Benfolly but decided not to move it up."

For the summer the Tates had rented James Waller's aunt's house, Westwood, across the street from Andrew and Edna at Monteagle. It would be easier, Caroline said, than opening Benfolly. Besides, life among the Meriwethers was so complicated, although it wouldn't be as complicated, she conceded, since her grandmother's death.

On their way to Monteagle, they went to Cincinnati to visit Ben Tate, and then to see Caroline's brother Bill, who was farming near Merry Mont. "One part of the agony of these visits," she wrote Katherine Anne, "is the rapid adjustments we have to make from having your clothes laid out for you . . . to, say, lending a hand with the manure spreader if your host hasn't finished his evening chores." Then to Merry Mont, where Caroline took Grandma Nancy Minor's portrait out of the parlor (she had it copied in Charlottesville and gave the original to her cousin Manny) and a broken blue vase that came from

Woodstock. The disposition of Merry Mont was still unsettled, but it was felt that Douglas Meriwether, Uncle Rob's son, would buy out the other heirs. The Tates went by Benfolly, where the hollyhocks she and Katherine Anne had planted two years before were flourishing. They were tempted, briefly, to stay at Benfolly, but rushed on to Monteagle.

There were so many difficulties moving into Westwood that they called it Wormwood. Once in, however, they found it very comfortable—cool and spacious with its five bedrooms. They had brought their cook with them from Greensboro. She was the best cook they ever had, they said. The dogs had a room of their own, and "the children"—Dot Arnett was with them again that summer—had a wing to themselves.

Andrew Lytle set a good example, working on his novel about Spanish explorer Hernando de Soto in a kind of cave under his porch from five in the morning until five in the evening. "We have a wonderful routine," Caroline wrote Katherine Anne. "It all hinges on getting up early. Then as Andrew says you really have infinite leisure through the day. If you fail on what you were trying to do in the early morning you have time for a nap and can go at it again before lunch time. Then there is a long afternoon still for work. Of course you fall in your tracks with sleepiness."

One day Edna came across the road to show Caroline an Associated Press story from Deauville in the paper—Ford Madox Ford had died on June 26. Caroline wrote an incoherent note to Janice Biala. "I am too upset," she explained. "We all are—we really can't quite take it in yet." Later she learned from Janice that Ford had been unable to lie down and had sat up all night for weeks before he died, while Janice played cards with him. Caroline immediately began a campaign at Scribner's to get them to republish Ford's best books.

The Tates and the Lytles quit work on weekends and went fishing or climbed in the gorges of the plateau on which Monteagle sat. One week they discovered a place they'd never seen before. They climbed down a gorge "and there at the bottom of a waterfall was the most wonderful pool I ever came upon, perfectly clear, perfectly green and very wide. I never had such swimming."

And that was the summer they met Ward Dorrance. At the suggestion of Maxwell Perkins, Dorrance, a professor of French at the University of Missouri, had sent the Tates copies of two of his books, one about three rivers in Missouri. Caroline had loved his description of the Black River, where her father used to fish, but had written to suggest that he might learn more about writing. They would be at Monteagle that summer, she had said, and he might come to see them there. Allen had written to him, too, making some suggestions about his writing. Dorrance did not answer either letter but turned up at Monteagle, a tenant of a servant's house nearby. With him was his servant, Vergil; when Ward came to dinner, Vergil came along to serve. Vergil confided to his master that he was romancing both the Tates' cook and the Lytles' cook. "Thank God!" said Allen. "Now they'll stay all summer."

At the end of the summer Caroline looked back and said that she and Allen and Nancy had eaten only one meal alone. Peter Taylor, the young man they had met in Memphis, was there and Caroline read his short stories and offered criticism. Her brother Morris and his son, Meriwether Gordon, came for a visit, as did Cleanth Brooks and his wife, James Waller, Lon Cheney, and a stream of others. This was the normal life for the Tates. The quiet time in Greensboro had been anomalous.

18

PRINCETON, 1939–1941

In 1939 Princeton was probably the most congenial spot in the Northeast for two Southerners. Since before the Revolution when John Witherspoon, president of the College of New Jersey, as Princeton University was then called, went down to Virginia to raise money and recruit students, it has been known as the most Southern of the Northern colleges, or the most Northern of the Southern colleges. In Nassau Hall the roll of Princeton Civil War dead lists as many Confederate as Union soldiers. In 1939 there were 2,500 undergraduates—all white, all male, mostly Protestants from private schools, an elitist group. President and Mrs. Harold Dodds lived on the campus in Prospect House and still entertained students for tea on Sunday afternoons.

Allen was struck by the architecture of Princeton and by its complacency. At first, he found the atmosphere of the university heady—Thomas Mann was lecturing in the humanities—but he was somewhat put out to find that he would not be a member of the English department. (As a resident fellow in creative writing, he was attached to no department.) "The bigwigs in the department think it is a 'very dangerous thing' to have Allen here," Caroline said. Another newcomer to the faculty that year was a young assistant professor of economics named John Kenneth Galbraith, who didn't like Princeton and later wrote disparagingly of its snobbishness and elitism.

The Tates liked their house on Linden Lane better than they expected to. The garden was much bigger than Caroline remembered and there was room for the two dogs to dig. The sun porch was pleasant and the library made a good study for Allen. They called the living room the salon because it was very French, with a woodland scene painted over the mantel, a pink rug, and blue chairs. In the library were their very own often-moved Confederate flag, Ned Meriwether's sword, the luster pitcher from Allen's family, and a portrait of Major Bogan, his grandfather. "The contrast between the two rooms is a bit startling," Caroline said.

As for the town, Albert Einstein called it a "quaint and ceremonious village." (Caroline saw Einstein on the street and wondered along with his other neighbors what he was wearing on the day his much-worn gray sweater hung on his clothesline.) Caroline liked the country-town aspect of Princeton and the way one could leave Nassau Street and be in a country lane in ten minutes.

The Tates went to New York to see the World's Fair before it closed and renewed old friendships with Edmund Wilson and Malcolm and Muriel Cowley. They went up to Connecticut to see Mark and Dorothy Van Doren, and over to the small town in northern New Jersey where Kenneth Burke lived. (When the Burkes came to Princeton to see the Tates, the Burke children spent the whole time running water and turning on the electric lights—enjoying wonders they did not have at home.)

Allen had many applicants for his writing class and had to winnow all but twenty. He planned to have them turn in their work in the middle of the week so he would have his weekends free. After the class started, he found his students "amazingly competent," but decided "their knowledge of life is what you would expect from the sons of commuters." Two of the students in his first class were Frederick Morgan and Joseph Bennett, who would later start *The Hudson Review*. Morgan recalls that Allen was a wonderful teacher, "gentlemanly, courteous, quick-tempered and easily offended," and that his class was "the most stimulating intellectual experience I had in my life up to that time. He introduced me to contemporary American poetry; the tradition of great prose writing of Flaubert, Henry James, and James Joyce; and the French symbolists and the English metaphysical poets."

Allen invited some of his students to the house on Linden Lane to read Dante in an edition with Italian on one side and English on the other. They thought Caroline was gracious, dignified, somewhat formidable, and handsome. She would say, "You boys . . ." the way a school teacher might say it, while Allen said, "You boys . . ." too, but with affection. The students could tell that there was tension in their marriage—they sensed two very strong personalities, not always in accord.

The older English professors were hostile to the New Criticism, for which Allen was an advocate, and Allen was contemptuous of them and their historical criticism. He made no effort to conceal his scorn for the older professors, including the chairman of the department, Hoyt H. Hudson, and Robert K. Root, who was dean of the faculty as well as a professor of English. The prudishness of the time prevailed in the department and when Allen pointed out sexual imagery in the work of the metaphysical poets, the students giggled.

Caroline said she had hoped that the wife of the resident fellow could live in quiet retirement, but she found that the faculty wives were worse than the hated clubwomen of Memphis. She was startled to find that the ladies made formal calls and left calling cards. She went to teas for faculty wives, and complained that two afternoons running of teas were too much. It was all pretty stuffy, she said, and they never seemed to stop calling. "If they know who you are they call on you because they like to know writers. If they don't know who you are they call more than ever to console you for being so obscure. I am known in the town as a writer of mystery stories under a nom de plume. I hope they think I am Mignon Eberhart." But she did her duty and stopped work on *Green Centuries,* on a day when she intended to kill twenty-six Indians, when Mrs. Gauss gave a tea for her and again when President and Mrs. Dodds invited them to dinner the very next day.

Willard Thorp said he never went to the Tates' house when there wasn't at least one houseguest and a crowd for dinner. Janice Biala came down from New York, bringing some of Ford Madox Ford's personal possessions so Allen and Caroline could have fitting remembrances. Allen got his malacca cane and Caroline ended up with a worn billfold that still had a penciled list of names and addresses in it. Mark and Dorothy Van Doren came for Thanksgiving (a week after Thanksgiving). After Robert Lowell and Delmore Schwartz visited, Caroline thought of hanging out a sign: "Young Poets by Appointment." Bob Daniel, a young writer they had known at Monteagle, asked if he could spend his spring vacation with them, and when Caroline said no, he came anyway and complained that he'd had to do so much household work at the Tates' he had no time to visit with other friends. Caroline, outraged, said that all they'd asked him to do was go to Kingston once and to check on the furnace once—"and not even put coal on, just look at it." Ben and Louise Tate came from Cincinnati for one football game, Bess (Ben's former wife) for another. Ben's son, Chuck, was a student at Princeton, and his girlfriend from Smith stayed with the Tates. Caroline's relations came, too—Manny first. When Pidie came, she and Caroline drove down to Toms River to spend two days and two nights with Cousin Kate Radford.

Caroline was delighted to have them all, but life was strenuous, and she was anxious to bring Cheryl, their cook, up to Princeton. As soon as Cheryl got there, they found she had both syphilis and gonorrhea. But the doctor said she was not at all contagious, and Caroline got her into a clinic where she received free treatment once a week. The poor woman, said Caroline, was so full of mercury her head reeled, but she did her work.

Later, when Caroline had to find a dentist for the cook, she was appalled to discover that only one white dentist would see a black patient, and then only with the stipulation that she come to his office after five o'clock. She wrote Andrew about this and added an anecdote about the English department. They were concerned, she said, about a graduate student who was Jewish—would he be able to get a job when he finished his Ph.D.? Never mind, said T. J. Wertenbaker, a historian from Virginia, I'll get him a job in the South where we have no race prejudice.

Henry Church, heir to the Arm & Hammer fortune, became a friend and supported the creative arts program at Princeton, funding the Mesures Lectures. Grace Lambert, a cousin of Sherman Morse, who was married to Caroline's cousin Little May, lived in Princeton; she and her husband, Jerry, became friends of the Tates. Lambert had made a great deal of money from Listerine (which publicized the word *halitosis*) and had helped finance Charles A. Lindbergh's flight to Paris. Caroline wrote to Little May that Jerry was an awful stuffed shirt. "He is what Ma used to call Grandpa Wilds, a 'circumstantial talker.' Sometimes it takes him two hours to answer a question." But she liked the Lamberts' house, "the best rich American's house that I ever saw."

Nancy, who by this time had attended innumerable private, parochial, and public schools in Clarksville, Chattanooga, Memphis, and Greensboro, was in the ninth grade at Miss Fine's School for Girls. She lost thirty-five pounds between September and Christmas, became a raving beauty, developed a scorn for people who had any bulges, and acquired sixty-five boyfriends from the Lawrenceville prep school and—when her mother would allow it—the Princeton freshman class. "I had always been a fat girl, and I saw all those cute boys and I just stopped eating," Nancy said years later. "I was so boy-crazy!"

At Princeton in those days, the English Club met regularly in the engineering building lounge, and members of the department read papers. Full professors sat in the front row, with the younger faculty members ranged behind them according to rank. Allen's turn to give a paper came in April 1940, when he read "Miss Emily and the Bibliographers," a violent attack on the historical method of literary criticism and on scholars for evading their responsibility to judge the text. The younger professors and the graduate students loved the talk, but the older men in the department were genuinely affronted. A legend grew that this paper, later published in *American Scholar*, launched the New Criticism, although Tate, Ransom, Cleanth Brooks, Kenneth Burke, and Eliot had published articles on its principles earlier.

The future that spring looked bright for the Tates. To Allen's intense relief, the committee appointed to oversee the creative arts program wanted him to stay a second year at Princeton, gave him a raise, and offered him an assistant. He asked for Richard Blackmur, who he said was the best critic in America. (Blackmur, reviewing Allen's *Reactionary Essays* a few years before, had spoken of Allen's "powerful . . . unusually integrated sensibility" and compared him to Hemingway.) Huntington Cairns, a lawyer with the Department of the Treasury, and an immensely learned man, invited Allen and Mark Van Doren to appear with him each week on his radio program, *Invitation to Learning*. Caroline was working on *Green Centuries*. John Peale Bishop wrote that he had seen Arthur Mizener, a young Princeton Ph.D., who was "certainly impressed—I might say awe-struck—by you two. He seemed to regard you a little short of the super human." Caroline and Allen were a couple who seemed richly blessed—amusing, successful, pleasantly eccentric in their nostalgia for the Old Confederacy.

As Allen became the better known of the two, Caroline sometimes had to fight for her identity. Anyone who looked up "Gordon, Caroline" in the first edition of *The Oxford Companion to American Literature*, published in 1941, would find "See Tate, Allen." Under Allen's rather full entry was this brief note: "Gordon, Caroline (1895–   ), his wife, is the author of novels about the South. *Penhally* (1931), *Alec Maury, Sportsman* (1934), and *None Shall Look Back* (1937), and many short stories."

In April the Tates went into New York for the wedding of Robert Lowell and Jean Stafford at St. Mark's in the Bowery, where Allen gave the bride away, then to a small reception at The Brevoort. In 1937, after he left Benfolly, Lowell had met Jean Stafford at a writers' conference in Colorado, where he had gone trailing after Ford Madox Ford. After the wedding, Caroline set about trying to find them a cheap place to live and a teaching job in a prep school for Lowell, perhaps at Miss Fine's. (Lowell went to Baton Rouge on a graduate fellowship at Louisiana State University, where he would work with Robert Penn Warren and Cleanth Brooks.) At the same time Caroline was trying to find a cheap house for Una and Phelps Putnam, but the cheapest she could find in Princeton was for eighty dollars a month, including coal, and too expensive.

And that spring Caroline took on William Slater Brown, one of the many people for whom she assumed responsibility and tried to help, giving freely of her time, her energy, her contacts, her hospitality. Bill Brown and his wife, Sue Jenkins, had stood up with Caroline and Allen when they were married. Now Sue had left Bill, and Caroline invited him for a visit. One night they were talking about Tory Valley, where Brown still lived. Caroline felt that he was obsessed by the valley, hating it and loving it, and decided that for fifteen years Bill had been unconsciously collecting material for a book. She asked him why he didn't write a novel about the valley. Bill, drunk by that time, said, twirling his mustache, "I will do it, Caroline. I will write it at once. I will write a thousand words every day and hand them to you every evening."

Caroline and Allen had frightful hangovers the next day, and Caroline spent her time taking Anacin; that evening Bill came down with a complete outline of his novel. He began writing the next day and, just as he had promised, wrote a thousand words a day. It went fast, because he had no research to do, and Caroline thought it was "marvelous stuff."

"Mama *made* him stop drinking and finish his novel," Nancy said later. "She *squoze* that novel out of him."

"He is working steadily, even while drunk, and it is going to be fine if he finishes it," Caroline wrote Ward Dorrance. "If he doesn't finish it I shall never speak to him again. Allen says he thinks it is a risk to urge him on. If he doesn't finish it . . . he will be dreadfully demoralized, but I have got so interested in the book that I don't care what happens to the man. Besides, you have got to take risks in this our life."

Bill and Nancy had long conversations about her tactics and strategy with her sixty-five boyfriends. "I don't think you're managing him right," Brown would say. "Try this . . ." Caroline and Allen were uneasy as the parents of a beautiful, popular teenage girl. Sometimes Caroline was calm and understanding and would order the other grownups upstairs so Nancy's beaux could talk to her. Sometimes she helped Nancy defy Allen when, for instance, he forbade her to go with an upperclassman to Princeton house parties when she was fifteen. (Neighbors saw Nancy crawling down a ladder from her bedroom window, while Caroline held the ladder steady below.) At other times she became hysterical, insisting that Allen go roam the streets to look for Nancy if she missed her curfew.

Allen wanted to spend the summer in the South, not Princeton, and the Tates had been talking of joining the Lytles at their farm in Tennessee. Caroline wrote to Andrew that she felt a little sheepish about settling on a bride, and offered to bring her cook if Edna wanted her. She could also provide a cow. The Normans had Daisy and Bill Gordon had Minnie, but Minnie's heifer had had a calf by then. Caroline hoped none of the lads on the next farm was the right age to take an interest in Nancy—they thought simple country life with no boys around would be just the thing for her. Her head had been pretty well turned by this winter's conquests. "It happens most of the girls in that school are dreadfully plain," Caroline said.

As the time approached, Caroline got a little scared. "Do you reckon you can stand up under the combined assault?" she wrote Edna. "I have taken a vow to help as much as I can but it's the planning for a lot of people that takes it out of you and I can't help you with that. However I can and will hoe and wash dishes and make beds. If it does get too strenuous, we will just trek over to Benfolly."

She then asked Edna if she would consider taking a boarder—Bill Brown. He was one of the most charming men that ever lived and one of the most soothing, Caroline said, and she was afraid if Bill went back to Tory Valley he would not finish his book because of Sue. Sue had been leading strikes but she had not had a strike on for some time, and Caroline felt sure she would go to Tory Valley to spend the summer and "take Bill to pieces and scatter him over those New England pastures." After this passionate plea for an invitation to Brown, she said, "Anyhow as Mr. Norman says, I thought I'd just name it to you."

Whether it was because of Bill Brown or not, plans changed, the Lytles came to Princeton, and the summer of 1940 was one of those comic communal experiences that occurred so often in the lives of the Tates. Andrew was still working on his novel about de Soto. Caroline was still struggling with *Green Centuries*. She wrote Lon Cheney to ask Fannie to send her at once Judge Williams's *Old Times in Tennessee* from the Vanderbilt library. "This library doesn't have it or anything else I need," she said. Bill Brown was writing his novel. Allen, perennially blocked, was trying to write anything he could. Edna kept house. "She spent less than Caroline and had two more people to feed. . . . There was no private life," said Andrew, who had not been married long. "The house was old and shaky and in the acrobatics of love I shook the house and woke everybody up. Nancy thought it was an earthquake." They all went swimming every afternoon at the home of Henry Church and had parties at night.

When the summer was over, the Lytles went back to Tennessee, and Richard Blackmur and his wife, Helen, arrived and settled in a house on Linden Lane near the Tates. Blackmur, whose mother had run a boarding house in Cambridge while he worked in a bookstore and audited courses at Harvard, was self-taught; he was thrilled to have a legitimate connection with a great university. Helen was a painter, with white hair and intense blue eyes. The Blackmurs were a wretchedly unhappy couple by all accounts, and the students felt that the Tates' marriage was made in heaven compared to the Blackmurs'.

Caroline had by this time accumulated a bushel basket full of notes and still had 40,000 words to go on *Green Centuries*, but she took time out to acquire a new hobby that would interest her for years and would provide her with one of the motifs in *The Women on the Porch*. Bill Brown taught her how to collect mushrooms.

They first went mushroom-hunting down by Lake Carnegie in Princeton, and then went to Washington's Crossing on the Delaware River and in a pine grove gathered one bushel of *Boletus subluteus*. "I never expected to find more mushrooms than I could gather but there they were . . . a wonderful sight. Brown *boleti*, charming little things, pushing up through the pine needles and right beside them hundreds of *Amanita muscaria*. (The *Amanita muscaria* is yellow with scarlet spots and is perfectly beautiful. Yes, it is deadly poison.) What Bill and I long to find now is the coral mushroom. We were quite cautious about the *boleti*. We tried them out first on a lot of Italians, the university head gardener, a negro, and the brother of the tailor. Then Bill and I ate a large bait. We wouldn't let Allen and Nancy have any that first night," she recounted to Dorothy Van Doren. She and Bill ate many of them, creamed on toast (with garlic and onion). "We rested nicely and arose the next day with an appetite for more."

Caroline took 170,000 words of her novel to Scribner's, where she thought everyone was taken aback by the size of her manuscript. Max rallied and took her to lunch at the Ritz and praised her Indians. He told her for once what Caroline said she would have said herself, "that they are the best Indians anybody has done yet."

She added that her path was very plain before her: "Just one novel after another. The other night I called for a little less noise on the plea that I was writing a book. Nancy observed that she had known me now for fifteen years and in all that time she could not remember a moment when I wasn't writing a book, 'except the three months that Daddy was finishing his novel and you were scared to start one.' "

Bill Brown was at his Aunt Lydia's, where he went to church and at night played cards with his aunt. Caroline said she missed Bill—he was fun to have in the house. (When Bill inherited some money from one of his aunts, Caroline remarked, "Old aunts in the North always leave people legacies. In the South, old aunts come to live with you.") Months later, in the summer of 1941, she was still concerned about him because he was drinking too much. She concocted complicated schemes involving Malcolm Cowley and Bill's brother Fritz, in which small amounts of money would be doled out to him at Tory Valley until he finished his novel, and she wrote urgent letters about these schemes. Every time Sue came back, Bill began to drink again and didn't write, Caroline said. At one point Caroline sent money to a storekeeper in Patterson with instructions to give Bill a certain amount of groceries each week. When Bill did finish his novel, *The Burning Wheel*, the next year, she rallied friends to help him get it published, and after it was published she badgered them again to review and to publicize it. She reviewed it herself in *Books*, and it was reviewed favorably in *The Nation*, *The New Republic*, *The New Yorker*, *The New York Times*, and *Saturday Review of Literature*.

PRINCETON, 1941–1942

In early 1941 Allen started seeing Dr. Max Wolf on East Seventy-ninth Street in New York, hoping for a cure for his migraine headaches. Dr. Wolf, recommended by Stark Young, was newly arrived from Vienna and treated Marshall Field, Elsie de Wolfe, the decorator, and Alfred Vanderbilt, among others, and charged them high fees. "Ordinary people," though, paid only twenty dollars a visit. Stark Young persuaded Ellen Glasgow to see Dr. Wolf, and she said she never felt better, and Allen sent John Peale Bishop and John Crowe Ransom's wife to him. Caroline hoped he was not a quack. While one friend said he was, somebody else told her other doctors made that claim because Dr. Wolf knew so much and "was up to all sorts of new tricks learned in Vienna." Wolf told Allen that the old-fashioned method of bleeding was of great value and that he bled himself at least once a month. At any rate, said Caroline, in one visit he took more interest in Allen's "liver and lights" than Rainey, the doctor in Princeton, had taken in two years.

It seemed for a while that Allen had been cured of all his ailments. His migraine headaches vanished. His blood pressure was up to normal. "All but four of the five flu germs that he was carrying around have disappeared," Caroline wrote to Katherine Anne. "I always thought

Allen was one of the laziest people I ever knew and now I begin to think he has been a hero all these years."

Allen was dismissed by Dr. Wolf and missed the visits. One morning he drove to work, felt faint, and had to leave the car and take a taxi home. He got into bed and Caroline telephoned Dr. Wolf, who said that the trouble was circulatory and that Allen must get up at once and exercise violently for ten minutes. Allen, all set for a day of invalidism, hopped out and did setting-up exercises.

Allen followed Wolf's orders to exercise the next time he had a fainting spell. Caroline wrote Edna Lytle that "he ran at a trot through the house (pausing occasionally to look in the mirror, Nancy says) . . . yelling, 'Call Rainey, call Burbidge, call Summers . . . no, call Wolf! I am dying. I am numb to the knees, have no feeling in my fingers now. Call Rainey. Call Burbidge.' Rainey finally arrived, took a look at him, pinched his ears which he said were the color of a healthy baby and told him to behave himself. Rainey has given him every test he can think of and says there is nothing the matter. But there must be we both think. My opinion is that it is either the thwarted migraine headache or else it is his subconscious protesting against writing the novel which he is trying to start. It sounds awful, these spells. . . . We're off to the Churches' pool. Harry is dreadfully jealous of Allen's spells but tries to conceal it."

Bibi the dachshund had been run over, and Bub got all of Caroline's attention. She loved to talk for him and said that Bub had another dreadful habit, taking his pulse and calling for the vet. " 'Call Sylvester,' he yells and trots through the house," she said.

Once Allen had another spell in the middle of the night. Caroline told the Lytles that it was mostly insomnia, "provoked by rage at Nancy. . . . When I commented on his healthy appearance, he said no wonder with the blood about to burst out of all his veins. He made me call the doctor at two o'clock. The doctor prescribed soda. The next time I am just going to hold down the receiver and pass on to him an imaginary line from the doctor. I know all the responses by this time."

Caroline went to Dr. Wolf about her back. "I have germs that are much more interesting than any Allen ever had—streptococcic, rheumatic," she wrote to Dorothy Van Doren. "He is curing them with some of his magic vaccines. Already I am out of pain and seem to be getting better every day. It is wonderful. Allen was a little jealous. He said as we were leaving the office, 'He said my tongue was a *little* coated.' "

They were relieved and pleased when Allen was hired for a third year at Princeton. "It is in the nature of a third term," Caroline wrote

Jean Stafford, referring to Roosevelt's unprecedented third term as president. "The committee met the other day and solemnly complimented Allen but the feeling is that it is dangerous for a man to remain too long. He might indoctrinate the students with his point of view.' Allen says he doesn't know what else in the name of God he'd indoctrinate them with, unless he had no point of view, in which case he might as well not be here."

Cleanth Brooks came to lecture at Princeton in May. "It was awkward, though," Caroline wrote Edna. "For several hours we were provided with two lecturers. Allen got the dates mixed up and Wallace Stevens and Cleanth were about to have a head-on collision. After much racking of brains we finally paged Stevens in the Penn station just as he was about to board a Princeton train. He was very nice about it, though everybody was scared. He is said to be so violent. Cleanth gave a fine paper." (When Wallace Stevens did come, he was "the queerest fish," according to Caroline: "one of the best poets writing in the world today and also a big business man.")

"I hurt Cleanth's feelings when he was here," she wrote Edna and Andrew on May 4, 1941. "I jumped on him about the way they have been turning my stuff down lately, with letters that might have been written by the editor of the *Atlantic Monthly*. [Brooks was coeditor, with Red Warren, of *The Southern Review*.] 'This isn't quite it,' or 'it doesn't quite jell' are the expressions that particularly infuriated me. I am one of their oldest and I thought most valued contributors and then suddenly I begin getting these letters which mean, if I know anything about editors, 'We wish you wouldn't send anything else but we are determined to be polite about it.' I won't send anything else, of course, but the whole thing is very puzzling."

Caroline wrote to Katherine Anne, sympathizing with what she considered the poor judgment of John Crowe Ransom, editor of *The Kenyon Review*. "Yes, it's like John Ransom to write at long last asking you for something and print that fake thing of Eleanor Clark's. He can't bear for women to be serious about their art. . . . That Clark girl, by the way, seems to me the 1941 version of Laura Gottschalk. She has the same carp-like mouth. I couldn't stand her." She went on to say, "This afternoon I killed off Dragging Canoe and Archy. Tomorrow I write Cassy's death scene, Deo volente. . . ." She hoped to finish the novel that week.

She finished *Green Centuries* in June. The title comes from the poem "Green Centuries," by John Peale Bishop, one of the four poems grouped under the overall title, "Experience in the West." The first lines are:

Courage and hope demand
For here the heart was sound.
The long man strode apart
In green no soul was found,
In that green savage clime
Such ignorance of time.

"Allen helped manfully towards the last," Caroline wrote Edna. "In fact he practically wrote the last chapter. I was off on the wrong foot, striking the folksy note, using too much clinical detail—Cassy dies of pneumonia. Allen stepped in, took a look and pulled the whole thing together with a passage that works in the symbolism of the constellation Orion—very boldly and I think successfully." To Edna again, "Allen has gone over the manuscript, taking out the 'thens,' 'theres,' and 'nows.' They were thick as fleas on a dog's back. He also made me take out some of the dialect."

She took the completed manuscript to Scribner's on Friday, June 13, in a driving downpour. There were six hundred pages, sixty-six chapters.

The Tates went to Nag's Head, North Carolina, with the Willard Thorps, hoping the salt water would be good for what they thought was bursitis in Allen's shoulder. "We are simply mad about Nag's Head," Caroline wrote Malcolm Cowley. "The water is wonderful. We bathed until we felt like sea weeds. If you ever want a cheap seaside place to go and can stand the old fashioned family hotel you ought to try Nag's Head. Allen says the First Colony Inn is like the old fashioned resorts of his childhood. There is not a private bath on the place and the screen doors are equipped with powerful springs and slam constantly. The first few days the slamming worried us but after two days you are so drugged by the water and the air that you don't care how much they slam and towards the end of your stay you find yourself slamming the doors yourself with pride in the amount of bang you can produce." They paid twenty-five dollars a week for room and board.

Since Allen said he couldn't go through another Princeton winter without a taste of Monteagle, they went to see the Lytles. They also wanted to read Andrew's novel about de Soto, which he'd been working on for five years.

Edna was expecting a baby in November 1941, and Andrew was in the very last throes of the de Soto novel, *The Moon's Inn*. "My conscience hurt me to be visiting them at such a time but I did enjoy being there," Caroline wrote to Una and Phelps Putnam. "We had two dusky maids in the cave below stairs. Mr. Lytle came up from the plantation every weekend with his truck loaded with melons, tomatoes, squabs, peaches, a young goat—any provender that he raised or found it exciting to buy along the way. We lived mighty well and everybody had fun except poor Andrew. He finished the book and sent it off while we were there. I feel a little sad about the book. It is a fine book, in places magnificent but it lacks the professional touch. I feel that if he had had a few months to work on it he would have had a memorable book. It is splendid but . . . We made him cut sixty thousand words. He said it was like losing a leg. . . . We tried to make him rewrite the beginning . . . but he was like a horse that falls between the shafts, almost incapable of further effort. And Edna, who after all has lived her whole married life with de Soto, couldn't stand any more de Soto. He was afraid, too, to hold it over another publishing season with the world in the condition it's in. . . . Poor Allen has had to read and edit two enormous novels this summer. Mine was six hundred pages and Andrew's five hundred."

That summer she collected mushrooms with Dr. Sedley Ware, a retired history professor known to everyone as Fuzzy, who said she was "very cultivated for a summer person." In twenty years of mushroom-hunting, he had found only one beefsteak mushroom and when he did he brought it to Caroline. "They grow out of trees, look like a piece of liver and taste like steak with onion on it," Caroline wrote the Putnams. "What I can't understand is where all the mushrooms were all the years I wasn't collecting them. I never remember seeing any except the dried puffballs which we called 'Devil's snuffbox' and now I never step out but I see some wonderful thing, like a *sparassis crispa* which looks like a head of lettuce and tastes as we mycologists say, 'Deliciosissima.' Mycologists all use the same style, a little like Lord Macaulay, only a little more florid."

She cooked one of Mr. Lytle's squabs with sour cream and wine and three pounds of mushrooms she gathered off the university's cow pasture. Mushroom-hunting was a wonderful sport, she said, agreeing with Andrew that it was accompanied by the necessary spice of danger. "People always seem to think that if you take up mushrooms you are either planning suicide or yearning to murder somebody but I am awfully careful, eating nothing that Fuzzy Ware hasn't eaten for twenty years," she wrote Una and Phelps Putnam.

Caroline's favorite mycologist was the one who was referred to as "the indefatigable McIlvaine." He had "a cast iron stomach and tasted over a thousand varieties before he went to his reward. I met a biologist yesterday who had sat at the table with McIlvaine. He didn't seem to realize that he had been in the presence of genius and couldn't even remember what he looked like."

Back at Princeton, there was the usual stream of visitors, the usual visits to doctors. Edmund Wilson and Mary McCarthy came and the Cowleys came for the Princeton–Harvard football game. Some of Allen's relatives came for Thanksgiving, and Nancy gave a party for "thirty-five howling young demons."

The cook went to the hospital and Caroline did the housework. "Isn't it fun?" she wrote to the Putnams. "I have been scrubbing the floors. I derange the dirt and push it to some other corner of the house but can never seem to get rid of it." The housework kept her from getting out on her bicycle in the fall weather.

She was about to start a new novel. "The life of a person who is not writing a book is too strenuous for me," she wrote to Little May, repeating an oft-spoken sentence. "I always have the delusion that I will have a little leisure and the minute I am through an avalanche of household chores falls upon me and stuns me. If you stick at it all day long you can sometimes get a thousand or so words written but you can never get the chores cleaned up and out of the way."

"The life of a person who isn't writing a book is too difficult for me," she wrote Lon Cheney. "I have never been so harried and so inadequate in my life as I have been these last few months. I realize that I will always be inadequate at the tasks I have undertaken lately and all I want now is to get back to that desperate daily stint at the typewriter and let the rest go hang."

Just as after she finished *Aleck Maury* she had thought of writing about bird dogs, after *Green Centuries* she thought of writing a piece about bloodhounds. She toyed with the idea of a detective story, "The Blue Boletus," with a Sewanee setting, the corpse a professor. "Hack work, but I begin to think it's time I did some," she said.

Allen, who had trouble with his shoulder all summer, had gone to various doctors, all of whom had diagnosed bursitis. "He was in the hospital twice," Caroline wrote to the Putnams. "They gave him so much dope that he took to having what he calls 'My spells.' He loves to 'doctor,' you know. I forget how many doctors he called in before he was through." When Dr. Wolf came back from vacation, Allen rushed to him. Wolf diagnosed it as a spastic colon. "Wolf took away the bursitis—it was hard after we had lived with it all summer—and centered Allen's attention on his colon where it ought to have been all along. He was convinced that he had acute heart trouble, and indeed his pulse would race, all due, Wolf says, to gas pressure. Wolf says these attacks have every symptom of heart trouble but that Allen is really in good shape. I really got quite worried about Allen for a while. He was developing such an invalid psychology. . . . Now that he knows he has only a case of 'academic guts,' he takes it easier."

She finally began work on the novel, *The Women on the Porch,* and made one "research" trip to Columbia. All her heroes had been strong, silent, and illiterate, she told Katherine Anne, but this one would be different, a historian. The action would shuttle back and forth between an old house in Kentucky and New York City. Since the leading male character was to be a Columbia professor, she "had to find him an office so I'd know what he looked out at, how the light fell, etc." On the way downtown in New York, she saw the *Normandie,* the French luxury ocean liner that had caught fire and keeled over while it was undergoing conversion to a troop ship. It looked, she said, like a wounded animal. She put it in the novel.

When *Green Centuries* appeared, Katherine Anne wrote that it was "a knockout. All of it is good and grand and a splendor to read." They were the first real Indians she'd ever known. "Even you must break down and admit you've done it this time." Christian Gauss told Caroline she had given "a clearer picture of frontier America than I have seen anywhere." She wrote Andrew Lytle that John Crowe Ransom had said he was sorry to see her going over to naturalism, "completely oblivious of the symbolism with which I feared it was too heavily loaded! But then he doesn't know or care anything about fiction." (Caroline still resented all those poets.)

One Sunday afternoon in December, Willard Thorp called to tell his friends about Pearl Harbor, and Caroline said, "I can't live through a fourth war." She thought she had lived through the Civil War. "I feel as if some horrible Grendel were lurking in the marshes and bellowing for a sacrifice of young men, and that all our business nowadays will be to pack them up and ship them off to him properly," Caroline wrote Ward Dorrance. "I am not a Pacifist and I know that war is spiritually necessary, but . . . I don't believe that when they were sending the youths off to the Minotaur each year the Athenian women went on about how nice it was for them to see the world."

The Churches were out of town and the Tates had to give a party every Thursday for three weeks for the Mesures lecturers, among them Red Warren. "Red gave a good one and people liked him though they all said they couldn't understand his Southern accent," Caroline wrote to the Lytles in May 1942. "Manson and Rose who had come down for the lecture got lost on the campus but located 28 McCosh when they heard the accent rolling out on the New Jersey air. It was pleasant having Red here but it was like having someone you had heard a lot about from a mutual friend or someone you had known a long time ago. I think he was much more interested in seeing Albert [Erskine] than in seeing Allen. He got pretty disgusted with Allen when he commented on the preposterous way Katherine Anne has been acting lately and informed the Lowells that never until the other night had he heard anyone speak ill of Katherine Anne—as if people hadn't been sitting around for twenty years talking about Katherine Anne. We decided that Cal Lowell [Robert Lowell's nickname since prep school was Cal, for Caliban and, later, Caligula], who is positively saintly since his conversion, was the only one of us Christian enough to associate with Red these days. I really don't think I ever want to see him again. When anybody prefers Albert Erskine to Allen I think they are pretty dumb."

James Ross, the writer they had befriended in Greensboro, quit his job with the IRS after his novel was published and set forth, as he said, to make a living as a full-time writer. He went to Princeton, where he stayed with the Tates until he moved into a room at Lahiere's Hotel on Witherspoon Street. That spring he decided to marry a Swedish physiotherapist, Alexandra Schaarp, and Caroline, who loved a ceremony, staged their wedding in the Tates' backyard.

She made it a formal ceremony, too, when Robert Giroux brought a contract for *Boston Adventure* out for Jean Stafford to sign, lighting candles for the signing and serving festive fare.

It became certain that Princeton would not hire Allen for a fourth year. The Tates thought at first that they could live off royalties from *Green Centuries*—but it did not earn enough to pay back the advance. Allen had no prospect of a job; he thought of going into the Navy but his bad shoulder kept him out. "Meanwhile he goes to New York a lot and lets it be known that he wants a job and sees people and so on. The job hunting trips usually end up at the Little Hotel on West Fifty First Street where Edmund and Mary Wilson have been staying for the past three weeks. They say they are so broke they can't get out of town," Caroline wrote to Una.

Caroline was outraged when she found out that Allen's successor was to be George R. Stewart, an alumnus of Princeton and author of *Storm*, a Book-of-the-Month Club choice. "He is a high class journalistic writer. . . . I think they ought to have gotten Gypsy Rose Lee—her detective story is exactly the same kind of writing. Allen says the thing that puzzles him is why they ever asked him here in the first place. It does leave rather a sour taste in the mouth. The devil of it is they could have got Eliot. Dick Blackmur is to stay on as a sort of bridge between old and new. I fear it will be rather a strain on him."

Later the Tates came to believe, as Blackmur's biographer Russell Fraser states categorically, that Blackmur helped to get Allen fired, going to Dean Gauss, who had suffered during World War I because of his German name and background, and implying that Allen was a fascist. Caroline spoke years later of "Dick's perfidious tales," but those who were familiar with the politics of Princeton at that time do not believe this for several reasons: one, Dean Gauss, the soul of honor, would not have paid attention to a scurrilous tale like this; two, Dick Blackmur, for the rest of his life, said only good things about Allen; and, three, it is much more likely that Hudson, Dean Root, and the other conservative English professors had had enough of Allen and what they regarded as his intransigence.

In New York one day, Caroline went into Scribner's bookstore and looked for a copy of *Green Centuries*. When she asked a salesperson, he referred her to the books on gardening. Furious with Scribner's for not pushing a book that she had thought would sell well, she decided to change publishers and put her affairs in the hands of Nannine Joseph, a literary agent they had first met at a writers' conference at Olivet in 1936. Caroline wrote to Dorothy Van Doren that an editor at Houghton Mifflin told her that after reading the first long chapter, he feared that her new book would be "light and popular and not one of the author's major works." "It may not be a major work but how I am going to make it light in tone with half the characters shades from the underworld is more than I can see," Caroline said. She had lunch with three people from Harcourt, Brace, and one of them told Nannine Joseph that it was a joy to meet an author who had the real author's approach. When Caroline asked Nannine what the person meant by that, Nannine said he meant that there was nothing commercial about her. In the end Caroline stayed with Scribner's, who agreed to a $1,200 advance; Caroline figured that "with what I owe them [that] makes an advance of twenty-two hundred, more than any other publisher would give on a book, sight unseen. Besides I know they will give me a little more towards the end of the book, if I have to have it." Caroline continued to work out her own book contracts.

George Haight, Andrew's Hollywood producer friend, said *Green Centuries* would not be good for the movies because it belonged to "the coonskin cap group" and verged on "the white wig group." It reflected on the British and reminded readers how we had treated the Indians. Caroline considered him amusing and acute.

Caroline said she and Allen were as "unsettled as a jaybird on a bough." It was amazing how unanimous the colleges were in feeling they could not afford Allen. There was some talk of making Allen editor of *The Sewanee Review* but Alex Guerry was scared of him, Caroline said. Meanwhile, she tried to get a job three days a week at Sarah Lawrence, supervising the college newspaper and teaching newswriting. She thought she had the Sarah Lawrence job in the bag, "but they were so insulting to Allen I withdrew my application."

Allen was offered a job at Louisiana State University but turned it down, declaring that he wanted to write another novel. Balch advanced him $2,000, and the Tates decided to go to Monteagle. "With our combined advances we would have as much money as the job would bring, more when we consider the difference in living expenses at Monteagle and Baton Rouge," Caroline wrote Mark Van Doren.

Robert Lowell and Jean Stafford needed a place to live and gladly accepted the Tates' invitation to join them at Monteagle. They all planned to write like mad. "We will just hole up in a cottage on the mountain until we have finished our respective books. The feather bed was nice while it was under us but now that it has been jerked out from under we find ourselves almost hysterically anxious to be in the South again. I go around grinning like a chipmunk at the farewell parties people are kind enough to give us—I hope they think it's the liquor I take on in large quantities to keep my strength up," Caroline wrote to Malcolm Cowley.

Gas was rationed, but they could get enough to go to Tennessee by pleading change of residence.

Gauss continued to write Allen cordial letters long after he left Princeton, and Tate came back to give the Mesures Lecture in 1943. On May 4, 1943, Gauss wrote him that the group Allen had picked the first year provided two valedictorians and one Latin salutatorian, thus demolishing the argument of the faculty who had said that if boys were allowed to write they would not keep up their grades.

Monteagle with the Lowells,
1942–1943

Caroline often described the winter she and Allen spent at Monteagle with Jean Stafford and Robert Lowell as an idyll. It didn't seem right, she told Katherine Anne Porter, for them to have such a winter when the world was in such a state.

The Tates and the Lowells shared a house called Immokalee (or "New Wormwood") next door to the Lytles' log cabin; Andrew and Edna and their baby were living in Sewanee, where Andrew was teaching at the University of the South. Immokalee had three stories, a dining room, and a kitchen in the basement, but the stairs were easier than those at Benfolly, Caroline insisted. Caroline and Allen had five rooms on the middle floor, and the Lowells and Nancy had the top floor. The Tates lived on $150 a month—their share of the rent was fifteen dollars a month, they had a maid, sent Nancy to private school, and weren't "cramping" themselves. Allen and Caroline provided most of the food that went on the table. (Boxes arrived from Robert Lowell's mother, however, containing fancy English teas and jams.) Caroline and Allen loved Monteagle so much that they were superstitious about it. Allen liked it that occasionally one of the old ladies who summered there would come up to him and say, "I haven't seen you since your Ma used to lead you by the hand over to the mall," but the real reason they liked Monteagle was the way they were consistently able to write. "We always start working like hell as soon as we get here," Caroline said.

All four of them wrote that year. Lowell wanted to write a biography of his great-great-grandfather, Jonathan Edwards, but he began to write a different kind of poetry and had turned out sixteen poems by March 1943. Jean worked on *Boston Adventure,* and had to endure "having [her] novel torn to pieces by fiends in the guise of friends," said Caroline. "We all took a whack at it, and there were three of us."

Caroline worked on *The Women on the Porch,* and felt it would not be like any of her other novels. For one thing, it was not a historical novel, and it would deal with a young woman who discovers her husband's infidelity in New York and flees to her family's home, Swan Quarter, in the South. Once more, Caroline was drawing heavily on her Meriwether background and, this time, on her own life. The heroine, Catherine Chapman, is thirty-five years old, owns a dachshund, and has an unfaithful husband. (Catherine's long automobile trip from New York to Swan Quarter with her dog, which opens the book, is not autobiographical. Caroline never fled alone to Merry Mont.) When the car stalls, Catherine and Heros, the dog, have to fight their way through thickets of brush to get to the old house, where she can see three women on the porch; the porch at Cloverlands served as the model. The women seem to be the three Furies, though they are really Catherine's grandmother (the widow of a Confederate veteran, like Caroline's grandmother), her aunt, and her slightly mad cousin who collects mushrooms.

Caroline was using the Orpheus and Eurydice myth as a framework, with Jim Chapman coming down from New York to lead Catherine back to the land of the living, and Caroline was equally pleased to discover a way of using the interior monologue to make it more dramatic by alternating slices of past and present. "Like 'broken colours,' to use a painter's term," she wrote to William Meredith, a young poet who had been a senior at Princeton the first year Allen taught there. She said she was as excited about it as Uccello was over the discovery of perspective.

Even Allen wrote, working at first on another novel, then abandoning it forever. He translated the "Pervigilium Veneris," ("The Vigil of Venus"), a short hymn to love and springtime by an unknown Latin author. In an introductory note he gave credit to Caroline for the translation of the first line of stanza 21 and to Robert Lowell "for constant criticism." He also wrote several poems, including "Ode to Our Young Proconsuls of the Air" and "Seasons of the Soul." Since he had written very little poetry over the past ten years, this furious production was heartening, especially to Caroline. "When one is married to a poet one always feels a little guilty when he isn't writing poetry," Caroline wrote to Katherine Anne, "the supposition being that he might be writing if he were married to somebody else."

They got up at six, breakfasted in the dark, and Allen took Nancy to meet her school bus. A "little mountain maid" came in at nine, cleaned up, fixed lunch, and left at five. After a morning's work, they ate lunch, and walked in the woods, Caroline looking for mushrooms.

At four o'clock they all went to have a Coke or a chocolate milk at the village drugstore. Before dinner they sat around the fire with drinks and talked about friends. It was "amiable venom" Lowell said. Caroline used Bub, the dachshund, when she wanted to be ugly about somebody, saying, "Bub thinks so and so." After dinner, Jean, Robert, and Allen played three-handed bridge. "I haven't come to that yet, though I will take a hand at setback occasionally," Caroline said. Bub also began to write verse. One effort:

> Zov, zov,
> He don't know
> What he's thinking of.

("Zov," short for "Karamazov," was a nickname that Allen acquired that year. He detested it.)

Another of Bub's poems went:

> I roll in manure
> To insure my glamour.

Caroline had always been fond of Robert Lowell, but she found herself liking him better all the time. He was a remarkable boy, not just a New England eccentric, 1943 model, she said. Allen had been afraid that Lowell's conversion to Catholicism would ruin his poetry, but he decided after a few months that Lowell would become a fine poet. Every Sunday the Lowells took a long bus trip to the nearest Catholic church.

Willard and Margaret Thorp came to Monteagle and ate dinner with the Tates and the Lowells every night. "They had lots of company, lots of picnics," Thorp recalled. "Donald and Theresa Davidson came and John and Robb Ransom—their hospitality struck me. Allen and Robert Lowell and I used to sit on the porch and play pinochle and dip snuff with a sassafrass twig. The college had one grand piano and we went over there every day to play duets. Allen played the violin very well."

Caroline enjoyed the country life. "It has been so long since I've lived in the country that I'd forgotten or can recall only with great difficulty all sorts of things: the sharp line that a shadow falling across a frost-covered bridge will make . . . the way woods look on a moonless night, when there is no electric light anywhere near," she wrote to William Meredith.

In spite of the healthy country life, Caroline picked up some kind of virus. After Nashville doctors put her on a liquid diet, her weight dropped from 139 pounds to 125. She rode the train to New York (thirty dollars round trip) to see "darling Dr. Wolf." Of course he cured her at once and told her to eat anything she wanted. (She dedicated the book she was working on to Dr. Wolf and his wife.) On the trip she ran into Philip Shirkey, one of Allen's students at Princeton. Shirkey had escorted the body of a fellow soldier, who was killed in a plane crash, from their base in El Paso to Bedford, Virginia. Planning to write a short story based on a tale Shirkey told her, she wrote William Meredith to ask him if he wanted to be her collaborator and provide her with details of barracks life. She usually gave collaborators a fifth of the proceeds—sportsmen and soldiers made ideal collaborators, she said.

Caroline took two baskets of mushrooms from Monteagle to Knoxville to show to "the only mycologist in the state," but while he could not identify all her specimens, she returned to Monteagle knowing some new ones. Another time she went to Asheville, North Carolina, to sit at the feet of Miss Emma Morris, who was seventy-three years old and had been feasting for twenty years on *Amanita chloronosma* and other mushrooms that the books said were dangerous.

"The first morning I said, 'Do you feel like taking a walk in the woods?'" Caroline reported about her visit to Miss Morris's. "She leaped from the breakfast table, paused in the kitchen long enough to snatch up a sharp knife—she always cuts specimens for fear of injuring the mycelium—and was off." Caroline had a hard time keeping up with the old lady who went, she said, exactly like a bird dog, and a rangy one at that. Caroline noticed that Miss Morris had trained everyone in the neighborhood to watch for mushrooms. The little children watched the stumps for miles around and came to say, "Miss Emma, there's a chicken mushroom over at such and such a place," and the rector would say, "Miss Emma, you'd better come over to the church yard today. Mr. Seely is pushing up a lot of *camestris.*"

Caroline wrote Fannie Cheney that she was going that day to pick an oyster mushroom she'd been watching for some time and that she was drying chanterelles—they smelled like dried apples and would be grand in spaghetti.

Always scrupulously conscientious about trying out new mushrooms herself before she gave them to anyone else, she ate a mess of *Russula crustosa,* broiled. Everyone was interested to see what would happen. Two doctors sent word they were waiting with stomach pumps. She was in fine shape the next morning and went out to get *Russulae* for the others.

In the middle of the winter the Tates had to go to Benfolly to prepare it for wartime tenants; Clarksville was a boom town. They had furniture reupholstered and cleaned up the place as best they could. "We washed, dusted, and polished practically every article in the house, with no help, of course—you can't get any now in Clarksville for love or money. Sometimes the articles we were washing froze in our bleeding hands. One night I was so weary that I only had strength to pull off my slacks and fell into bed with the rest of my clothes on. I had a spool of thread in my pockets and some buttons. We woke in the morning, tangled like Venus and Mars, in a net of ONT 60 studded with small pearl buttons. If Allen had been a wild beast, taken in a snare, he couldn't have been more furious. Benfolly did look nice, though, when we got it slicked up—unbleached domestic curtains, chastely trimmed with cotton balls, at all the parlour windows and the floors all waxed and the old quilts on the beds."

The worst thing that happened that winter was the quarrel with Andrew Lytle, their closest friend for fifteen years. There were several reasons. Some trouble occurred over the editorship of *The Sewanee Review,* in which both Allen and Andrew were interested. "He regarded me as a rival," Lytle said many years later. "We quarreled." Another reason was more personal and more incendiary. The Tates heard that beautiful Edna Lytle was having an affair with a Sewanee college student, and they were incensed. Caroline made Allen write a letter to Andrew; she wanted him to horsewhip the student. Allen preferred to ignore it, but they both loved drama, and they loved to participate in their friends' lives. There was much driving back and forth to confer with others on the matter, much writing of notes between the two families.

On March 15, 1943, Caroline wrote to Andrew, explaining as she began the letter that she had given him a chapter in *The Women on the Porch* to read because there were some aspects of his father's character she wanted to discuss with him.

> I was impressed by the fact that on his last visit here he solved for me a technical problem that might have held me up for days, weeks. That is, there were some difficult problems of timing involved in that chapter, the whole thing being conditioned by the fact that the hero was dead drunk when he wandered into the cafe. I had to have something damned

good after that 'I have lost my Muse by being silent' passage, or the whole thing would have degenerated into a drunken monologue. I felt that Mr. Lytle's stories about Sawney Webb did the trick better than anything I could ever have thought up for myself and I have felt very grateful to him for supplying them just when they were needed. . . .

She then went on to say that she and Allen had been worried about Andrew that winter. Allen, she said, sometimes foresaw that Andrew would quit writing and degenerate into a sort of country squire who would entertain Nashville people and undergraduates and be popular with successive generations until his stories got too stale for them. On the other hand, she wasn't worried about Andrew anymore; he had two great raconteurs among his forebears—his father and his aunt—and she expected that this power from his family and his own great and original talent would push him inevitably forward. "It is evident that you are in a kind of backwash now but it is probably the prelude to a great surging forward," she said.

She was saying this, she wrote, because she didn't expect to see him and Edna anymore:

> We have been rather dumb about this but we have at last got the point. Don't feel that you have to make a trip over here for another of those evasive talks. There is no use in that—and don't invite us to any more duty dinners and we will reciprocate by not inviting you. I don't expect ever to be friends with you and Edna again, for art is long and life is shorter even than we can imagine and time is rarely given for the kind of adjustments and readjustments that would have to be made in this case. . . . You told Allen that you wanted to stand on your own feet, and that is praiseworthy, I suppose. But few artists have ever succeeded in doing it. Baudelaire used to pray to Poe before beginning his day's work. . . . Find somebody who will take Allen's place in your life. . . .
>
> I will only say now that I have loved you very much in the past and grew to love Edna too and will always cherish the memory of that affection. I am baffled by the fact that the affection you both seemed to have for us . . . has vanished so suddenly. . . . So, Brother, ave atque vale—but remember what I say about your talent. It is the great thing in your life, the thing to which everything else must be subordinated if you are not to rot—and lilies that fester smell far worse than weeds, you know.

"I never answered it," said Andrew forty years later, still chuckling over the last line. "I never paid any attention to her temper. She got over it." Caroline and Andrew were never as close, even though in 1949 Andrew offered one of the warmest, most appreciative reviews ever written about the body of her work, in *The Sewanee Review*. Allen and Andrew eventually resumed their close friendship.

In the midst of all this, Caroline wrote Mark Van Doren a really hateful letter about his new novel, *Tilda*. She wondered why he wrote "these novels," when he knew so much about the art of fiction. While "these novels of yours get a respectful reviewing in things like the *Times* and the *Tribune* . . . none of them have ever had serious reviews. Some day some young poet who has been much influenced by you and has come to resent it in the way that many young men have come to resent Eliot's influence, say, and wants to get quit of you is going to tuck into these novels and boy, won't your fur fly!"

Allen helped Robert Lowell get his poems published in *The Sewanee Review* and *The Kenyon Review* and urged him to send them to Cummington Press, a small publishing company in Cummington, Massachusetts, that specialized in small editions of beautifully designed hand-printed books. Harry Duncan, who operated Cummington, asked for a few more poems to make a book and wanted Allen to write a preface. Lowell's first book, *Land of Unlikeness*, with Allen's preface, would appear in the summer of 1944.

The Tates, as usual, had plenty of company that year. Eleanor Ross, Caroline's student in Greensboro and now a graduate student at Vanderbilt, came the weekend of April 25 to see the Tates. That was the same weekend that Peter Taylor, in the Army and stationed at nearby Fort Oglethorpe, arrived to visit his old Kenyon roommate, Robert Lowell. They all went for a picnic at Fiery Gizzard, and Peter Taylor and Eleanor Ross fell head over heels in love.

They decided to get married on June 4, although they had known each other only a few weeks and had seen each other only on weekends. Both sets of parents were outraged because they were marrying so soon, and they refused to come to the wedding. At the last minute, Taylor's father, mother, and sister arrived from Memphis with a case of champagne. "My father couldn't stand to miss a party," Taylor said. Father James Flye, mentor to James Agee and rector of St. Andrew's in Sewanee, performed the ceremony; Allen gave the bride away; Robert Lowell was best man; and Caroline put on the reception—in spite of the fact that she had spent hours the night before trying to urge the bride to call the whole thing off.

Nancy, Percy Wood, and Jean Stafford lurked in a corner at the reception and got very drunk. "Jean wanted Peter to stay single," Nancy remembered. Shortly afterward, Nancy was engaged to Percy Wood, who had finished college and was about to go into the Navy.

The Lowells left in June 1943, Jean for Yaddo to finish her novel, and Robert for New York, where he hoped to find work as a missionary in Harlem. "I fell in love with Caligula," said Jean, "and now I'm living with Calvin. He's become a fanatic."

In the spring of 1943, Archibald MacLeish asked Allen to become Consultant in Poetry at the Library of Congress beginning August 1, 1943. While Allen told Katherine Anne that he was to be a consultant in American poetry and was to check and evaluate the holdings and to recommend titles for purchase, Caroline wrote her that MacLeish wanted to make a critical collection "inside the vast welter," adding that Allen "and Archie have disagreed a good deal in public but they are both very amiable in private so doubtless they'll get along." Allen assured Caroline that they would not be forced to go about and see people. "The worst thing about Princeton was the long, dull, expensive dinners one had to give and go to."

As usual, Caroline hated the idea of leaving the country for a city. She worried about where they would live. There was hardly an unoccupied cranny, she said. She had been to Washington to see Grace and Jerry Lambert, who had moved there temporarily from Princeton, and late in the evening the butler came in to drape linen on the brocade sofa, making up a pallet for the other dinner guest. She realized then that there was a real shortage of living space in Washington.

Besides, Caroline had taken up painting. It was the worst thing to happen to her, she told Katherine Anne, worse than gardening, sewing, or even mushrooms. She used pastels at first; Jean Stafford had brought her some from Nashville. She started at six o'clock in the morning on a portrait of Bub confronted in the woods by a turtle and worked on it until after midnight. She heard Allen say to Nancy, "Look at Mama. It's right pathetic, isn't it?" He was astonished to see that she, who had never held a crayon in her hand before, could produce something that resembled either Bub or a turtle.

Caroline yearned to try her hand at oils, but Allen said she could have no oils until she finished her novel. Caroline went to Nashville to visit Fannie Cheney—Lon was in Washington, working for Senator Tom Stewart of Tennessee—and seized the chance to buy paints. Her first painting was one of Fannie on a green sofa with a yellow shawl behind her. Through the curtained window in the painting one could see a woodland scene with satyrs and nymphs. Allen's old English professor Dr. Mims, horned and hoofed, peered out of a bosque about to pounce on a nymph a younger satyr thought he was going to get. (Robert Lowell once told Caroline that her descriptions of her paintings were much better than the paintings.) "The woodland scene is very interesting," Caroline wrote Katherine Anne. "It looks a lot like the pictures Allen's grandfather and other gentlemen of his vintage used to paint. You know, those cows and sheep in the shade of trees or beside a river, all very shiny and melting into each other. I used to think they strove for that effect but now I see that it comes from

having to do things over and over. I had a hard time with my nude
. . . she kept crying out for umber shadows and nipples and navels
and as soon as I'd get them in she looked like a corset ad. I finally
compromised by making them all sort of mauve and now she doesn't
seem to be advertising lingerie, though I cannot say much else for
her. My, the problems of art! If I finish my novel this fall I'm damned
if I don't take a few lessons, not many, just enough to pick up a few
tricks."

Lon Cheney found the Tates a house at 3418 Highwood Drive,
Southeast. Allen and Caroline set out for Washington, leaving Nancy
behind in Sewanee to stay with friends, Margaret Myers and her husband, George, an Episcopal clergyman.

Washington, D.C., 1943–1944

Everything in the house in Washington was gaudy and undersize, and Caroline promptly named it the Bird Cage, referring to a whorehouse with that name in one of Lon Cheney's novels.

As soon as she had made curtains and contrived shelves for their books, Caroline located a mycologist at Catholic University and discovered a wooded park nearby where she was sure she could find mushrooms. She worried about Jean Stafford, who was ill, finishing up a novel, and expecting her husband to be drafted or jailed as a conscientious objector. Caroline wrote to Jean five or six times, urging her to come to Washington and live with them or find a room near their house. Concern about Jean's health led her finally to write to Robert Lowell's mother. "I tried to make it a very tactful note," she wrote to Jean. "I deplored the fact that the children (I spoke of you and Cal as if you were babes whom I had had under my care all winter). It was too bad that the children had had such heavy doctors' bills. I myself was not very good at managing my own affairs so hesitated to give advice but it had occurred to me that it would be better to have a doctor's bill to end doctor's bills. Our doctor in New York was a celebrated diagnostician, catering to Rockefellers and the like. I felt sure he could get at the root of your trouble and felt sure his charges would be very moderate, since he takes pride in putting artists on their feet. I felt sure he would take you for nothing but we hesitated to do that since we'd sent so many people there. What did she [Mrs. Lowell] think? Should I force my advice on you or not? Etc., etc. Allen pondered the letter and said he thought it was tactful, but of course he's not much of a judge. If she doesn't offer to pay the bill after the letter, she's a—rock-ribbed New Englander. I hope I haven't done wrong to horn in but I have been so worried and felt that something ought to be done."

Jean reported later that Dr. Wolf's magic medicines seemed to be working, but he charged her his regular rate. Caroline was outraged. "Whenever Allen has sent anybody to him who could pay his fancy prices he has said so explicitly. The fact that you were recommended by us should have protected you." She advised Jean to send Dr. Wolf a small token payment at intervals, "very small, very token. That will teach him to go charging artists fancy prices. I'm disappointed in him."

Robert Lowell, who had been paying little attention to Jean's distress, was shocked at what he considered Caroline's intrusion, but the shock was healthy. He, too, wrote his mother about Jean's condition. Mrs. Lowell regarded the letter as further evidence that the Tates were to blame for Lowell's behavior. At any rate, Jean's illness seems to have cleared up.

Almost as soon as he started work, Allen found he could have an assistant. "What about Mrs. Cheney?" he asked. The people at the Library of Congress thought Fannie Cheney would be wonderful, and she agreed to come. The Tates and the Cheneys could share the Bird Cage.

"The Tates set the tone," recalled Lon Cheney. "Fannie and I hadn't lived outside the State of Tennessee before. We drank right smartly." (People who visited the Bird Cage recall parties at which guests were each served a bottle, not a glass, of Jack Daniel's sour mash whiskey.) "It was quite an establishment—incessant company, so much that we had to sleep some of them in the attic and some in the basement. Bill Meredith slept on the floor of a screened porch. Robert Lowell came." Allen told Lowell he could get him a job either as a doorman or a guard at the Capitol. "A doorman has lots of time to read," Caroline wrote Jean. "A guard has to step around more. The guard-ship is under Stewart's patronage and Lon has that in his pocket. . . . I think in some ways it might be pleasanter than office work."

On their way to Washington from Monteagle the Tates had come through Chattanooga, where Caroline had picked up Jessie McGehee, Pidie's maid, to bring with her. Jessie was bored in Washington, and Caroline used precious rationed gas to drive her around to amuse her. One Sunday she took Jessie to a black church, and when the preacher asked the visitors to introduce themselves, Caroline stood up and said, "This is my friend Jessie McGehee and she doesn't have any friends." Jessie made two friends at church that day. Shortly, however, she became very ill and began to hemorrhage. Fannie Cheney remembers that Caroline washed out the bloody sheets without complaining, took Jessie to the doctor, and finally took her back to Chattanooga.

After Fannie arrived, Caroline said she was floating like a cloud above the household cares. She wrote Jean Stafford that she would not be worth killing when the year was over, because living with Fannie was very demoralizing. Fannie, without grumbling or apparent effort, did all the things that Caroline said she was used to doing with clenched teeth and curses. After Caroline finished her novel they would have to make some other arrangement, but for the present it was a dream come true. "She insists on doing the shopping since the breadwinners have the car and I have to walk a half mile when I do it. . . . Once I am out of touch with the shopping I can't seem to take hold anywhere."

At work Fannie worked on the bibliography for Allen's *Sixty American Poets, 1896–1944,* and at home she did most of the cooking, all quite cheerfully. In fact, she recalls that when she arrived, "Caroline had done all the dirty work of pulling down the tacky things and putting up simple curtains. Caroline did most of the cooking, even while she was working on her novel. We had food rationing. Herring roe weren't rationed. We never had company that we didn't have herring roe in sour cream. You could get Smithfield ham and she'd get one pound sliced for a dollar. You could serve five or six or eight people. We had kidneys a little bit too often. They weren't rationed, but nobody liked them. And if Caroline was really pressed, the kidneys came bleeding to the table. That spring, she went out early to get poke salad [wild pokeweed] before the leaves came out—there were some little woods six blocks from our house—and she served it with lemon butter, like asparagus."

Marcella Winslow reported to her mother-in-law in Memphis on a dinner at the Bird Cage. "When Caroline invited me she said the Huntington Cairns were the only other ones coming; that she was wearing a long dress, because she never felt much like 'a dinner' if she didn't dress." Marcella, arriving in a long dress and pearls, was met by Caroline in a shirtwaist and skirt and moccasins. "What's more, the shirtwaist was hanging out the back," said Marcella. Mrs. Cairns had on what looked like hunting boots and a tweed suit. Fannie Cheney wore slacks, but changed into a velvet dress after dinner. Allen read his "Vigil of Venus" and Caroline displayed her pastels for criticism and smothered

Bub with phrases of love from Allen's poem. "Everyone decided that he, or she, had at some time contemplated suicide, except me," said Marcella.

Marcella could tell that the Tates were somewhat disconcerted by the success of Mrs. Winslow's book, *The Dwelling Place*, which had just been published, when Mrs. Winslow was in her late sixties. "To have such good reviews at her age for a first book!" recalled Marcella later. Mrs. Winslow would astonish them further by going on to publish four novels in her seventies.

Nancy arrived and began work at the Library of Congress, earning $1,700 a year. "Imagine an untrained little twirp like Nancy making a hundred and forty a month!" Caroline wrote Jean.

Caroline finished *The Women on the Porch* and turned it over to her housemates. Allen and Lon had no hesitation about criticizing it, but Fannie restricted her activities to looking up facts for Caroline in the Library of Congress. Caroline felt that Allen and Lon had saved the book, if not her life. "But God, I got worn out with it all," she wrote Jean. "In fact, I have a white streak up the front of my hair that wasn't there two weeks ago." Maxwell Perkins told her that if she wanted spring publication she had better get the manuscript in. "I turned from the kitchen table to my desk and scarcely rose therefrom for eight days. I thought I knew something about working under pressure but there is always something to learn about human endurance in this trade of ours. I had already rewritten the chapters in which Chapman is introduced twice but I scrapped them and wrote two more, then revised the train chapter drastically and corrected the whole manuscript. It was all about young love. You can imagine the grim visage I bent over the task."

In the midst of final revisions, Caroline had to go to Florida to see about her father, who was in Orange General Hospital in Orlando with a prostate infection. She wrote to the group at the Bird Cage, urging them to keep up their walking. "If you could see Dad's sufferings, you would be frightened of what a sedentary life can do to you," she said. Her father was delirious, and a beast—once a lamb, then a polecat—hung over his bed. The urologist was "mean" and wouldn't answer her questions.

While Caroline was in Florida, Nancy and Percy Wood, now in the Navy, were married. "Daddo agreed to the wedding because he was bored," Nancy said many years later. "He liked to buy cases of champagne." Percy's mother did not approve of Nancy and objected strenuously to the wedding. Nancy outtalked her. Lon Cheney was kneeling by the phone while Nancy talked to Amelia Wood, and he was so impressed with her common sense and tact in handling Mrs. Wood that he was convinced that Nancy, although she was only eighteen and had not finished high school, was mature enough to get married. The wedding took place at the Episcopal chapel in Garrett Park, Maryland, on January 3, 1944, a day of torrential rain.

Caroline wrote for news of the wedding but said that she was not going to worry about Nancy and Percy anymore. "So far as I know their kidneys function all right. That is the main thing in this life. I discerned that when Nancy was born and every day with Dad confirms the impression."

While Allen was having wedding announcements printed and mailed, Caroline wrote to him and to Lon with instructions about patching up the manuscript, and sent them a new passage to end a chapter. "Now, Zov," she wrote Allen, "if you are ever going to help me, this is the time. I want some quotation from Ovid, something about love. The bum murmurs one or two words of it, looks away, makes another effort, and comes finally with the whole quotation. You will have to read the manuscript carefully to see where it fits in. Also please put in the name of the university for me. Fill in anything that needs to be filled in. Punctuate or change in any way you want to, but get it off to Max. Change the bum's name for me if it doesn't sound right. . . . You will find a duplicate manuscript lying on the floor of my study."

Her father was still delirious, alternately bellowing like a bull or snarling like a tiger. "His long study of animal life enables him to make the sounds quite realistic," she wrote Jean Stafford. "I am kept busy every second, attending to his real or imaginary wants. It is not a dull life, but a strange one. I feel quite goofy myself sometimes." Caroline ate her meals at a drugstore, and was often miserable, but in her letters home she characteristically described the flora—the orange trees and palm trees—around the lake near the hospital.

Mr. Gordon grew worse. "Last night he wanted to get up to the ceiling where all those animals were," she wrote to Allen. "He is dying . . . the same way Cousin Robin and Uncle Jimmy died—only they were worse—calling all the time for guns to shoot themselves with. He curses horribly."

When her father died, Caroline took his body back to Kentucky for burial—and rode the train from Nashville to Monteagle, where she spent one night with Nancy and Percy, who were honeymooning in a friend's cottage. She stopped off in Chattanooga to see Peter and Eleanor Taylor before returning to Washington.

With the manuscript of *The Women on the Porch* off her hands, she plunged into painting, enrolling for lessons with Karl Knath and C. Law Watkins at the Phillips Gallery in Washington. Caroline always praised Watkins and regarded his book, *The Language of Design,* which explains the emotions that geometrical forms can convey, as nothing short of a masterpiece. She continued to paint, mourned when her lessons with Watkins were over, and loved taking visitors to look at pictures at the National Gallery. She painted a picture of Janice Biala, who came down with her new husband, Alain Daniel Brüstlein, an artist who did a great deal of work for *The New Yorker,* signing with only his first name, to visit. Caroline also painted Bub as a sleeping gypsy. "The Phillips people say I am not a true Primitive, just naïve," she wrote to Jean.

Nancy came to Washington while Percy was in training. When John Peale Bishop, who had been asked to be resident fellow in comparative literature at the Library of Congress, came to stay, his appearance shocked them all. At fifty-one he had suddenly turned into an old man, Caroline wrote to Jean: "He totters, gasps and heaves. Very much like Ford he is, these days. Has developed the same trick of suddenly sitting back on his hunkers and being an old man while he regards the passing show with a fishy eye. Allen feels awfully sorry for him but his plight leaves me pretty cold. I am fond of John but he always did make me tired." Bishop stayed at the Bird Cage for a while, then rented a room across the street and ate his meals with the Tates and the Cheneys. "He got a bad cold and everybody—except hard-hearted me—was afraid he'd get pneumonia so we turned Nancy out of her bed and installed him there, and he gasped and wheezed for several days and finally got strong enough to move. Margaret ought to come down here and look after him."

Bishop left soon for his home on Cape Cod, ill with a fatal heart condition. "And we may have brought his death on," Lon Cheney said years later. "We had a lot of steps leading to our house, but the house across the street had eighty steps. I think that brought on his heart attack."

"Thank God, I only criticized John behind his back," Caroline wrote to Jean. "I really slaved for him while he was here." Allen went up to Cape Cod for the funeral, and Caroline went as far as New York, where she saw Janice, but missed Jean Stafford.

Katherine Anne Porter, separated from Albert Erskine, was asked to replace Bishop as resident fellow at the Library of Congress. She arrived without a cent and lived in the basement playroom of the Bird Cage. Caroline admired and loved Katherine Anne. "She would walk miles to get you a bouquet of flowers or a jug of wine and present the gift gracefully," she wrote Jean. But she thought Katherine Anne undependable and—far worse—insufficiently passionate about her art. It maddened Caroline that Katherine Anne would spend hours putting on makeup and getting dressed or while away an entire day cooking an elaborate meal when, Caroline felt, she should have been writing. One morning when Katherine Anne was sleeping late in the basement, Caroline went down and shook her awake. "Get up, get up," she shouted. "You have a God-given talent. Get up and use it."

When young men came to call on Nancy, Katherine Anne was apt to hang around and flirt with them. Allen felt that Katherine Anne simply talked too much. At any rate, she and Caroline had a huge quarrel that began, according to Nancy, when the two of them were discussing their Southern childhoods and began to argue over how an old verse went:

> The turkey was so cool and ca'm
> She did not give a damn. . . .

Marcella Winslow thought the quarrel began over a bottle of perfume. Allen told Katherine Anne's biographer forty years later that Caroline was jealous of Katherine Anne's fame and the fact that the Cheneys were more interested in Katherine Anne than they were in Caroline. Whatever the causes, the two women ended up screaming at one another. Caroline was perhaps the angrier of the two. As one of her friends said thoughtfully about another outburst, "Caroline was subject to an *abstract* rage." Her temper flared spectacularly, and then disappeared. The next day she would literally not remember the angry things she had said the night before. She would begin letters to friends by berating them for some misdeed in insulting terms and end with expressions of affection and offers of help if needed in the future. Both sentiments would be sincere. In this particular case, it was plain that Katherine Anne would have to fly the Bird Cage, but with the wartime housing shortage she could find no other place to live. Allen went over to Georgetown and asked Marcella Winslow if Katherine Anne could stay with her.

The Women on the Porch appeared that spring. It is a novel full of people without hope. Cousin Daphne, the mushroom collector, has led a lonely life since she was abandoned on her wedding night when her husband found out she had no money. Aunt Willy's life will be equally bleak; she will have to nurse her mother, who has a stroke toward the end of the book, and she turns down a proposal of marriage from Quentin Durward Shannon, the tenant farmer who is helping her train her horse. The horse, a discard of Elsie Manigault, a neighbor modeled on the rich Mrs. Hunter Meriwether, blossoms under the care of Willy and Quentin. When the horse is electrocuted, Willy's one remaining interest in life is gone. Elsie Manigault has built a new house, for which the architect was Roy Miller, a homosexual from

New York; he has to leave after he makes advances to a black houseboy. Catherine has an affair with young Tom Manigault, in an episode that was certainly not autobiographical. She returns to New York when Jim Chapman—Orpheus—comes to fetch her.

There are so many interior monologues—the reader goes into the minds of Catherine, Willy, Daphne, Jim Chapman, Tom Manigault, Elsie Manigault, even Maria, the cook—that the narrative energy is diffused. In Jim Chapman, the ineffectual man of letters makes his first appearance as Caroline's new heroic type. Daphne and Willy are two of the most interesting women in all of Caroline's books, and both are doomed to bleak, unfruitful lives. The author condemns Roy Miller's homosexuality so harshly that the reader recoils. In spite of these faults, the brilliant writing and the close observation of nature redeem the book.

Orville Prescott in *The New York Times* called it a "cryptic and peculiar novel." He added that Caroline had more power over words than most and was also equipped with greater perception into the secret depths of human psychology than most, but that the novel was wholly unsatisfactory as a story about human beings.

Edmund Wilson wrote to Caroline to tell her that he could not review her book favorably for *The New Yorker* because he thought it was a failure. Stung to fury, Caroline wrote him that the problems involved in her book were posed by Henry James. "I was trying to solve the problems that he doesn't often succeed in solving in some of his short stories. . . . I call it the circumnatural for lack of a better label. . . . As to the use of local detail, isn't all detail local? . . . If you can find one detail in my book which is used for picturesque effect, and not to give immediate reality to the scene of action, I shall be grateful to you; for only if my detail is picturesque may it be called 'local,' in your sense. . . . I know that Orpheus and Eurydice is an awfully old story, but I thought that if I let hell yawn between husband and wife there might be some little interest in the situation. But I see that I was wrong. . . . You know, Edmund, I have sat around for nearly twenty years listening to you talk, often about the novel. I don't think it ever occurred to you during that time that I might possibly have something interesting to say. But I think you'd do well to listen occasionally to what fiction writers have to say. It seems to me that both in conversation and in your criticism you show great interest in novelty of subject and almost no interest in technique. . . . But please, in memory of all those hours that I have listened to you talking through your hat, don't have my book reviewed in the *New Yorker* at all."

Caroline, defending her book with spirit, makes a point that many a married woman has wanted to make to many a man who paid attention to her husband's opinions but not to her own. Indeed, it should have occurred to Edmund Wilson that Caroline "might possibly have something interesting to say" about the novel.

Allen often cited *The Women on the Porch* as an example of how little Caroline knew about marriage. He asked her why Jim was unfaithful to Catherine, and when Caroline said she didn't know, Allen said that proved his point. Caroline conceded in a letter to Sally Wood that relations between Catherine and her husband were not defined clearly enough. There should have been more of their life together, she said. "None of my books ever seems round enough. They are always too lean somewhere." She complained that critics said she was obsessed with the past, that her present seemed pale. She was, on the other hand, extremely proud of her use of the "circumnatural," which she defined for Sally as "the intangible verities that lie about us and are yet not supernatural." This might be a real contribution to the art of fiction, she said, confessing that her ambition was to be an "inventor" in fiction, not just an "innovator," as Ezra Pound defined the terms. She wrote Jean Stafford that she had been "writing very lucidly about something that is quite complicated, and there is nothing that annoys people more."

She was thinking next of writing a book about a black Guggenheim fellow, a painter, she told Sally.

As Allen's year at the Library of Congress drew to a close—he had found the job rather boring—he was at last named editor of *The Sewanee Review,* and Caroline happily began house-hunting in Sewanee.

Before they left Washington, however, they had a big party. "Willard Thorp and Mark Van Doren were here . . . and we had a case of Jack and a Kentucky ham. . . . It seemed to be quite a success. Denis Devlin [a poet and first secretary at the Irish embassy], always the last to leave, went to sleep in our bed. Nancy, who had been asleep for hours, woke up, found her father and mother sleeping on a cot in the basement, grew very indignant and went upstairs and routed the sleeping Denis, who, she complained, was snoring like a hog. [Alexis] Leger was here and talked to an admiring circle—the chairs stayed in the same position and people slipped in and out of them— about his adventures with Stalin, Mussolini and other worthies."

Sewanee, 1944–1945

The Tates called the house they rented in Sewanee The Robert E. Lee, and, like the Memphis police chief, it was named not for the general but for the steamboat. Big and white, with a curved front piazza, it appeared to be steaming down the Mississippi. The house had been built in 1890 and its many bay windows seemed to pull the sunlight indoors. It stood on the edge of dense woods, not far from a bluff from which, on a clear day, you could see for thirty miles. Nancy, pregnant, came over first to begin getting the house ready. When the Tates arrived, they hung their Confederate flag on the stairwell, put the luster pitcher from Allen's family on the mantel, and began to collect furniture to fill up the nobly proportioned rooms.

Caroline and Allen went to Benfolly to pick up what furniture they could for the Robert E. Lee and to get Benfolly ready for the new tenants, three USO hostesses. It was an arduous task. Benfolly was hot and dirty, the water was turned off, and they had to sleep on bare mattresses and could not take baths. They stopped in Chattanooga to visit Pidie, who wrote to a relative, "Isn't it awful the way they move around? No wonder Carolyn's head is turning gray." (Caroline's family continued to spell her name the old way.) They bought a mahogany sofa and six chairs when a Monteagle cottage was sold, and brought some things from Washington. The Robert E. Lee began to look furnished.

Caroline and Nancy used plant-bed canvas, only a little thicker than cheesecloth, to make curtains for the windows in the living room. "We dyed them red," Caroline wrote to Jean, "and of course they warped, and getting the hems even was the devil's own job. The stuff is so thin it took four curtains to each window." The walls were painted gray and hung with the family portraits and Janice Biala's painting of Good King René's castle at Tarascon. On the mantel with the luster pitcher was the bullet mold that had belonged to Allen's Greatuncle Benny, who died at the age of eleven. Allen said his mother had always kept it where she could put her hand on it and he liked to do the same.

Sewanee suited Caroline. Although it was not Monteagle, there was still the same coolness, the same feeling of "rustic ease." She liked picnics at Fiery Gizzard and enjoyed Sewanee characters like Fuzzy Ware. It suited her to live near the low stone monument to Confederate General Edmund Kirby-Smith, who had refused to surrender when the Civil War was over and had led his men off to Mexico. (The general eventually came back to the United States and ended up at Sewanee, a math professor.) She plunged into picking and canning blackberries, anticipated mushroom-hunting, and painted a picture, *Dream of Fiery Gizzard,* that showed Bub seated beside a casement opening on a mass of wild magnolia leaves. There was great excitement that summer in Sewanee because a group of men had discovered the remains of a saber-toothed tiger embedded in limestone in a cave. (Allen went to the cave with them and couldn't sleep that night, Caroline said, for reflecting on the dangers he had undergone during the day.)

While Percy was off at midshipman's school at Columbia, they all waited for Nancy's baby, which the doctor said was due October 1. With wartime shortages, they had a hard time collecting enough diapers, but they finally managed. Nancy grew more unwieldy every day. The baby, said the obstetrician, was far too fat. They would all be glad when he was there, or would they be "laughing out of the wrong sides of our mouths"? Caroline tried to remember what it was like to take care of a small baby—and went blank. She hoped that Nature would "twang the right chords in the Fat Girl's bosom." It would be grand if she could take care of him herself, Caroline said. She was going to try to be one of those grandmothers who don't interfere, and she was glad to see that Nancy, who was not quite nineteen, seemed to be maturing so rapidly that she might be equal to taking care of a baby. To Allen, Nancy appeared as complacent as Io. Everybody was sure the baby would be a boy. Caroline's brother Morris came for his annual visit and suggested Nancy name the baby "O jocund day" and call him Jock. A neighbor told Caroline that when her baby was born her mother collapsed and took to her bed. "I hope to do better than that," Caroline said.

Allen loved his job as editor of *The Sewanee Review* and began immediately to line up contributions from writers he admired—T. S. Eliot, Wallace Stevens, Alexis Léger (writing under the name St.-John Perse), W. H. Auden, Denis Devlin, John Crowe Ransom, Kenneth Burke, Herbert Read, Dylan Thomas, Katherine Anne Porter, Richard Blackmur, Randall Jarrell, Wyndham Lewis, Robert Lowell, Jacques Maritain, Marianne Moore—and to open the door to younger writers like Peter Taylor, John Berryman, and Elizabeth Hardwick. (Hardwick was a young woman born in 1916 in Lexington, Kentucky, and educated at the University of Kentucky in Lexington. She came to New York, much as Caroline had twenty years before, to become a writer. When her first novel, *The Ghostly Lover,* was published in 1945, she attracted the attention of several editors, among them Philip Rahv at *Partisan Review* and Allen.) Allen had the *Review* redesigned by P. J. Conkwright of the Princeton University Press and obtained pledges from donors so he could pay contributors. Within a few issues, *The Sewanee Review* had changed from a sleepy academic journal into a leading literary magazine. He needed an assistant/secretary and Caroline helped him locate Mildred Haun, a twenty-two-year-old former student of Donald Davidson's who had studied writing at the University of Iowa, taught school, worked as an editorial assistant at the Methodist Publishing House in Nashville, and written a novel, not yet published, *The Hawk's Done Gone.* Mildred was not beautiful—far from it—but she was fanatically devoted to Allen.

Pidie wrote to Caroline asking her to invite a friend of Pidie's daughter, a young paratrooper stationed at jump school at nearby Tullahoma, Tennessee, to see them, since he was interested in becoming a writer. John Prince, who received a warm and immediate invitation from Caroline, hitchhiked to Sewanee. Looking out the window, Caroline watched Prince pass Nancy without looking at her. It was so different now that Nancy was pregnant, she thought. Men used to always look at Nancy.

Caroline wrote several people about Prince's visit and said she planned to use the parachute jump as a symbol in her next novel. "Allen said he made him feel closer to the war than any soldier who's come our way. He described the jumping in detail for us. They are commanded to sing as they go up. He made his first jump singing, 'Hail, hail, the gang's all here.' Just before they jump, the jumpmaster calls, 'Everybody happy?' It's all pretty grisly." Prince also told them that he had watched a man jump whose parachute failed to open. "He screamed all the way down."

Prince returned the next Sunday and told them his group had been alerted and this would probably be his last leave. At six o'clock Nancy and Caroline realized that they ought to have a farewell party for him, and they borrowed a quart of liquor from a neighbor's son-in-law and gathered together a group to play charades that included the son-in-law and a sixty-five-year-old former actress. "The house was a wreck the next day," said Caroline, "as we had to take that frizzly stuff Nancy's wedding presents were packed in to make hair for the cannibals who cooked Red Beall in the laundry tub when he sought to convert them. The paratrooper assured me he had never had a better time in his life."

Forty years later Prince recalled the warmth of the occasion and the fact that when he left, Caroline threw her arms around him.

Nancy's pains started at three o'clock the morning of October 5, but she did not tell her parents until seven and then she told them there was something wrong with her digestion. Caroline went next door to wake up Nancy's obstetrician, Betty Kirby-Smith (granddaughter of the Confederate general), and took Nancy to the hospital about eight-thirty. She was in labor more than twenty-four hours—the baby was not born until seven the next morning—and Caroline stayed with her until she went into the delivery room (the "living room," as Caroline noticed that the hospital cook called it). Then Caroline went and took a tub bath. She was so tired she was afraid she was going to float down the drain—and the baby would be minus a grandmother.

As they had predicted, the baby was a boy. He was named Percy Hoxie Wood III and called P-3.

"People talk a lot of nonsense about new-born babies being ugly," Caroline wrote the new father. "He is a rich color all over but he is just as cute as he can be." They had been afraid that the baby would be a girl and have Allen's forehead "and consequently never have a beau, but he didn't." Caroline was enchanted with his "darling little chin and rather fat cheeks." His feet, she said, were lovely "and seem to be covered with the best quality purple satin." When Nancy and the baby met, they opened their mouths as wide as they could and yawned at each other. "They looked so funny," Caroline said. "Nancy is crazy about him and thinks he is perfectly beautiful." She was pleased to see that Allen, who had kept saying that the baby was no affair of his and that he would have nothing to do with him, "had a very maudlin look on him" as he inspected the baby.

By chance the first copy of *The Sewanee Review* under Allen's editorship came out on the same day the baby was born. "Allen got his first copy that day and bound it himself," Caroline wrote Fannie Cheney. "He is in a perfect dither over it, more excited than he has ever been over publishing a book." (A few months later, Cummington Press published Allen's new book of verse, *The Winter Sea,* in a special limited edition of 300 at five dollars each. Thirty especially beautiful ones were ten dollars each. Allen could afford only two, one for himself and one for Nancy and the baby.)

Nancy shocked the old ladies of Sewanee and Monteagle with what was considered her disgracefully quick recovery from childbirth—it wasn't quite ladylike, they felt. Caroline never flagged; she rocked the baby and sang to him and warmed his bottles. In fact, she cheerfully took over the full care of the five-week-old infant when Nancy decided to leave him behind and join Percy, by then stationed at Harvard for communications training.

When Katherine Anne wrote that there was nothing as wonderful as holding a little baby in one's arms, Caroline calculated that she held one in her arms something like a hundred times a day. Giving him his bottles took almost five hours a day, and then there was the sterilization of bottles and the mixing of formula, the twenty to thirty diaper and garment changes a day. But Caroline forgot all that when he began to smile—real smiles and not just gas pains—and displayed a knowing, gaminlike look. "I was gorged on babies," said Caroline, "what with all those young cousins I didied but I must admit that he is as charming a baby as I ever saw."

Even with the care of a baby, she read F. O. Matthiessen's *Henry James: The Major Phase,* which inspired her to reread *The Wings of the Dove.* "God, that James!" she wrote to Jean. "He is like Dostoievsky and Tolstoi in one respect, different every time you read him—if you allow yourself a few years between readings. . . . *The Ambassadors* seems almost fumbling beside *The Wings,* or rather lacking in force. It is Kate Croy, I believe. James gets such a lot of evil into her."

Later that year, Caroline wrote to a newspaper reporter who had submitted some written questions to her that she admired Gustave Flaubert more than any other writer of fiction and she thought most modern fiction writers worth their salt "had gone to school to him." Flaubert "teaches among other things the necessity for verisimilitude in detail," she wrote. "Falsification of detail seems to me the unforgivable sin in a fiction writer. Mr. Faulkner for instance has a livelier imagination than Mr. Erskine Caldwell and swells his characters to monstrous proportions or shrinks them below human level, but he never falsifies sensuous details. I know that the insides of his country stores smell just the way he tells me they smell and have the same things on the shelves. But when Mr. Caldwell tells me that four of the best hunting dogs in the county stayed at the bottom of a well for hours because nobody would rescue them I just don't believe him." In answer to another question from the reporter, she wrote that Faulkner was the only contemporary fiction writer she knew who approached the stature of a major artist. She added that she thought Malcolm Cowley's "William Faulkner's Legend of the South" was the only criticism of Faulkner that made any sense and Cowley was the only critic who had discovered that Faulkner was really writing legend and not making a sociological report on Mississippi.

As for her own writing that winter, she asked Fannie Cheney to dig her up a good book on vampires, "the kind of thing Bram Stoker evidently boned up on." The Tates were so hard up (the move had been expensive, and they had bought Nancy her flat silver) that she was thinking of doing a horror story about Dracula in Princeton and had even proposed it to the publisher William Morrow. (When they lived in Princeton, the Tates had entertained Frances Phillips of Morrow. They liked to hear her gossip about the New York publishing world.) Her hero would meet Dracula on a train and tell him about the distinguished refugees in Princeton, and Dracula would smile sardonically, thinking that he is more distinguished than Thomas Mann or Albert Einstein.

After several weeks of caring for the baby, Caroline carried him on the train to Boston, an exhausting journey on packed wartime trains that lasted about thirty-six hours, and delivered him to Nancy. Returning home, she stopped in Westbury, Long Island, to see Jean Stafford and Robert Lowell; Lowell had finished serving his term as a conscientious objector. She paused in New York City to do some shopping—a brown furry coat, a brown dress, gray flannel skirt, red flannel coat, purple sweater, and silk jersey blouses—and in Washington to pick up Loulie and bring her home with her. Loulie was dying of cancer and Caroline thought she would be better off with them at Sewanee than with Manny in Washington. In Washington, Caroline borrowed money from Lon and Fannie—and was unable to pay it back right away. She had borrowed from the Lowells earlier and had a difficult time paying them back. The Tates' finances were always in a mess, but they never let that stop them from taking people in.

Caroline said with what might have been an understatement that it was the damnedest trip she ever took. There was a train wreck at Roach's Run and the Tennesseean sat in the Washington station for many hours, while she and Loulie, knowing how hard it was to get on the train, stayed aboard. Loulie refused to go to the dining car or to lie down—she wanted to be on her feet quickly in case of a wreck. Old ladies, said Caroline, were the devil on trains.

At Sewanee Caroline installed Loulie in the nursery, which she had been dreading to see empty. Loulie did not know she had cancer, and she began to feel better, creeping downstairs each morning at eleven to try to help with the cooking. She baked bread and desserts and showed Caroline how to make her famous potato pancakes. Caroline said she had heard her talk about cooking for a lifetime, but with only half an ear. Now that she knew Loulie was saying things for the last time, she listened more carefully.

Caroline received a royalty statement for *The Women on the Porch* and a check for thirteen dollars. Scribner's charged her several hundred dollars, she told Jean Stafford, for printer's corrections, a charge they'd never made before. Furious, Caroline wrote Jean Stafford that she was going to tell Max Perkins she had made a Plasticine model of Whitney Darrow, the executive vice-president at Scribner's, and every morning she would "stick a long, sharp pin in the place where his bowels ought to be."

But Christmas was coming, and Sewanee was the only place Caroline had ever liked to celebrate Christmas. She managed very well this last wartime Christmas. She and a friend who had some precious gasoline drove to Fiery Gizzard to get Christmas greens. The Tates went to a Christmas Eve dinner party and gave an eggnog party on Christmas afternoon for thirty people.

When Nancy and the baby returned, Caroline was enchanted to see P-3 again—he had doubled in size and looked, she wrote Jean, "exactly like that fat man in *The Maltese Falcon,* if you can imagine that fat man composed of the most beautiful, pink, dimpled flesh." He was at last sleeping through the night. When Percy was sent to Charleston for a brief stay, Caroline kept the baby again so Nancy could be with her husband until he went to sea. Loulie was no longer able to come downstairs "to do the cooking" but she wanted to take care of the baby. This meant that Caroline had to stand over Loulie while she lifted P-3. As Loulie grew weaker, the situation became more strained. Loulie refused to take any medicine, saying that Henry Kirby-Smith, the Tates' doctor and the brother of Nancy's obstetrician, was drunk when he prescribed for her. Loulie paid no more attention to Betty Kirby-Smith. She refused to take even an aspirin, since she had heard that people with heart trouble should not take aspirin. Soon Loulie was in bed all the time, and Caroline was glad to see Manny, who came down to help look after her mother. When Percy went to sea in March and Nancy came back to Sewanee, Caroline immediately went to bed with the flu.

With all this going on, Caroline invited the Lowells down to live with them. They could have a bedroom, she said, and Cal could have the little cottage in the yard for a workroom. The Lowells had other plans. Jean's novel *Boston Adventure* appeared and was an immediate success. With the money she intended to buy a house in Maine. Caroline managed to paint a portrait of Nancy and P-3, as Nancy took on "quite a Madonna aspect"; she did a portrait of Allen called *Thinking Nothing, Nothing, Nothing All the Day*, and yearned for the time to paint a picture of P-3 as the center of a sort of chromatic rose, with the different times of day raying out in a color sequence. Early-morning "bolly-wolly" time would be gray, and she would work through "changy-wangy" time to "percomorphy" time (percomorph, which was like cod liver oil, was given to babies at that time) and "juicy" time and "bathy" time and "kicky-wicky" time and "nappy" time to the high point of the day, the noon meal, which would "have to be a fine purple as it included prune juice and pablum." Such is the decay into which ordinarily hardheaded writers can sink when they become grandmothers.

Somewhat to her own astonishment, Caroline wrote a short story in the midst of all this. She was lying in bed, "having flu," and suddenly a line said itself in her head: "And rear the olive garden for the nightingale." "I wrote it," she told Jean, "rough draft in two days, with Allen playing the violin and Manny adoring the baby on her highest notes." For "The Olive Garden," which is about a man returning to France immediately after the war, she used details of Cap Brun, Ford's villa, and the Villa les Hortensias. Allen thought it was one of the best stories she had ever written and wanted it for *The Sewanee Review,* but he realized she could get more money elsewhere. Caroline was gathering together her short stories for publication that fall in a volume to be called *The Forest of the South.* For it she revised one of her first short stories, "Chain Ball Lightning," and called it "Hear the Nightingale Sing." In the story, after a Yankee soldier takes a Southern girl's pet mule by force, the mule bucks and the soldier is killed. Caroline wrote to Jean Stafford that Marian Ives sold the story to *Harper's.* "Nannine never managed to sell a thing for me," she said.

The short story collection was something Caroline had wanted to see published for a long time. Her version of events has it that she told Maxwell Perkins that if Scribner's didn't want them, maybe he'd just as soon Prentice-Hall published them, "which, of course," she wrote to Jean Stafford, "brought an offer in the next mail. . . . What really hurt was my comparing him to Lord John Russell who always told the Confederacy . . . give us a victory and then we'll help you. Scribner's contracts are the most generous of any to authors, but what good does it do the author if he never sells enough to take advantage of all the benefits they offer?" At any rate, she was glad to get the stories off her chest, she said. Revising things one wrote twenty years before was a grisly business, but a good way to learn something about the short story.

The State Department expressed interest in hiring Allen as a cultural attaché in France. Allen, who found it hard to resist a trip if his fare was paid, went to Washington for talks but decided against the job. He would have liked to take the job, he said, if he could have it for just a few months—he would learn a lot and have a chance to line up foreign authors, but neither Sewanee nor the State Department was interested in a short-term appointment. Also, Allen's views on literature were quite different from those of the State Department. He asked an official from the Office of War Information why they were exporting James Hilton instead of William Faulkner, and the reply was that they hardly liked to back a man like Faulkner. "Who in hell do you want to back?" Allen asked.

With Manny and Loulie on the premises and her relatives coming to see Loulie, perhaps for the last time, Caroline "went completely Meriwether," as Marcella Winslow wrote to her mother-in-law. "Allen and Nancy have to get out and leave them talking clan," she said. When Caroline "went Meriwether," it always drove Allen mad. In the summer of 1933 it was her "going Meriwether," and her obsession with her Uncle Rob that he said caused his escapade with Marion Henry. Now here she was doing it again, after their home had been invaded by a new baby and a terminally ill old woman. Going Meriwether added one more stress point to a marriage strained almost to the limit.

As the bluebells and iris and narcissus bloomed on the mountain, Loulie, who was suffering hideously, asked them to telephone her brother, Rob Meriwether, to come and poison her. "He will gladly do it for me," she said. "You are afraid of a little electric plate on your head." Allen replied that he certainly was afraid of the electric chair. Loulie finally called for an ambulance to take her on a trip, destination unknown. Caroline and Manny rode with her in a hearse—they told her it was an ambulance—that took her to Pidie's house in Chattanooga. She died two weeks later. "That family," Caroline wrote to Katherine Anne, "came near cracking up during those two weeks. Pidie has been ill ever since and we wonder if she'll ever be herself again." Actually, it was Caroline's family, not Pidie's, that was about to break apart.

As summer drew near, Caroline began to read about Vedanta philosophy. She wrote Jean Stafford about her new interest and said she looked forward to "many a rousing talk on religion" with Robert Lowell. "This Vedanta business is wonderful. Fits in with all my intuitive certainties—my feelings about animals, for instance. It is comforting to know exactly where my poor, dear Loulie is at the moment. She is in the moon, enjoying the society of gods. She will stay there as long as she can pay her hotel bill. She pays it with the good deeds she did in this life. When she has used up all but a certain percent of her credit she leaves the moon and embarks on another existence. She, lacking the higher cognition—none of the Meriwethers have much mind—is treading the path of the fathers."

Caroline and Mary Phillips Kirby-Smith, wife of Henry Kirby-Smith, who lived about three-quarters of a mile from the Tates, almost embarked on a career selling plants like ginseng, star grass root, sumac berries, and peppermint stalks to the L. B. Penick Company, botanical chemists. They began gathering mint, used a needle and thread to string it up, and hung it in a little cabin behind the Tates' house. Then they found that the vast quantities of mint they had collected would bring only eighty-seven cents.

Caroline's interest in the natural world was still vivid in Mrs. Kirby-Smith's memory decades later—as was Caroline's hot temper. "It was her only fault," she said. "One time we went on a picnic with Allen and Caroline and my husband killed a copperhead. She chewed him out. 'This is his home and you had no right to kill him. I shall never think the same of you.' "

Nancy came down with appendicitis and had to have surgery, forcing Caroline to forgo a month's vacation in North Carolina with a friend who had a cottage and two servants who liked to serve breakfast in bed. Instead, she hired a nurse and considered that a vacation.

The war ended and V-J Day was celebrated in Sewanee. "The church bell rang like mad and we all trooped into All Saints, including P-3 . . . who howled his head off when they sang 'Rejoice,' " Caroline wrote Katherine Anne. "God, it is wonderful not to have to lie awake nights, worrying about boys."

The picnicking season was in full swing. The Willard Thorps from Princeton were spending a month in part of a ramshackle building known as Old Doc's Place—Old Doc, the local pharmacist, had once had his shop there. Allen had rented the place for them and had painted the walls of their rooms before they got there. Allen went to New York, and Caroline waited for Eleanor and Peter Taylor, who was about to be discharged from the Army, to arrive any minute. Sam Monk, already discharged, was on his way. The Lowells were to come in October.

Allen returned, and with the landscape, as Caroline said, "thick with figures hurrying toward the Tates, expecting a little fun and frolic," the Tates' marriage split asunder.

23

DIVORCE, SEPTEMBER 1945–APRIL 1946

When the Thorps reached Sewanee, they saw immediately that their happy time in Monteagle in 1942, when they had eaten dinner every night with the Tates, was not to be repeated. The situation at the Robert E. Lee was far too strained.

Willard Thorp remembered for years the morning he was writing on the screened porch at Old Doc's Place. He had just seen some cadets from the military academy walking through the woods toward the college and he reflected that Confederate soldiers probably had looked like that as they walked through those same woods. The next time he glanced up, he saw Caroline coming around the corner of the house. She was crying.

"Willard, can you take me to Winchester?" she said. "Allen wants me to get a divorce."

Thorp got the car out and drove her to Winchester, the county seat. "I fooled around town while she went in the courthouse," he said.

Some years later, Caroline said that she was just out of bed after a bout with Ménière's syndrome, which can cause deafness, vertigo, and loss of vision, and had gone to the movies. When she got home, Allen met her at the door and told her she must leave town on the next train, that they must get a divorce.

There had been terrible fights between Caroline and Allen that summer. Years later, Sally Wood would say that both Allen and Caroline had told her that Allen had tried to kill Caroline, and Nancy hit him with a slipper. Nancy saw her mother with a knife in her hand. At any rate, Caroline—tearful and angry—told Nancy, "I'm going to New York."

Fourteen years later Caroline wrote about her arrival in New York. When she got off the train, she could not see because she had had, she said, a relapse from the Ménière's. There was still a wartime shortage of hotel rooms and she could not find a place to stay. She asked a red cap to read the telephone book for her and he called twenty hotels with no success. Finally, he suggested she go to Travelers' Aid. "They got me into a third rate hotel called the Aberdeen. I was so frightened and sick that I telephoned my husband and asked if I could come home. He said I couldn't."

Everyone but Caroline knew that Allen's name was linked with those of other women that fall and winter, among them Elizabeth Hardwick, the young Kentucky writer whose work he was publishing in *The Sewanee Review,* and Alida Mayo, wife of a professor at the University of Virginia. Caroline was ignorant, if not blissful, for a long time. "One usually looks for the other woman," she wrote to Malcolm Cowley. "In this case I think there are two: Allen's mother and my muse. I'd have done better if I hadn't been so absorbed by my own work and so drained by it. Allen's mother looms larger in the picture. She so tortured him when he was a child that he is literally afraid to commit himself to any woman. I might have done something about that years ago if I had been wiser, but it is too late now. It's a wonder that we've lasted this long. However, it's really been fine while it lasted."

Nancy and her baby stayed in Sewanee, where Nancy became her father's confidante. "Your mother's been so cruel to me," Allen would say. When Elizabeth Hardwick called he would say, "Speak to my beautiful daughter," and hand the phone to Nancy. "Hello, Elizabeth," Nancy would say, and Elizabeth would say, "Hello, Nancy." When Percy Wood landed in California, not long after Caroline had left Sewanee, he urged Nancy to join him. Sam Monk, who had come to Sewanee after three years in the Army and expected to see both Tates, found, instead, a confused and distraught Allen and Nancy and the baby. He urged Nancy, who felt perhaps she should stay with her father, to go. Nancy left the baby with the cook, Louella, acting as nurse and flew out to meet Percy. Two weeks later she received a telegram: "Baby neglected. Seriously ill." When she got back to Sewanee, Allen said, "I was lonesome. I didn't have anybody to talk to." Nancy took the baby and went to California and spent the winter there.

Caroline at first tried to put a good face on things, writing to Jean Stafford and Robert Lowell that "Nancy and Allen got tired of having me tottering about with this and that ailment and have shipped me off to New York for a vacation, or rather, a rest. I don't know that I'll be home by the time you all get to Sewanee, so am writing in the hope that I may see you before you head that way. I may stay in New York or go up to Connecticut to stay a while with a cousin." They could always reach her through Janice Biala in New York, she said, since she would keep in touch with Janice wherever she went. "Part of the cure is being foot-loose and irresponsible! (I feel positively wicked, acting this loose way.)"

Far from footloose, Caroline was beside herself with anxiety and depression and anger. Allen had thrown her out—there was no other way to put it—and she was alone in New York with, as usual, very little money. When she left Sewanee, they had had $500—she had just sold a short story—and Allen later borrowed money from Huntington Cairns, the man who had asked him to appear regularly on *Invitation to Learning*. Caroline spent "ten hideous, expensive days" in New York. The hotel asked her to leave—there was such a room shortage that guests had to limit their stays—and she finally found a furnished room after tramping the streets for two days. Allen wrote to her every day—"long letters examining my character"—and followed her to New York, but sent a letter to her lodgings saying he did not dare see her and went back to Sewanee.

Caroline hated her life in New York and went to Princeton, where the Thorps found her a bed-sitting-room in the home of the widow of Professor Malcolm MacLaren on Boudinot Street. It was a good place to write, she said. She had persuaded Maxwell Perkins to release her from Scribner's so she could write, under a pseudonym, the novel about Dracula for Morrow, which had given her a $700 advance. She looked for a job, and wrote Jean Stafford to ask her if a job at Queens College, once offered to Jean, was still open.

She began to tell people the truth. "We are getting a divorce in December," she wrote Jean. "It all came up quite suddenly, though, of course, we have had trouble off and on, like most married couples. It is his idea, not mine. And I do not think he understands himself, or is frank with himself. At any rate he feels that we can no longer live together. I do not bolster his ego in little ways, he says—I have too high an opinion of him, an opinion he cannot live up to. I have pointed out that there are a good many men whose egos I have bolstered for years: Lon, James Ross, Stark Young, and that I might have treated him the way I treat them if I had realized he needed it. The truth is, he is not himself right now. Twice before I have seen him like this, completely irrational. When it is over he has demanded that I make these seizures be as if they had never been. I have tried but evidently have failed. But there's no use in discussing it now. Some day I'll want to talk to you both about it more fully."

Caroline spent her fiftieth birthday on October 6 with Malcolm and Muriel Cowley in Sherman, Connecticut.

From Princeton, Caroline wrote to Katherine Anne: "Allen and I are getting a divorce in December; we manage these things fast in Tennessee, you know. And there's plenty of mental cruelty to go around. However, it's Allen's idea. He sprang it on me rather suddenly a few days after his return from New York. I have often threatened to divorce him—as who hasn't?—and could only say, 'All right, it's your turn.' I left as soon as I could."

Allen had showed a fine sense of drama, Caroline said bitterly. Now she had stacks of letters to answer. Their friends simply could not believe it. Katherine Anne Porter said she felt as though the Rock of Gibraltar had split and slid into the sea. "Evidently we gave the impression of a devoted couple," Caroline said. Allen said that anyone would have thought they were a museum or a university, an institution run for the public service.

The separation came as a shock to everyone except Nancy. Percy had predicted that Caroline and Allen would be divorced as soon as Nancy was married. The only time they were united, he said, was when they were castigating Nancy.

Caroline felt that some of the letters of condolence struck quite a selfish note, with people saying plaintively, "What am *I* going to do now?"

"I, of course, am like a person who's had both legs cut off but will probably learn to get around quite spryly on crutches," Caroline wrote Katherine Anne from Princeton. She would try to learn how to lead a single life from Sam Monk, whose wife had drowned recently. "It's rather bewildering when you've had dozens of people around and sort of dependent on you to be suddenly on your own. Of course none of this would have happened but for my aunt's being there this year. She exuded a poison which is still hanging over the place. . . . He has conceived a violent hatred of the Meriwethers. I always realized they bored him and [I] tried to keep them off his neck as much as possible. But it seems it wasn't boredom as much as a deep-seated resentment. I think that, louts as they are, as he is always saying they are, they still have something that his family has lost. That deep sense of insecurity is the real motif of *The Fathers*." She decided that Allen had come to the time of life when he thought he could have a new life if he had a new wife, like Sinclair Lewis, Ernest Hemingway, and Louis Untermeyer.

Allen at first told all their friends that the whole thing was his fault. He admitted he had betrayed Caroline in 1933 when he had the affair with Marion Henry (he said he had retaliated because Caroline had punished him for not being a Meriwether) but he resented Caroline's refusal to forget it and the way she would not stop bringing it up. He admitted to several people that he was in love with another woman but insisted that this was not the reason for the separation but a result. Then he said he was no longer in love with that woman, but mentioned a new love, Lida Mayo.

Caroline thought about *The Women on the Porch* a great deal and wrote to Sally that she had always had the feeling in the back of her mind that Catherine "in herself didn't amount to much, but that the thing she had in back of her, even in its decadence, made her in a way the equal of her intelligent, gifted husband. . . . The woman represents the earth. It may be fine, rich soil or it may be barren. But anyway, it is earth. The man represents the mind of the modern, rootless American. You remember when he comes out of the house he says, as if surprised, 'I don't belong anywhere.' "

Allen worried, too, about Caroline studying the Vedanta. He did not think she had the kind of mind to enlarge her consciousness through the Vedas. Caroline would not allow him to open a door for her over the years. He was still in love with her, always would be, but he could not live with her. It would take a religious conversion in her to make it possible. On and on, he would go, harking back to 1933 again and again.

It appeared that Allen might have to give up the editorship of *The Sewanee Review* because of the separation. He had submitted his resignation on October 15, but the vice-chancellor of the University of the South at Sewanee, Alexander Guerry, who presided over an Episcopal school, had not accepted it. Someone said he was waiting to see how much pressure the bishops exerted. "Allen, really, seemed to have everything in his lap when this storm came over him. Poor darling," said Caroline. "I reckon it's his age."

Allen's life became more complicated. Mildred Haun, who worked for Allen at the *Review*, went to Guerry and told him Allen had seduced her, but nobody believed her. His friends said it was too bad that Allen, who was guilty on other counts, should be unjustly accused of dallying with Mildred Haun. (Peter Taylor tells a wonderful story about Allen: Donald Davidson called him and said, "What's this I hear about you and Mildred Haun?" and mentioned that Mildred's brothers might come looking for Allen. Allen hung up the phone and said dramatically, "We must arm ourselves.")

Desperate for money, Allen sold Benfolly, and the purchaser immediately sold the timber on the land for more than he'd paid Allen for the whole place. Ben Tate, who had bought Benfolly for Allen in 1930, put the money from the sale in trust. Both Caroline and Nancy were furious with Allen for selling Benfolly, although they had not lived there for eight years. A great many possessions were lost when Benfolly was sold, including some of Caroline's family's furniture and Andrew Lytle's books on Civil War history.

Robert Lowell wrote Caroline a letter that she found touching, inviting her to spend the winter with him and Jean in the house they had bought in Damariscotta, Maine. One of them would even go down to Tennessee with Caroline in January for the final divorce hearing, Jean wrote to Allen. (Allen appeared very concerned about Caroline's welfare and wrote to their friends asking them to help her.) Caroline gratefully accepted the invitation to Maine. The Lowells were good company and it was possible to work while living in the same house with them. She was tired of Princeton, where she knew too many people and where she could not work.

Lowell came down with appendicitis and Caroline went to Maine alone while Jean stayed with him. The house was beautiful, with a lake behind it and the tidal river in front, but Caroline discovered that the only stove on the place was in a room completely bare of furniture. The water was not turned on; there was no food in the house, and it was a Sunday before a holiday. She dragged a few pieces of furniture from another room and set up a rude study. A neighbor across the road got someone to haul coal for Caroline, who had been bringing it in a piece at a time, and persuaded her to sleep under an electric blanket at her house, although Caroline insisted on working in the Lowells' house. She bought a small airtight stove she saw in the window of the general store where she went for groceries.

It was a love of a house, she wrote to Jean, and it would be wonderful in the spring and summer with the lake right behind them. She was mad about the little terrace at the back of the north room. It would be grand to sit there in the summer. She thought she was going to be crazy about Maine. She walked to the village and circled back through hemlock woods, and then walked up the road past the church. It was beautiful country, she thought, with wonderful walks all about.

She wrote to the Lowells next that she was having a hard time keeping enough oil in the drum. The regular once-a-week delivery would not keep the stove in oil, although she said she was burning only one burner. As it grew colder, the neighbors told her the pipes in the bathroom would freeze unless she put a heater in there. Perhaps they could get one in New York or Boston. "I would let the fires go out over here and stay across the road but I hate to have the water turned off just as you may be coming. It takes several days sometimes to get hold of Harry Seidlinger [the handyman]. . . . Turning on the water is more of a chore than you all realized. It took him two hours. He says that if you had left it the way you had it there would have been trouble. The traps were not drained and would have burst. I have taken cold. I may be able to shake it off. I usually do. But if I really get sick it is going to be hell, keeping up fires in both houses. For God's sake, let me know when you intend to come, so I can decide what to do about the water."

Tending the fires became a heavy burden. The kind woman across the road went away for Thanksgiving, and Caroline had to keep fires going in her house as well as the Lowells' to prevent the pipes from freezing. "Thank God for that winter in Tory Valley," she said. If it had not been for that experience, she would not have known how to handle the fires. A northeaster came while she was there by herself, and she had just started to work at four in the afternoon when the lights and telephone went dead. As she walked downtown to call the telephone company, she almost stepped into a tangle of live wires where a car had knocked down a light pole. With only the firelight and the stub of a candle she made it through the night, although the house shook until it rattled and her bed trembled so she could not sleep. The next day the tide was so high that the rats ran out of the cellars of the stores in Damariscotta. Still, she managed to write the first chapter of her book, which cheered her. She felt she had mastered the mechanics of living in a Maine winter when the Lowells arrived right after Thanksgiving.

What happened next is hard to piece together. The Lowells evidently mentioned Allen's love affair. Robert Lowell left. While Jean and Caroline were alone in the house Caroline kept asking Jean for details about the affair, and Jean gave them. Caroline became angrier and angrier; she was, quite literally, out of her mind with rage at Allen. This was a repetition of the affair with Marion Henry, another unbearable, unbelievable betrayal by Allen. She turned on the bearer of the bad news, and told Jean that there was no hope of a reconciliation between her and Allen after what Jean had told her, whereas there had been hope as long as she had not known the facts. Jean had ruined the lives of two valuable artists.

As Caroline lashed out, Jean began to cry. Caroline threw a glass of water in her face and, according to Jean, threatened to "break everything in the goddamned house" and began to throw dishes, glasses, pitchers, jars of mayonnaise and peanut butter, the sugar bowl, and everything else she could lay her hands on. She broke a window, leading Jean to fear that she might try to destroy the house.

Jean ran next door and asked Mrs. Cabot, her next-door neighbor to call the doctor. The doctor could not come, but the neighbor's daughter, an Anglican nun, said they must call the sheriff. When the sheriff arrived, Caroline had gone across the road where she had been spending the nights; she returned, assuring everyone that she had merely had a girlish tantrum. Jean spent the night next door; she said she found bloodstains on her bedroom door the next morning and was sure that Caroline had tried to kill her.

Caroline called Allen, who was in New York, and agreed to meet him "to talk things over." Jean cowered at Mrs. Cabot's and would go home only after Lowell returned.

Allen was disgusted with Jean. "You don't call the sheriff on your friends," he said over and over.

After she saw Allen in New York, Caroline decided to go back to Sewanee with him, and letters full of dignified outrage flew back and forth between the Tates and the Lowells for some time.

"I do not think that either of you . . . realize, or will admit, the enormity of Jean's offense," Caroline wrote Lowell. "What she did puts her beyond a pale within which we all move and have our being. Only a genuine act of contrition could bring her inside the pale again. I was wrong to burn up her letter after only one hasty reading, but when I read it I saw no sign of such contrition. I do not believe that she was frightened in the way she maintains she was. I think that after she realized that what she had done might have extremely unpleasant consequences, she grew frightened. But that is a different kind of fright from the kind she maintains she had."

Back in Sewanee, the Tates' reconciliation did not last. "The issue between us is so deep that it may be no human affection can resolve it. God knows there is enough affection on both sides," Caroline wrote to Ward Dorrance. No matter how things turned out, Caroline told Ward, she was going to take more time for friendships and for personal correspondence. "It has been years since I enjoyed that luxury!" she wrote. "Allen's reactions to life are so complicated that I have kept my own life as uncomplicated as possible. We have a great many friends and a great many people come to our house, but, though it sounds strange to say and may seem incredible to you—I have forgone many friendships that I would have enjoyed. It seemed better for me to have as little personal life as possible. I think now that that was a mistake and did neither of us any good. It took a third person to make me see it. A man wrote me the other day that he had always admired me but had been compelled to do it at a distance. As he was a young man, who for years had had the run of our house, I was surprised. But he explained though he had seen me, off and on, for fifteen years, I was, in a sense, never really there, and I had to agree. It was not just being married—though, that, of course, brings certain deprivations—but another, extra deprivation that I see now was unnecessary."

She invited Ward to spend Christmas with them in Sewanee, but a few weeks later wrote to withdraw the invitation. The attempt at reconciliation was the "worst idea I ever had in my life," Caroline said. "What went before was child's play compared to the last ten days." At the end of two weeks, both she and Allen said, things were worse than ever before.

Maybe it was all for the best, Caroline said. "We are both cured. We realize we can never stay under the same roof again, and it is something to have that settled."

"Allen was such a liar," said Mary Phillips Kirby-Smith, Caroline's friend and neighbor in Sewanee. "There was no truth in him. Caroline never told anything but the truth. She was a truthful, moral woman. When they were getting the divorce, Allen told us about it. 'Caroline has violated her oath never to bring a certain thing up to me,' he said."

Mrs. Kirby-Smith drove Caroline to see her lawyer in Winchester and asked her what was the thing between them, and Caroline said, "Allen thinks I feel morally superior to him."

"Can't you disoblige him of this misconception?" Mrs. Kirby-Smith asked.

"It's not a misconception. I am morally superior," Caroline said.

Caroline liked her lawyer, a seventy-year-old man who had a happy home and a mistress named Fluffy. He gave Caroline a little talk on how bad it was to break up a marriage of twenty years, but as soon as he discovered she was in earnest "he was marvellous about smoothing out difficulties."

As soon as they decided to go ahead with the divorce, Allen and Caroline were marooned together in Sewanee when an ice storm made the roads impassable. The little town talked of little else but the Tates. Caroline's nephew Meriwether Gordon, just discharged from the service and just back from overseas, arrived for a visit just before Christmas.

"I have bad news. Allen and I are getting a divorce," Caroline told him after she fixed supper. "Will you drive me to Elkton so I can leave Bub with Cousin Ross McCuddie and then drop me in Nashville with the Starrs?" The Starrs were old friends of Allen and Caroline; Alfred Starr had been a member of the Fugitive group, and Mrs. Starr had been a pupil of Caroline's at Clarksville High School. Starr had just lent Allen $1,000 at no interest. "You can bring the car back here," Caroline told Meriwether, "and stay with Allen as long as you like. He'll be delighted."

Meriwether, who did as Caroline asked, recalls that Caroline said to him on the way to Elkton, "Allen has been back at me with the old fury." Meriwether drove back to Sewanee, but he did not feel that Allen was delighted to have him. Allen played the violin constantly and seemed distraught until he drove Meriwether to the train.

While Caroline waited for the divorce hearing and worried about where she would live, she stayed with the Starrs in Nashville. She could not go back to Maine, and there was nothing for her in Nashville, so perhaps New York City was the best idea. Surely she could find an apartment if she began looking far enough ahead. She asked everybody she knew in New York to be on the lookout for a place for her to live. All she needed, she said, was a large room to work in and some sort of kitchen, since it was too expensive to eat out. Allen asked his New York friends, like Philip Rahv, a founder and editor of *Partisan Review,* and Vivienne Koch, a critic and teacher, to help Caroline find an apartment. She put lines out in Florida and made a few inquiries about Columbia, Missouri, where Ward Dorrance taught.

While Caroline was waiting, Janice Biala called to tell her she had found a cold-water flat for her in New York at 108 Perry Street—a flat with four rooms and a marble mantel, one cold-water faucet and no heat. The rent was only twenty-five dollars a month. "I don't mind wrestling with a stove," Caroline said. She was excited about the apartment: Willem de Kooning lived right around the corner, and Janice Biala was lending her her painting of the quai Malaquais.

Friends, speculating over the breakup, decided that in addition to Allen's infidelities, real strains came from lack of money and the pressure on Caroline to entertain constantly, making it hard for her to do her own writing. Allen's playing his violin while Caroline was trying to write was considered another possible contributing factor.

A few days before the hearing, Caroline began to plead with Allen for another attempt at reconciliation, but he was obdurate. The divorce came up the morning of January 8, 1946, and the court proceedings were over in fifteen minutes. Caroline left immediately for New York. Allen, in the hospital in Sewanee with flu, said he was not at all pleased with the symbolism of his situation.

"It is such a relief to have that over, to be convinced that there is absolutely nothing I can do for Allen any more, and am at liberty to pick up the pieces of my own life," she wrote Ward Dorrance, as she settled in at 108 Perry Street. She realized almost immediately that she had to have a job, and not just for financial reasons. She needed a routine to struggle against, she said. "One has to have some kind of framework and to be suddenly quite alone when one has been used to fighting like a tiger to get a few minutes to one's self is disconcerting."

Mark Van Doren helped her get a job teaching a creative writing course in the general studies program at Columbia University and she found another job teaching at New York University. She also read manuscripts for Macmillan. The first manuscript she read was a novel almost good enough to be published and Caroline wrote the author a letter with suggestions; the young woman replied that she had stolen a copy of *The Women on the Porch* from a drugstore because she didn't have enough money to buy it.

Her first class at NYU was on Friday night from six to eight. Fifteen pupils came from as far away as Larchmont. (Caroline thought Larchmont was in New Jersey.) She was afraid they would not be able to understand her Southern accent, but they got along fine. Nobody went to sleep in class. Caroline said she was as limp as a rag afterward.

She liked her cold-water flat with its stove, even though she had to bathe in a laundry tub. Sally Wood found furniture in her attic in Rochester and shipped it down to Caroline. Dorothy Van Doren's cook, who said Caroline was the only person who treated her as an equal, took Caroline under her wing and introduced her to the grocer and the other tradesmen in the neighborhood. Caroline was thus able to get bacon, although it was still scarce.

She began to entertain, and one night had three women writer friends to dinner—Eudora Welty, in town from Mississippi; Marguerite Young, who was working on *Miss MacIntosh, My Darling;* and Vivienne Koch. For her first big party without Allen, Caroline invited twenty people to hear Fletcher and Margaret Collins sing ballads. She had first met the Collinses in North Carolina; she wrote Ward Dorrance that they "fair draw the heart out of your bosom." In the same letter, she confessed, "Ward, I don't think I'm doing well at all. I'm just treading water as best I can. I have to be somewhere—unless I commit suicide, and I reckon I'd still be somewhere then—and New York seems to be the best place for me right now, for the reason that I can so easily pick up a job. But I loathe living here. I loathe everything about it."

She was able to survive in New York only because of Tory Valley. She renewed her friendship with Sue Jenkins Brown and every weekend began going out to Patterson and Tory Valley, where she could dig in the ground. When spring finally came to the valley, Caroline lay on her back and gazed up into the branches a good part of one day, but she also worked so hard that weekend that she staggered when she got on the train to go back to New York City. She planted nicotiana, gourds, onions, hollyhocks, tomatoes, and cress. She wanted to raise them in the open row, the way an old market gardener had shown her, sowing the seeds and thinning the plants out. She felt that plants grown that way bore sooner than the transplanted ones.

Peter and Eleanor Taylor, meanwhile, had heard nothing of the divorce and took the bus to Sewanee for a much-delayed visit with the Tates. "When we got there, the Tates had been divorced," said Peter Taylor. "We hadn't heard a word about it. It was like hearing that your parents had gotten divorced." The Taylors stayed with Allen for several months. "A Mrs. Mayo from Charlottesville had gotten a divorce because of Allen," Taylor said, "and they would have long talks on the telephone. Then Allen went off to New York and came back and said he and Caroline were going to be re-married. I went with him to buy a ring."

And Caroline wanted a ring. She wrote to Allen from New York. "I am convinced we are rid of the humors that plagued us. . . . Every now and then somebody makes a casual comment that shows me that he or she realizes that we have a very special bond. My difficulty was the doubt that you loved me, but that came from a feeling of inferiority I have toward you. It was so wonderful to have you love me that I couldn't believe it was true. But I believe it now, and I want the ring. It will serve to remind me of how important our love is."

Allen, too, looked to New York; he had a new job at $6,000 a year with Henry Holt & Company. Joseph Brandt, the president of the publishing house, who had been with Princeton University Press, had offered Allen the position.

By mail they discussed the best way to get married again. Caroline suggested Washington, if no blood test was required. Princeton was a possibility, but one had to be there a few days ahead of time to apply for the license. "Or we could spend a few days in sin here and then go to City Hall," she said. She was happy. "Yes, it would have been better, in a way," she wrote to Allen, "if this cataclysm had taken place years ago. If I had been convinced that you loved me, or if you could ever have brought yourself to tell me certain things that you tell me so easily now there would have been no trouble. But we couldn't seem to do this. We are not ordinary lovers. We are Equilibrists, like the lovers in John's poem."

In John Crowe Ransom's poem, "The Equilibrists," the one John Berryman had recited for Caroline in the summer of 1938, the lovers are dead. One stanza of the poem reads:

> At length I saw these lovers fully were come
> Into their torture of equilibrium;
> Dreadfully had forsworn each other, and yet
> They were bound to each, and they did not forget.

And the last stanza is an epitaph:

> *Equilibrists lie here; stranger, tread light;*
> *Close, but untouching in each other's sight;*
> *Mouldered the lips and ashy the tall skull.*
> *Let them lie perilous and beautiful.*

Caroline's letter to Allen continued: "Or perhaps we aren't. Our love has been progressive. It is flowering now when most people's love is getting ready to wither. . . . I don't know. I just know that I love you. . . . I honestly think that we complement each other in an almost mathematical way. . . . Stark Young said almost the same thing. . . ."

Allen went to New York, abandoning all the furniture in the house in Sewanee, some of which belonged to them, some to Manny, and some to James Waller. Nancy later rescued all of the Tates' furniture and took it to Memphis, where Percy was in medical school. Caroline managed to get Allen to salvage the portraits of her great-grandmother and great-grandfather and Ned Meriwether's sword.

"From the beginning he said everything was wrong between us and that the only hope was to shatter everything and start fresh," Caroline wrote Sally, telling her Allen had appeared in New York and they were going to get married again. "Of course, a lot of things got shattered in the process, alas, but not my affection for him. I'd have that no matter what happened to the poor devil. . . . He says that the animus he had against me has quite died out in him, and he has been finding out what a desperate business it is to cut through the affections and habits of twenty years. One thing that makes it possible for me to go back to him is that through the whole business, even when he was saying the most awful things to me, he stoutly maintained that he could never love anybody as he loves me."

Allen and Caroline were both excited about the wedding. On his way to New York, Allen had stopped in Washington, and Marcella

Winslow noted that he was as "excited as a new bridegroom and bubbling over." After Allen reached New York, he and Caroline walked around to see Mark and Dorothy Van Doren. "We want to come in," they said. Once in, they said, "Guess what! We're going to get married!"

The wedding took place in Princeton at the home of Willard Thorp on April 8, 1946. The Reverend Wood Carper, the Episcopal chaplain at Princeton University who had performed the ceremony when Nancy and Percy were married two years before, read the service.

The Tates went back to New York City and Caroline, on her way to teach at Columbia that night, met a colleague, William A. Owens, as she was coming out of the subway. "Guess what!" she said. "Allen and I just remarried." She met her class and told her cousin Danforth Ross and Tommy Mabry, two young men from Kentucky who were taking her class, "This is a wonderful day. Allen and I just remarried. Let's go out to celebrate." So the four of them went out for drinks and food and back to the Tates' apartment on Perry Street.

NEW YORK, 1946–1947

After the second wedding, there was a brief period of euphoria for Caroline. Bub traveled from Cousin Ross McCuddie's in Elkton, Kentucky, to New York to be reunited with his mistress. In May Caroline wrote the front-page review of *The Portable Faulkner,* edited by Malcolm Cowley, for *The New York Times Book Review,* a piece that marked the beginning of the Faulkner revival. She went to Bethany College to receive an honorary degree and promptly had herself listed in the Columbia course descriptions as "Dr. Gordon." She abandoned the novel about Dracula—Dracula himself kept changing, and she found that she did not know as much as she needed to know about the devil. Allen went to Utah to teach at a writers' conference and wrote Caroline tender love letters.

T. S. Eliot came over from London and, though they arranged for him to sleep at the Van Dorens', the Tates were his hosts. Caroline thought Eliot "literally one of the most charming men I've ever known. He's looking quite ravaged . . . but he's still extremely handsome. And a brilliant conversationalist. He seems just to pluck the right word out of the air, and usually one word does the trick where somebody else would use half a dozen. We were all talking about a book that nobody particularly liked the other night, trying to say what it was, and after everybody had talked around it a while, Eliot said quietly, 'It's edifying.' "

In fact, there was the usual procession of out-of-town visitors through the cold-water flat, from clergy from Sewanee to writers from all over. Peter and Eleanor Taylor spent the summer in New York and saw a good bit of the Tates; Allen had helped get one of Peter's stories published in *Partisan Review*.

Caroline read *Cloud of Unknowing* by an anonymous fourteenth-century monk, a book she admired not only for its content but for its prose style, and she talked about it to everyone who would listen that summer. Although it was long out of print—an Episcopal clergyman had taken her copy from some library long before—she recommended it enthusiastically to Robert Lowell.

The Lowells had spent a hard summer at Damariscotta, entertaining the same kind of stream of poets and their wives or mistresses that the Tates used to welcome. Jean Stafford was drinking too much, and when Gertrude Buckman, former wife of Delmore Schwartz, came to visit, she and Lowell began a romance. In the fall of 1946 Lowell abandoned both Jean Stafford and the Catholic Church. Jean fled to a hospital in Detroit, to her sister in Colorado, and then to Payne Whitney Clinic in New York for treatment for psychological troubles that included alcoholism. Lowell's second book, *Lord Weary's Castle*, appeared in December 1946 to ecstatic reviews.

That fall Caroline began to look better than she had in years. She did her hair differently, lost weight, and bought new clothes. She taught a novel workshop and a short story workshop at Columbia. She was a fierce teacher, repelling some students, driving some to tears, and winning the wholehearted admiration and loyalty of others. She taught the way she had at Greensboro, combining the reading and analysis of great works of fiction with the criticizing of students' manuscripts.

You had to give the students something they could sink their teeth into, she said; most of them came to class "as ignorant as catfish." Most of them had some "horrible novel" they had been working on and what they really wanted was help in getting it published. She set *Madame Bovary* before them to show them how bad their own work was. It was not a book, but a method, she said, and in writing it Flaubert perfected a method, rendering everything through appeal to the senses. She stressed, too, the agility with which Flaubert shifted point of view, being sometimes at Emma's shoulder, sometimes right inside her head.

Caroline became almost obsessed with point of view. She admired Henry James's "central intelligence," the superior mind placed at the center of action. The central intelligence, she told her classes, combined all the advantages of the other three possible points of view—the omniscient narrator, the first-person narrator, and the author identifying with one character.

Specificity of detail was another canon. "You can't say the men at Vicksburg ate rats and make the reader see it," she used to say. "You have to show a specific man eating a specific rat. And it should be good eating, too."

John Prince, the paratrooper who had visited at Sewanee, took her class at Columbia; he found her an inspired teacher and thought everybody adored her the way he did. He was therefore shocked when another student said to him, "If I didn't have respect for her knowledge, I'd spit in her face." For some students, she was the right teacher at the right time. Madeleine L'Engle took her class when she had been living in the country for ten years with nobody to talk to about writing. "We started out hating her," L'Engle said. "She made us feel we weren't good enough to be in her class, but I invited her for tea and got to know her." L'Engle credits the class with helping her to a turnaround in her own work. For the final examination, Caroline asked her class to write an answer to one question: What, if anything, have you learned in this class? "I still teach writing classes using my final exam," said L'Engle.

Another student found her "the most stimulating and informative teacher I ever had." Bette Bentley, who later took Caroline's class in Seattle, said she learned more in one short quarter than she had managed to pick up by trial and error in the five or six years she had been writing fiction. That class was small and most students were displeased that Caroline made them learn first to write a sentence and then a paragraph. Bentley thoroughly enjoyed "the almost word-by-word analysis" of Flaubert's "A Simple Heart" and Joyce's "The Dead."

William Price Fox and the playwright Murray Schisgal stumbled on a class of hers at the New School in New York and remained, transfixed by the way she read and the way she could recite whole pages of Flaubert and Joyce from memory. Fox wrote his first story for that class. When he turned it in, Caroline told him, "You're a natural. Don't go to school any more." Fox took her advice and wanted to dedicate Southern Fried to her. Caroline asked him not to. She thought the title was awful.

Teaching was good for her, she decided. "It has made me do a lot of reading I wouldn't otherwise have done and to some extent it has clarified my ideas," she wrote to the Cheneys the summer of 1947. "I find Percy Lubbock's The Craft of Fiction very helpful in my classes. In fact, I don't think anybody has beat Lubbock yet, and I am amazed to see how all the James commentators ignore the things he tells us about James so plainly."

At Christmastime she and Allen met Nancy, Percy, and their baby in Sewanee for a three-week reunion. Nancy was impressed with her mother's looks and her new air of detachment. They had a picnic at their winter picnic site, Natural Bridge, where if it rained picnickers could stay dry in a cave while they looked out at the miniature natural bridge, "so much more charming than any of the more advertised natural bridges." They built a good fire, heated lard in an iron kettle, and tossed quail into it. They were thoroughly cooked in ten minutes, "the most delicious quail I ever ate," Caroline said. In spite of all the fun and Caroline's good looks, Nancy knew that things were terrible. "I had been married long enough to see that things wouldn't survive," she said.

The marriage was indeed in trouble: Caroline was jealous and fiercely possessive of Allen. "Allen was her monomania," said one friend. William Slater Brown was at Perry Street when Allen and Caroline came back in a taxi from a party where Léonie Adams had been. "Allen's face was scratched," Brown said. "He had been making passes at Léonie Adams. Caroline had a satanic expression on her face, as though possessed. It scared me."

She had never had a confidante, Caroline wrote Ward Dorrance, and perhaps she'd made a mistake trying to handle Allen alone. She had persuaded Allen to go see their "darling Dr. Wolf," who told her that an imbalance of the glands had been responsible for Allen's "antics" of the past two years, but now she was convinced that psychoanalysis would help Allen—he needed a father confessor. The year before she had felt rather guilty, as though she had failed Allen, but now she thought he was the victim of a "castrative impulse." He had suffered so at the hands of his mother that he lived in deadly fear of women. At the same time he could never fall in love with any woman who could not have real power over him. He was incapable of making the kind of marriage that most people made. She sometimes wondered— treacherously, she thought—"whether he might not be better off with another kind of marriage."

Sally Wood, who probably knew more about the Tates' marriage than any other person, knew that Allen had attacked Caroline in Sewanee, and she was concerned for Caroline's safety. "I was worried about Caroline, thinking that what had happened once might happen again, and went to New York to see them," she wrote years later. "Mr. Tate had tried to kill his wife again. They had both gone to a psychiatrist who is a friend of my husband's and mine, Dr. Lawrence

Kubie, who had advised them to stay apart for a while while there was so much tension between them. Mr. Tate had moved to The Brevoort. . . . From both Mr. Tate and Mrs. Tate I had accounts, separate accounts, of this incident, which coincided."

Sally arranged for them to see Dr. Kubie, described in *The New York Times* as an orthodox Freudian psychoanalyst, and worked it out so that they would not be charged.

While he lived in a suite at The Brevoort, Allen told his friends the trouble was more serious this time. Caroline's temper had gone from bad to worse, and the neighbors complained that they heard her scream at night and throw dishes against the wall. Her behavior does not seem inappropriate to one who knows that Allen had embarked on a series of love affairs, mostly with women who were poets and writers but once with a sculptor. Caroline did not know about all of them and even invited the sculptor to go on a trip with them. "She never gets the woman right," Allen complained once, but it was inevitable that she get some of them right and react with violence. Wives do not have a great many choices in situations like this. They can cry. They can go mad. Caroline reacted with memorable fury.

On the other hand, she tried to keep up appearances. She would make a joke and suggest that they find a way to signal their friends whether Allen was in residence or not—perhaps with the small Confederate flag flying from his great-grandfather's picture.

Bravely, she wrote to Mark Van Doren about the separation. It wasn't that Allen couldn't get along with her, she said, it was that he was in a blind alley at Holt, the worst place he could be. She did not want to move on, she said—her Columbia job was just right for her and the cold-water flat was so cheap that she could hang on to it through almost any domestic upheaval. If only Allen could get his affairs straightened out. "I think he ought to have a teaching job again. . . . If you hear of anything in any of the colleges in New York will you please keep Allen in mind? He'd rather take some two by four lectureship here than go out to Iowa, say, where Cal Lowell is going on Allen's recommendation."

She was determinedly cheerful in April 1947 when she wrote to Fannie and Lon Cheney. "Allen and I have been going through another of our tail spins," she said, "and this one makes the antics of the past two years look like child's play." She insisted that she was quite hopeful about the outcome since their relations were franker and more cordial than they had been for some time. Allen, she said, had "a very bad mother fixation, as you know. He finally turned on me all the hate he had been bottling up all these years. I have become so identified with his mother that he simply couldn't disentangle us." She conceded that it was partly her fault because of her "jealous, suspicious nature and violent temper."

Caroline decided that Allen should have had psychiatric advice years before, and she had been maneuvering to get him to a psychiatrist. They were both seeing Dr. Kubie, the most expensive psychiatrist in New York. "He has given us some advice which changes the whole picture and we are slowly picking up the pieces of our common life, with that picture in mind," she told the Cheneys.

One of the things Kubie brought up with them was the possibility of latent homosexuality in both of them—a diagnosis that neither of them was able to contemplate. Caroline told the Cheneys that she found psychiatry, "this modern substitute for prayer," no real improvement: you stood some chance of getting hold of God when all you had to do was to kneel down at your bedside, but getting hold of your psychiatrist took skill and energy and then he could give you only an hour, less five minutes.

Allen moved back to Perry Street and the Tates maintained an uneasy equilibrium.

In a letter to Ward Dorrance, Caroline observed acutely that when Allen "can't write—and lyric poets can't write all the time—he is in a very devil of a fix and can't keep from taking it out on everybody around him. And he doesn't seem to be able to refresh himself or renew himself through Nature—or even through other people." She told Ward that their life together was more satisfactory, because "I pay less attention to Allen than I used to. I go ahead and lead my own life, deliberately do things that will give me pleasure, or see people whom I enjoy seeing, even if he doesn't enjoy them."

One afternoon in June 1947, Caroline went by Maxwell Perkins's office, and they had what Perkins liked to call "tea" at the ladies' bar at the Ritz. Perkins was enthusiastic about Caroline's idea for a book on the novel to be called "The Figure at the Window," recalling a phrase in one of Henry James's prefaces. Caroline asked him for some money in advance. He refused. As she left, she said, "That's all right, Max, I don't need it."

Perkins went home that night, Friday, became ill with pneumonia, went to the hospital on Monday, and died Tuesday. "I simply cannot realize Max is dead," she wrote Ward. "It has done all sorts of things to me. I am still talking to him. I mean we both understood that we were terribly occupied and all that, but we saved up things to tell each other, and now he is dead, and all sorts of things—some of them rather silly—I can never tell anybody else. What I mean is, for twenty years, there was always Max, and now there isn't any Max. Well, my father's death hit me in much the same way, but I guess I said to myself, 'You've still got Max,' but I don't have him any more. He wasn't terribly interested in my work. He liked other people like [Thomas] Wolfe or Marcia Davenport—they gave him an opportunity to exercise his extraordinary talents but you could always approach him. You could always say, 'Hey, Max, what I'm trying to do is awfully hard. How do you think I'm getting along?' and then he'd put his whole mind on it and tell you what he thought. [His] suggestions were damn good."

Caroline's idea for the book on the novel was turned over to Tom Walsh in Scribner's textbook department and he thought it would be best if it were written in collaboration with Allen so both their names could be on the title page. Walsh also wanted them to do an anthology of short stories under both their names, "with suitable annotations and introduction, for the education market." Scribner's would pay an advance of $500 for both the book on the art of fiction and an option on the anthology if Allen would be willing to consider the $500 he owed them as an advance against his half of the anthology. Allen liked the idea, planned the anthology, which was called *The House of Fiction*, wrote three of the commentaries, and left the rest to Caroline.

At Allen's urging she went to the University of Utah to teach at a writers' conference in the summer of 1947. He had gone the year before and told her he would never forget the scenery. Any scenery that Allen noticed, she decided, was worth going to see. And she did like the Utah landscape, where she felt the light was "classical" and there was some shade of lavender everywhere she looked. The teaching at the conference was on a high level, she told Katherine Anne Porter, but perhaps more important, there were plenty of places to swim and picnics were held at ranches where everyone could ride horseback.

Life in New York City was hard for Caroline, and she continued to go to Tory Valley on weekends during 1946 and 1947, whenever, as she put it, her chlorophyll deficiency became acute. She had to have country air, and Sue Jenkins's old house that she went to as freely as if it were her own, she wrote Ward, was a godsend to her, now that she had to live in New York. There was still an outdoor privy at Tory Valley; there were kerosene lamps, and a pump in the kitchen sink. She disapproved of the Cowleys and the Matthew Josephsons, four miles away in Sherman, with their oil heaters and "hygienic white walls." Sue's place had "just the touch of ruin about it that makes a place attractive to me." She usually went alone, although Allen joined her for the Fourth of July celebration, a holiday festival they had first attended in 1925. She enjoyed the rugged aspects of life at Robber Rocks and quite late one fall took a bath in the spring, pouring three buckets of water over her "not really shivering frame, while two frogs . . . applauded."

She spent a couple of long vacations there too, and was a part of a group that included Sue Jenkins, Eleanor Fitzgerald, an old radical and a former staffer at the Provincetown Playhouse in New York who had a house nearby, and Eva Parker, the local handywoman who wore men's clothes, lived in a one-room cabin, and used her car for storage and as a mobile workshop. According to her obituary in the local weekly paper, Eva could "use a scythe, plow a field, plant a garden, 'cumber' a road, read the tracks of birds and beasts in snowy woods and in the dust of roads, paint a house, 'point up' a stone foundation, install a culvert." Each of the women had her own tools, her own work gloves, her own tasks. And after Caroline got her honorary degree from Bethany, she was Dr. Gordon, Sue was Dr. Jenkins, and Eva was Dr. Parker. Eleanor Fitzgerald, apparently, was always Fitzy.

They did heroic work on the grounds in the spring and summer of 1947 and rejoiced when they could see results. Since she was impervious to its effects, Caroline was the poison ivy expert, and she worked on the old stone walls and in places where nobody else dared go. One day she freed an apple tree from a great tangle of grapevines and poison ivy and stood on the porch to admire how the tree stood out. One beautiful moonlit night, after numerous guests had left, Caroline and Sue went for a walk; when they came back to the house the moon was still so heavenly that they could not bear to go indoors, so they made up beds on the porch.

Wherever she was, Caroline wrote. She fitted up Sue's woodshed for a study, but when it got too hot she moved back into the house. And wherever she was, Caroline always traveled back in her imagination to her childhood summers at Merry Mont. A short story published in the fall of 1947 in *Mademoiselle* called "The Petrified Woman" described the Fayerlee family reunion "at Arthur's Cave." It was a description, too, of the annual Meriwether reunion at Dunbar Cave, where Meriwethers "of the name and of the blood" came back to the Old Neighborhood to breathe the sacred air. The narrator, a little girl named Sally, mentions a pet squirrel she used to have named Adji-Daumo, the same name Caroline had given her own pet squirrel. The story is about people full of suppressed fury with one another, genteel people who drink too much, a husband who accuses his wife of unspecified offenses, of being petrified. It ends, inevitably, in violence.

In France, 1932: Caroline, Allen, and
Sally Wood.
(Princeton University Library)

Katherine Anne Porter and Caroline
Gordon on the trip the Tates took
from the Olivet writers' conference
back to Benfolly by way of Bethany
College and Virginia.
(Princeton University Library)

Pidie (Margaret Douglas Meriwether
Wilds Campbell), Caroline's
grandmother ("Miss Carrie"
Meriwether), and Moggie (Margaret
Douglas Campbell Carden), Pidie's
daughter, at Merry Mont in 1938.
(Nelson Sudderth)

Monteagle, 1942–1943. Caroline is at far left, once more apart from the group: left to right, Anne Goodwin Winslow, Andrew Lytle, Edna Lytle, Nancy Tate, Allen Tate, Robert Lowell, Jean Stafford. *(Marcella Winslow)*

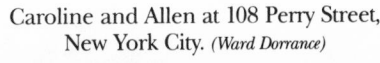

Caroline and Allen at 108 Perry Street,
New York City. *(Ward Dorrance)*

Bill Gordon and his father, James M.
Gordon, the model for Aleck Maury.
(Princeton University Library)

The Tates' Christmas card for 1949, with
a photograph of their latest house,
Benbrackets, in Princeton.
(Van Pelt Library, University of Pennsylvania)

Caroline at the Kenyon School of Letters in Gambier, Ohio. *(Ward Dorrance)*

One of Caroline's paintings, *St. Cuthbert and the Otters.*
(Nancy Tate Wood)

The Red House, Caroline's "perfect house," on Ewing Street in Princeton.
(Ann Waldron)

A festival of Southern literature at the University of
Alabama in the sixties. Left to right, Andrew Lytle,
Caroline, and Robert Fitzgerald.
(Princeton University Library)

Caroline at the Red House with Melusina.*(Polly Gordon)*

Caroline teaching at Emory University in Atlanta, spring 1966. *(Nancy Tate Wood)*

Three generations: Amy Wood, Nancy Tate Wood, Caroline Gordon. *(Princeton University Library)*

Caroline at San Cristóbal de las Casas. *(Nancy Tate Wood)*

THE CATHOLIC CHURCH,
1947–1948

Caroline had been reading about Eastern and Christian mysticism since 1945 and in 1947 went on to Aldous Huxley's *The Perennial Philosophy*. Although it suffered from its semipopular approach, she said, its few hundred pages held information that would take people years to get for themselves. She began to think of joining the Catholic Church. She asked her student Tommy Mabry to write to Robert Fitzgerald— a Catholic, a poet, and translator of Sophocles and Homer—to say that Caroline would like to talk to him. One morning Caroline walked over to the Fitzgeralds' apartment on York Avenue in New York City and said she had decided to become a Catholic and wanted to talk to a Catholic writer. Robert Fitzgerald and his wife, Sally, encouraged her and became good friends.

The climate was favorable for conversion just then; there was a boom-let in Catholicism after World War II. Francis Sheed, an Australian convert, and his wife, Maisie Ward, a British cradle Catholic, were writing furiously, publishing Catholic writers at Sheed & Ward, and even preaching on street corners. Bishop Fulton J. Sheen had become a television personality and had personally instructed converts like Hey-wood Broun, Fritz Kreisler, Grace Moore, Henry Ford II, the glamor-ous Claire Boothe Luce, and even reconverted Louis Budenz, managing editor of *The Daily Worker*. The Catholic Worker movement and French worker priests made the news magazines. It seemed easy, almost chic, to be a Catholic.

Caroline gave different people different reasons for her turn to the Church. She told Bill Brown, who had become a devout Anglican, that once at Tory Valley when she idly took the old calf-bound Brown family Bible down from the shelf and read two sentences in Jeremiah— "The heart of man is desperately wicked" and "It is not in man that liveth to direct his own steps"—she knew that she was going to join the Catholic Church. It had taken her fifty years to get to that point. During those fifty years, her faith, revealed to her in a lightning flash, had been slowly assembling itself, as if her soul had been some small animal crouched on the banks of a mighty river that put out a paw and dragged what it needed to the bank. For example, she said she got her first notion of the grandeur of the Archangel Michael from the Baron de Charlus's boasts about what a mighty patron he had. She told Andrew Lytle it was from *At the Moon's Inn*, his novel about de Soto, that she got one of her first glimpses of the power and the majesty of the Church. She told Nancy that Sigrid Undset's books "had something to do with my conversion. When I read them I never gave a thought to the Catholicism implicit in them—because I didn't have the least idea what Catholicism was." To Dorothy Van Doren she said it was St. John of the Cross, whom she read casually and then found it "gripped her by the soul."

An important incident had occurred in Rouen when she stayed in the car while Allen went into a store to buy cigarettes. A beggar woman approached the car, hand extended. Caroline gave her some francs, the woman scuttled down the street, only to return to ask Caroline, "Have you faith?" and Caroline had responded, "No."

She spoke movingly of the Normans, the tenant farmers at Benfolly who were Holy Rollers, who believed that every day was Pentecost, who lived in the light of continual revelation. "Everything they did was done with grace and dignity, because it was done for the sake of pleasing God. . . . Mr. and Mrs. N., although we did not know it at the time, were constantly instructing us in the theory and practice of the theological virtues of faith, hope, and charity. We were not apt scholars."

Perhaps the person who most influenced Caroline's spiritual growth was Dorothy Day, whom she had known as a "forlorn girl, somewhat raddled from knocking about Greenwich Village," but who was now transformed. Caroline had been profoundly impressed when she found out in Memphis that Dorothy had converted, taken a vow of poverty, published *The Catholic Worker*, and operated soup kitchens for the poor.

Perhaps Allen's contention during the first divorce that only a religious conversion on her part would make it possible for him to live with her helped goad her into the Church.

Caroline was baptized on November 24, 1947—the feast day of St. John of the Cross—at the Church of St. Francis Xavier, 30 West Sixteenth Street in New York City, by the Reverend Martin J. Scott, S.J. Her sponsors were Frederick Morgan, a student of Allen's at Princeton whom she called at the last minute, and his wife, Constance. For her name in Christ, she chose Monica—the mother of St. Augustine, who prayed him into the Church. Allen was there for her baptism and afterward the Tates and the Morgans went back to Perry Street for drinks.

Her spiritual adviser was a jolly eighty-three-year-old Jesuit at the College of St. Francis Xavier, who gave her a copy of *Your Mass Made Visible* to help her follow the service. She chose Our Lady of Pompeii, an Italian church at the corner of Carmine and Bleecker Streets, for her parish, instead of the Irish St. Joseph's on Sixth Avenue.

A year later, after a great deal of effort, she was confirmed at Holy Name, a church on Riverside Drive. The idea of confirmation, she said, almost takes you off your feet, if you stop to think what it means—having an indelible and eternal seal upon your soul.

She always saw a close connection between religion and the art of fiction. "I am a Catholic, I suspect, because I was first a fiction writer," she wrote Lon Cheney. "If I hadn't worked at writing fiction for so many years I doubt if I'd have made it into the Church, but working at writing fiction all those years taught me how god-like a trade it is. We are actually trying to do what God did: make our word flesh and make it live among men." On another occasion Caroline said that the writer of serious fiction had the same goal as the contemplative and the mystic. He needed the patience of Christ. Writing a novel was also a little like trying to get to heaven—to get there, the writer had to exercise faith.

She thought that writers like Faulkner, "who are muddled in their heads and know no doctrine," or writers like Henry James, who on the surface do not seem to be religious, all use the Christian myth in their plots. "It is what we are all writing about," she said. Not understanding the Christian myth handicapped the work of all novelists, including herself, she said. Dostoevsky, on the other hand, was able to achieve such miraculous effects because he rested squarely on the Christian myth. He did not have to create a new heaven and earth, and so he had more energy left for his characters. In Eastern religions, she was fond of saying, there were two ways to truth, one a lower path for the simple-minded and one the way of cognition for the intellectual, but in the Christian religion truths that were hidden from the wise and prudent were often revealed to babes and sucklings.

Once converted, she set out to convert others. She wrote to Andrew Lytle (the Lytles and the Tates were now speaking again, after their long quarrel, which Caroline now believed arose because Edna Lytle had taken an intense dislike to both the Tates) and offered to give him a St. Andrew's missal if he would read the Mass for every day and the exegesis. "I am an artist," Andrew told Lon Cheney. "I've got enough on my hands without taking on religion." She worked on Ward Dorrance by mail, ceaselessly urging him to read the newly published *The Seven Storey Mountain;* she sent him quotations from St. John of the Cross and told him that she did not think he would attain his full stature as a fiction writer until he understood the Virgin Mary better.

She flung herself into religion with all the fervor she had given to hunting mushrooms, painting, and the writing of fiction. She went on retreats. She ate fish on Fridays. Sam Monk said that when she ran out of fish for dinner she said, "Sam, you take this cold lamb and I'll take eternal life."

All the trappings of Catholicism, like rosaries and crucifixes, appealed to her, and they lay about the rooms wherever she lived. The lives of the saints caught her fancy, and, remembering the Meriwethers' Douglas ancestors, she was especially delighted when she discovered a new saint, John Ogilvie, whose mother was a Lady Douglas of Lochleven. His feast day was March 10, but it was kept only in Scotland by Jesuits.

She came to detest Protestantism. When she first lectured at a Catholic college—the College of St. Thomas in St. Paul, Minnesota—she proclaimed that Catholic audiences were far superior to Protestant ones. Protestantism "not only has no apparatus for keeping you in touch with the supernatural, it, in effect, denies the supernatural. I was told about Mary's Little Lamb as a child. . . . I was never told about St. Colette of Picardy who had a little lamb that accompanied her to church and always knelt down at the Elevation of the Host," Caroline wrote Nancy. She agreed with Jacques Maritain's thesis that the three men who made the hated modern world were Luther, Descartes, and Jean-Jacques Rousseau; later she was convinced that John Calvin was even more of a villain than any of these. She decided the Meriwethers had fallen because they were heretics, and she became consumed with the desire to be buried at Meriville, the Meriwether burying ground. One Catholic in a cemetery could redeem the whole lot, she believed.

She read St. Teresa all the next winter, and "What a psychologist!" she said; St. Teresa made Freud and Jung look like schoolboys. "She will just calmly announce as a fact something that takes the top off your head. . . ."

Caroline was delirious with happiness in May 1948 when she thought Allen was about to be baptized, but the priest, detecting arrogance, told Allen he was not ready.

In the summer of 1948 Caroline read the Bible for the second time since her conversion, while Allen read *The Iliad* in preparation for a class. Caroline realized that the Blessed Virgin came from a long line of women who couldn't have children without supernatural assistance—Sarah, Rebecca, Rachel, and Elizabeth, mother of John the Baptist. "Yet Robert Graves in his *White Goddess* objects to the Christian Myth because it doesn't go in enough for goddesses!" Caroline wrote to Katherine Anne.

Caroline told Bill Brown that she prayed for him often. "It is simply wonderful to be able to pray for people. I have three girl cousins who committed suicide when they were still quite young. The thought of them has been like a stab in the heart for years. But now I don't have to feel that way. I can just try to pray them out of Purgatory. . . . The chief trouble with the Anglo-Catholic church, from a practical viewpoint, at least, is that you never see any truck drivers praying in them. Learned men, old and young, and pious ladies, yes, but not truck drivers."

Immediately her conversion affected her fiction. She wrote a short story, "The Presence." "It's the last Aleck Maury story and shows him being converted," she wrote Fannie Cheney.

26

NEW YORK AND CHICAGO,
1948–1949

In the spring of 1948 Allen wrote to Donald Davidson that he and Caroline were coming back into the world again and he believed their abysmal troubles were over; a new life awaited them.

Terrible weather had marked the winter just past, and because of the shortage of cannel coal, Caroline and Allen had a hard time keeping the Perry Street apartment warm. The snow that fell on November 26, Caroline wrote to Katherine Anne Porter in January 1948, reinforced with worn-out Christmas trees, rotten banana peels, and tin cans, was still lying on Bleecker and Perry and Hudson Streets, freezing up every three days, thawing, freezing again, but never leaving. Caroline cut herself bangs and said she looked like a cross between Alice B. Toklas and John the Baptist.

Allen decided he could manage with part-time teaching at New York University and resigned from Holt early in 1948. He felt his NYU job was ideal. He earned $2,000 a year at NYU and Caroline made $2,500 at Columbia; he could not have afforded to leave Holt if Caroline weren't working. It was the best arrangement they had ever had, Caroline told Katherine Anne. They each taught two classes a week and they made enough to live on and still had time for their own work.

There was a steady flow of guests in the cold-water flat on Perry Street—Marguerite Young, still working on *Miss MacIntosh,* Van Wyck Brooks, E. E. Cummings, Paul Engle, Cleanth and Tinkum Brooks, Robert Lowell, Léonie Adams, Denis Devlin, Eleanor Clark, and Vivienne Koch. The Tates renewed their acquaintance with William Faulkner, whom they'd met years before at the writers' conference in Charlottesville, and he came to dinner at Perry Street. He must have been more sober in New York, because Caroline wrote Ward Dorrance that she was pleased to find him exactly the way he ought to be, a little diffident, rather old-fashioned in his manners, with sort of a touch of Edgar Allan Poe about him. He admired Aleck Maury, and when he heard she had written the last Aleck Maury story, in which Maury foresees his death, he said, "Don't kill him off." On another occasion the Tates had T. S. Eliot and John Crowe Ransom for dinner at the same time—a first meeting for those two. Caroline thought the evening somewhat spoiled because Robert Lowell came in, drunk, and monopolized Eliot. Caroline felt that neither leaving the Church nor divorcing Jean Stafford had improved Robert Lowell; he was belligerent even when he wasn't drinking. While the Tates were hospitable to guests for meals, this was one period in their lives when they could not manage houseguests. "Mr. Tate and I cook and bathe in the kitchen," she explained to Ward Dorrance when she urged him to come to New York for Christmas but to stay at The Brevoort.

In the summer of 1948 Caroline and Allen went by train to spend two weeks with Nancy, Percy, P-3, and the new baby, Allen Tate Wood, in Monteagle (Percy was still in medical school in Memphis) and to visit the Cheneys in the old white-columned house in Smyrna, near Nashville, that Fannie had just inherited. There they drank Jack Daniel's and ate fried chicken and brown-sugar pies. "People are always saying you can get the best food in the world in New York restaurants. It just isn't so. You can't get good food in them for money or love. I am tired of their sour vichysoisse and chef's salads made with inferior oils. You know, we really have the best food in the world in the South," Caroline wrote the Cheneys later.

They spent a week with Ward Dorrance at his house, Confederate Hill, near Columbia, Missouri. Caroline conceded Ward was one of the strangest people she had ever known but "he had turned into a very good writer." His house had sixteen rooms, with various galleries, all wreathed with wisteria vine; a terrace where the house party sat and watched the moon come up through the mulberry leaves; a garden where Caroline pulled weeds; a Newfoundland manservant who looked like something out of Dickens, said, "Sorr," but couldn't cook; a Louis Quatorze bed; a bathroom off at the end of a long wing where nobody could get to it. Caroline left her girdle in the bathroom; the manservant said, "Looks something like a gym strap, sorr. Shall I send it on to the lady?" Caroline's brother Morris came from St. Louis while they were there, and she tried, to no avail, to convert him to Catholicism.

Then, as Caroline said, it was time to get down to work at a writers' conference in Lawrence, Kansas.

"Kansas is not at all what I was led to expect," she wrote to Bill Brown. "Lawrence, a town settled entirely by Black Abolitionists from Massachusetts, is perfectly beautiful—huge elms interlacing over all the streets, and the mourning doves so tame they sit in the streets cooing at you. Quantrill, the [Confederate] guerrilla leader, whom I was brought up to revere, had a special hatred for Lawrence and he and his men used to come over, hitch their horses on the bluff, raid— and sometimes sack the town—they burned it to the ground once, then saunter back to their horses carolling 'Lovely Annie Lyle,' a melody to which the university has set its alma mater."

At Lawrence the Tates saw Katherine Anne Porter for the first time in years. The director decided that not enough people had heard of Katherine Anne Porter, Caroline Gordon, and Allen Tate. "We must have a drawing card," he said, and brought in Erskine Caldwell, who looked, Caroline and Katherine Anne agreed, just like a goat. The Tates did not admire all Southern writers, and Caldwell was one for whom they had no use. (Another was Truman Capote. Caroline spelled his name Kapote, and Allen called him "the impotent foetus.") Caroline liked the fact that they were staying in a Catholic fraternity house. Allen respected the writers' conference in Lawrence since nobody tried to tell the students how to get their work published.

Allen left after one week and went to Gambier, Ohio, to teach at Kenyon College's School of English, directed by John Crowe Ransom. When Caroline joined him there she went into the hospital for an exploratory operation—she had hemorrhaged in Lawrence—and was much relieved to find she had a fibroid tumor, not cancer. She was glad Allen had persuaded her to wait to have the operation until she got to Gambier. She liked her doctor and the small, cozy hospital, run by the "gabbling" nuns, the Sisters of Mercy, who urged patients to take communion every morning. "Might as well get the extra blessing," one of the sisters said to Caroline. "A young Jesuit father, one of the School of English students, came in and talked to me about subjects I am deeply interested in, like the mystical Body of Christ. It is so seldom one finds a priest who knows what one wants to know and has the leisure to impart his knowledge," she wrote to Katherine Anne. She wrote Bill Brown at the same time that one reason she was so happy being a Catholic is that "along with everything else, little bits of the Middle Ages are crystallized in the Faith and are always popping up, on one's bread and butter, so to speak. And I do so love the Middle Ages, and hate this one."

In the middle of July Caroline had a second operation, this time to remove the tumor. While she was still in the hospital, Allen received a telephone call saying that Bub had been injured in an automobile accident. He was afraid to tell Caroline for fear she would try to go to Bub, no matter what her own condition. Bub had an operation, but died anyway. Caroline was desolate until a priest told her that Bub was perfect, an adequate mass of corruption, not disproportionate, like Caroline, so he didn't have to bother with another life, just consumed himself and went back into the Potentiality of Nature, whence he could emerge again. Would he, she wondered later, emerge as some darling puppy?

Back at Tory Valley, Caroline was able to work in Sue's garden fifteen or twenty minutes a day. The poison ivy she had worked so hard on the summer before was flourishing again. She and Sue had more help that summer—John Prince had finished college at Chapel Hill and had come to New York that summer. John and Caroline met at Grand Central every weekend and rode the train to Pawling, New York, where Sue kept an old car. They went first to the bank and the liquor store and then out to Sue's place. With John's help, they finished clearing the lawn to the old stone walls and built a terrace for cocktails. Léonie Adams and her husband, Bill Troy, who lived nearby, gave them "enough forsythia roots to ruin the place with" and they set those out.

With $300 from *Mademoiselle*, Caroline made a down payment on three acres of Sue's land. The site was an old orchard, completely encircled by stone walls, and although it was quite near Sue's house, it was out of sight from the house. The view was magnificent; they had often had picnic suppers there to watch the moon pop up over the mountain. Caroline said she wasn't worrying about building a house for some time, but when she did build, she wanted to use the ancient method, *pisé de terre*, or rammed-earth walls. You put the earth into a form and ram it, she explained. The method had been in use since Hannibal's time and was highly recommended by Pliny. She wanted a sod roof so she could grow leeks there, as Charlemagne recommended. She conceded that she would have her work cut out to convince Allen of the superiority and cheapness of this method, but she thought he would fall for this process because it sounded exotic. They were considering spending seven months of the year in Sue's house, helping her to bring electricity in and fix up the plumbing, until they could build their own house.

Caroline brought nicotiana plants in from the country to grow in her apartment—all the Meriwethers grow tobacco, she said—and she experimented with various kinds of hydroponic gardening.

Caroline worked on her critical essays for the anthology, some of which she was able to sell as separate pieces to *The Sewanee Review*. When she was in the country without the books she needed for work on the anthology, she would turn to work on a new novel about the Tates and their guests at Benfolly and the Normans in their tenant house. In the late summer of 1948 she wrote to Ward Dorrance that she had planned all the key incidents and then decided to do it in a different way. "One thing I have learned from James—in theory, at least—is that a character can often be rendered more dramatically when handled objectively. . . . I found myself asking whether the action might not work better if seen through the eyes of another person than the main character."

The hero (or villain), she wrote Ward later, was Edmund Wilson: Uncle Tubby Martin (later Tubby MacCollum), who comes to visit Aleck Maury's daughter and son-in-law at a place like Benfolly. Uncle Tubby was to be in love (hopelessly) with Katherine Anne. The central intelligence would be that of the little girl, Lucy. "A central intelligence has to be superior, or it won't work. Hers is superior to that of the grown people because it is pure. I shall not use a child's language for the narrative parts, but that of an omniscient observer. After all, we all speak Johnsonian English when communing with our souls, as Faulkner has shown many times." The Normans, the tenants, would be having a bush arbor meeting in the locust grove beside their house, and the singing would reach the ears of the wassailers at the big house. They would plan to attend the meeting—Uncle Tubby was curious about local customs—but after supper they would get too drunk to go. The germ of the story came to her, she said, when she found herself amused by the way the Normans used to say, "Let's go up the hill and watch," and then "Crouch in the bushes and observe the goings on in the big house (much the way we go to the zoo) while the guests would hang over the balcony of the big house and observe the Normans with an equal amount of curiosity and lack of comprehension."

Allen was offered a job—"fabulous salary [$5,000], one preceptorial a week and every other concession you can think of," according to Caroline—at the University of Chicago in the spring term of 1949. He left New York in January, taking all his summer suits with him since they would not be back in New York until September. Caroline, on leave from Columbia, followed in February. The university had found them an apartment at 5631 Kenwood Avenue—"almost too good to be true, equipped with every gadget known to Western Man"— with separate dining room, sun porch, modern kitchen, and a cleaning woman.

Caroline liked Chicago better than New York, she said, because one was always conscious of open fields outside the city. It didn't seem to "swing in a balloon the way New York does." Allen found the university huge, rich, cosmopolitan, but still nicely provincial and Midwestern. Writers were still curiosities there, and the phone was always ringing.

They finished up the anthology quickly and sent it off to Scribner's. Tom Walsh wrote that the English professor to whom he had sent it for reading had what Caroline called "the usual objections"—why didn't they use Steinbeck, Katherine Mansfield, and a lot of other what she called second-rate writers?

She began to paint again and did Cardinal Jozsef Mindszenty in prison with the Archangel Michael beside him while she wasn't working on the Benfolly novel, *The Strange Children*.

Robert Lowell, on the road to a total emotional breakdown, had left Yaddo after demanding that the director be fired for harboring communists; he was now generally outraged at the evil in the world. He felt, for one thing, that Allen's life needed straightening out and he called Allen and told him to come to New York to hear the will of God. Allen said he couldn't come East. Caroline wrote to Lowell, inviting him to come and stay with the Tates for the rest of the semester and go to Kenyon College with them that summer. She urged him to see and talk to Father Dan Walsh, who taught philosophy at Manhattan-ville College and at Columbia, a man of "utter simplicity and great learning." She told Lowell that Allen "was himself again" but had not yet joined the Church, though he had been on the point of baptism once before.

Lowell arrived and proved an exasperating, even frightening visitor. Caroline, who was home alone with him in the daytime, was thoroughly scared. He kissed her every five minutes, began to embrace and kiss Allen, too, and talked about how much he needed them both since he was weak. Then Lowell implored Allen to repent of all his sins, including all his love affairs. Allen must know his sins, he repeated, and so must Caroline, and he gave Caroline a list of Allen's lovers. Allen and Caroline were both furious with Lowell. Lowell, twice Allen's size, came up behind him, squeezed him, and lifted him off the floor. When the Tates took him out to eat one night, Lowell made a scene in the restaurant. When they got him home, Lowell opened the window and began to shout out obscenities. Neighbors called the police and it took four policemen ten minutes to subdue and handcuff Lowell and take him to the university psychiatrist. Allen, in spite of his rage at Lowell, persuaded them not to take him to the police station. The psychiatrist thought Lowell should be taken into custody, but again Allen persuaded the police to let him come back to the apartment. The next day Lowell announced that he was going to see Peter Taylor in Bloomington, Indiana. With relief—and uneasiness—the Tates put him on the train. In Bloomington Lowell was jailed until his mother and his psychiatrist could fly out and take him to a hospital outside Boston.

Talking it over afterward, Allen and Caroline agreed that Lowell's troubles were due to his meteoric success as a poet (in 1947 he had won the Pulitzer Prize, a Guggenheim Fellowship, and an award of $1,000 from the American Academy of Arts and Letters), his leaving the Church, and his divorcing Jean Stafford—but mostly, the quick success. "So maybe we're not so unlucky after all to be only moderately famous," Caroline said. She said for days after Lowell's visit they walked around as if they had bad attacks of rheumatism; their muscles were still tied in knots. Their real concern for Lowell was apparent to the British poet Stephen Spender, who met them for the first time at a dinner party in Chicago. He noted in his diary that the Tates felt almost as though Lowell were their adopted son.

Caroline left Chicago on May 31, 1949, to visit Ward Dorrance at Confederate Hill. Allen picked her up there and dropped her off at the writers' conference in Kansas, where she began putting Catholic tracts under the doors of the other faculty members. Allen, meanwhile, drove to Memphis to pick up Nancy and her two little boys to bring them to Gambier, where he was again teaching at the Kenyon School of English, and where Caroline would meet them later.

Nancy took Yvor Winters's class at the School of English (she wrote a "brilliant" examination paper, Winters told the Tates) and Caroline kept the children. Gone were the days when P-3, now known as Peto, was an angelic baby. Four years old, he woke up at six every morning and started yelling. His little brother, Baby Allen, who had Allen Tate's head, blond hair, and black eyes, always yelled everything that Peto did. "The constant yelling gets on my nerves," Caroline told Robert Lowell when she wrote him. Then she tried to encourage Lowell, who was still in the hospital. "Everybody has a nervous breakdown at some time in his life—at least our kind of people do—and it is a relief to get it over with," she said.

Princeton Again,

1949–1950

The Tates abandoned their plans—if they had ever had any—to build a rammed-earth house at Tory Valley. They decided instead to buy from Louis Coxe, whose poetry Allen had helped get published, a tiny eighteenth-century house in Princeton, across the street from the Willard Thorps. Ben Tate let them have the Benfolly money back and they named the house Benbrackets. They could easily commute to their two-day-a-week teaching jobs in New York, they said.

In 1949 the house, at the corner of Riverside Drive and Nassau Street, was almost in the country. What is now Riverside Drive was a country lane that ran back to the Howe Farm. Benbrackets had too few rooms and stairs that were too steep, but it had, Caroline said, "touches of Benfolly on a Lilliputian scale." Like all the houses the Tates acquired, it had its own peculiar charm. They moved in the fall of 1949, ten years after they had come to Princeton the first time, and Caroline said how wonderful it was to be where she could set her foot on the ground any minute she pleased.

"The last few weeks have been simply hell," she wrote Stark Young right after they moved in. "You know—consideration of every object and whether it ought to be shellacked or painted or thrown away and where is my grandfather's gold tooth pick and that communication from Columbia and while you are going in that trunk will you just look for last year's tax returns etc. This is the sixth house we have inhabited since last February. One more would push me over the edge."

While she wrote, Allen was running around the house, directing the man who was going to mend the roof and put on the gutters and also drive out the hive of bees in the south wall.

Allen's study was tiny but he said he liked it better than any study he ever had. Although her study was dark, Caroline said she liked it better than any she had ever had. (She always said that.) The front door didn't open—they had to put the sofa against that wall. The hearth was made partly of bricks and partly of a huge stone, sunk in the middle, which had UNION carved on it. The Tates thought the house might have been an underground railway station. It was really a glorified Negro cabin, Caroline said.

She planted dozens of Merry Mont jonquils and snowdrops and fifty wood hyacinths and spread leaf mold and manure. Still the yard looked awful, she wrote to Nancy. "It ought to be fine next spring, though," she added with her eternal optimism.

At first, commuting seemed a breeze. Allen went in on Wednesdays, taught one class at NYU, spent the night at the Perry Street apartment (which they had turned over to Sue Jenkins, who gratefully let them continue to use the bedroom), prepared for his Thursday class, and came back Thursday night. Caroline repeated this routine on Friday and Saturday. She laughed when she had to borrow thirty cents from the conductor to pay for her ticket the first time she went in to teach, but then she began to feel "run literally off my feet," trying to keep house, teach, and write a novel. Still it was better than living in New York, she thought, and she started going to Holy Roller meetings with the cook (who had worked for the Tates when they lived in Princeton ten years before) to do research for the bush arbor scene in the Benfolly novel.

Jacques Maritain, who had just moved to Princeton to teach philosophy at the university, and his wife, Raissa, became valued friends of the Tates. Maritain, sixty-five years old, was a convert to Catholicism whose writings had been one of the cornerstones of the Catholic Worker movement. He spoke fluent English, but Raissa, after fifteen years in the country, spoke none. Caroline used English to her and Raissa spoke French to Caroline, and they got on fairly well. Caroline admired Maritain's *Art and Scholasticism,* in which he said that all great novelists were mystics, and recommended it that fall to Ward Dorrance. The mere sight of Maritain's face, Caroline said, "worked wonders in the pagan breast." He was the most charming human creature she had ever known, and the pope had referred to Maritain as "that soul that uses a human body."

They resumed their friendship with the Thorps. Richard Blackmur, who had been Allen's assistant in the Princeton University creative writing program, now directed it, and had as his assistant John Berryman, who had visited the Tates in the summer of 1938 in Connecticut. Eileen, Berryman's wife, was curious about Allen—she had heard him described as a superb poet and critic, a kind mentor, an urbane host, and a literary politician who recently, while he had not been able to write poetry, had become jealous of the success of others. When she met him, she "was struck by the size and curve of his forehead, . . . the slim build and gait of a much younger man, his mustache, which he used as a weapon in literary criticism. When he commented unfavorably on a poet's most recent publication, he twitched it up to the side and sniffed through one nostril."

Although Eileen had heard from many people that Caroline was formidable and sharp-tongued, she was disarmed immediately by Caroline's attempts to establish that they were kin to one another. Surely they had a cousin in common, Caroline said. How could they? asked Eileen. She was a Northerner while Caroline was a Southerner. But wasn't Eileen a Catholic? asked Caroline, the recent convert. They became friends.

That fall, an old friend, Andrew Lytle, wrote a long, appreciative review of Caroline's work in *The Sewanee Review*. Called "Caroline Gordon and the Historic Image," it pleased her immensely. Nevertheless, she could still write Andrew years later that she "could not appear in any anthology edited by you. Our literary paths diverge too widely." He really should have asked her permission before he dedicated a book to her, too, she said. Then, as though unaware of the wounding tone of the first paragraphs of her letter, she told Andrew that she heard good things about the work he was doing. "And if I can ever be of any help to you, don't hesitate to call on me." She signed the letter, "Love, Caroline." As she said in the letter, "How complicated these matters are!"

In Princeton the Tates were as hospitable as ever. Caroline gave a gala fiftieth birthday party for Allen. Although none of the guests could understand how so many people could be fitted into the doll-sized living room and be given food and drink, it was a great success. Caroline plaited a laurel wreath and put it on Allen's head. After the toasts and the cutting of the cake, they played charades. John Berryman and Helen Blackmur acted "parnel," a priest's mistress. While Helen reclined on the couch like a *maja*, John, with a towel around his neck to look like a Roman collar, knelt at her side. Allen heard talk about it the next morning at the Baltimore Dairy, but Caroline was very pleased with the game; she needed an exotic word for the charade game in *The Strange Children*. Houseguests came and went. John Prince and T. S. Eliot were once there the same weekend. Edmund Wilson, with whom they had been out of touch since Caroline wrote him the angry letter about his refusal to review *The Women on the Porch*, had his mother's chauffeur drive him over from Red Bank. He had missed them, Wilson said, and he stayed from one o'clock in the afternoon until midnight. Allen called the Berrymans and said, "Bunny Wilson is here. Come and have a drink." Louise Cowan, who had earned her Ph.D. at Vanderbilt and was writing a book about the Fugitives, came to Princeton with her husband, Don, to interview Allen. "Allen was utterly charming and brilliant," Louise said years later. "Caroline liked Don, but she didn't like me—she didn't like women who were working on their doctorates. She said she never learned anything important that a man didn't teach her." Stark Young came to visit, as did the Malcolm Cowleys. Tommy Mabry, who had worked for *Time* magazine but wanted to write fiction, came and went, "white and wan" after two sessions with Caroline on his novel.

Between visitors Caroline worked on her own novel. She was vain about the "method" she was using in *The Strange Children* and said over and over that she didn't think anybody had ever used Henry James's central intelligence, plus the innocent eye. "I use Lucy's eye more, much more than her mind," she wrote to Ward Dorrance on Octave Day of All Saints, 1950. "But I wanted the innocent eye for the sake of the brilliance of its recording—not to mention the innocent ear. I haven't had the difficulties I anticipated, have had others, instead. For instance, I find that Lubbock was absolutely right when he said that you could sometimes shut an intelligence off to great effect. Sometimes Lucy hears things she can't understand. But a child, I imagine, registers tones of voice, registers, that is, anything that is important, anything that is said with feeling, even if he or she doesn't understand the feeling. When Nancy was four years old she reproduced what I'm sure was my grandmother's intonation when, fancying she was alone, she used to mutter: 'I've got to die some time. I've got to die some time.' Nancy tossed it off gaily, but I could hear the old woman's voice through hers. Lucy's story—what happens to Lucy—is the basic theme, but what happens to four other sets of people is intertwined with her story. They are all strange children, as it says in the Bible. [The title, she said, came from Psalm 144.] Lucy's name, of course, is significant. She is smarter than the average child—at least she sees farther. Why is St. Lucy always represented carrying her eyes about if she can't see farther than the next one?"

Ward warned Caroline not to try to write the French passages herself so she wrote them out in English and sent them to Sally Wood to translate for her. Sally had then shown her translations to a French professor at the University of Rochester, who made some corrections. But Ward, who taught French at the University of Missouri, found more errors.

She found one thing easy about *The Strange Children*—the setting. She said she used Benfolly straight; it made a splendid stage setting. In fact, she told Robert Lowell that Benfolly had always struck her, even when she was living there, as a sort of stage set. "So I used it straight and then just took some of Nancy's traits, some of Allen's traits and some of my own traits and used them for my purpose." For the scenes in France, she used the Villa Agatha at Toulon, where she used to steal flowers in 1932.

The House of Fiction came out in the summer of 1950, with both Caroline and Allen listed as authors. Allen freely conceded that it was mostly Caroline's, since she had written most of the commentaries on the stories and a large portion of the appendices, discussions of point of view and tonal unity in fiction. He said that he had wanted to include one of her stories, but that she felt that it would be improper.

In her commentaries, Caroline used a great many of Henry James's ideas, ideas that she had articulated, shaped, and refined in her classes. She stressed the value of technical analysis to identify the "central intelligence," the "omniscient narrator," or the "effaced narrator," the "long view" and the "short view." Her commentaries are informed by a moral sense. She sees the devil as the controlling symbol in Faulkner's "Spotted Horses," and God serving the same function in Flaubert's "A Simple Heart." Although she had always claimed that she was no more a critic than she was a poet, she proved without a doubt that she was a very fine critic indeed.

The reviewer in *The New York Times Book Review* said the anthology contained "the intensive technical and symbolic analysis that the New Criticism developed for poetry," and noted that six of the nine living American writers included were Southerners. (They were Warren, Welty, Lytle, Faulkner, Porter, and Peter Taylor.) Used for years in colleges across the country, the anthology was a success, and there are many people whose ideas of fiction were formed by it.

While Allen went back to Kenyon College to teach that summer,

Caroline visited Ward at Confederate Hill and Lon and Fannie in Smyrna, and spent several weeks with Sue at Tory Valley.

Back home in Princeton she gardened with enthusiasm. She walked to confession at St. Paul's, and thought nothing of walking on downtown to the hardware store to buy "a thing to sift soil in," something she had wanted all her life. Ward sent quantities of advice on planting, and she went around reciting to herself a kind of litany: "Cranesbill, Jack-in-the-pulpit, cardinal flower . . . statice, aconite . . . *Scilla hispanica, Veronica longifolium.* . . ." What could she plant around the shady terrace now monotonously fringed with ivy? Ward suggested ferns, and Grace Lambert told Caroline she could dig up all she wanted in her woods. She decided to put out *Lobelia siphilitica*—it would be a conversation piece, she said, especially if Madame Maritain asked what that *joli* herb is. She stole *Vinca minor,* or myrtle, from a place across the street about to be occupied by a Saks Fifth Avenue magnate, estimating that, since fifteen plants cost a dollar at the nursery, she had taken fifteen dollars' worth in one morning.

"Are you *sure* it won't tear such a little house down?" Caroline asked when Ward recommended wisteria. "I knew a man who had a barn he wanted torn down and he said he just planted two wisteria vines on it and told them to go to work." She recommended angel's trumpet, or cultivated jimson weed, to Ward. It was "simply divine, with blossoms that smell like a lemony magnolia." Even the burrs, she said, were attractive. A young man, a junior at Princeton who read St. Augustine and St. Thomas in his philosophy course, worked in her garden for seventy-five cents an hour. "No use trying to get any work out of Allen, except on some fine day when anybody would be a fool not to garden."

As always, she had nicotiana (all those Meriwethers and their tobacco!) and phlox, daylilies, iris, and foxglove. She dug up wild columbine and maidenhair at Tory Valley and brought them back to Princeton. When she visited Stark Young's country place, she brought back wild flowers. She ordered daffodils by the carload, and changed her milkman in order to have access to a barnyard full of manure.

Caroline wrote and rewrote a long review of *Parade's End,* which, with an introduction by Robie Macauley, collected four of Ford Madox Ford's out-of-print novels: *Some Do Not* (1924), *No More Parades* (1925), *A Man Could Stand Up* (1926), and *The Last Post* (1928). Her review, on the front page of *The New York Times Book Review* of September 17, 1950, called Ford "one of the most brilliant and faithful recorders of his time" and "the best craftsman of his day." Caroline wrote Janice, Ford's widow, that Harvey Breit of the *Book Review* staff inserted a sentence to the effect that there was too much in Ford's novels. "This sentence could not have been written by anybody who understood the novels," she said. "He also cut out what to me was the heart of the review. I said, as I remember, that Ford's was a voice calling in the wilderness of contemporary letters, saying that letters is a kind of life of the soul and must be passionately and stubbornly defended." It would have been much easier, she told Janice, to write the review for a literary magazine, for she had "to calculate and translate my meaning into language for the simple-minded."

That fall the Tates started remodeling Benbrackets in order to add a combined kitchen and dining room downstairs and a bedroom and bath upstairs. Since they would be without a kitchen and bathroom for some time, they moved the refrigerator into Allen's study, set up a sort of kitchen in the living room, and ate on the terrace while the weather was still warm. The bathroom was more of a problem. Since the toolshed had once been a one-hole privy, they had thought they might return it to its original use, but the workmen ripped the privy to pieces before the Tates could stop them. They could use the Hesperides' bathroom next door or the Thorps' across the street, but Caroline warned Nancy not to bring the children for a visit during the next six weeks. Caroline came home one day to find that the workmen had ripped off one end of the house, including a closet, and all their clothes were thrown all over their bedroom. Allen, unable to get at his desk for two months, formed the habit of rising at four o'clock to write necessary business letters before the workmen arrived.

Caroline said Allen hung over the workmen as they drove each nail. With Bill Brown's help, Allen painted the inside of the little house; they had the outside painted white with green shutters. "The very peculiar little chimney at the west side we have left unpainted—the bricks must be two hundred years old and are that wonderful rose pink," Caroline said.

"The last two months have been hellish," she wrote Fannie. "I'm experienced in upheavals but this was the worst I ever sustained. Plaster powder an inch thick over every object in the house and whenever I contrived some rough kind of order the workmen would rip out a wall and the center of equilibrium would have to be reestablished."

The remodeled house was so convenient Caroline began to worry for fear it would affect her prose style. The kitchen and the bathroom were the best parts, she said, and made washing dishes practically no trouble. The living room was even nicer with the bookcases out of it. They had five closets and she was a little worried over having everything so fine. "It really is the cutest little house you ever saw and you won't ever see another house like it, so you'd better just come up and see it," she wrote Fannie. It wasn't good for artists to live too easily, but paying off the loan at the bank would keep their noses to the grindstone. "I guess we won't be tempted to enjoy the house too much," Caroline observed.

As soon as she could get to her typewriter, she wrote to Nancy about the most interesting book she had read in years, a biography of St. Teresa by a Catholic author who told you all the little things about her that you never knew. She wished Andrew Lytle had had it when he was writing his de Soto book—it told so much about sixteenth-century Spain.

Dorothy Day spent the night with them in Princeton late in 1950. Allen, as well as Caroline, was mightily impressed with her. "She is quite a sight," Caroline wrote Nancy. "The figure is deplorable—farinaceous food does spread one out so—but her head and shoulders are magnificent. And the clothes she gets out of the 'clothes room' look wonderful on her. It is particularly interesting to us to observe her because we remember so well what she looked like in the old days: the same features but transformed because they have been put to such a different use."

The Thorps had brought the Tates gin from Poland Spring, Maine, in a bottle in the shape of Moses. When Dorothy admired the bottle, Caroline gave it to her to take to her chapel to be filled with holy water.

They marveled that the forlorn girl they had known in Greenwich Village was now the editor of *The Catholic Worker*, which had a circulation of 65,000 and was read with attention by cardinals and, no doubt, said Caroline, the pope himself. Dorothy had acquired two mansions in New York, using them for *The Catholic Worker* office and places to feed 500 men a day and sleep as many as she could. Then there were the Houses of Hospitality all over the country—some of them farms, run like medieval communes, where people lived and worked, making their living as best they could. "She always has a few broken down priests on her hands so she has a private chapel and can have sung masses any time she wants to, not to mention Prime and Matins and Lauds and Sexte and None and Vespers and Compline," Caroline wrote to Nancy.

Caroline went down to speak at Dorothy's flophouse—Dorothy would not allow her to call it a mission—and decided she coveted Dorothy's library. "All the books I want to read and can't get in the university libraries are on her shelves. As a gesture toward voluntary poverty, chastity and obedience, she has put all her books on the open shelves, where the bums can take them out and sell them for liquor if they are so inclined. She is awfully glad to lend them to me for an indefinite period. I reckon she feels that for a time at least they are safe from the bums," Caroline wrote.

Nancy and Percy would not have to worry about her in her old age, at least, if her present plans worked out. She was going to live in Dorothy's community if she got too feeble to teach. "She is fixing up cells in the barn, any one of which would suit me to a T. Zov can live there, too, if he wants to. No doubt he will be converted to Catholicism himself by that time."

28

PRINCETON, 1950–1951

With Jacques and Raissa Maritain as his godparents, Allen was baptized into the Catholic Church on December 22, 1950, at St. Mary's Priory, run by the Benedictines in Morristown, New Jersey. Caroline wrote Ward Dorrance that Allen had prepared for his baptism in characteristic fashion, plowing through two huge volumes of *The Catholic Faith*, stopping occasionally to convict her of various heresies. The things he knew about the Holy Ghost and Original Sin! She was, she said, in a dither of delight over his conversion.

Nancy and Percy had been taking instruction in Washington (Percy had finished medical school in Memphis the year before and was interning at the United States Naval Center in Bethesda) and had hoped to join the Church on the same day, but their instructor, whom Caroline described as "a careful Jesuit," thought that they were not fully informed.

It was said that Allen joined the Church so he could write, "as a Catholic," a letter to *The New York Times* protesting Cardinal Spellman's attempt to suppress the movie *The Miracle*. The cardinal's efforts were not necessary, Allen said, because bad art did not endure. Friends of the Tates were much amused by the letter when it appeared. Peter Taylor said the letter should have begun, "As a Catholic of many weeks,"

Randall Jarrell said he didn't know what the cardinal thought of being called a heretic, "but he might as well get used to it."

Caroline wrote to Robert Stallman, a writer and professor who directed a writers' conference at the University of Connecticut, that Allen was getting plenty of fan mail about the letter. "It seems that entering the Church doesn't change one's nature overnight. He is as controversialist in it as he was out of it but he sure is enjoying being in it. He is awfully strict about observances and scolds me roundly if I slip up on a Holy Day of obligation."

Allen was happy and said he had longed all his life to be a Catholic. He acquired a vast store of Roman Catholic trivia that enchanted Caroline. She marveled that he knew what Ebionites were and how the Greek Orthodox Church and the Roman Church split over the *filioque* clause. When Nancy and Percy and all their children, as well as several of the Tates' friends, joined the Church, Jacques Maritain said that Allen's conversion was like that of King Clovis of the Franks when the whole country followed him in.

Caroline was afraid that Nancy, when she did join the Church, would be disappointed in the priests at confession. They took it as a routine matter, Caroline wrote her. "I have decided, though, that the trouble— at least my trouble—all along has been me and not the priest. The priest—any priest—is ready to hear a good confession. I didn't know how to make one until recently and am only beginning to suspect how to do it now. I think perhaps the best thing is to make a general confession. For instance, my worst sin is self-love. It is better to tell the priest about that than to tell him how I forgot and ate meat on Friday, but he is willing to listen to any confession of either sin."

Caroline enclosed a little tract of St. Ignatius's exercises for Nancy. He was certainly one of the greatest geniuses that ever lived, she said, and his prayer, Anima Christi, contained the whole doctrine of the Church. Many Protestants had the idea that saying a prayer like that or the Hail Mary or Our Father over and over all your life—was mere rigamarole . . . but you could say the Anima Christi every day of your life and not fathom its whole meaning because it was the work of a miracle. St. Ignatius was miraculously inspired when he wrote it. It had taken Caroline four years to even begin to surmise what was meant by the phrase "Blood of Christ, inebriate me."

She urged Nancy to read St. Catherine of Siena's *Dialogue*. She had already ordered a copy from Sheed & Ward for her. "Right now this seems to me practically the best book I ever read in my life," she said. Saint Catherine "could have been probably the greatest fiction writer of all time if she had thought it was worth her while."

Catholicism affected every thought Caroline had and even made her recast her views of the Civil War. She wrote Lon Cheney that a chapter left out of *None Shall Look Back* had been devoted to the thesis that only a few of the men in high command knew what was going on, "or, rather subordinated themselves to the action. Forrest and Sherman subordinated themselves to the action. That is, they acknowledged that the issues at stake were bigger than they were. So did Stonewall Jackson. Lee didn't. He remained always outside of the action, judging it, weighing it, while the others flung themselves into it, to be saved or destroyed, according as things turned out. I don't know that I'd see things just the same way now. Lee's attitude, for instance, it seems to me now might have been dictated by the fact that he was a Christian."

While Caroline worked away on *The Strange Children*, the seed for another novel was germinating in her imagination. Reading the *Dialogue* of St. Catherine of Siena, she had been struck with the resemblance between her image of the bridge as Christ and Hart Crane's images of the Bridge. When Crane was writing his poem *The Bridge* at Tory Valley, Caroline had thought that the Brooklyn Bridge was too frail to stand up under the imagery he loaded on it. After her conversion and her discovery of St. Catherine, Caroline decided that Hart Crane had seized on an archetypal symbol. She tried, without success, to sell this idea to various graduate students. In 1950 she wrote Sister Bernetta Quinn, a Catholic scholar, who began to develop the idea further for an essay that would eventually appear in her book *The Metamorphic Tradition in Modern Poetry*. Sister Bernetta wrote Caroline that Crane and St. Catherine were both intense personalities and "the tremendous implications of the Incarnation must have stirred him as well as her, despite his lack of contact with the church." Caroline still reflected on the idea and was getting ready to convert it to fiction in the next book she wrote, *The Malefactors*.

Early in 1951 she wrote Stark Young that she had finished *The Strange Children* and was now starting on the revision. She boasted of her technical feat in using the central intelligence for its moral effect and the innocent eye for the brilliance of its recording. "I wanted more range than I could get through the child's intelligence or sensations but hadn't even considered how I'd get it. Then you came to see us that Sunday. I don't know whether that had anything to do with it or not, but the memory buried at least fifteen years rose to the surface the next morning. I remember, years ago, reading *River House* and admiring the way you managed the denouement—by a sudden change of view point in the very last paragraph of the book, as I remember it. I think I had probably been pondering your tactics, underground, so to speak, all these years, for the next morning I was handed the solution of my problem, on a platter, as it were. Isn't that interesting?"

About the same time she wrote to Lon, who was working on a novel that also had Holy Rollers in it, that there was an "unholy prejudice against Holy Rollers." It was part of the prejudice against regional writing, she said. She had run into it with her Indians in *Green Centuries*. Frederick Lewis Allen had written her about her settlers, "We can't get much interested in 'Hit war' people." She was still writing about "Hit war" people, but she had a colleague at Columbia who had written a book about a black Holy Roller preacher who had run through communism and other isms and had gone back to his Holy Roller faith. Editors refused to believe that an educated Negro would do such a thing. "Therefore it seems to me that anybody who has such a theme as you and I and this man must manage some way to dramatize it so that they can't keep from believing it."

Her novel was, Caroline said, a story of a man's conversions, but she had stated and dramatized the theme in five different ways. She listed the "strange children" in her novel—Lucy; Lucy's parents; "Uncle Tubby" MacCollum, Lucy's father's best friend, who has just made a lot of money when Hollywood bought his long poem, *If It Takes All Summer*, for the movies; Kevin Reardon, another old friend, immensely rich, who has recently been converted, and his wife, Isabel, with whom Tubby is in love. Lucy, Caroline said, falls in love with Tubby and is shocked when she comes on Tubby and Isabel making love in the woods.

The MacDonoughs, the tenants who are believing Holy Rollers are the fifth set of "strange children." Always impressed with Mr. Norman's sincerity and true spirituality, Caroline said she had tried to convey some of this in the novel. "I want to show people that these Holy Rollers have really got something, something that the reader presumably hasn't got and had better start getting. But when you write about Holy Rollers you totter on the verge of the 'regional novel.' Nobody but Donald Davidson approves of the regional novel. But the virtues the regional novel exalts are timeless and not bound to any locality. In my novel, Mr. MacDonough and Kevin Reardon are exactly the same kind of man."

When Percy Wood finished his internship in February 1951, he and Nancy and their two little boys came to Princeton. Percy, who had put off doing anything definite about a residency in psychiatry, the next step in his medical career, thought he had Hodgkin's disease and believed he would be dead in a few months. (Later he said this was why he had joined the Catholic Church.) Caroline made a bargain with God: she would quit smoking and Percy was *not* to have Hodgkin's disease. It must have been efficacious—Percy did not have the disease.

Percy realized later that he had been dragging his feet about a residency because he was basically afraid of commitment to adult things. He had put off taking his state boards and didn't have a license. Caroline was nervous about her son-in-law, but she was very realistic, helpful, and intuitive. She had Ken Wallis, the only psychiatrist in Princeton, to dinner; Wallis told Percy about the Trenton State Hospital's residency program, which was associated with the University of Pennsylvania. Percy was admitted to the program.

Allen urged Nancy and Percy to live at Benbrackets, telling his daughter that they would be a valuable buffer between him and Caroline, who was, he said, more and more difficult to live with. Alcohol was now a problem for both Caroline and Allen. When she was having dinner in New York with Léonie Adams and her husband, Caroline passed out, and Léonie took her to Perry Street, where Sue Jenkins put her to bed. "The truth is," Caroline wrote apologetically to Léonie, "I am a bit of an alcoholic. I have had to give up whiskey entirely. I see that sherry will have to go, too." Often when Caroline had too many drinks, she became quarrelsome, and sometimes there were recurrent temper "fits," mayhem, and broken crockery. It was these rages—inexplicable, it seemed—that Allen complained about to Nancy. There is a theory, rather attractive to partisans of Caroline's, that anger and violence were her reaction to Allen's philandering, but the theory is too pat; the Tates' situation was more complex than just action and reaction.

Sam Monk, their old friend who had been with them at Southwestern and was now at the University of Minnesota, offered Allen a job teaching there, to begin in the fall of 1951. Allen took it, grateful that he would have tenure for the first time in his life and that he would no longer have to live like a wandering scholar in the Middle Ages. The College of St. Catherine in St. Paul asked Caroline to teach one class and she accepted with pleasure. "You are getting a letter from a woman who has achieved her worldly ambition," she said when she wrote to Ward Dorrance about the invitation to teach there. "I have a particular devotion to St. Catherine. She seems to me the most admirable woman that ever lived and it seems almost too good to be true that I am going to be allowed to teach under her aegis. [The College of St. Catherine was not named for Caroline's favorite, St. Catherine of Siena, but for St. Catherine of Alexandria, a martyr who was ordered broken on the wheel.] To tell the truth I was pretty damn sick of teaching under Protestant aegises." It was settled that the Woods would remain at Benbrackets, rent free, after the Tates went to Minnesota in the fall.

Meanwhile, in February 1951 Fannie Cheney went to Japan for a year and a half on library business and Lon was at loose ends. He drove up to Princeton and he and Caroline racketed around the country in his car. They spent a couple of months in the summer of 1951 at Tory Valley with Sue Jenkins, went up to Stockbridge, Massachusetts, to see Tommy Mabry and his wife, Ethel, drove through Canada, and came down through Detroit on their way to Bloomington, Indiana, where the Kenyon School of English had moved and become the School of Letters.

In Ohio the car broke down. "We suddenly began to boil and almost exploded," Caroline wrote to Nancy. "We stayed in a motel for twenty-four hours while the car was being mended. It was a mile to town and we were broke. We wired Allen for money but it was most embarrassing until it came. The garage people said they would take Lon's check for the car but we didn't like to ask them for pin money, so we had to count our ten-cent drinks of beer at 'The Batt's Nest' most carefully, and just spent most of our time sleeping."

At Bloomington the writers' conference started, while the School of Letters had been going on for two weeks. Caroline said that everybody they ever knew was there—Glenway Wescott, Peter and Eleanor Taylor, Eric Bentley, Delmore Schwartz, Robert Fitzgerald, Francis Fergusson, and Philip Rahv, who kept asking Caroline for Dexedrine. Rahv was so insistent that Caroline wrote Nancy and asked her to look for an old prescription she had for it—it was probably in that old leather billfold that belonged to Ford, she said.

The Tates and Lon stayed in the house that belonged to the chairman of the art department and stumbled over the statuary in the garden when they came in late at night. Caroline gave herself up to a "debauch" in painting, fearing it was the last chance she would get for two or three years, as she intended to start a new novel as soon as they got to Minnesota. In the afternoons, they swam in a limestone quarry that looked, Caroline said, like a swimming pool some pharaoh had started and quit in a pet. They saw a lot of Dr. Alfred Kinsey, and Caroline, fascinated by his language, threatened to call people when she got back to Princeton and say, "Could you and your Sexual Partner pop in for a drink Tuesday afternoon?"

When the term was over, the faculty had what Lon Cheney called "the wildest party"; it went on almost all night. The house where the party was held had wooden Indians and a sculpture of a horse, and for the rest of his life Lon carried with him the picture of Caroline, inspired by D. H. Lawrence's story "The Rocking-Horse Winner," astride the horse, whipping it into a lather at three o'clock in the morning.

She and Allen left Bloomington the first week in August to drive back to Princeton and ready themselves for Minneapolis. Before they left, Allen went to his first retreat, conducted by Dom Hubert Van

Zeller at St. Mary's Priory. "He's been going about in a daze since he got back," Caroline wrote to Stark Young.

When *The Strange Children* appeared in 1951, it struck most readers as cold and unfeeling and seemed to be about people lacking in common decency. Her earlier novels—tragic and full of despair though they were—had characters who were colorful and passionate and alive. There was energy in the story of Orion Outlaw crossing the mountains in search of new land, in the story of Penhally and the generations who lived there, and in the story of the men who rode with Forrest and the women who stayed at home in the Civil War novel. *The Strange Children* is arid.

Many reviewers disliked it, saying that relations were unclear and watery, that Lucy was odious and her interpretations of adult talk more stupid than childlike, that Caroline had pushed her bent toward cerebrational motivation to a point where readers would wonder what it was all about, and that there was too much symbolism and high dramatics. On the other hand, when a British edition appeared a year later, Anthony Curtis, writing in *New Statesman and Nation,* said that "the sly irony springing from the child's perceptive nine-year-old mind is sustained for the whole of Miss Gordon's unusual and poignant novel." Although he found an "artificiality, a self-consciousness in her symbolism," he said that Caroline was "the most original and suggestive of writers. I have not come across anything so daring, so free from the burden of dead tradition in a long time."

Caroline turned from her own novel to the work of two young Catholic novelists, the first of whom was Walker Percy. Orphaned at thirteen, Percy was raised in the Greenville, Mississippi, home of his Uncle William Alexander Percy, a poet, a lawyer, and author of *Lanterns on the Levee,* who died in 1942. The Percys had spent their summers at Monteagle and young Percy had looked with awe upon the Tates, Andrew Lytle, Robert Lowell, and Jean Stafford. After he left medical school, Percy wrote a novel and sent it to Caroline. "She was the only literary person I knew. She wrote me a thirty-page single-spaced letter," he recalled. "It was an extraordinary kindness. She told me everything that was wrong with the novel." Did he take her advice? "Not really," Percy said. "The valuable thing was the relationship with her. She had an extraordinary personality."

Walker Percy, Caroline wrote Lon Cheney, "had sort of disappeared from Sewanee after stirring up a lot of commotion in the dove cotes up there and all we'd heard about him since was that he'd got married and joined the Church. It is evident now that in the five or six years he's been lying doggo that he's done a lot of reading and thinking and writing. The [manuscript] is five hundred pages. My heart sank when I saw it. I feared a Wolfe had got into the fold. [Caroline used to keep Wolfe-bane nearby when she read young people's manuscripts in those days, since they were often influenced by Thomas Wolfe.] But not so. It is . . . a sample of what the next development in the novel will be according to me! And it *will* be something new. At least something we have not had before. Novels written by people consciously rooted and grounded in the faith. People who don't have to set the universe up fresh for every performance, people who don't have to spend time trying to figure out what moral order prevails in the universe and therefore have more energy for spontaneous creation. I feel quite certain about this."

Percy, who had joined the Catholic Church about the same time that Caroline did, kept in touch with her the rest of her life.

Also in 1951, Robert Fitzgerald sent Caroline a manuscript by a young Catholic writer from Georgia, Flannery O'Connor. It was *Wise Blood*. Caroline always said that she knew genius when she saw it. She wrote Fitzgerald that she was quite excited about the manuscript: "This girl is a real novelist. (I wish that I had had as firm a grasp on my subject matter when I was her age!) At any rate, she is already a rare phenomenon: a Catholic novelist with a real dramatic sense, one who relies more on her technique than her piety." Caroline told Fitzgerald that she would like to make a few suggestions. Her suggestions do not survive. Flannery rewrote the book, had it retyped, and asked Fitzgerald if Mrs. Tate would read the revised version. Mrs. Tate would. Flannery told the Fitzgeralds that Caroline had sent the revised manuscript back with nine pages of comments "and she certainly increased my education thereby." One of the points that Caroline always hammered away at was the necessity for the omniscient narrator to speak in Johnsonian English, avoiding expressions like "green-peaish color" or "squinched."

Flannery replied gratefully, saying that she needed all the help she could get. There was no one around Milledgeville, Georgia, she said, "who knows anything at all about fiction (every story is 'your article,' or 'your cute piece'?) or much about any kind of writing for that matter. Sidney Lanier and Daniel Whitehead Hickey are the Poets and Margaret Mitchell is the Writer. Amen. So it means a great deal to me to get these comments."

It was a friendship and a "master class," as Flannery's biographer Sally Fitzgerald calls it, that endured until Flannery's death in 1964. Caroline read and commented on every novel and every short story that Flannery wrote.

"It is no accident, I'm sure," Caroline wrote Lon, "that in the last two months the two best novels I've ever read have been by Catholic writers." The two novels, she continued, marked a turning point. "The Protestant *mystique* has worn out," she said, "but people would have gone on forever writing those curiously dry novels (like Lionel Trilling or . . . Truman Capote) . . . if something new hadn't come along. And Walker's novel and Flannery's novel are IT. They are both so damned good!"

29

MINNEAPOLIS, 1951–1952

Another town, another house. How many had there been? New York, Paris, Benfolly, Toulon, Benfolly, Memphis, Monteagle, Greensboro, Princeton, Monteagle, Washington, Sewanee, New York again, Chicago, Princeton again, and now Minneapolis.

Joseph Warren Beach had just retired as chairman of the English department at the University of Minnesota and gone to Europe, and Sam Monk rented his house for the Tates. Near the campus, it was big, ramshackle, dark, dingy, dignified, and comfortable, and placed on the lot, Caroline said, so that there was not a pleasant prospect from any window. Still, it was wonderful to have room for all her papers after having them mixed up with Tinker Toys and marbles for all those months with the Woods in Benbrackets.

Caroline wrote to her friends that she was mad about the country. Everything was so big, and the sky was the highest and widest and the cleanest blue she had ever seen. The Mississippi River, which ran right through town, was steel blue, except when it was bronze or green or scarlet from the trees along its banks. The earth was rich and black and the farmers all had round, red faces—so different from that gaunt look that Southern farmers have, she wrote Lon Cheney. Even the first snow was beautiful to her and she marveled at the Mississippi

River after it froze. Northerners loved to hear her tell how she tried to melt the ice on the front steps by pouring boiling water on it.

Early on, she said she felt another novel closing in on her and by the time of the first snowfall had finished the first chapter. This was to be the story of Tom Claiborne, a forty-eight-year-old blocked writer who shuts himself in his study every day pretending to work on a long poem, actually nonexistent. Tom's rich wife, Vera, owns the Bucks County farm where they live and raises purebred red poll cattle. There was much talk of Vera's champion bull, Blencker's Brook's Best Man, or Bud, and a great deal of discussion of artificial insemination, of which Caroline violently disapproved. She was so lucky, Caroline wrote to her editor at Scribner's. When she was writing her Civil War novel with Nathan Forrest as the hero, she went to live in Memphis on Forrest Avenue a few blocks from where his great sword hung on the wall of his granddaughter's bungalow. When she turned to her pioneer novel, she went to live in North Carolina, sixty miles from where Daniel Boone lived. Now she was at the University of Minnesota, "a fountainhead of artificial insemination."

The faculty wives came to call on Caroline and admired her peculiar charm, "an ingenuous quality that was not unconscious," as one of them put it. The faculty found both Tates, by and large, entertaining and attractive, even if Caroline was a bit dotty about the Catholic Church. A story made the rounds that she had gone into a church and genuflected in front of the drinking fountain, but then everyone conceded that Caroline might well have started the story herself. Caroline's superb skill with the sweeping statement left them dazzled. At a party, Caroline was overheard telling the artist Gyorgy Knepes, a visiting lecturer, "Of course, you must admit there has been no worthwhile painting since Piero della Francesca." The faculty, who thought all Southerners had aristocratic tastes, was agreeably surprised to find that the Tates willingly drank cheap bourbon.

The housekeeping was nothing, she wrote Nancy. Simply nothing. A student came once a week for a dollar an hour and vacuumed the whole house. She turned a bay off the living room into an oratory. It had two sunny windows and a little sofa where Mr. Beach, the Tates were told, used to lure the prettiest young faculty wives; the Tates' crucifix was now on the wall. It made a splendid oratory, she wrote Nancy. "I keep my breviary there and say Matins in the morning while my egg is boiling and then say Lauds after I have consumed the egg." Later, she ordered birdseed and put up a bird feeder at the oratory window. "I must have some wildlife around here," she said.

As always, they were worried about money. After they paid the rent and the installments on expensive storm windows for Benbrackets "and a few other things," Caroline and Allen had about $200 a month to live on. "It sounds absurd, when you consider the good salary Allen is making, but that's the way it is," she wrote Nancy. Caroline told Nancy all this because she had promised to send her the money she would get for speaking at a library dinner—and she did not get paid. Since she could not send this money, she said she would pay for the boys' clothes Nancy had charged to her at Best's. Sue Jenkins wrote to ask Caroline if she didn't want to sell the land in Tory Valley back to her. Allen, who handled their money, wrote Sue without consulting Caroline and said she did. Sue's check came in the next mail. "It was so badly needed that I had to keep it," Caroline told Nancy, but she hoped to pay Sue back the next year. She wanted to keep that land— it was such a lovely situation.

They visited Hunt Brown, a professor in the English department who lived on the Lake of the Isles, and his wife, Bid. While Allen and Biddy played the violin, Hunt, Sam Monk, and Caroline walked around the lake, three and a half miles. Sam dined with the Tates every Tuesday, and the Tates entertained and were entertained by David and Virginia Erdman, the Louis Coxes, Danforth Ross, a cousin from the Old Neighborhood who was now a graduate student, and his wife, and the Leonard Ungers, among others. Caroline wrote Lon that she liked Leonard Unger immensely; he had been brought up in Nashville by his grandparents "who gave him the orthodox Jewish viewpoint—as Allen says, it's a little like being brought up by a Confederate, only much more formidable." Like Caroline, Leonard did not drive, and she said to him, "We're too fine." Once when they had the Ungers to dinner Caroline came out of the kitchen and announced, "I cooked this duck and I'd looked forward to cooking it, but I forgot it was Friday. Well, it's cooked, and we might as well eat it." When they got home, the Ungers discovered it was Thursday. The Tates went on a picnic with the Coxes but it was so cold they sat in the car and drank martinis and ate their sandwiches. They gave a dinner party for the younger faculty members in the department.

They invited Lon Cheney up to visit (Fannie was still in Japan) assuring him there was plenty of room in the house for three novels to be written. They rented the attic bedroom to a graduate student named Edwy Lee. Harry Duncan and Paul Williams of the Cummington School came out for a protracted visit. (Their Cummington Press had published the beautiful edition of Allen's *The Winter Sea*.) Harry and Paul were ardent converts who had chosen Allen and Caroline for their godparents. Caroline said it was a great relief they had given up their sinful way of life and were in the Church. "They were always rushing down to Princeton to tell us about their lovers' quarrels. Now they just worry about our souls."

Caroline, infatuated with everything Catholic, thought the atmosphere was delightful at the College of St. Catherine. She wrote Lon that the president, Mother Antonine, looked like Caroline's mother might have looked "if she had espoused Jesus Christ instead of my father." For her seminar every Monday from 3:30 to 5:15, twelve girls gathered around a table surrounded by an outer circle of nuns. One of her auditors was Abigail McCarthy, an alumna, who was the wife of the congressman from that area, Eugene McCarthy.

But Caroline's high standards caused infinite problems for Sister Maris Stella, chairman of the English department, who discovered that Caroline wanted in her class only people who could write. One of the girls in the class wanted badly to write, but she had dyslexia. After Caroline read her paper, Sister Maris Stella had to tell the girl she could not come to the class. As the semester passed, fewer and fewer students came, until there were only three girls. Since Caroline could not drive, Sister Maris Stella found a student to drive her back to Minneapolis from St. Paul; as time went by and the weather got worse, Caroline asked for a man—she didn't feel safe with a woman driver.

She threw herself into painting, and worked on a picture of St. Cuthbert and the otters. The natural history museum was nearby and she could go there to make sketches of the animals for her paintings, but it was harder to get models for the saints. She started sewing again and wrote for Percy to send her sewing machine.

In the spring of 1952 Allen was invited, along with William Faulkner, James T. Farrell, Katherine Anne Porter, Glenway Wescott, Louis MacNeice, and W. H. Auden, to be a delegate to a festival of modern arts, sponsored by the Congress for Cultural Freedom in Paris. The festival, designed to show "what man can create when his mind is not subject to totalitarian constraints," lasted from April 30 until June 1. Allen borrowed $350 from Scribner's for the journey, promising to repay the loan when he was reimbursed for his expenses. The writers played just a small part in the show, which included art exhibitions, concerts, ballet, and opera. Genêt, reporting on the conference in *The New Yorker*, remarked that "few writers talk well and most talk too long." Faulkner, she said, "muttered some incoherent phrases about how American muscles and French brains could form the coming cultural world and sat down, small, reserved, and inarticulate behind his little Southern mustache." Years later, in 1966, *The New York Times* revealed that part of the funding for the Congress of Cultural Freedom's festival had come from the Central Intelligence Agency.

After the festival Allen went to London, where he spoke on the BBC, was guest of honor at literary parties, decided he was in love with Natasha Spender, Stephen Spender's wife, and felt that they were enmeshed for life after spending "three perfect days" together in the Cotswolds. He was delirious with happiness when he wrote Katherine Anne about the "treachery and glory of life" that would find him in such a state at his age.

Meanwhile, in Minneapolis, Caroline went to parties, gave the Phi Beta Kappa address at St. Catherine's, and built a herb garden with Edwy Lee. She and Edwy resolved not to drink after dinner. In fact, Caroline had promised God that if He would get Allen safely back and forth across the ocean and onto the ground and also "take care of" a friend of theirs who was being tried for sodomy, she would never touch hard liquor again.

Allen came home, bringing Caroline an antique cross encrusted with sapphires and diamonds, a "slightly obscene" Gaudier-Brzeska drawing, which Sir Osbert Sitwell had helped him pick out, and many stories. Caroline wrote to Nancy that "Gpa had a marvelous time both in Paris and London. The climax of the festivities was a dinner party given in his honor by Dr. Edith Sitwell at which Dame Myra Hess played Beethoven. No, that was the party Mrs. Spender gave—Dr. E. gave a luncheon party. Mrs. S. told him to do his homework before her dinner and made him memorize the titles of at least five of Dr. Sitwell's poems. He worked away at Dr. Sitwell with a will and they got on fine, but he fears he spoiled it all by saying to Louis MacNeice in the gents' room of Dr. Edith's London ladies' club, 'Do you think I flattered Edith enough?' and then looking up to see Sir Osbert standing a few feet away."

By this time the Tates' marriage was as ramshackle as the Beach house. Most of the world saw them as an amusing couple, once a bit cracked on the Old Confederacy and now obsessed with the Catholic Church, but still, in spite of one divorce, a viable couple. They were as generous and helpful to their friends and to other writers as they had always been; Caroline still wrote six- and eight-page single-spaced letters to Lon Cheney about his novel and to Ward Dorrance about his short stories, while Allen continued to find jobs and fellowships for poets and to help them get published. They went out together and they had company, as always.

Behind the façade, however, lived two people who were in great pain. They drank immoderately. Caroline would say, "Just one ice cube, please. Ice is bad for my ulcer." Once Virginia Erdman watched her lean against the wall, sipping a drink, then slide gently to the floor, drink in hand. But there was no scandal, no talk that either of them drank excessively. With Natasha Spender, Allen abandoned all discretion; he talked openly of his great love with colleagues and friends. Edwy Lee recalled that W. H. Auden warned his friends to keep their wives away from Allen. Allen retaliated with a limerick whose last line was "How different, how different is Wystan."

Caroline, who had always been fiercely jealous of Allen, was for a while unaware of the way he felt about Natasha. She was angry about Allen's flirtations, in general, and worried about the state of his mental health. He had what she called "his attacks." She lost her temper. He reacted to her temper with "violence"—they both used the word. On the other hand, they were dependent on each other in different ways, and, incredibly, they still loved each other.

Allen left for the School of Critical Studies at the University of Vermont on June 6. Caroline went to Utah to teach at a writers' conference. She wrote Nancy that Percy must get her some Dexedrine so she would have it for the conference. From there she went to Princeton to see Nancy and the children. There were now three—a daughter named Caroline had been born in January, and Grandmother Caroline much admired her namesake. She predicted that little Caroline would be like her—a homely little girl with two handsome brothers. But then she was smarter than her brothers, and surely little Caroline would be, too. Benbrackets was so full of children, bottles, and diapers that Allen and Caroline rented Richard Blackmur's apartment for July and August. She was upset by the amount of work Nancy had to do and arranged to sell one of her de Koonings so she could give Nancy money for household help.

Lon Cheney appeared, fresh from successfully managing the election campaign of Frank Clements, a spellbinding young orator, for the governorship of Tennessee. He brought a play he had written for Caroline to read and stayed until he got word that Fannie was home.

The Tates thought of selling Benbrackets but decided to keep it so Nancy and her family would have a place to live as long as Percy's training kept him in the Princeton area. This condemned them to living "in a balloon" in Minnesota, Caroline said. She didn't care much what kind of house she had as long as she could stay in it long enough to plant a few bulbs. "I have never stuck a bulb in the ground that I didn't move on the next fall," she said. "What I crave is the opportunity to garden. I am really hardly human without it."

Allen had managed to get another trip abroad in the late summer, this time as a delegate to a UNESCO conference in Venice. The only reason Caroline objected to his going abroad again, she wrote Robert Lowell, was that the trip would interrupt his work on his long poem *The Buried Lake*. To see him off, she left a retreat at Dorothy Day's Maryfarm near Newburgh, New York, that was, she said, "the finest experience I ever had." Dorothy Day called it the "basic retreat," and said it was modeled on one she had attended in Canada. The approach of Father Casey, the "retreat master," was "frankly mystical," Caroline wrote Allen, "and all based on that passage from St. Augustine . . . 'spiritual gravity.' He taught the way I try to teach, resorting to graphs every now and then, starting out with the circle as a symbol for God and then tri-secting it with the Trinity." She admired the brilliant way he used geometry and fairy tales throughout and the way he quoted as Jacques Maritain quoted. She made notes—ten single-spaced type-written pages—on Father Casey's talks, illustrated with her drawings of his charts.

After Allen left, she went back to Maryfarm, and had a dreadful shock when, breaking their silence at noon on the fifth day, people all over the dining room began chatting. She wrote Allen that they must someday build a little house up in Dorothy's orchard. "I know quite well we can't do it—but there's no harm in just saying what you'd like to do, is there?" The house could be far enough away not to see too much of Dorothy's bums but near enough to frequent their chapel. "Living where the liturgy goes on every day makes life entirely different. . . . And the chapel built by Dorothy's old seaman, Hans, is really lovely. . . . Their Way of the Cross is wonderful. One of those old country lanes, bordered on each side by stone walls. We made a procession through it with the statue I gave them singing Salve Regina." She closed by saying, "I love you more than I ever did."

She and John Prince went up to stay with Sue Jenkins at Tory Valley, where the cuisine, which in the past had run pretty much to tunafish straight from the can, took a radical turn for the better: John had learned to cook. He turned out *arroz con pollo* and cold cream-of-broccoli soup while Caroline worked on an essay on Henry James in a little shed they called the "Professional Building," the kind of hermetic re-treat every writer longed for, she said. The walls were paneled in "those lovely silvery boards from the old barn. John Hall Wheelock wrote her from Scribner's that Bantam Books had bought *Green Centuries* for paperback publication for $4,000, of which she would receive half. "Imagine not owing Scribner's money—if only for a few weeks!" she wrote Allen. That same letter to Allen reflects her continuing struggle with alcohol. She had "slipped," she told him, the night before and had three beers. Sue had drunk half a bottle of Scotch, though, and nagged her about the different kinds of graces.

Caroline and John then went on to Confederate Hill in Missouri to see Ward Dorrance. She almost wished they had spent the summer there, she wrote Nancy. It was so beautiful, with Ward's garden at its peak—old brick walls, a hedge of rue in the herb garden, a cunning finial atop a dovecote, a duck named Sir Francis Drake, and peacocks that ran away. Caroline soon solved this problem by sprinkling holy water on their tails. "It was amazing, the effect it had on them," Caroline wrote to Nancy. John Prince cooked wonderful food for them; Caroline and Ward took to calling him Saint-Ange because Madame Saint-Ange's cookbook was his holy writ. There was herring roe on toast made from John's homemade bread, and later perfect omelets and lobster tails with two of Madame Saint-Ange's sauces.

While Caroline was at Confederate Hill, Nelson Heath Meriwether, a cousin who had written the Meriwether genealogy, brought his family to visit her. She was enchanted with his book, which he had printed and published in his own print shop. When Caroline asked Meriwether how he had done on the book financially, he was startled; he laid his hand upon his heart and swore that no Meriwether should ever pay him a penny for the book. Through the book Caroline discovered that John Prince was related to her through the Minors—he was so nice that she had always thought he must be a cousin.

Caroline was out of money, and Allen arranged from Italy for Scribner's to send her enough to last her until he got back. John Prince drove her from Missouri to Minnesota.

ST. PAUL, 1952–1953

The Tates rented the house of David and Virginia Erdman, who were away that year, at 1908 Selby in St. Paul. Caroline liked St. Paul better than Minneapolis because it was Catholic. As she did every time they moved, she said the new house was the nicest one she had ever lived in, with its sun porch and sleeping porches. It had a good stove, she wrote Nancy, a good refrigerator, and "the most imposing sink—yards and yards of it." She kept a roomer that the Erdmans had had and rented another room to a College of St. Thomas student on condition that he shovel the snow. Soon Harry Duncan, back for another long visit, occupied another room. Caroline bought a steam iron and learned to use it. She did her own laundry and sent the money she saved to Nancy to pay for household help.

Eugene and Abigail McCarthy lived down the block. He was, Caroline said, the only man in American politics who understood St. Thomas. She always accepted when Abigail called and asked her to pour at a ladies' political tea.

Tommy Mabry came over from Iowa City to help Caroline with her novel. She was thinking of having Cousin Mary dying upstairs, she wrote Nancy. It was going to be one hell of a big novel, "but if you can't write a big novel at the age of fifty-eight I think you might as well shut up shop." Aunt Mary turned into Aunt Virginia in the novel, which indeed had a multitude of characters based on real people, living and dead, whom Caroline had known—Hart Crane was to become Horne Watts and Dorothy Day would become Catherine Pollard. Tom Claiborne, the failed poet, would leave his wife for an ambitious young poet, who could be said to be based on several young women Allen had known. There was to be a homosexual painter, an aging priest, and even a woman psychologist based on Mary Shattuck Fisher, a contributor to *Who Owns America?* and the type of woman intellectual Caroline particularly detested.

Allen, meanwhile, traveled across Europe, from Brussels to Paris to Rome; he had an audience with the pope at Castel Gandolfo, which he found rather disappointing because of the pope's lack of English. He loved Italy and felt, Caroline said, as Nancy did one day in Paris in 1929, when she rolled on the floor yelling, "No more milk, Mama. *Du vin!*" He was saying, "No more Paris. *Du Rome!*" In Venice he saw the Spenders again, as well as Robert Lowell and Elizabeth Hardwick, married since 1949, who sent Caroline a piece of Venetian glass.

"I am convinced that, in line and colour, it surpasses Elinor Wylie's 'Venetian Glass Blower' or any other piece of Venetian glass ever blown," she wrote, thanking the Lowells, adding that she would not be likely to see it except through the eyes of the imagination, since Allen had left it in the New York airport.

Caroline chatted in the letter about the fine time they all must have had "under those Italian skies and all that Palladian stage setting." She was still ignorant of Allen's feeling for Natasha Spender and told the Lowells that the Spenders would be at the University of Minnesota that fall.

Allen was late getting back to Minneapolis and when he did finally arrive, he was exhausted. Later Caroline would tell her friends that when he came back his eyes glittered like Robert Lowell's and he was clearly manic, but at the time she wrote cheery letters saying that all he could talk about was Italy. "Catullus' lake seems to be the spot he loves best—he has an *albergo* all picked out where you can get board and room for three dollars and a half a day on the lake," Caroline wrote Fannie and Lon Cheney. "The fresco towns, Venice, Florence, Rome—well, he's seen 'em all. And can hardly wait to get back." He had wangled a Fulbright professorship at the University of Rome for the next year and the two of them would go in the fall of 1953.

Allen, still working on his long poem, wrote 120 lines in one week, the greatest poetic seizure he ever had, Caroline said. He asked her to substitute for him at the College of St. Thomas in a lecture on the Catholic revival in literature. Caroline read and reread Catholic writers and gamely set out to prove her latest thesis, for which she credited Maritain: that Joyce and Flaubert were more Christian writers than François Mauriac because they were better writers. She promised to send Nancy the money from the lecture for Peto's tuition in private school, and then sold the lecture to *The Sewanee Review.*

Caroline went to visit Tommy Mabry in Iowa City and sat in on a writing class he conducted with two other teachers. She disapproved of the way the class spent two hours discussing a story by a student named Mr. Salazberg. "Not one word—or hardly a word—about what might be right or wrong with it, just round and round about what his 'meaning' was," she wrote to Fannie and Lon Cheney. When time came for me to speak I said I thought we'd get on faster if Mr. S. told us what he meant so we could get down to brass tacks, whereupon Mr. S. replied with some hauteur that what he meant was for him to know and me to find out, whereupon I, with some acerbity, complimented Mr. S. on his head still being a normal size, for, says I nastily, 'I have been writing fiction for over twenty-five years and I feel sure the entire body of my work has never received as much speculation on its meaning as Mr. S.'s short story has received.' . . . Tommy says these sessions just drive him crazy and he can't stem the tide all by himself. . . . As Allen says if they gave any real technical criticism in those sessions the class would boil down to the few students who mean business. As it is, they pack them in—just for the show."

When Dorothy Day came through on a cross-country bus tour of her Houses of Hospitality, Allen said again that she was the most impressive person he had ever met. "He went to sleep one night murmuring, 'Mysterious, so mysterious. Isn't she *mysterious,* Sweetie?' " Dorothy Day traveled with what she called "my suit"—her suit for at least five years, Caroline knew for a fact—and one dress and a supply of reliquaries that she left with people who needed them. She left Allen one containing a bit of flesh of Pope Pius X to help him finish his poem. Allen rejected a reliquary of the Little Flower, all done up in roses, on the grounds that it might cause his style to deteriorate.

Caroline, Allen, and Dorothy worked out plans for a new kind of writers' conference, one where the liturgical life was lived each day, to be held at Maryfarm. They would sing prime, vespers, compline, and the Mass each day. There would be no tuition and students would eat food grown at Maryfarm. And when a student would bring her a manuscript and ask her what was wrong with it, Caroline said, the answer might be, "What's wrong with you?" Allen thought the school should be called "Newburgh Conversations," after a similar affair that French poet Charles Péguy started called Entretiens à Pontigny. Dorothy thought it was a wonderful idea and said, "One thing we must not worry about is money. That will be provided. Leave that to St. Joseph."

Caroline had not stopped performing generous acts for young writers and old friends. In January 1953 she wrote to John Hall Wheelock at Scribner's about Walker Percy and his new novel, "Charterhouse." She wrote two pages about young Percy and praised his novel, saying that she and Allen both thought his was the best talent to come out of the South since Faulkner. A few weeks later she wrote to Wheelock, asking him to help Sue Jenkins get an editing job. Sue, who needed to get out of her "high-powered job as civic secretary of forty-nine neighborhood houses," had been an editor at Macaulay when they put out *American Caravan*, she told Wheelock.

Allen could not pass the physical for the Fulbright; his pulse was 111. One doctor recommended he exercise less. This would not be possible, said Sam Monk, unless someone met Allen at his car every morning and carried him piggy-back to his office.

Caroline, meanwhile, was planning to go to the University of Washington as visiting professor for the spring quarter at a salary of $2,000 for ten weeks. She hurried to type her novel and pack for Seattle, Princeton, the summer, and a year in Europe, as she would not be coming back to Minneapolis. She went by train to Seattle, where some old friends from Paris days, Jackson and Marthiel Mathews, had rented her an apartment in the building where they lived at 4337 Fifteenth Avenue, N.E. She promptly named the apartment the Moated Grange, because her window overlooked a moss-covered roof where snails lived. If she were going to stay there, she would get herself a turtle, she said.

She wrote immediately to Allen about the jonquils, forsythia, and flowering fruit trees she saw all around her. "I miss you so, darling. But I think that maybe God wants us to have this separation. You say the last few months have seemed like a new life. We both got a new life when we were baptized, but it takes a long time to realize you've got it, evidently. Anyhow, I do feel that things between us are different—and better than they have ever been."

But Allen still saw Natasha Spender; he drove her to Washington and took her to Marcella Winslow's house. When Marcella suggested he turned to Mrs. Spender because he was frustrated in his work, he told her he was at the top of his powers and had just written the best poem he had ever written and his recent critical writing was his best, perhaps anybody's best. All he asked was to be loved without question. The trouble between him and Caroline was that she could not say that she loved him no matter what he did. People would understand as soon as they knew how empty his marriage was.

Caroline wrote to him several times from Seattle about their drinking, and when she heard he would be seeing the Spenders she wrote Allen that she was afraid he would fall off the wagon. In the same letter, she told him about the Tau Delta sorority, a group of women who were pledged to have no more than two drinks. (The Greek letters tau delta stood for "two drinks.") If he could just stay off liquor, she wrote him several times, lecture trips wouldn't be so hard on him. "The trouble with us is that we are too greedy. We want to take in every party and work, too," she told him.

Somehow Caroline heard about Allen's trip with Natasha Spender. "Darling," she wrote him, "there is something I want you to do for me, without getting angry about it—because I love you. I want you to examine your conscience about the Spenders. . . . They seem to come on the scene every time we have a reconciliation. I had felt that the reconciliation we had just before I left was real and final in a way that no other had been. It was a shock to find that you had taken the car in order to drive Natasha to Washington without telling me." She added that she thought that the malicious gossip about Spender was not wholly without foundation. "And I must say that it infuriates me to think of his sneering at Ben [Tate]—who is worth fifty of him," she said.

Spender was a sycophant, she said, but what was a sycophant to do except hang about his betters? "I don't know that he can be criticized for that. At the same time—well, I have the same feeling about him that I used to have about Laura Gottschalk, a kind of fear and distrust. I imagine that if we hadn't broken with Laura we would have been in for even more trouble than was waiting for us. There is nothing more trying than these women who set up to be Norns, I know. It is up to you, now I have got this off my chest. I shall be entirely guided by you in my relation with the Spenders. If you tell me you think I ought to be friendly with them I shall certainly meet any overture."

A little later she wrote to him not to worry about her and the Spenders anymore. The apprehension she felt about Stephen might be simply a reaction to his worldliness. She certainly was not going to ask—in cold blood!—that he not see anybody.

Meanwhile, she loved Seattle, which was right between two huge lakes and Puget Sound, with snow-covered mountains rising all around it. When people said, "Rainier is out," it meant it was a fine day, clear enough to see Mount Rainier. The poor mountain hardly got out before it had to go back in again, like a cuckoo clock, Caroline wrote the Cheneys. She was thrilled when it was "out" for three days.

She went to church every day during Holy Week. Her apartment was within walking distance of the university, shops, and Blessed Sacrament, a Dominican church. On the feast day of St. Catherine of Siena she lit a candle for Allen's poem, Harry Duncan's book, and her own book. "I go to Mass by way of the alleys, so I can inspect the little back gardens. They are just the kind I like. Bristling with vegetation. Every inch of ground used. I never saw anything like the rhododendron and azaleas here unless it is the flowering fruit trees. And the rock gardens! They overhang the terraces 'like great baskets of flowers,' as Uncle André [Gide] says of the gardens in Africa." Three days after she got there she had started writing a short story based on correspondence between André Gide and Paul Claudel, which Walker Percy had called to her attention. She drew heavily on Gide's journals and the memoir he wrote about his wife. She worked on "Emmanuele! Emmanuele!" for some time and sold it to *The Sewanee Review.*

She decided to write a book to be called *How to Read a Novel,* for which she signed a contract with Viking, before she finished her novel. For one thing, she said, she might read something that would prove helpful. Allen showed what she had written on the novel to Denver Lindley at Harcourt, Brace. Lindley liked it very much and said that a novel that was "humanly fascinating" and also had religious appeal was a natural in those days.

Allen had been maneuvering for them to leave Scribner's since December, when he had asked for a formal accounting for both of them. John Hall Wheelock replied that Caroline still owed $780.47 on the unearned advance on *Green Centuries.* Allen owed $1,012.72, plus a $500 advance for the introduction to poetry. However, when the money for the paperback edition of *Green Centuries* reached Scribner's, Caroline's $2,000 would reduce these loans and advances to $293.19. There was a debit of $161.93 on the books for *The House of Fiction,* but this would be erased by royalties. Allen wrote to Wheelock in December that he wanted a publisher who would publish everything he wrote— essays, as well as poems—and Henry Regnery, a small publishing company in Chicago, would bring out his essays in full, a small book on Dante and Poe, and the long poem when it was ready. He would never have another book that sold well, he said. (His novel had sold 15,000 copies, he told Wheelock, and his biographies 20,000 each.)

In February, thanks to royalties from *The House of Fiction,* the Tates' debit balance at Scribner's was only $492.81; the advance payment was still to come for *Green Centuries.* Wheelock wrote to tell Allen that the $500 advance for the poetry book had not been included in this reckoning. Allen pointed out that the *Green Centuries* money would wipe this out too. In April Caroline wrote to Wheelock that she had had an offer from another publisher and would be leaving Scribner's.

Wheelock replied with regret and said he was sorry that they had not been able to win the large distribution for her books that her work deserved. By this time, he said, both her and Allen's loan and royalty accounts had been merged into one account.

Caroline had contributed to the family income ever since she and Allen were married in 1925. She worked hard, submitted her essays and stories regularly. She was completely professional about rejections and became angry with the young writers she was advising when they did not behave in the same stoic fashion when their work was rejected. Their incomes were as tangled and knotted together as their lives. No one seemed to think it unfair that money Caroline earned should be used to pay debts that Allen had made.

Allen's Fulbright was finally approved, and Caroline said she hoped to be able to do some sightseeing in Rome. In France she had always worked so hard on her writing that she never saw anything, and she wanted to see Rome. She hoped she could work in the mornings and get out in the afternoons.

Caroline and Allen were not to see each other that summer. Allen was teaching at the University of Vermont and the University of Connecticut until July 3, and he left for Oxford, where he would begin teaching in the American studies program, on July 12. Caroline arrived in Princeton on June 20 to spend two days with Nancy and Percy and the children before she went up to Tory Valley, where the annual Fourth of July party was rather quiet. She told Nancy she stuck to temperance drinks—except for two mild shots of gin at the last.

Bantam's edition of *Green Centuries* appeared in July.

She visited the Mabrys at Stockbridge, where she and Tommy began a play about Gide. They went to Jones Beach, which she loved. "It is divine. I never saw anything finer," Caroline wrote to Allen. "Wonderful sparkling sand, handsome bath houses. Everything immaculately clean. Beds of flowers all about. It was heavenly. We got in three swims, but worked under the umbrella." She and Sue drove over to Maryfarm for the retreat, conducted this year by a Father Judge, who was not, she told Allen, as much fun as Father Casey—no quotations from St. Gregory of Nanzianzus. Sue was impressed with the retreat but she would stay for only one night and would not go to Mass because she said she felt hypocritical when she knelt and conspicuous when she didn't. "I pray for you when I make the stations of the cross and I make them several times a day," Caroline told Allen. When she wasn't working on Tommy's novel or their play, she turned to a short story, "Feast of St. Eustace," based on the first chapter of her novel. Sue thought the bits about artificial insemination were hilarious and agreed to retype it after Caroline left and submit it for her. (It was published in *The Kenyon Review* in the spring of 1954.)

Back at Tory Valley, she learned that Allen had barely reached London before he had to have two teeth pulled, the two from which his bridge depended. He became ill and had to go to the hospital for two days, and delayed his lectures at Oxford until July 17.

She sent Nancy the money for the essay on James, which Monroe Spears had bought for *The Sewanee Review,* and promised to send her the money for "Emmanuele! Emmanuele!" when the *Review* paid for that. The money would be for Nancy's maid, Christine, and "DON'T YOU DARE FIRE HER," she wrote her daughter.

ROME, 1953–1954

Caroline sailed for Southampton from New York in late July on the *Flandre*, sharing a cabin with three other women—two schoolteachers and a fashion designer, one of whom worked out a system whereby each woman got up and bathed at a different time. Caroline took Nembutal every night so she could sleep and nursed a sunburn, but didn't get seasick and ate "good meals with lots of red wine." All her tablemates, she wrote Nancy, drank themselves into a coma at lunch so they could sleep all afternoon. In this same letter, she asked Nancy and Percy to destroy any letters they had from Allen that he might have written during one of his "attacks." She tried to protect him, she said, but she would lose heart if she thought there were damaging letters from him floating around.

Before Caroline arrived in London, Allen, now recovered, had gone to Hastings with Natasha Spender, where she had a concert. On the day Caroline docked, he took Natasha to lunch and then went with John Prince to meet the boat train. (A neighbor of Ward Dorrance's in Missouri had sent John Prince to England to retrieve Dorrance, who had gone abroad to recuperate from an illness and had simply stayed on.)

The Tates stayed in Oxford until Allen finished his teaching stint and then went to London, where they were lent a house at 14 Edwardes Square with a topiary teddy bear in boxwood that Caroline trimmed and watered while she stayed there.

One day Allen asked John Prince and Ward Dorrance to take Caroline to lunch and to the zoo so he could have lunch with Natasha and break up with her. (When Natasha called him later in Rome, Allen said he said to her, "Talk to Caroline," and handed the phone to his wife. Allen would tell this story to his friends with glee and pride.)

The Tates spent one weekend with Herbert Read in his house at Stonegrave in Yorkshire, and Caroline admitted that "envy reared its head often in this bosom." The house was a long building, twice the size of Woodstock, she said, and she would gladly settle for one of Read's chicken houses or privies. A pear tree was espaliered against the wall of one of the wings. A long terrace ran the length of the house in back; here Herbert could sit and look down at his trout stream and watch his ducks, his fantail pigeons, his pony and donkey. His gardener raised tomatoes, grapes, and figs in several greenhouses. Stone walls enclosed the whole thing.

Herbert's wife, Ludo, was a dynamo of energy, and Caroline thought she dressed very smartly, unlike most British women. Ludo had been converted to Catholicism and nine months later met Herbert. Caroline was sympathetic with Ludo, who was out of communion, since Herbert's first wife was still alive. "But she is an ardent Catholic," Caroline said, "and the children are practically raised at Ampleforth, the Benedictine Abbey and school two miles away."

Herbert took them to the earl of Faversham's parkland, which was open to the public for a fee. They later went for a closer look at the ruins of Rielvaux Abbey, which they had seen from the Faversham park. "It gave me the most vivid impression of the Middle Ages that I have ever had," Caroline said.

After a look at York Minster, they caught the train back to London, where they had dinner with Maisie Ward and her son, Wilfrid Sheed, who was still recovering from polio. Later they went to hear Maisie speak at Hyde Park.

Caroline wanted to go to Scotland, home of the Gordons and Douglases, but Allen persuaded her to stay in London instead and go to his dentist. The dentist gave her sodium pentothal while he pulled two teeth. "If you ever have a tooth out ask for it," she wrote Nancy. "It is divine, like sitting down on a sofa beside a friend, getting pleasantly tight immediately and having a conversation that doesn't seem to get anywhere but is nevertheless pleasant. Maybe parties would be better if everybody had a shot of sodium pentothal before turning up!"

The Tates went on to Paris, where Caroline revisited all the places where they had lived in the twenties. They sat in their favorite cafés and "all the old haunts around the Odéon." The Hotel Corneille was being torn down, but she saw the window where she had sat with one eye on her novel and one eye on Nancy, who was playing with the little English girl (paid by Caroline) in the courtyard. They went to the Closerie des Lilas for lunch, ate *choucroute garnie* at Lipp, and toasted Ford. She went to Mass at Saint Séverin, "the holiest church in Paris," and saw a stained-glass exhibition at the Louvre.

Jackson and Marthiel Matthews and John Prince were with them in Paris and the Matthews introduced them to Princess Caetani, an American woman married to an Italian prince and editor of *Botteghe Oscure*, an international literary publication. The princess invited the whole party to dinner, after which Caroline remarked that Margherita was just a nice Yankee woman.

In Rome, Laurance Roberts, director of the American Academy, offered the Tates one of the apartments that "cling to the skirts of the . . . stately Villa Aurelia," built by the Farnese family and now home to the Academy's director. The rent was only forty-five dollars a month, and for a pittance they had the services of Giuseppe, the gatekeeper, and Assunta, his wife. Assunta was hurt if Caroline tried to do any of the marketing, cooking, or washing. Their apartment had once been a bowling alley, and they had plenty of space, plus a terrace from which they could see the whole city.

They joined in the social life of the American Academy—cocktail parties, dinner parties, and even a formal dance for which Allen wore tails and Caroline a new gray designer ball gown. She had been wearing her hair pulled up on top of her head with bangs in front, but now she got a permanent and had her hair styled the way she had worn it in North Carolina, parted in the middle and curled around her face. The Tates saw a great deal of the painter Franklin Watkins and his wife, Ida; William Styron; and William Faulkner, who asked Caroline at a dinner party where Mr. Maury was. Thinking he meant Rufus Morey, a Princeton art historian, she told Faulkner that he spent his days in the Vatican cataloguing the pope's collection of gold-glass medallions. "I wish I could have met that man," Faulkner said. "That is a wonderful story." Caroline realized then that he was asking about Aleck Maury.

Caroline loved Rome on sight and thought being there different from any experience she'd ever had. It was like "walking down the street talking to your brother or sister and discovering that your grand-mother and grandmother [*sic*—an interesting slip] are walking along with you, and then you stumble and fall into a hole and there are your great-grandmother and great-grandfather. Ruins are every-where. . . ."

With *The Wonders of Italy* and *Pilgrims and Martyrs of Rome* in hand, Caroline walked the streets, marveling at the saffron-colored buildings, wallowing in holy places, regarding the remnants of Imperial Rome with a kind of pity, and looking. St. Peter's was "practically incredible." The Church of Santa Pudenziana, which had been Pudenziana's house until her conversion by St. Peter, was a place where "St. Peter must have said Mass." Santa Maria sopra Minerva was where "St. Catherine of Siena's . . . and Fra Angelico's bones lie." The Pantheon was "in a square that swarms with cats." The sight of the Forum and the Colos-seum made "you realize that the ancient Romans really perished of pride." The Arch of Titus was "one of the most impressive sights" she had ever seen. In fact, Caroline said, what made Rome so fascinat-ing was the contrast between the Cross and the pride of the Empire. "You are also struck by the way Peter and Paul seem to hold the city in their hands."

She liked the way ruins were left in situ so that one could see frag-ments of ancient statues and inscriptions in a wall of stucco in the courtyard of a modern apartment building. Allen suggested that they build an addition to Benbrackets, not of rammed earth but of rubble and stucco.

"Grandpa and I have decided we want to spend our old age in Rome," she wrote Nancy. She said she realized now that everything she liked about France or any other place was the way it resembled Italy. "Like Nietzsche, I was a 'Southerner by conviction' long before I got here. I simply love every inch of the country."

In a frenzy of spiritual ardor, Caroline picked up the shinbone of a Christian martyr in the catacombs and brought it back to the apart-ment. When Allen pointed out she could be excommunicated for this theft, she was aghast and wondered what to do. She tried to get Allen to take it back, and asked various other friends, and finally sneaked it back herself, slipping it in among its fellows.

Just a few blocks from the American Academy, Caroline discovered the Convent of the Perpetual Rosary, where American nuns said the rosary constantly in honor of Mary. "The first time I went there," she wrote Nancy, "the gate was opened by a middle-aged woman who, it struck me, must have been converted from being at least a Hard Shell Baptist, Sister Mary. In the world, she was a widow by the name of Girty from Bloomington, Indiana—the kind of woman who has given me a lot of trouble in my time, the kind who 'wants to write' and she actually used to write feature stories for newspapers, 'But this,' says she, 'is so much more important.' She is not a nun, but is what they call 'a familiara.' The nuns being cloistered up to the gills—up to the grill, I mean—they can't have many dealings with the world. So Sister Mary goes for the mail, answers the door bells and tends the candles at the altar. . . . It is really wonderful to live so near this place. If you wake up in the night you can just tune in on the Rosary with the sisters instead of taking phenobarbital."

She reread *The Marble Faun.* "It is great fun," she told Ward Dorrance, "reading it in Rome. Like Allen, Hawthorne was not able to work in Rome and had little use for the Eternal City. 'A long decaying corpse . . .' 'ugly, crooked streets paved with little bits of lava' etc. The Tiber is 'a mud-puddle in motion.' " She much preferred Stark Young's description of the city: "Universal, earthy, gross, golden—in short, a mystical body."

She went with the American journalist Mary McGrory to see St. Benedict's sacred cave at Subiaco. They took the train to Mandela and found that it would be three hours before they could get a bus to Subiaco. The people of Mandela were so astonished to see a couple of pilgrims turning up at that hour that they left their work and followed Caroline and Mary around in what Caroline felt was an admiring throng, smiling and making suggestions about what they could do next. The only person who was not crazy about them was a jealous baby who danced up and down and howled to get attention. On the way up the road toward a restaurant where the *padrona* was supposed to speak English, they passed a sign that said "Grotte di San Benedetto"; Caroline recalled that when St. Benedict fled Rome at the age of fourteen, "disgusted with its lasciviousness," he spent a year in a cave. This must be it. They made their way over horse, chicken, and sheep droppings to the church and rang until a Franciscan monk appeared, wearing the dirtiest habit Caroline had ever seen. St. Benedict's first cave looked "like something you'd find off in a field in Kentucky," she said. The Franciscan took them on a tour of the garden and plucked enormous bunches of grapes for them and "the most heavenly figs" Caroline ever ate.

They were having such a heavenly time in Italy, Caroline wrote Nancy, that they felt guilty every now and then. They hired a car and drove with Richard Blackmur and Margot Cutter of Princeton to the Villa d'Este and to Hadrian's Villa at Tivoli, eating lunch at a restaurant, Sybilla, with a square temple to the sibyl beside it, as well as a round temple to Vesta. "The whole restaurant was covered with wistaria vines springing from a trunk so gigantic that it might have belonged to the sybil's [*sic*] time. If you looked off anywhere you saw waterfalls gushing out from the mountainsides." The Villa d'Este was the most pagan spot she was ever in, Caroline went on, and it was "simply divine—well, not divine, either."

After they acquired an Austin, they drove to Naples and Pompeii, and Assisi. Allen, who gave up eating fruit and vegetables and subsisted on pasta and meat, fell prey to all sorts of ailments that prevented them from going on a trip to Sicily.

When Bernard Berenson invited them to Florence—at the age of eighty-eight, he still remembered the first piece of Allen's he ever read—the Tates could not go. Allen had a sty on his eye, because, said Caroline, he didn't want to look at all those works of art. However, they went later, in February 1954, and Caroline found I Tatti just as fabulous as people said, with marvelous gardens, a library larger than the libraries some colleges have, and a picture gallery before which words failed her, where she spent every minute she could before Sassetta's *Glory of St. Francis*.

She admired Berenson, who, bearded and very small, moved with a kind of grave dignity in the midst of his own aura. Inside that aura he was, she felt, furious and dismayed and beginning to suspect that he might die any minute without finding out what it was all about. The suspicion made him slash out in sudden, seemingly unaccountable rages. Caroline granted him his profound insights about art but she considered his opinions on literature puerile. She found his situation, however, interesting. His wife had been dead for some years and an old friend, Nicky Mariano, acted as his hostess. Her family had been the great family in the Lithuanian village where Berenson was born.

"The Allen Tates staying with us," Berenson noted in his diary. "She bulky and opulent, novelist and critic in her own right, but do not know under what name, nor what she writes. He slender, alert, with a head recalling those supposed to be Plotinus or Chrysostom, and with dazzling expressive eyes. Both Southerners, knowing all the American writers of today. She kept butting in, but he managed to tell me a good deal about most of them. Penn Warren had been a friend of their youth, married a rather difficult wife and, persisting in covering her conduct from others, ended by stiffening and getting opaque. Edmund Wilson on the whole a jolly giant. Mary McCarthy better critic than novelist. Capote of small account, etc. One gets from them the impression of a very busy, buzzing, bustling literary life, whatever its values may be. . . . All in all, a most interesting couple, a good investment."

They went to Ninfa, south of Rome, to have lunch with the Prince and Princess Caetani. In antiquity Ninfa had been a nymphaeum and shrine to Aesculapius. In the Middle Ages the inhabitants of the small town got tired of the Caetanis fighting among themselves and demolished the town. The house of the prince and princess, which was the old town hall restored, sat beside a rushing stream in the midst of the vine-wreathed ruined walls of the old town, including the remains of seven chapels. Here the princess had made, with a firm American hand, what Caroline called "the most wonderful garden I ever saw. Every flower you can think of: iris, anemones, daffodils, those little single hyacinths my grandmother called 'roman,' peach, pear, almond trees, and, of course, mimosas everywhere. We lunched outdoors beside the stream on trout from the brook. Mine was lavender with pink spots on him. So beautiful I could hardly bear to eat him."

After lunch they went up to the Cyclops Castle at the top of the mountain that hangs over Ninfa. The peasants had turned odd corners of the ruins into stable yards, cow lots, and pigpens. A donkey stood on top of the mountain, silhouetted against the sky, and brayed. There were, Caroline said, sheep, a hen with a new brood of chickens, and "a darling little black, chthonic pig. When you looked down on Ninfa from the Cyclops Castle it looked like a huge bouquet somebody had flung down on the Campagna."

At Ninfa, she was disconcerted when the toilet in the huge bathroom would not flush. She was in despair, she wrote Pidie, until her Merry Mont training told her that in a place that had been inhabited as long as Ninfa there were certain to be old-fashioned "conveniences." She opened the doors of various cupboards until she found what she needed—a chamber pot of vast dimensions. "I filled it with water and hefted it over the toilet and all was well. Three cheers for Merry Mont!"

A few days later the Tates went to Florence and Venice, which she considered "too much of a confection, except for the inside of St. Mark's." The Tuscan landscape, however, was the country of her dreams, "the country you always knew existed." They went to see the frescoes at Arezzo, the mosaics in Ravenna, and, in a sort of lumber room in the town hall of Sansepolcro, Piero della Francesca's *Resurrection,* "which for a good many years now has been my favorite picture."

On Christmas Eve Caroline wanted to go to the Church of Sant'Anselmo for pontifical matins, followed by pontifical Mass and lauds, but she and Allen went to an official dinner at the Villa Aurelia and got trapped into church-hopping with other American Academy people. They went to Aracoeli, because Ida Watkins had heard they had bagpipes from the Abruzzi there, and then to Santa Maria Maggiore, brilliantly illuminated for a change, and got to Sant'Anselmo for the Mass.

On Epiphany Sunday Father Anselm Strittmatter took them to the Byzantine rite monastery at Grottaferrata. "It was the most beautiful rite I have ever witnessed," she said. After that, she said, she felt the Roman Catholic ritual was like that of a Methodist church. Father Anselm took them, too, to the chapel in the convent of Benedictine oblates of Monte Oliveto, founded by St. Frances of Rome. (Nancy had a particular devotion to this saint, she told Lon Cheney, perhaps because St. Frances was married at the age of eleven and had eight children.)

While Caroline was in Rome, she learned that Douglas Meriwether, the son of her Uncle Rob, had lost Merry Mont. A Cumberland mountaineer named Shem Hamlett bought it at auction and made it a profitable farm, bulldozing down the trees and bushes that had screened the house from the road. In Rome Caroline brooded that it marked the end of Meriwether landholding begun in 1690. In the same mail came news that Jack Miller of a seed and farm supply firm in Clarksville was on a trip around the world and would look them up in Rome. The tradesmen, who were townspeople, had triumphed, and the landowners were prostrate. As in *Penhally,* the agrarian cause was truly lost.

Caroline tried to write every morning, then take a siesta, and start out at four o'clock with Allen to look at the sights. "The day is so long here—we dine so late—that there is time for everything," she said at first. Although Allen could write nothing, Caroline did manage to get some work done before being caught up in a whole new interest— Jungian analysis. It began because of, she said, her concern over Allen's "drinking problem." Earlier, she had written to Sam Monk that he would be pleased that she and Allen had come simultaneously to the belief that they both drank too much. She asked their doctor to recommend a Catholic psychologist so she could perhaps learn what to do about Allen's "maniacal drinking spells" and also find out why "they make me so damn mad," she told Ward.

When she found the apartment of the "psychologist," Dr. Dora Bernhard, on via Gregoriana near the top of the Spanish Steps, Caroline discovered she was not a Catholic. An Austrian, the daughter of a scientist who had been transferred to Germany, Dr. Bernhard and her husband, Ernest Bernhard, were both Jungian analysts. Caroline decided that therapists in Rome were very different from therapists in the United States. They didn't have as many patients—Italians were perhaps better able to cope—and had all the time in the world to give their patients. Dr. Bernhard had "one of the most powerful and subtlest imaginations I ever had to do with," Caroline said. Still, she was reluctant to take the plunge into intensive psychotherapy and told Dr. Bernhard that if she stopped writing her novel to "work" with her, it would be the first time she had ever voluntarily stopped writing. Dr. Bernhard replied that the work she did with her might be the "most important novel you will ever write."

When Caroline first went to her, she explained regretfully, as nine out of ten patients did, that she never dreamed. "But my husband has wonderful dreams," she said, and began to recount some of them. The *dottoressa* said firmly that she would be very interested in Allen's dreams if he were her patient but found them irrelevant at that time.

"The idea is that the human psyche has in its deepest level . . . the powers necessary to heal itself," Caroline wrote to Ward. "A neurosis is, according to this view, . . . an effort of the psyche to cure itself. . . . The only way to get in touch with the unconscious is through the dream which gives the only accurate report of what is going on. Dr. Bernhard listens politely to whatever I have to say but her expression changes when we start on one of my dreams." The dream was the text, the *dottoressa* said, and Caroline told her she was a real New Critic.

Instead of long single-spaced letters about books by Catholic writers, Caroline began writing her friends long expositions of Jung's ideas and even longer descriptions of her dreams and Dr. Bernhard's comments about them.

"We have got a whole series of my dreams and, as she said, they make a novel. A novel, with the preparation for the denouement planted in exactly the same place that James would have planted his 'stout stake.'" In another letter, Caroline described her dreams as a serial, with clues in the earlier ones explained in later ones.

She described one dream to her psychiatrist son-in-law: "Allen and I were climbing either up or down a big hill and came to rest on a spot half way up. We had been walking on a sort of country road—at least wheel tracks were perceptible. There was a huge tree, an oak, I think, growing beside the road. I seem to have been conscious of a beautiful view in front of us—it was almost as if we had turned around to look at it, but we were not looking at the view. At least, I wasn't. I was absorbed in admiring the pattern of light and shade that was made by sunlight filtered through the leaves of the tree. It is a phenomenon that always gives me a feeling of well-being—I have often tried to portray such a scene in my novels. At any rate, watching the sunlight fall, almost like gold coins, on the road, I was overcome by a sense of well being. At that moment Allen said that we had to decide what we would do next, or perhaps where we would go next. I said, 'Why not just stay here until we get the money the Old Lady left us?' [Dr. Bernhard] says that in dreams money rarely means money or material goods, but rather opportunities for growth or spiritual enrichment. 'I have no idea who this old lady is,' she said, 'but I feel sure that she will turn out to be somebody very important in your life.' She suggested that the old lady may be wisdom."

"My! It certainly is fascinating," she wrote to Ward Dorrance. "One of the things that fascinates me is that my 'little, darling nature,' as Bub used so aptly to term it, is apparently so different from what I, and I think my friends and family, have always thought it. . . . I do feel that meeting this woman, at least becoming acquainted with the Jungian technique is the most tremendous experience of my life, next to falling in love and being converted, and of a piece with both."

Caroline wrote to Nancy about the *dottoressa*'s interest in her childhood:

> When she got to questioning me . . . she was much interested in my relations with my grandmother, and of course, with Mother. The key to it is masochism—no news to Percy. But I had not realized how much I have been influenced by the fact that I could not "identify" with my mother. It was next to impossible, since Mother was a bit beside herself all her life. We all learned to discount almost everything she said, but of course it affected us just the same. I remember Dad's taking me aside and saying, "When she says, Black is white, I say Black is white, and that is what you have got to do." I thought to myself that that was all right for him because he was a man and in love with her but since I wasn't a man it didn't seem my duty to take her that way.
>
> Of course Mother was married at seventeen and had a hard life herself, and I have come to feel towards her almost as if she were a younger sister who hadn't had much of a chance, but La Dottoressa says that the really religious attitude is to take each moment for itself, as unique, and that put in the spotlight as my mother she failed. She says that I feel as if I have never been recognized for my true self and that any violence I commit is, au fond, a clamoring for attention. I pointed out that I had had a good deal of recognition, in my work, for instance, but she says it isn't so much the quantity of recognition as the quality. A very little will do if it is the right kind. Anyhow, she was much interested in my relations with my grandmother. I was, of course, the favorite, but remember that being the favorite brought great embarrassment—it used to burn me up the way Mama treated Manny and Mil. She says that nevertheless the fact that the old lady accepted me as something mighty fine had a great effect on me, and cites a dream I had yesterday as the fulfillment of a clue in the earlier dreams.
>
> But first I will have to tell you an even earlier dream. I dreamed that

Allen and I and some other people were out on a *scavi,* as we had been several times recently. The men were digging in front of us and Allen and I were standing there talking about a stone face that had been discovered and that we had agreed had better be put in a box and stored away somewhere. She asked what expression the face had. I told her that it was a sort of archaic face and had a serene expression. . . .

She says that the old lady in the first dream is my grandmother, who was the first person who recognized me (to over-simplify it) for my true self. The serene archaic face that Allen and I have agreed to put away some place is my true self, the self I have got to get back. The Merry Mont dream is "a good prognosis." I had no feeling of sadness when I saw that the house was gone. The wealth of apple and pear and peach blossoms seemed to more than make up for it.

. . . People in your dreams are, of course, often projections of certain aspects of yourself, sometimes a part of your self you don't want to recognize. Tom Mabry was in one of my dreams, representing, she says, my professional self, but also figuring as himself. . . . Anyhow, working with her is fascinating and, for me, at least, immensely profitable. After all, an artist spends his time working with symbols.

Once that winter Caroline dreamed about Mrs. Winslow, the woman in Memphis with the Italianate mansion and the peacocks. She explained to the *dottoressa* that Mrs. Winslow looked a great deal like her own mother, "so much so that I sometimes (in actual life) have a frisson when I look at her. On the surface she is entirely unlike my mother. She is, in a way, worldly, while my mother seemed very unworldly. Mrs. W. was a beauty and a belle and in her early married life wrote poetry which attracted the attention of discerning critics. She could have had a career as a poet but, I think, deliberately chose not to. She was frank in her enjoyment of A.'s and my society. At the same time, she had reservations about our work. In a kind of autobiography she wrote in her late sixties she spoke of us as being charming and intelligent and so on, remarking parenthetically . . . that she did not like our work. . . . When she was sixty-seven or sixty-eight years old she became a professional writer and has had a best seller every three or four years since then. An astonishing achievement.

"I suspect that one reason she was able to achieve this feat was that she rejected her real self (which might have made a real artist) and lived most of her life as her shadow and was therefore 'possessed' in much the same way my mother was. I suspect now that this woman and my mother—and K.A.—have one thing in common: a rejection of the real self for the shadow self. . . . K.A. . . . has become such a 'great woman' that many of her friends find it impossible to communicate with her. . . . A. has pointed out her fame is out of proportion to her accomplishment."

In her notes, Caroline says that the *dottoressa* concluded that Caroline saved herself by not identifying with her mother. "If I had identified myself with her I'd have been a goner. I saved my self by turning to my father, cultivating talents I inherited from my father, but I naturally paid a heavy price for this. . . . Consciously, at least, I have no resentment toward her. The dottoressa says that this is all very well but that when you consider my mother as a mother she must be judged only as a mother. As a person she was remarkable, admirable in many ways. But she was a bad mother, she says. Bad because she applied 'collective or conventional' judgments to moral problems. The old fashioned 'I'd rather see you in your grave than smoke cigarettes' is a version of this attitude. My mother said that I must never marry. Having such a bad disposition, I would be sure to leave my husband, which would be mortal sin. Therefore I had best not marry. She did not scruple to suppress letters and once even a telegram from my beaux. . . . By living with Pidie and working on a newspaper I managed to stay away from my mother and also wrote my first novel in Pidie's attic. The dottoressa says that such a period in my life corresponded to the years the early Fathers used to spend in the desert and that I would not have survived if I had not undertaken some such desperate measure."

At one session Dr. Bernhard told Caroline that she was too "identic." Caroline, who had always considered herself the most self-centered mortal, was surprised, but the *dottoressa* said that one of Caroline's difficulties was that she could identify herself with practically anybody.

Caroline made notes on the dreams and the notes turn into a plea to Allen: "You are firmly established as my animus. I look to you for guidance and wisdom. At the same time life with you has meant great suffering for me, for you do not seem to know how to deal out joy. I hardly have time to recover from one wound before you deal me another. . . . I am so tired of being hurt and of anticipating being hurt that in the last few years I have been tempted to live apart from you. When such thoughts occur to me I salve my conscience by telling myself that if I live apart from you I could probably do more for you than when I am living with you—by praying for you I might be able to pray for you more effectively if I did not live in constant apprehension of encountering some suffering greater than I can bear."

Allen, Caroline said, had quit drinking as soon as she started seeing the *dottoressa,* and "was dying" to go to her himself, but "she won't have him till she is quite through with me, and as she says, 'We still have a lot of work to do.' "

Dr. Bernhard remembers that Caroline was "hostile toward her husband" when she first came to her. "I had to educate her so that she could understand and live the symbolic life." Dr. Bernhard, who later saw Allen as a patient, recalls also that Caroline was "more intelligent and more clever than her husband." The Tates lived, she said, "too much extrovertedly. They never came to the kernel."

Dr. Bernhard's work with Caroline was interrupted in late March, however, when Percy called Caroline and asked her to come to Princeton. Nancy had had what he called "a psychotic episode."

32

Princeton and Minnesota,
1954–1955

Caroline was in Princeton within three days of Percy's call. Although Nancy had already improved a great deal, Caroline was still appalled at what she found. Nancy and Percy had been living in Benbrackets, a miniature house that was delightful for a middle-aged couple but a "torture chamber" for a woman with three children. Nancy had had a nervous breakdown from simple overwork, Caroline said. "Excessive fatigue is toxic," she told Pidie.

Nancy suffered from more than fatigue; she and her husband say it was a true schizophrenic breakup. She was under many pressures. Still young, not yet twenty-nine, the mother of three small children, living on slender finances, she was worried about her husband. Obviously brilliant, Percy had finished medical school at the top of his class, done his internship, and done well in his residency—but had never taken the examination for his medical license. Years out of medical school, he was having to review everything to take the exam. Allen had not helped. Ever since his trip to Europe in 1952, he had been telling Nancy and Percy that he was in love with Natasha Spender, "this wonderful woman" who was going to leave her husband and marry him. When Natasha and Stephen Spender came to Princeton to see Muriel Gardiner, a Vienna-trained psychiatrist and analyst, it became clear to Nancy that Natasha was not going to leave Stephen Spender. Nancy felt as though she and Percy were at the center of a battle. She broke down.

Fresh from her Jungian analyst and unaware of many things, Caroline was full of psychological theories and curious theology. "Nancy's spending sprees are her way of making Percy choose between her and his mother," she wrote to Allen. "Of course, my troubles have upset Nancy, and of course your violence has upset Nancy. . . . But this is not the cause of her illness; it merely makes it worse. Our troubles are testing us and that may be the means of redemption."

Allen, meanwhile, wrote that Nancy's trouble was caused not by their trouble but by the failure of Percy's mother to give him and Nancy money. He urged Caroline to stay with the children for six weeks and send Nancy to Rome so he could put her in the care of the *dottoressa*. He had started seeing Dr. Bernhard as soon as Caroline left Rome and reported a new dream in which his mother had appeared as an Amazon, while he was much smaller than lifesize—he could hardly wait to take it to the *dottoressa*. He was drinking nothing but wine, he said, and he was sure he and Caroline were entering a new phase. He did not add that he was also seeing Natasha and Stephen Spender.

Caroline tried to bring some order out of the chaos at Benbrackets. There was no place to put the laundry, Caroline said, and "we sort of walk around on top of it, diving down every now and then to extract a diaper or some other such needed object." Caroline thought about adding a prefabricated garage "so Nancy would at least have a place to sort the laundry," and went to the bank to see about a loan. She mentioned to the banker that maybe she should buy an ugly old house that was for sale on Hodge Road. That was a much better idea, he said.

So, using an advance of $1,000 from Viking for *How to Read a Novel*, she bought a house at 54 Hodge Road for $23,000. She was assured that Benbrackets would "move" quickly, and she and the Woods worked like mad to get it in shape to show it to prospective buyers. The first person who saw it fell like a ton of bricks, she said, and she sold it for $20,000 to R. W. B. Lewis, who would later go to Yale to teach and write a prize-winning biography of Edith Wharton. Caroline said that if she had had more money in hand she would have held out for $25,000, but she couldn't wait. Since they had a smaller mortgage, she and Allen felt they had made a profit of $3,000. She had turned the whole financial problem over to St. Joseph, she wrote Allen, and he had been very helpful. She could not have gotten through "without enormous supernatural help," she said.

Caroline's handling of the real estate deals impressed everyone. Jack Wheelock said he was going to turn all his affairs over to her, and Allen praised her.

The house that Caroline bought had been built by a Princeton professor, Alexander Phillips, to please his wife, who wanted the latest thing in architecture. The architects were the Charles Addams brothers, Caroline said. It was the latest word in Victorian architecture gone perverse, so hopelessly out of date, Caroline wrote Pidie, that nobody else would buy it. Although it was on the right side of town, in the heart of "Old Princeton," it had been rented out for years and was a mess.

Into the chimney were bolted iron letters: DULCE DOMUM. "It is a nice test of whether anybody has had a classical education. People over fifty get sort of glass-eyed when they see them—you can actually hear them declining 'Domum' under their breaths," she wrote Pidie. Dulce Domum, "Sweet Home," became one of the house's names, the other being the Hodge Horror.

Caroline rather liked its "architectural marvels," and she turned the breakfast room, which had been known as the stained-glass room, into an oratory in honor of St. Thomas More. Caroline wished to emulate St. Thomas More in his relations with his son-in-law.

There was, in fact, quite a lot of stained glass and oak paneling, and a side porch shaped like the "bandstand at a county fair," wreathed in wisteria vines. There was a large living room, a huge dining room, a butler's pantry, "which bristles with closets, including one for the maid's uniform," and "the kitchen of Nancy's and my dreams." Nancy said there was nothing sanitary in it but the refrigerator. Immediately after moving in, Caroline and the Woods ripped up the linoleum and put linseed oil on the floor. The kitchen had plenty of closets, including one for the laundry. There were six bedrooms and three and a half bathrooms.

Percy had an office in the house where he could see his psychiatric patients. Caroline bought him some tree ivy to screen the windows instead of curtains. She was glad there were back stairs; the boys were forbidden to set foot on the front stairs because the front hall was the doctor's anteroom. When Percy had been in private practice two weeks, a pleased Caroline wrote Pidie, "He started out with four patients. One lady, so deeply disturbed that she has to see him four times a week, has moved to Princeton in order to be near him. Four times a week at fifteen dollars an hour! We sorrow not as those without hope. I think we really may get out from under in the next few months."

Upstairs, Nancy and Percy had a big bedroom with a private bath. Little Caroline had a room of her own. Allen and Caroline each had a room and their own bathroom. Caroline told her grandsons, "If any boy ever sets foot in my bathroom I will cut his head off, shrink it, and hang it on the Christmas tree." How would she do that? the boys asked, enthralled. The boys' room and a guest room were on the third floor.

Caroline bought secondhand furniture for the house, including a wicker chaise lounge for the room they called the Gun Room. ("It stands rather high, looks like some long-legged animal, startled and about to take flight and does something indescribable for the room," she wrote Allen.) She bought armchairs for five and eight dollars apiece and slipcovered them in Bemis bagging. The books were as prolific as rabbits, she wrote Phyllis and John Hall Wheelock. If she left two books on one shelf, in the morning she found four or five, even six.

The garden was a jungle but had pink and white dogwoods, the biggest Japanese magnolia Caroline had ever seen, a "wonderful" star magnolia, a "beautiful" crab apple, and a "silver chain" tree. The riding stable was near, and "we can get all the manure we can cart off— free. I have realized one dream of my life—a compost heap." A painter wanted $400 to paint the downstairs rooms so Caroline, Nancy, and Percy rashly decided to do it themselves. "At first I was thought to be too old to climb up the twelve-foot stepladder, but after the doctor had put in one weekend painting he decided I was just the right age for such work!"

By August Caroline thought Nancy was a great deal better, but still not herself. "I had never dreamed that a human being could work as hard as Nancy does. She does not even sit down to eat lunch—when she eats lunch. And during the day she has not one moment for reflection or recollection," Caroline wrote to Pidie. She supposed Nancy had had what old-fashioned people would call a nervous breakdown, although the psychiatrists had other words for it now; the wonder was that she had not had one before.

Although Caroline's consideration for Nancy was very real, there was a certain amount of tension in the house that summer. It was hard for three generations to live together. When Nancy and Percy were invited out to a small dinner party, Caroline insisted that they go. Alone, she destroyed a picture of Nancy, explaining when they returned that the photograph was taken at a time when Nancy had caused them so much trouble. There was friction over decoration of the house and cultivation of the garden. Percy cut the branches of a spruce tree that screened the garbage from the terrace and caused a great commotion. Nancy cried, and Caroline called Ben Tate, still the financial angel for the Tates' housing.

There was friction over the children's education. Peto had finally learned to read at the age of nine, the age when, Caroline said, she was laying the foundations of her prose style by studying Latin. "Allen has not yet been allowed to learn to read, though he has done a lot of painting and papier mache work at his school. He is seven." She saw little hope for him.

But little Caroline was "an enchanting child," she said. In late summer, she took care of her while Nancy and Percy and the boys went to the beach. She was amused when she heard little Caroline calling, "Whar you, Omma? Writing a check?" because that's what she felt she'd been doing all summer.

Caroline and the Woods had people in to dinner. John Prince brought his fiancée by to meet them. Lon and Fannie Cheney drove up from Tennessee to see the new house. Peter and Eleanor Taylor came by with news of Robert Lowell, who would have to stay, they said, in Payne Whitney for a year. He was all right on some subjects, but not on money, marriage, males, females, and religion. In fact, Elizabeth Hardwick, Lowell's second wife, wrote Caroline to ask if she had sent a priest to see Robert. Caroline wrote back that no, she hadn't, then she remembered that she had sent Ivan Illitch, who was a priest. "I am sure, however, that he never mentioned religion during the course of his visit. I asked him to go because he seems to me the most remarkable person I have ever met and I thought Cal would enjoy knowing him. He liked Cal immensely." In another letter to Elizabeth, Caroline beseeched her to call in a Jungian analyst. She was convinced, she said, that Jungians were better able to help the poet in his daily battle, since they dealt daily with the same material—symbols and archetypes—that the poet did.

At the end of the summer, Percy was offered a job at the Carrier Clinic, a psychiatric hospital on the outskirts of Princeton, and he decided to take it, although the hospital required him to live in a house on the hospital grounds. The Woods moved out of the house they had just moved into, and the Tates left Princeton for Minneapolis. Dulce Domum was rented out, and Caroline regretted very much ever leaving Rome. She should have spent the money she used to come home and buy the house to pay a maid to help Nancy out, as Father Anselm had advised her to. Allen, however, said dire calamity would have befallen if she hadn't gone to Princeton.

That year in Minneapolis, where the Tates lived at 1409 East River Road, must have been terrible for the two of them. Drinking was such a problem that Allen told Caroline they both should regard it as an occasion of sin, nothing less. Caroline mistrusted Allen and continued to go through storms of temper, which Allen found unbearable.

Caroline wrote few letters during 1954 and 1955, a sure sign that her life was in disarray, but she kept up a brave façade in the ones she did write. Allen could work better in Minneapolis than anywhere else, she wrote Stark Young, probably because the landscape was veiled in snow for seven months of the year and he didn't have to look at anything.

They both read the works of Jung that fall, and Caroline felt she was understanding Allen better. "It seems to me that just one idea of Jung's, 'the shadow,' man's darker side which grows more and more menacing until it is confronted and come to terms with, has done more for Allen than I could have hoped," Caroline said. She was also reading "all the time now in *La Divina Dottrina* of Santa Caterina da Siena. She seems to me the most wonderful woman that ever lived, next to the B.V.M."

That spring Allen was gone for weeks on a lecture tour while Caroline stayed in Minneapolis, working on *The Malefactors*. Conditions for work were ideal, she wrote to Allen in March, but she was having "the most devilish" time with her last chapter. (The ending of the book was to be very melodramatic, with Tom Claiborne, the failed poet, about to be converted to Catholicism.) "So far I have succeeded in writing a page and a half and I'm not sure I can use that. I don't think now I can make publication this fall. However, I have worked, or tried to work every day. I can't do more than that. Tommy was a wonderful help but there is one thing he isn't any help on, which you are infallible on: tone." She was staying by herself, and if Allen couldn't get in when he came back, he would realize that she was dead, "fallen on my typewriter."

When Dorothy Day visited for a few days, Caroline took time off from her novel and they sat doing handwork all day, like Victorian ladies. Caroline embroidered a dress for little Caroline, and Dorothy, as befitted a holy woman, said Caroline, knitted bandages for lepers.

While Allen went to Bloomington to the School of Letters, Caroline made her annual visit to Tory Valley in June, earlier than usual; she felt that she got in three weeks of the most satisfactory weeding ever. She wrote to the Lytles that she was reading Erich Neumann's *The Origins and History of Consciousness* and thought it "about the best book I ever read, next to Holy Writ."

While Caroline was at Sue Jenkins's, Flannery O'Connor came up for a weekend and they gave a party for her. Guests were the Malcolm Cowleys and the Van Wyck Brookses ("dear old Malcolm Cowley and dear old Van Wyck Brooks," Flannery said). Brooks insisted that Flannery read one of her stories. She started to read "Good Country People," but Caroline could not see the guests swallowing the scene in the hayloft, in which the Bible salesman tries to seduce the one-legged

Ph.D., and suggested "A Good Man Is Hard to Find," which was shocking enough, Caroline felt. "It was interesting to see the guffaws of the company die away into a kind of frozen silence as they saw which way things were heading," Caroline wrote to Fannie Cheney. Brooks said later that it was sad to see such a talented young writer have such a pessimistic view of life; he felt the experiences of her characters were "alien to the American way of life," according to a letter Caroline wrote the Lytles.

That spring Caroline had reviewed Flannery's collection of short stories, *A Good Man Is Hard to Find,* for *The New York Times,* which held her to a mere 500 words, to her intense disappointment. She admired Flannery's work and wanted to explain it to the world—she felt that none of the critics understood what Flannery was trying to do.

Caroline flew out to Bloomington to teach at the writers' conference, which started later than the School of Letters. Allen went to Europe after he finished at Bloomington, and Caroline went to Princeton. They had decided that she would go back to Rome in September, after Allen came back to the United States, to finish her course with the *dottoressa.* Allen's biographer states that they "agreed to separate" in 1955. It was not that simple. Caroline said later that she went to Rome the second time at Allen's insistence. "My husband would not allow me to return to my home, even to pack my belongings," she said. At the time, they told their friends they lived apart because Caroline's work demanded it. During the next few years, they would stay together briefly in places where Caroline's jobs took her, in Princeton, or at friends' houses.

Sue came down for a visit at Dulce Domum, and the two friends of thirty years quarreled. Caroline, edgy and bitter, felt that Sue was criticizing everything she did—buying too much expensive meat for the children, serving ice cream for dinner (people don't need desserts, Sue said), and spending too much time in the kitchen when company was coming. It was like having Loulie around, Caroline wrote Allen, when every move was an error. Caroline said she let her infantilism take over and asked Sue for God's sake not to give so much advice. Angry, Sue left Princeton. It all went back, Caroline thought, to the time earlier that summer when Flannery had been at Tory Valley. Sue had driven Flannery and Caroline to Mass and read the *Times* while she waited for them. As they were driving home, Flannery told Caroline about Romano Guardini's *The Faith and Modern Man* and Caroline told her about the Neumann book. "Sue felt left out," she wrote Allen. "How childish can grown women get?" (Sue and Caroline soon made up and were friends again.)

Caroline kept the children while Nancy and Percy went to the beach for a week and later wrote to Allen that she had not done a lick on her novel. In this letter to Allen, dated August 17, 1955, she commented on what Guardini said about indissoluble marriage, which, she said, "conforms to the most profound sense of nature and, in the final analysis, even with all the suffering and destruction it entails is the only practicable form of marriage—not the beginning, but the end of Christian effort, and must be formed by the same power behind virginity: a renunciation made possible by Faith." If one could accept the other as he really is, then a second love would come, the real mystery of marriage. "One thing I have learned from the dottoressa," Caroline's letter went on, "is that you see farther than I do, if sometimes by a peculiar route. When you said that I admired you too much you were saying in essence the same thing Monsignor Guardini says here but I was too distracted by the violence with which you said it to take it in. And anyhow you can't understand something like that overnight." (Caroline had found Monsignor Guardini's book "one of the most profound things" she had read in her life.)

ʼ A few days after writing the letter, she finished revisions on the novel. Nancy made a brilliant suggestion, she told Allen, and she followed it. "All that information about everybody's first and second marriages, originally presented in dialogue, is now put into a soliloquy of Claiborne's as he drives to the train."

She and Pete Wood, aged nine, went to New York to deliver the manuscript of *The Malefactors* to Denver Lindley. "It is, I suspect, not the end of four long years' work," she wrote Allen, "but of thirty-three years' work. I began to think seriously about the writing of fiction when I was twenty-seven. I feel that I have learned almost as much as I will ever learn about it in writing this book. It may seem wasteful to stop writing fiction just as you learn how to go about it, but after all, one does, or should die, soon after one has learned a little something about how to live. James hit his stride when he was older than I am but he was never married and was never a parent or a grandparent. I certainly don't intend to stop writing but I feel that this novel marks a dividing line in my work. From now on I will be writing about the same things—the same thing, there being only one—but I will use a different method of attack. If I had envisioned the method of attack which I now envision, I doubt if I would ever have written any fiction. But the Lord has to use even our blindness his wonders to perform."

She was truly glad, she said, to get the novel off her chest so she could put her whole mind on her work with the *dottoressa* when she got to Rome. "I have been thinking very seriously about my shortcomings whenever I have had a chance to meditate this summer. Monsignor Guardini has been enormously helpful in pointing them out to me. Viewed from the theological point of view my trouble is essentially lack of faith. If I had faith in the promises of Christ I would never be disturbed and would never do things that disturb other people. The psychologists say that when a person is frightened it's 'fight or flight.' I don't flee but I am too quick to fight. If I had enough faith I wouldn't feel that I had to fight, I wouldn't feel menaced."

Just before she left for Rome Caroline went to Maryland with Anne Fremantle, a Princeton friend who was born a Catholic in England but was now an American, a writer, an editor at *Commonweal,* and a teacher at Fordham. They went to visit some Catholic friends of Fremantle's, Marion and Ivan Stanicoff, whom Caroline liked instantly. Their house was twice the size of Mount Vernon, bigger than Herbert Read's, she wrote to Allen, with a long veranda back and front and wisteria climbing up the pillars and sprawling on the upper veranda the way it did at Benfolly. The living room was many times the size of the parlor at Benfolly, and there were wardrobes in the bedrooms instead of closets. The Stanicoffs had twenty-five people for lunch and thirty-five or forty for dinner. One of their seven children brought home fifteen friends. "The house has got something that every house I ever liked has and more," she said. The Stanicoffs had everything the Old South had. "Everything we ever tried to bring back to it, is on the hill being preserved by this Christian family. There is no nonsense, no romantic illusions about country life being a 'way of life.'" There were no idolatries that Caroline could discover.

She had seen this venture that the Stanicoffs had embarked on several times before. "My father tried it in Virginia—but was vanquished by Mother's fancy for speaking only in Negro dialect for a solid year! It would have got anybody down. And we tried it in a modest way at Benfolly and poor old Andrew tried it. But it won't work without faith. It is faith that animates every one."

Ivan Stanicoff had all the prejudices Allen had, she told him, and he was the soundest man she'd met in years. She pointed out other parallels between the Stanicoffs' house and Benfolly. "Uncle Doc was there disguised as a Polish classicist waiting for a post in India," she said. Also the dog at Benfolly known as the Soup Hound was there, she said, disguised as a beagle. "They spoke of him as a 'stray dog,' but he confided to me he had been there three years and intended to spend the rest of his life there."

Caroline closed this letter to Allen with a paragraph that is painfully moving: "I want to see you so much and would be so happy if we could go back to Minneapolis together. . . . But I know I have things to learn from the dottoressa too so I am going on to Rome. You say you have hope for our future. I think that if I could learn not to get angry no matter what happened our life would be different. And if you could forgo deception at the same time I was forgoing anger we'd probably be as happy as any two people could be."

ROME AND KANSAS,
1955–1956

On the same day that Allen left Rome by plane on his way to Minnesota, Caroline sailed for Italy aboard the *Independence*. Robert and Sally Fitzgerald met her in Genoa, collected the rubber pants, baby food, and Multicebrin tablets she had brought them, and took her to the Church of St. Catherine of Genoa to see the saint's incorrupt body.

In Rome Caroline settled into a *pensione* at via Nicola Fabrizi 11A, a few blocks from the American Academy, where she would eat dinner every night, went off to early Mass at San Pancrazio, and telephoned the *dottoressa* to make an appointment for the next day.

With no car, she said, she learned more about Rome in two weeks than she had the whole year she was there before. She visited catacombs, among her favorite attractions in Rome, walked along the Appian Way, bought putti and gilded candlesticks in the flea market, celebrated her sixtieth birthday, and went every evening to benediction at the Convent of the Perpetual Rosary at via Giacomo Medici 15—it was "such a splendid place to pray for Percy." She began to work in the convent's garden, keeping garden shoes and an apron hanging on the door in a room in the guest suite. When she got tired of writing, she said, "I just nip around two corners and dig a little in the garden." The garden, the fourth she had worked in that year—none of them her own—became almost an obsession. She asked the gardener at the American Academy to save roots and cuttings for her, and he brought a wheelbarrow-load of plants to the convent. With some of them, Caroline made a triple crown of "the little daisy-like plants you see in Fra Angelico's landscapes." She traveled to Subiaco to get from the monks there a cutting of one of the roses that St. Francis of Assisi grafted on the wild rosebush that St. Dominic rolled on to subdue the lusts of his flesh. She persuaded somebody else to obtain roots and bulbs from the garden near the catacomb of San Callisto and she bought two rose trees and ivy plants. She asked Allen to become a member of Mary's Guard of Honor. All he would have to do was spend an hour a month in prayer or contemplation, but the hour and day must be registered with the convent sisters. She thought of taking up mosaics and making a "catacombian sort of fish" at the bottom of the Virgin's pool with tesserae embedded in wet cement.

She urged Allen not to paint the apartment in Minneapolis until she got there. "Remember that I am a paintress, myself, and have decided ideas about *decor* and no mean reputation," she wrote. One of the worst features of the apartment, she said, was that it wasn't on the ground floor. "I do so hanker to have even a few feet of dirt to plant things in."

When Stark Young came to Rome, Caroline went to Grottaferrata with him, although she found him grossly fat and disliked his obscene jokes about the Church. She beseeched him to go to Santa Maria sopra Minerva and have the sacristan show him into the little room where St. Catherine of Siena stayed when she was in Rome. She wanted Stark in the Church. Life, she said, was just so damn dull outside it that she hated to see a dear friend condemned to such boredom. She thought St. Catherine had a wonderful way with young men and she was certain that she had something to tell Stark. He must read the *Seraphic Dialogues*—extraordinarily like Hart Crane's stuff since both St. Catherine and Crane were haunted by the image of the Bridge.

Meanwhile, Caroline was seeing Dr. Bernhard twice a week. The "work," the *dottoressa* reported to Allen, was going better than last year. Caroline was busy and happy, the *dottoressa* thought, and she hoped this would last. Allen had apparently written Dr. Bernhard to ask her if it was fair to Caroline to commit himself as he had done to a younger woman. Dr. Bernhard said years later that she had tried to help Caroline come to terms with Allen's affairs with other women by pointing out that many societies—specifically, ancient China—had approved polygamy. On the other hand, she said, relationships were not Allen's strong point, and "other women found this out."

The Tates were turning over Dulce Domum to Percy and Nancy—

Percy was paying them $10,000 in cash, and Caroline wanted to use the money to get a place for her and Allen. "More and more I feel handicapped, both in my work and in my life, by not knowing . . . where I'll be tomorrow," she wrote Allen on November 3, 1955. "I have just realized that I have never answered a letter I got from Bill Owens at Columbia over a week ago, asking me—and you, too—to teach there this summer, because I have no idea where I'll be this summer. The dottoressa has thrown considerable light on this craving of mine for a place of my own. She says that unconsciously I had a deep resentment against my father for keeping the ground always shifting under my feet and that the fact that my life with you duplicates to a great extent the circumstances of my life with my father tends to keep that resentment alive and that I often use you as a 'screen' on which to project that long-cherished resentment. I am sure she is right. She says that one reason you don't have as deep a craving for a place of our own as I do is that you have me and that to you I represent 'earth' but she thinks that if you lost me you would jolly well feel it and very quickly."

News came that the Cheneys, perhaps bringing Flannery O'Connor along, were coming to Rome on December 1 to stay until after Christmas. Following the Tates' lead, the Cheneys had been baptized on March 16, 1953, with Allen and Caroline as their godparents. Lon said he had always considered Caroline his literary godmother and now she was his godmother in the Church. One owed as much to one's godchildren as one did to one's grandchildren, Caroline said, and wanted to guide them to the holy places herself. Besides, it might be Flannery's last Christmas out of a wheelchair. The ACTH she was taking for her lupus was softening her bones and she was already on crutches. Although she was tired of pension life and hated to miss the family Christmas at Dulce Domum, Caroline canceled her passage home, which had been booked for December 11.

She wrote to Allen again about a place of her own. "The dottoressa says that my passionate desire to have a roof of my own over my head, or, at least, a desk of my own, under my typewriter, which appears in various forms in my dreams, is very significant. . . . She says that my longing to have ground under my feet represents that most feminine side of my nature, a side which has been dangerously suppressed and frustrated by our wandering lives. She says that everything you have ever done that I resent is, in a way, a posing of this same problem. Never having any security of any kind goes contrary to my deepest instinctual desires. On the other hand she thinks that I was right not to try to make you stay in one place. (I wanted very much to stay in Greensboro—that is, I wanted it for myself, but I thought and still think that it would have been bad for you.) Both as man and poet it was necessary for you to range, but the time has come when we ought to bear and forbear with each other better. I ought not to want my own way all the time but you ought to let me have it some of the time."

Not only did Dr. Bernhard see that Caroline felt cheated in never having a place of her own, but she also saw in Caroline an adventurer that made her want to go on to new places. While they were hammering this out, there was a crisis in the therapy. Allen told Caroline something the *dottoressa* had written him about her and Caroline was justly furious with them both. The *dottoressa* was again indiscreet and wrote Allen that Caroline took him as a child she would not allow to grow up.

Next Caroline was angry about a passage in one of Allen's poems. "You are right in what you say about my reaction to that passage," she wrote him. "I can see that it had awful effects for you and I have been worried about that for some time. . . . You are wrong about one thing, though. I did not react so violently because I saw myself in your poem but because I saw—or thought I saw—another woman pictured as the object of your desire. I reacted, the dottoressa says, from 'a primitive level,' a level that is at the bottom of every woman's consciousness."

She asked Dr. Bernhard to take her three times a week, but the doctor said Caroline needed the time between appointments for reflection. They were getting what Caroline called "pretty far underground" and were coming upon an underground type who was probably Hecate, according to the *dottoressa*.

"I think you and I are each beset on occasion by a demon," Caroline wrote in this same letter to Allen. "My demon does not want me to be happy with my husband so it tells me I can't be. Your demon doesn't want you to write poetry so it tells you you can't."

When she wrote again on November 13, she harked back to the passage in the poem:

> Once, when you were very upset, you said you wished that I had had affairs with other men. I can see how you would. If I had it would lessen your sense of guilt. But we can't have things the way we want them in this life. Once Bill Brown, after making a pass at me and failing to get anywhere, said, "You'd rather have Allen than any man you ever saw, wouldn't you?" and I said, "Yes." Several of our friends tried to console me when we were separated and came to the same conclusion. But let's put it that I have betrayed you on a higher level: in my violent reaction to a passage in your poem. It was a worse betrayal, coming from me, who am myself an artist, than it would have been coming from another

woman, but it came from a level where I am not an artist, but just a woman. I know it is a lot to forgive but I feel sure that if you can forgive it you will receive grace—maybe even grace to finish your poem.

One of the things that I think we are both learning from the dottoressa is that neither you nor I, being the kind of persons we are, can operate on what she calls "the conventional" level. From birth we have both been committed to another approach to life. When one of us falls down the other ought to help him up. You have said this to me. It is the implacable Hecate in me that has kept me from giving a full assent to what my mind tells me is all too true. But the dottoressa sees evidence in my dreams that she is crumbling into newer shapes.

. . . I think the fact that I am an artist, too, has complicated our life together. On the other hand, I had little choice: art was for me a way of surviving, of going on drawing my breath. If I hadn't become an artist I'd have gone under under the family pressures, the dottoressa says. When you helped me become an artist—and I could never have done what little I've done without your help—you saved my life.

There is one thing, though, that I think we both ought to take under consideration. My work as a novelist is over. . . . I feel a little relieved, as if somebody had told me I didn't need to sit around, waiting for messages any longer but could go on and do something else. . . . It is all very different for you, not only because you are a man but also because you are a lyric poet who cannot go at things the way a novelist does.

Caroline wrote Allen what the *dottoressa* had told her:

Our situation is like that of two children, clutching at each other on the edge of the abyss. She says that if we would only retreat to another level we would be safer, or as she puts it, when you gain access to another level the problem which was so frightening either disappears or presents itself in a more soluble form.

I did not realize until these last sessions with her just how badly frightened I was as a child. She finds it significant that I have three first cousins who committed suicide. There is no use in my speculating as to whether or not my family would be better off if I hadn't been a writer. She says that if I hadn't had my talent, that is, if I hadn't had something my cousins didn't have, I'd have gone their way or been locked up. At the same time, she has showed me why my mother turned against me. My likeness to my father—the qualities I inherited from him, which were the qualities that saved me, were too much for my mother. She had enough of that sort of thing in him and yet she was too deeply committed to him to turn against him so she took it out on me.

. . . The dottoressa has led me to face the fact that my mother really did reject me. She says that I perceived that when I was very young and that it was as if an abyss had opened under my feet and I have been scared to death ever since.

Dr. Bernhard thought that one of Caroline's earliest memories contained the germ of her life's central problem. When she was four years old at Merry Mont, she thought suddenly that it was all going to be too much for her to take and immersed her face in a basin of water on the washstand. She remembered being surprised when she came up for air still breathing. But she realized there was no way out, as she told Allen. "That is one reason I have demanded so much of you, I'm sure. (You realized this long before I did.)"

As well as having been rejected by her mother, Caroline had been, the *dottoressa* felt, greatly disappointed by her father, and this disappointment added to her problems with Allen. It is clear from the letters that Dr. Bernhard wrote to Allen and to Caroline that she liked Allen better than she did Caroline—Allen's charm always worked—but she conceded that she admired Caroline's struggle to understand herself, as well as her strength and magnanimous qualities that showed through even in attacks of violence and despair.

Caroline often talked to the *dottoressa* about homosexuals, about whom her feelings were confused. Many of her friends were homosexual, but Caroline disapproved of their sexual orientation. In fact, she had always detested homosexuality, and now that she saw everything in the black-and-white terms of religion, she viewed it as a sin. Once she told Dr. Bernhard she thought Allen had had an affair with Stephen Spender as well as Natasha. The doctor brushed this aside, pausing only to wonder if there were so many homosexuals in America because the women were so rigid.

November 24 was the feast day of Caroline's patron saint, St. John of the Cross, and she made her way through a cold rain to Santa Maria della Scala, where there was a chapel dedicated to him. When Caroline went past the Convent of the Perpetual Rosary the next morning, she saw that Alberto, the gardener, had planted all the rose trees she had bought with money sent her by Jerry and Grace Lambert. Sister Mary, the "familiara," had made him do it, telling him that it was Caroline's feast day. There were fifteen rose trees, one for each of the mysteries, and Caroline had them planted in honor of certain people. Jerry and Grace stood at the entrance. Allen was a Pace rose, Stark Young an Eterna Giovinezza, Katherine Anne Porter a Mirandy, little Caroline a Climbing Caroline, Nancy another Pace, and Percy a Gloria di Roma.

Mother Immaculata sent word by Sister Mary that she wanted to see Caroline to thank her for all she had done in the convent garden.

While Mother Immaculata remained behind the grill, Sister Mary served Caroline tea and cake and gave her a relic. "You know," said the voice behind the grill, "that we have the flesh and the hair and the bones of Pope Pius Tenth." Caroline vowed she would wear her silver reliquary with a fragment of the pope's remains the rest of her life. In spite of all this gratitude, in one of Caroline's dreams recounted to the *dottoressa* people resented her planting too many flowers. (The sisters later left Rome and sold their convent to an order of Barnabite brothers; Caroline's garden is now gone.)

On December 5 Caroline wrote to Allen that when she had come to Rome in the fall she realized that their differences were affecting their lives but she thought that they were gradually learning to surmount them, with the help of Dr. Bernhard. "But the differences—the difficulties, rather—are even more profound than I had realized. . . . In fact, I agree with practically all of the charges you bring against me. You have been sorely tried and in ways more intangible and hence in some ways harder to bear than the ways in which I have been tried. I agree with you about this."

An offer from the University of Kansas for Caroline to teach there during the spring semester seemed providential, since in Rome her money was melting away. The pay would be good but it would be hard-earned; she would have to give one public lecture a week, as well as conduct a writing workshop. She told Allen that when she came back to the United States she would not go to Minnesota before she went to Kansas. If she did, she said, it would be falling into the "trap" the *dottoressa* talked about. "I fell into it when I went back to Sewanee with you," she said. "It would have been much better for both of us if I hadn't gone." She would need a period of recuperation in the United States to get her lectures ready. After a brief stop in Princeton, she would get a room or an apartment in New York. (Years later Caroline would write that "my husband would not allow me to return to my home—even to pack up my belongings.") Close friends who were aware of the true state of the Tates' marriage were certainly under the impression that Allen did not want her in Minnesota.

For a while, in Rome, Caroline felt a momentary surge of confidence. She would be able to help Allen because she was less in need of help herself. "A pressure under which I have laboured all my life seems to have been taken away," she wrote Allen. "I *have* asked too much of you but one reason was that I felt so poor and forsaken myself. The dottoressa said that apparently neither of us had a happy childhood but that people who did have happy childhoods often had a harder time than we have—it is harder for them to face reality. . . . You are having a devil of a time about your work but you have yet to repeat yourself, as Hemingway does, or make an ass of yourself, as Faulkner did in his last book, or fall from your own high standards."

When he read the galleys of *The Malefactors,* Allen cabled her that it was wonderful. Caroline wrote, "I want to say one more thing, in defense of poor old Claiborne." Claiborne, third in Caroline's series of frustrated intellectual heroes, is clearly based on Allen. "He is, indeed, but a pale reflection of you but I think he's admirable. There were two effects I got that particularly pleased me. First, that he was nearly always right, even when he didn't know it, even when he [was] doing the wrong thing. That is, I think I showed in him the seer that is in every poet. The other effect was that everybody he met, from the leading characters in the book to people he met only once, like the girl he met in the hall or the young man who was writing the editorial and also the priest—all of them not only liked him but recognized that he had remarkable qualities."

Denver Lindley, Caroline's editor at Harcourt, Brace, sent page proofs of *The Malefactors* to Dorothy Day, in the hope that she would promote it in *The Catholic Worker.* Not only would Miss Day not promote the book, she was deeply displeased with the character of Catherine Pollard. Caroline had dedicated the book to Dorothy Day, one of the few women she genuinely admired, and made no secret of the fact that Miss Day was the model for the figure of Catherine Pollard. Miss Day objected especially to the fact that Catherine Pollard had participated in Black Masses in her youth. Lindley took out the dedication and the reference to the Black Mass, and Miss Day said that did a lot to remove the offense. She still found the alchemical experiment with "consecrated wine obtained from some friendly priest" so fantastic that it was unbelievable, but she could see that the idea of the "precious blood" and Horne Watts's perversion and his desire for blood were so tied together that there was no way to edit it. Horne Watts, a poet in the book, was modeled after Hart Crane. Dorothy Day could see what Caroline had tried to do and she respected her attempt to show the profound aspect of the Church in reference to the most loathsome sins, but she wished that Caroline had not described Catherine on Mott Street, on the Bowery, and at the farm—all Dorothy's bailiwicks—so precisely. And she thought it unfortunate that Peter Maurin appeared in the darkness of his last years without the light of his earlier years. (Peter Maurin was an old French peasant who had come to this country to spread the gospel of the Green Revolution and had helped Dorothy Day start her Houses of Hospitality. He reminded Caroline of the Agrarians.) But of course, Dorothy said, she would not dream of taking "action." Lindley told Caroline he found Dorothy Day impressive, even more impressive than Caroline had said she was.

The Cheneys came to Rome—without Flannery O'Connor—and they came strictly as pilgrims, Caroline said, "such a relief after all one's tourist friends!" They had what Caroline called "such fun," including an audience with the pope, whose eyes impressed Caroline mightily. Then the Cheneys got a telegram that Lon's nephew, the only child in the family, had been killed in an automobile accident. They all three took the next plane home.

Caroline saw Allen briefly in Princeton before he went back to Minnesota in early January. He told her that they had to face the fact that they both had deep neuroses that might be sublimated but never eradicated; they would have to make concessions to each other, hoping for grace to help them. She needed ground under her feet and he needed a response from her that would not plunge him back into the arms of Magna Mater. Caroline copied out passages on the "transformative character" of the feminine from Neumann's *The Great Mother*, which she thought illuminating, and read a "wonderful commentary on St. John of the Cross by a Benedictine named Bede Frost."

Never did a couple seek the help of God and His Church more devoutly and more earnestly. And never did God and His Church seem more impotent or less interested.

Caroline was unhappy the minute she hit Kansas in early February. She hated the "hideous" place where she was staying with "delinquent old ladies," where the furnace thermostat was always set at eighty degrees. The linoleum on the floor and the paper on the walls crawled with huge hideous flowers. "I tell myself they represent basically the same impulse that created the milles fleurs tapestry but it is hard to make the notion stick," she wrote Nancy. It was too far to walk to the campus and she had to take a bus. She planned to spend her spare time painting a portrait of St. John of the Cross, who "asked and obtained of God the privilege of suffering every day. I think of him every time my eye lights on one of these walls." However, what with preparing a weekly public lecture, there was no spare time. She talked the first week on the structure of *Oedipus Tyrannus*, the second week on Beatrix Potter's *Jemima Puddleduck*.

She told Allen she was glad he was seeing Father Casey, his new spiritual director. She continued to romanticize Allen's role in her life. "We were born . . . in a jungle of misinformation and prejudices and lies," she wrote. "You took machete in hand and hacked a way out for both of us when we were young but you have got to hack another trail in the next few years, or, I think, we are both lost. I don't think that when we went to Minnesota either of us took enough thought about the danger involved in a poet's getting a good safe job."

The Malefactors appeared in the spring of 1956. While she was writing it, Caroline had regarded it as her chef d'oeuvre, her "big novel," and she was proud of her use of Henry James's "later method." Critics did not remark on her use of this technique, she said, because they did not know what James's later method was. She was proud, too, of the way she, a convert, had written a thoroughly Catholic novel. She told Stark Young she also thought it was the first novel in which the Jungian "underground" actually provided a setting for action. "I am a little vain of that passage in which Horne Watts indicates to Claiborne that Catherine Pollard wants to speak to him, but Claiborne finds only a stalactite when he approaches her (in the dream), and has to seek her out and continue the conversation above ground, where they take it up as if it had not been interrupted. That sort of thing is not easily brought off, as you well know."

Allen expressed admiration for the book many times. Later, when he was on a committee to judge the best work of imaginative literature published in 1956 for the American Library Association, he could not understand why Caroline's publishers had not entered *The Malefactors*. (He would have withdrawn from the committee if they had, he said.) He thought that her novel and Elizabeth Spencer's *Voice at the Back Door* were the only good ones he had seen that year. On another occasion, he listed *The Malefactors* among great books that had been underrated.

There were some very good reviews. Vivienne Koch in *The Sewanee Review* called it a "profoundly conceived, incandescent story," with which the author emerges "as the best woman novelist we have in this country at this time." Arthur Mizener in *The New York Times Book Review* praised it, as did John W. Simons, a priest, writing in *Commonweal* and Willard Thorp in *The New Republic*.

On the other hand, *Saturday Review* called it a picture of sick intellectuals and a bitter dose. In the most unfavorable review of all, *Time* attacked the book's "semi-autobiographical overtones" and called it "one of those Mary McCarthy–like exercises in intellectual cattiness in which one claws one's literary coterie in public," but added that the book might inadvertently reveal that the "Lost Generation was born to be led astray and taken in."

Caroline wrote Allen that she did not take the reviews seriously— "but still they are interesting, viewed as the reaction to thirty years of hard work."

She considered a letter from Jacques Maritain more valuable than any of the reviews. She had his letter copied to send to her friends and to people who complained about the novel. Maritain wrote that few books had moved him so deeply. It was full of poetry and of admirably sure design. "The fact of your characters being haunted by real figures very close to us, Hart Crane, Dorothy Day, Peter Maurin, gives them a very strange dimension and renders them curiously familiar to us. This has nothing to do with the *roman à clef*. It is rather a use of overtones which seems to me very new and bold and very successful." He was proud that she had used some words of his for an epigraph, although he did not remember having uttered so profound a sentence.

The epigraph, from Maritain's essay "The Frontiers of Poetry," reads: "It is for Adam to interpret the voices which Eve hears." When Caroline wrote to Maritain to thank him for his letter, she quoted from the review John Simons wrote in *Commonweal;* his review, she said, took the epigraph to a higher, or deeper, level. "The poet is nourished by his intuitions, but is the critical intelligence (Adam) which must decide on the authenticity of what the soul (Eve) experiences," Simon wrote.

Ashley Brown, who had done his dissertation at Vanderbilt on Caroline's work, in an essay observed that she had written a Christian comedy, in the sense that Dante's *Divine Comedy* was a Christian comedy. Her *Commedia*, he said, "follows something of the plan of Dante's poem. . . . She has attempted something almost unprecedented in modern fiction: she has made the dead characters as important as the living. . . . The Dantesque scheme thus informs *The Malefactors* to a considerable extent." George Crenfrew, Claiborne's psychiatrist cousin, is a kind of Virgil, Brown thought. He praised the "controlled point of view, the carefully modulated time shift, the adjustment of style to subject, the precision of details—all of these technical procedures are made to work." Caroline was charmed and startled at these ideas. She said she had not read Dante.

Caroline and Allen continued their intense correspondence. "You are right when you say we must no longer put our fears and inadequacies off on each other," she wrote him in a letter dated Septuagesima Sunday, the third Sunday before Lent. "I don't think you asked too much of me. I think you asked the wrong things. . . . I am constantly tempted to apply the conventional standards to things to which I know very well they shouldn't apply. It drives me wild when you make us cut *brutti figuri* [*sic*] in public. Your temptations take place on a high plane. . . . You may be farther along the Unitive way than I am or you wouldn't be confronted with the temptations you are confronted with."

On Quinquagesima Sunday she wrote him that the period in Oxford was the first break they had had and a "time when we were sure of each other's affections." It was "at Benfolly that things first began to go really wrong between us—when you told me what you told me about Sally." She closed the letter: "Love, darling, I can't tell you how happy I am about things now."

Allen and Caroline had a brief, ecstatic reunion when he came to Kansas City to lecture. "They were mad for each other—when they'd been apart," a friend of theirs in Kansas City observed. During his spring break, Allen came again and moved her out of the old-ladies' home and into a more suitable place. Caroline spent her spring vacation in Minneapolis, but that reunion did not go well. "I am sorry if I seemed unsympathetic and hard while I was in Minneapolis," she wrote him on April 11. "I know I was. That night you appealed to me I was just stubborn because I was drunk. I am worried to death about you. It is one thing that makes me nervous."

In that same letter she appealed to him for help. "Darling, I am going through a strange and terrible time, so please be patient with me. A certain enthusiasm, a kind of vigorous response to life which I held on to through all sorts of trials has left me. I can hardly face each day. I long only for night. It is, doubtless, some kind of night of the soul, a trial sent me by God for a much needed purgation. I am sure of that. But it is very disconcerting to suddenly feel yourself become almost another person. I cannot muster any of the responses to life I once had. I feel like a zombie. . . . The one comfort I have is that you have come through to another level. I firmly believe this and I believe, too, that I will come through very soon. Pray for me, please."

In Kansas hyacinths, tulips, and narcissus burst into bloom, along with hedges of Japanese quince, cheering Caroline somewhat; it was time to make a quick trip to Nashville. The Rockefeller Foundation was sponsoring a reunion of the Fugitives in May, and Allen and Caroline were going to appear together. Caroline was also bringing friends from Kansas City, the Joseph Kellehers and the Howard Adamses. (Kelleher was on the staff of the Kansas City Art Museum and Adams was a rich young man who was interested in Caroline's work.)

The Tates stayed with the Cheneys in Smyrna, where, Caroline said, "marvelous food seemed to leap upon the table and Old Jack Daniel flowed like water."

There was a formal dinner one night at the Belle Mead Club, and on another night John Crowe Ransom, Robert Penn Warren, Donald Davidson, Merrill Moore, and Allen Tate read their poems. There they were, Allen said, "all but stuffed."

Back in Kansas to finish the semester, Caroline wrote to Allen: "I keep your letter you wrote me before we went to Tennessee by my bed and read it over every day. . . . We have been ill and now we are well. We happen to be two rather remarkable people and because of that have been subjected to great trials."

Allen was less sanguine. He simply did not feel that he could provide Caroline the complete reassurance she needed. He needed it too much himself.

As soon as the term was over, Caroline went to Princeton, expecting to spend the summer in Anne Fremantle's house at 154 Mercer Street—the Tates had leased the house for the summer months for seven years and intended to spend every summer there—but Anne Fremantle had forgotten that her tenants' lease was not up until July 1. Caroline was furious. And then she found the perfect house to buy.

GROUND BENEATH HER FEET,
1956–1959

The "perfect house" was small and old; part of it had been built in
1780, part in 1830. It was on Ewing just off Harrison Street, two blocks
from a shopping center; not the best of neighborhoods, but it had an
acre of ground. The young couple who owned it had added all the
modern conveniences, but not, said Caroline, a single modern vulgarity.
"One would not have to spend a penny on it, not even for a coat of
paint," Caroline wrote Stark Young. "We could just move in and have
the luxury of arranging our books and papers without any great upheaval such as we have had now every two years since we married. I
am not going to cry if we don't get it but I'll sing paeans of praise if
we do."

This house was to be the ground beneath her feet for Caroline—if
she and Allen could get it. But it looked for a while as if they could
not manage it. It cost $21,000. Even with some of the cash left from
the $10,000 that Percy and Nancy had paid them for their share of
Dulce Domum, they needed $2,000 more for a down payment. Allen
had to teach at an international seminar directed by Henry Kissinger
at the Harvard Summer School, but he came back to Princeton on
weekends to try to get the purchase through.

They went to Avalon on the Jersey shore to spend one weekend with Franklin and Ida Watkins, and there Caroline had one of her "fits," screaming at Allen all night and tearing the sheets to shreds. (Allen had been involved with Ida Watkins in Rome in the fall of 1953, he told John Prince.)

Caroline thought she lost her temper because she had missed Mass. Allen disagreed and felt it was because she was insecure about the future; he hoped they would be able to get the little house and bring off a permanent reconciliation.

Virginia Erdman called Caroline to say that she had looked at the house and thought it was wonderful. She and David had sold their St. Paul house and moved to Princeton, and they were in no hurry to buy another house. They would be glad to lend her the $2,000 the Tates needed to get the house. Allen came down the next weekend to sign the contract, and Caroline moved in. She expected to live in the house the rest of the summer, rent it for the academic year, and go back to Minneapolis with Allen.

She loved the house. It had three levels, "none of them split," she wrote to the Cheneys. It was a sort of miniature Benfolly, only more practical. There was a little terrace in back, half enclosed with "ancient lilacs and syringas," Caroline wrote to Flannery O'Connor. At the end of the stretch of back lawn there was a grove of young locusts and two huge willow trees. It was hard to believe they were in Princeton: one could sit on the terrace and watch the rabbits on the lawn.

They named the house Sabine Close, "after another poet, only *he* had a farm but this place is as near a farm as people like us can expect," Caroline wrote to Ashley Brown, who had become a warm and valued friend. Caroline, thinking about the Sabines, knew only that Horace had a farm in the Sabine country and that some Sabine women had been raped. Searching the encyclopedia, she found that the Sabines were "very, very autochthonous and that their first great chieftain . . . was named Tatius."

When Caroline walked up to Nassau Street, she felt like her grandmother driving in the buggy from Merry Mont to Clarksville. She immediately began having dinner parties and houseguests. Sue Jenkins arrived for a surprise visit and declared that the terrace was "a magic enclosure." Sue, according to Caroline, was a great axe-woman; she wanted to cut down the big wisteria, but Caroline let her do a little delicate pruning and chop down four arborvitae. Then Sue wandered down a little wooded path in the back and said, "I suppose you're going to have the Stations of the Cross here?"

Caroline had never thought of it, but she immediately said, yes, indeed. They set to work and before Sue left, the "Way of the Cross" was finished. They marked each station on a wild cherry tree with a cross and a neat Roman numeral in aluminum outdoor paint. When someone told Caroline it was "unliturgical," that the stations had to be a different material from their supports, she declined to listen.

When Allen came back from Harvard in August, they invited Caroline's cousin Kate Radford to come up from Toms River on the Jersey shore and spend the night. Allen would drive her back if she had a ride up to Princeton, Caroline said. Allen left about three o'clock, saying he had to go to the library. Mrs. Radford arrived at four, and she and Caroline talked until they became worried about Allen's absence. About seven Caroline went into the kitchen and found a special-delivery letter lying on the floor. It was from Allen, announcing he was leaving her. The thing that Caroline always remembered was the rat in the trap. Allen had set a trap the day before and now there was a rat caught in it, struggling, its back broken. Neither she nor Mrs. Radford had the will to get rid of the rat. Instead, they listened to it struggle all night long. When the sun rose, Caroline called her handyman to come and get rid of it.

Allen wrote from the Princeton Club of New York to say that he was not coming back because he could not live with her recriminations, her temper, and her jealousy. They would live distinguished lives away from each other. He could live without women if he did not live with her; it was living with her that had driven him to other women.

After several letters that discussed their separation in implacable, lofty terms, Allen sent helpful criticism on the draft of the first chapter of *How to Write a Novel*.

He assured her that she had plenty of money—$300 in the bank. He was going to India for the Department of State, and while he was gone he would have the university send his check, just under $400 a month, to a Princeton bank. He had arranged to give up the apartment in Minneapolis; their clothes would be shipped to Princeton, and everything else sent to Hunt and Bid Brown's house in Minneapolis.

That fall, when Caroline's checks began to bounce, she called the English department at Minnesota. The secretary told her that Allen had personally addressed the envelopes for his paychecks to be deposited in his account at a Minneapolis bank. Caroline, penniless, scrambled to find teaching jobs at Columbia and the New School and borrowed $500 from Sally Wood and smaller sums from other friends until her paychecks started coming in. It was up to her to meet the mortgage payments on Sabine Close and pay the insurance, as well as her own expenses.

She began, as best she could, to make a life for herself, working in her garden and writing letters that put up a brave front. "Allen and I are separated again," she wrote when she sent a chapter of *How to*

Read a Novel, to Philip Rahv at *Partisan Review.* "We do it every now and then, you know, and it is awfully tiresome of us! Too bad this time as we had just bought the house of our dreams in Princeton. I intend to stay in it the rest of my life and be carried out feet foremost."

Marcella Winslow saw Allen in Washington and wrote to her mother-in-law that she was sorry to say he had not improved. "He wants to go back to Caroline, but dreads living with her. He says all is well for about two weeks and then all hell breaks loose. . . . He is a lost soul without Caroline and I don't know what the solution is. He isn't writing—will go back to Minneapolis, I guess. Looks so old and thin but still has the wit and sparkle."

By December 28, 1956, Allen was back in Minneapolis living in an efficiency apartment. He had signed a separation agreement, promising to send Caroline $300 a month and to keep her as his insurance beneficiary.

For three years the Tates lived apart, Caroline in Princeton and Allen mostly in Minneapolis. Most of their friends did not realize they were formally separated. They saw each other from time to time, talked on the phone, and wrote to each other over and over, professing their love for one another, their despair at the present situation. Sometimes one of them would attack the other. Caroline often quoted long passages from Catholic writers to Allen—Fénelon, St. John of the Cross's *Spiritual Canticle* and Jean Pierre Caussade's *Abandonment to Divine Providence.* And they discussed money.

"I imagine you have put the Bollingen money on a new car," Caroline wrote him in January 1957, after he won the Bollingen Prize in Poetry. It was all right with her, she said. "When you told me you would pay off the Erdmans with it you were tight and therefore hardly responsible for what you said." She did not see how he could manage without a car, she conceded, although he had moved from an apartment to a seedy hotel.

Caroline's teaching load was heavy. She added City College and taught a Monday-night class at Columbia, two Tuesday-night classes at City College, a Wednesday-morning class at the New School, and two Thursday-night classes at City College. She broke the journey to City College at a church in Harlem dedicated to St. Joseph and the Holy Family. Somehow she finished *How to Read a Novel;* Sue Jenkins did the final editing and typing job for her.

In her letters to Allen, Caroline often said that they had special gifts, that she had learned everything she knew about writing from Allen, and that this was proper: "Man is supposed to lead, woman to follow." They discussed drinking and their need for spiritual directors. A priest told Allen that his periodic drinking was due to the intermittent belief that he had been abandoned by God. He managed to go five weeks without a drink that winter. When Caroline gave a dinner party and invited the Lamberts, Jerry sent her a case of Old Grand-dad, "but I stick to one drink," she told Allen.

They both felt that each should be seeing a priest and a Catholic psychiatrist—no couple ever worked harder at self-improvement. Caroline saw a Dr. Giorgio Lolli ("the finest Catholic psychiatrist in New York") who told her that he felt sure alcohol had played a large part in their troubles; Allen saw a Dr. Regan in Minneapolis, who told him that his trouble since the age of about fifteen was centered on his brother, Ben, as surrogate father, rather than his mother and father directly, and that he had tried to make Caroline into his mother.

In the spring of 1957 Caroline was almost reconciled to the idea of a formal separation, until Jacques Maritain told her that he thought it was right for them to be together. She was so anxious for Allen to talk to Maritain that she offered to turn the house over to him and stay with Sue if he would come to Princeton. Allen was seeing other women throughout this period, and when Caroline heard gossip about him that spring, she called him in a rage. The call made Allen decide not to go to Princeton for spring vacation but to visit Andrew Lytle in Florida instead. Caroline referred to her "little outburst the other night" and said, in explanation, "I received such wounds in my childhood and got into such a panic as a result of them that everywhere I go and particularly in any contact with you I am frantically demanding reassurance."

She asked Allen to return the money from the sale of her de Kooning so she could repay the Erdmans, who needed their money by June 1, 1957, to buy a house. She wanted what she called her professional library back; she had been handicapped in doing *How to Read a Novel* without Henry James's notebooks and she needed the other books by James, those by Joyce, Balzac, Dostoevsky, and Tolstoy, Aristotle's *Poetics,* Ford's books, and her own copy of *The Wonders of Italy.* She took time to tell him how beautiful the garden was, with "lilacs, apple trees, peach trees, pear trees and wistaria all in bloom and the big syringa bush in bud. The chestnut tree is in bloom and dogwood." A brook ran out of the mouth of a stone lion she had bought at the flea market in Rome and spilled over the rim of a fountain. The banks of the brook were covered with ferns and white violets and the water flowed past a bed filled with pansies, grape hyacinths, and petunias toward a bed of lilies, tulips, and roses. Caroline was eating Bibb lettuce, onions, and radishes from her little vegetable garden. "I am crowding all the gardening I have longed to do for years into this one spring," Caroline told him. She planted pussy willow cuttings and Merry Mont poplars.

Two gifts from Fannie Cheney provided endless diversion—a book of Persian miniatures and a copy of *Lives of the Saints*. "I find that the best way to prepare for Mass is to read the life or lives of as many of the saints of the day as I can get in before Mass. That Attwater is certainly a wonderful editor. Every now and then I come on some historical fact that nigh takes the top of my head off," she wrote Fannie.

Allen was at Sabine Close briefly at the end of the summer of 1957. That fall Caroline taught only on Tuesdays and Fridays and as soon as the garden was put to bed for the winter she looked forward to an orgy of painting.

On November 3, 1957, Allen wrote to compliment her on *How to Read a Novel*. The book distills a great many of Caroline's ideas about the novel, and pays tribute to Flaubert, James, and Joyce, her second Holy Trinity. She used Joseph Warren Beach and Percy Lubbock to buttress her arguments. It is perhaps excessively concerned with the technique of a novel. ("It is barely possible that there are other considerations than method in the enjoyment of novels," wrote Louis D. Rubin, Jr., in the Baltimore *Sun*. "What they might be, Miss Gordon does not say.") Nevertheless, the book is still wonderfully instructive and entertaining for any aspiring writer or serious reader.

Caroline and Allen still corresponded regularly. "I see my own life now that I near the end of it, as largely a conflict with daimons," she wrote him on November 13, 1957. "One of the first things I remember is fear of mother's other worldliness, that hearkening to and preoccupation with inaudible voices that made her deaf to anything any of us said to her. I don't think this is my fancy. . . . Of course, I had to marry a man who, being a poet, was necessarily preoccupied with daimonic voices. . . . I have spent most of my life half paralyzed with fear of those voices that other people hear. I realize now—theoretically, at least, no matter how long it takes me to put it into practice, that these voices are dangerous and I was right to fear them—but I took the wrong way to combat them. They came from evil spirits, who, being fallen angels, have angelic intelligences and the only way to rout them is to call in other angelic intelligences—to let the mind of Christ dwell in us. I am indeed far from that but at least I know what I ought to try to do. There have been times in my life—and they have been the worst and most terrifying times—when I didn't even know what I ought to try to do."

The Tates took Kitty Morgan, a Princeton friend of Caroline's who was an editor at the Rutgers University Press, with them to spend Christmas 1957 with the Cheneys, who were unaware of the separation. Allen told Nancy that Caroline had one of her fits of anger, a terrible exhibition, but Fannie Cheney remembers only that Caroline was excited and fun to be with and "made our Christmas—she went to the dime store and bought all these decorations and put them up. She always made life exciting. That little business didn't amount to a thing."

"I am sorry I marred the merry making by making a scene," Caroline wrote to Lon after the visit. "The truth is that the Devil (doubtless) has been tempting me to try to get a formal separation from Allen— I get so weary of his antics sometimes that I feel I simply can't stand any more of them. My advisers, including our Roman psychiatrist, Dr. Giorgio Lolli, are all against this and Allen, himself, is infuriated at the idea, so I guess I'll push the temptation into the background and try to behave myself a little better from now on."

A little later she wrote to Fannie. "In my long and misspent life I have had two of those hysterical seizures, such as I had at your house— in which an abyss seems to open right under my feet into hell," she said. "I had the other seizure at the Franklin Watkins' place on the beach. I was walking along with the others and suddenly had convulsions which lasted a long time. Ida and Watty were very kind and sympathetic to both of us."

To Allen she wrote that he put his finger for the first time on the place where their angers interlocked and ministered to each other. It occurred when he said, as he had so many times, that whenever he received the slightest reproach from any woman he saw her as seven feet tall, menacing his life. She would pray every day, Caroline said, that God would "set a watch before my mouth and a door round about my lips that my heart may not incline to evil words and seek excuses in sins." Dr. Lolli told her she was inclined to look on the dark side of things. "I know I am," she told Allen. "Certain attitudes of mine were the cause for your ill treatment of me. I have long known that this was so. . . . Dr. Lolli says that I am inclined to make too harsh judgments. . . . For years I had nobody to make judgments for me except myself and you. . . . Now that I am in the Church I see—with my mind's eye—that I do not need to make any judgments at all. The Lord attends to all that—if I can only realize it. But putting these realizations into practice takes time as well as unremitting effort."

Caroline began reading about the Carmelites, and Kitty Morgan drove her to visit the Discalced Carmelite nuns in Flemington, New Jersey, so Caroline could talk to Mother Beatrice, heavily veiled and behind bars. Caroline decided to study to become a Carmelite tertiary. "The postulancy lasts a year," she wrote to Allen, "and is pretty tough. But . . . better to try and fail than not to try. And in our difficult family situation I desperately need some outward discipline to help order my inner life." (Third-order Carmelites are not cloistered but devote themselves to teaching, care of the sick, and other charitable works.) Everybody had an affinity with some orders, she explained later, and she was convinced that the Carmelite order, which St. Teresa of Avila, with the help of St. John of the Cross, had reformed in the sixteenth century, was the one for her. Caroline regarded it as providential that she lived within driving distance of the nuns.

Again she asked Allen for some of the money from the sale of her de Kooning. She had let her bills accumulate; when she got home from New York one night she found the gas had been turned off. She cooked breakfast on the fireplace. City College was the only one of her jobs that paid before the end of the term, and it paid less than she had expected. "It was stupid of me about the bills but I just let them pile up thinking I'd get enough money from City College to pay them. But I didn't. I really have hardly had time to count them up. I have to spend most of the day getting my lectures up and then run for the train and I don't get back here till midnight, so exhausted that I couldn't count if I tried."

She made $299 a month from Columbia, $60 a month from City College, and her pay from the New School depended on the number of pupils she had. She had to make mortgage payments, pay taxes and insurance for the house, and she had still other expenses. It was clear she needed money from Allen.

She asked for a third class at Columbia, one in remedial creative writing, but did not get it. She wanted to concentrate her classes at Columbia and the New School to cut down on the commuting. It was not the teaching but the commuting that was wearing her down. As hard as she worked, she stayed some nights after class to study painting with Julian Levi, who had been one of Ford Madox Ford's group in Paris and an editor of *Gargoyle*. "He even remembers *Broom*," Caroline wrote to Allen.

She was excited and happy when Allen began to talk about getting a job at Columbia so they could "get organized and live at Sabine Close." A few days later she wrote him that Dr. Lolli had recommended Étienne Gilson's book on St. Thomas. She could not find it and went to the Princeton Seminary library, where all "the young men have the same expression on their faces, a kind of warped nobility." She found *Letters from Cambrai*, Fénelon's letters to the countess of Mountberon, "so much like me that the letters scare me." She quoted: " 'The basis of the trouble which you have nourished since childhood . . . is self-love disguised in the semblance of sensitiveness and brave generosity. This is a touch of the romantic. . . . On the one hand your sensitiveness and generosity are as unbounded as your jealousy and suspicion on the other.' " She added that this was mighty stout stuff.

Allen was like Fénelon, she said, "dry, hard and irregular. Some of the sufferings you went through in childhood have left dry, cold places in your heart. I ought to have tried to warm them to life instead of letting my self-love demand that they glow for me."

Her professional admiration of Allen remained undamaged. In March she wrote, "You *have* emerged into a new phase for which you are just beginning to find the equivalent in criticism. How much better to have got, as it were, a new mind, instead of giving people pieces of your old mind, over and over."

Allen received two medals for "Christian culture" that spring. He sent Caroline a picture of him having his medal pinned on by Basilian fathers at Assumption College in Toronto. "He went up to Assumption and made a big hit—they don't like Cardinal Spellman any more than he does," Caroline wrote Lon Cheney. Assumption offered Allen a job but, to Caroline's disappointment, he turned it down.

When Allen received a Fulbright offer for 1958–1959, Caroline did not want him to take it. If he wanted her to go with him, it would be difficult. She said her hold on her job was precarious; her two friends and protectors at Columbia, Vernon Loggins and Bill Owens, would leave the next year and she was afraid of a new broom. Another reason she did not want to leave was that she was studying the manual for Carmelite tertiaries. Furthermore, she thought she and Allen had lost a great deal of spiritual gains by following their parents' patterns of restless moving about. If they could establish some family pattern of physical stability, she believed, it would help them to attain spiritual stability. Allen had been working on a long poem for years, and Caroline hoped he could finish it in Princeton, just as he had settled down and produced a great deal of poetry during the winter at Monteagle with the Lowells. "I have felt this Sabbatical year is for you a kind of repetition of the year we had on the mountain. You acted then with a boldness and decision which I admired."

All that spring she worried about money and sent her curriculum vitae to four lecture bureaus, hoping to get speaking engagements. She took in a "gentleman boarder" whom she promptly set about trying to convert. Instead, he ended up committed to a mental hospital. She was troubled, too, by Nancy and Percy, who, she said, made her feel unwelcome at Dulce Domum.

On Holy Thursday, 1958, she wrote to Allen that yet another priest "made perhaps the most acute summing up anybody, priest or psychiatrist, has made of my troubles. He listened to me for an hour and then made only one remark: 'Caroline you want to be loved, don't you?' And of course that's it. But I would be rid of my troubles if I could only realize that I have already been loved immeasurably by Christ and that all I have to do now is to return that love as best I can to as many people as possible."

She was optimistic again. "Allen has been through a very hard time— one of the worst—but is in better shape now than I've ever seen him," she wrote to Mark Van Doren in May. "It was a Jesuit pulled him through."

Allen went to a writers' conference in Utah and Caroline, who, because of her garden, declined an invitation to teach there, drove to Canada with Kitty Morgan and returned to teach summer school at Columbia. Allen told her he had turned down the Fulbright and left for Harvard.

Tom Mabry and Ward Dorrance called Caroline from Massachusetts; they said that Sally Sidgwick, a woman in Boston, had told Tom that Allen was going to England. "Oh, no!" screamed Caroline. "Oh, yes," said Tom, "I saw her two days ago." Caroline described the incident in a letter to Fannie Cheney. "Unfortunately, I had been drinking a bit," she said. "I called Sally Sidgwick up and bawled her out. She is a nice woman and had a crazy husband, too. The next morning I called her and apologized and she forgave me freely. But Allen's familiar had at last accomplished what he had planned and took complete charge from then on."

To Allen she wrote: "Your discourtesy in failing to notify me of your change of plans, your unexplained absences, . . . references to long letters that never arrive have been pretty upsetting. Tommy's message seemed to throw a lurid light on this whole matter and I simply blew my top. But I would not blow my top like that if I did not go always in such fear of receiving a mortal wound."

Allen told her that he had to go to England because Minnesota expected it. They had no one else to send. He was committed to Minnesota for life. If she felt that she could live with him again, they would go together to Minnesota in the fall of 1959, renting out the Princeton house.

Caroline was in despair. She told Fannie Cheney, "My opinion of Allen is that he is the most wonderful man I have ever known but that he is a bit crazy." She thought he had been crazy since he got back from Europe in the fall of 1952. She believed that Allen had turned all their friends, as well as Nancy, against her. On the other hand, she said, "The opinion Allen professes to hold of me does not coincide with reality, for he expresses one opinion to one person, one to another. I have had three letters in one day from priests, to whom he had expressed contradictory opinions."

By September 30, 1958, Allen was in London and by October 23 at All Souls, Oxford, writing poetry, lecturing, seeing a Dr. Layard and a Dominican priest. In November 1958 he had a Minneapolis lawyer file a divorce suit, charging Caroline with cruel and inhumane behavior. Caroline hired Robert Barnett, another Minneapolis lawyer, to represent her and prepared to contest the divorce suit. Allen offered to pay Caroline $350 a month instead of $300 and told her this was about $300 a year more than his salary after deductions. His pension would still go to her, she would still be his insurance beneficiary, and in his will he would leave her all his personal property and papers.

Caroline was devastated. "The letter from Caroline today was pretty bad," Flannery O'Connor wrote the Cheneys. "It doesn't look like you can do anything for them but pray!" Caroline turned down an invitation from Fannie for Christmas and wrote to Allen that he should talk to Dr. Layard (John Layard, the Jungian analyst he was seeing) about the part Christmas had played in his life. "We had our first quarrel at Christmas time, shortly after Nancy's conception. In 1945, I spent Christmas with the Starrs, waiting for our divorce." Allen was already writing friends in America that he expected to be divorced by the first of the year, that things could not go on the way they had been going, since neither he nor Caroline could endure it. He would not marry again, he said; he could not afford it.

Caroline was frantic. She told her lawyer that if she cabled Allen she would not contest, he would drop the action, and she thought that his offer of a financial settlement was better than she would get in court. Later, however, she wrote to Allen: "I have consulted several priests. Each one has said unhesitatingly that it is my duty to actively oppose a divorce, so I feel that I have no choice. . . . I find myself inclined to make less and less emotional demands on you, as time goes. You are perfectly free to live apart from me if that is your wish. But do you feel that it is morally right to inflict considerable hardship on me in my old age?"

"Old age" was not something in the distant future—she would be sixty-four years old in October 1959—and she would have to retire from Columbia at seventy. "I am hanging on to my job at Columbia by a shoe-string," she continued. "They have asked me to do twice the amount of work this summer for the same pay I got last summer. My lapses of memory are a decided handicap." (She wrote Fannie that she was about to be fired from the New School on account of a bad memory lapse—she had given the lecture intended for English 653 to English 607. It would be the first time she was fired for incompetence and, while she was sure it would be awfully good for her, it was "damn inconvenient.") To Allen she declared, "I am going to work as long as I can but if I get to the point where I can't work you will be legally responsible for my whole support.

"Our present financial arrangement is unrealistic. You allow me thirty six hundred dollars a year ordinarily. The mortgage, taxes and upkeep on this house amount to twenty five hundred dollars a year. We own it jointly. The money I pay out is a saving for you as well me. You have been allowing me actually $2400 a year. It is not enough to live on. It is all right for me to earn my own living but it is a hardship on me to have to start doing it so late in life."

Her lawyer urged her to continue to contest the divorce action in order to save the marriage and keep Allen in the Church.

In the midst of this horror, she struggled with revisions for a new edition of *The House of Fiction,* enraged that she "had to do all of Allen's work" as well as her own. (The new edition, like the first, would carry both their names on the title page, and Caroline would do most of the work for the second edition, as she did for the first.) At Scribner's she pounded on the desk of her editor, Erik Lanngjkear, "a Dane with eyes like blue marbles," and said, "Damn it, I don't want to do this. I want to paint."

"You say you're penniless?" he said.

"No, I want to *paint,*" she said. "I'm very talented. My teacher says so."

"When an author uses a word that begins with *p* I always think he's saying 'penniless,'" Lanngjkear said.

On December 12, 1958, she sent Allen carbons of some of what she had written, commenting, "Lanngjkear returned to the attack with Isak Dinesen. I said she wasn't good."

Good news came. She wrote Allen that "a friend of ours" had offered to pay $3,000 on her mortgage and take over the rest of the mortgage herself without interest. "It would be a great relief because I know she wouldn't foreclose if I defaulted on the payments. But there is, as always, a catch. She won't take the mortgage over as long as the place is owned jointly. I wonder if you would be willing to sign it over to me? I don't see how you'd lose anything, really. My will provides that it would go to you if I die first and I give you my word that I will consider the place as belonging to us both just as jointly as if a paper hadn't been signed."

Allen did sign over his interest in the house to Caroline, and the friend, who was Grace Lambert, did as she had promised.

"I feel as if I could stretch my wings and flap right down to Nashville," Caroline wrote to Manny, who was back in Nashville, working at Ward Belmont College. "Isn't it divine? . . . What it comes down to is I will own the place outright year after next and for the next two years I will pay fifty dollars a month on the mortgage as opposed to one hundred and twenty. . . . Ain't it wonderful?"

In that same letter, she beseeched her cousin Manny to come and stay with her. "Now, Manny, don't let me down on this. I really need you. I've gone through a lot in the last year or two and I need the companionship and support of some member of my family." Manny did not come.

One morning, in the midst of all this, Caroline was lying in bed with a bad hangover. "I said to myself," she wrote Lon Cheney, "that I'm not as young as I once was . . . and I decided to stay in bed all morning. Unfortunately I had put the typewriter on the night table. As I recall, I sort of turned over in bed—and the first thing I knew I had eight pages of 'The Narrow Heart' written. Had another whack at it later and I now have twelve pages, so I am committed. The gaff, as my father would say, has been slipped home." She also told Lon, who thought the letter sounded more like the old Caroline, that she was seeing Father McCoy on Wednesday, redoubling her efforts "to see if I can't find some way to give Allen a divorce."

"I have finally found a priest who is willing to help me and expert enough to advise me how to contest the suit without injuring Allen's reputation. Father Horace McCoy at St. Francis Xavier . . . ," she wrote Father William Lynch, a literary priest at Georgetown who was a friend of Allen's.

Expecting to contest the divorce, she called for all the moral support she could get, writing and visiting priests and old friends.

Robert Lowell, just back from Europe and briefly in Princeton, told Caroline the latest gossip: Allen was living with a poet named Isabella Gardner McCormick and wanted a divorce so he could marry her. Lowell reported that Allen fancied himself as Lord Byron and that Isabella was his Countess Guiccioli. She was, Lowell said, "bone stupid." Furthermore, Lowell told Caroline, Allen was "engaged" to Isabella but he had asked Natasha Spender to marry him; Allen's ulcer had flared again and he looked awful, but he was sending everybody photographs of himself and Isabella falling in and out of gondolas in Venice. Caroline reflected that the worse Allen got, the more the priests praised him.

Isabella Stewart Gardner was born in Boston in 1915 (twenty years after Caroline, sixteen years after Allen). She had attended the Foxcroft School and studied for the stage in East Hampton, New York, and in London. When her stage career fizzled, she turned to writing poetry and worked for a time on *Poetry* magazine in Chicago. She published a book of poetry, *Birthdays for the Ocean*, in 1955. She had been married three times, the third time to Robert McCormick, Jr., of a rich Chicago family. As soon as she met Allen, she said, she made up her mind to marry Allen—and divorced McCormick.

When Caroline told Father McCoy about Allen and Mrs. McCormick, he told her that she, Caroline, had "helped to create evil" by condoning her husband's adulteries. Her uncle Paul Campbell, a lawyer in Chattanooga, heard about her troubles and called to see if he could help her. He agreed with Father McCoy. She told Allen that the minute she heard about Mrs. McCormick she had decided to stop contesting the suit.

"The gossip is that you are being given the Dylan Thomas treatment," she wrote to Allen. "I think you would do well to remember that the sycophant is always a murderer at heart—as poor Thomas's fate shows."

Caroline's friends tried to help her. Sue Jenkins wrote to Flannery O'Connor. Flannery wrote to the Cheneys. They all thought that if Mrs. McCormick thought Allen was going to marry her she had another thought coming, as Flannery put it. The Tates' first divorce had startled everyone; this one was like a slow and agonizing death. Ashley Brown, who was staying with Caroline that year, told Flannery not to mention the divorce when she wrote to Caroline. She had turned against practically everyone, he said. He listened to her and that was all anybody could do.

Allen told Léonie Adams it would be impossible for him and Caroline to live together after Robert Lowell's "wild gossip," and he could not contemplate a future in which he lived in a vacuum in Minnesota and made brief visits to Princeton.

On the advice of priests and lawyers, Caroline filed a countersuit. Details had to be hammered out and the matter of permanent alimony settled. Caroline's lawyer wanted to know all about the purchase of the house: whose money had made the down payment, who had made the payments, who had taken over the mortgage? He also asked for the names of people who had witnessed Allen's cruelty over the years. When Caroline said she wanted to keep Isabella McCormick out of it in order to protect Allen's professional reputation, Barnett told her that withholding evidence was not the way to win a lawsuit. Caroline rallied her friends to write to Barnett—Sally Wood, Léonie Adams, Kate Radford, and Isobel Howell from Nashville, who had seen Allen disposing of Caroline's belongings when he sold Benfolly ten years before. Barnett wanted Allen's admission of his infidelities in writing, and Caroline sent Barnett the letter Allen wrote to Sally on March 31, 1959, from All Souls, Oxford.

In this astonishing letter, Allen spoke freely of his infidelities in

1933, 1945, and 1947. As always, he blamed Caroline for his unfaithfulness to her. It was her fault for retreating into a mythical Meriwether world. She never forgave him. He had tried reconciliation and it was impossible.

"Allen will not like my divorcing him. He enjoys divorcing me, not the other way around," Caroline wrote Barnett. Allen wanted a divorce, and Allen did not want a divorce, she said. If he got the divorce, he would be faced with the problem of whether to marry Mrs. McCormick.

Caroline might toy with the idea of becoming a Carmelite tertiary, she might be embroiled in a bitter divorce from a husband she worshipped, she might be doing anything in the world, but she always came back to the writing of fiction. In May, the dust not settled from the revelations about Mrs. McCormick, Caroline wrote a letter applying for a Guggenheim Fellowship, saying that she was writing a book, for now entitled "The Narrow Heart," in which she hoped to accomplish something totally new for the novel form. "This sounds bold but I believe I can do it; over the years I have acquired considerable technical skill," she said. She added that her work had not been generally understood but the pattern of the whole body of her work had become apparent to a few critics. She was sure that Jacques Maritain, Herbert Read, Arthur Mizener, Francis Fergusson, Willard Thorp, and John Hall Wheelock would recommend her. She did not get the Guggenheim.

Caroline flew to Minneapolis for the divorce trial on August 18, 1959. Ashley Brown drove her to the airport and picked her up when she returned. Allen and Sam Monk met her at the Minneapolis airport, and in court she was flanked by priests. Allen had agreed to everything her lawyer asked, chiefly permanent alimony.

It was not long before she received a letter from Allen saying that he had married Isabella McCormick on August 27 on Cape Cod. Andrew Lytle had been best man.

In September, Caroline had a final session with Erik Lanngjkear on *The House of Fiction*. She had the house in Princeton painted—she started referring to it as the Red House instead of Sabine Close; she flew to Columbia, South Carolina, to visit Ashley Brown, and then returned to her painting and her gardening, writing Fannie that she must plant some sorrel. "Cream of sorrel soup is the best and most delicate soup ever made. And sorrel is a wonderful plant—turned from an annual to a perennial to oblige St. Kevin one winter when he was making a prolonged retreat. You just simmer some onions and stock and thicken with some cream and there you are. Of course, St. Kevin probably ate it raw but we don't have to."

Notwithstanding the house and garden and her resilient nature, the ground beneath her feet had been cut away. "The divorce was the tragedy of her life," Walker Percy observed. She—and the Catholic Church—still considered that she was married to Allen Tate, but she was never quite the same again.

35

Princeton, Dallas, San Cristóbal, 1959–1981

The divorce and Allen's remarriage almost destroyed Caroline. They had had not just a marriage but a comradeship and a partnership, more than thirty years of sharing poverty, parties, charades, house-guests, grants, houses, apartments, bourbon, friends, feuds, the perfidies of publishers, and a passion for the written word. She felt abandoned, bitter, and angry; she considered herself the most ill-used of women; no one knew what it was like to have loved, lived with, and lost Allen Tate; she could talk of little else.

They continued to write to each other from time to time, signing their letters "Love." Allen pushed Caroline for membership in the National Institute of Arts and Letters, asking Robert Lowell and Malcolm Cowley to propose her. He tried to get her foundation grants. He read every word she published and wrote her letters about her work. In 1963 he wrote to praise her essay on Ford Madox Ford and said he was sending it to Graham Greene, who was associated with a British publishing house. When she substituted for Allen on rather short notice when he was to give the Hopwood Lecture at the University of Michigan, he called a friend to see how she had done. "She always does better when I'm not there," Allen said. In his letters he urged her to pray for him, as he did for her. He reassured her that none of the money he sent her came from Isabella. Allen wrote Scribner's twice, urging them to reprint *Aleck Maury*. He told her he was saving $5,000 a year from his salary; by the time he retired he would have $30,000 and that would go to Caroline if he died before she did. He asked her to believe that he would provide for her. In 1965 he wrote her that "Cock-Crow," a section of her new novel that appeared in *The Southern Review,* was the best thing she had ever written.

A generous tone prevailed throughout the years he was married to Isabella, whom everyone liked. Then he divorced Isabella and in July 1966 married Helen Heinz, a nurse and former nun who had attended his classes at Minnesota. (Friends and relatives marveled. "A registered nun!" cried one. "He wanted to cuckold God himself," said another.) In August 1967 Helen gave birth to twin sons, Michael and John Allen. Allen had already told Caroline he was postponing three of his monthly payments. He was trying to get together money to build a small house in Sewanee for his retirement. With the help of a bequest from Helen's aunt, they were able to build a spacious house on Running Knob Hollow Road in Sewanee. Allen's financial picture had changed radically. He needed more money to provide for his young wife and small children. It was increasingly difficult to pay alimony, and by 1971 he stopped it.

In a dreadful accident, one of the twins, Michael, fell down and choked on a toy telephone, and while the nurse was bathing little John Allen, Michael died. Helen and Allen had another little boy the next year and named him Ben. Meanwhile, Allen's letters to Caroline became testier. He asked her repeatedly for financial statements and copies of her income tax forms, and finally in 1970 asked her to make over the Red House to him. Nancy did not need it, he said, and it would help provide for Helen and his little boys after his death. At almost the same time, he wrote to praise her story "Cloud Nine," about Heracles. Caroline—who was still writing him things like "You are the only editor I have ever been dependent on, for criticism as well as encouragement. You taught me practically everything I know about writing"—for once refused him. She would not make over the Red House to him. For years he kept up the campaign to get it, but Caroline never gave in.

More than one person heard Allen say—sometimes in Helen's presence—that no matter how many times he married, Caroline was his only wife. At some point they had what Caroline considered a kind of reconciliation. While Helen was out, Allen managed to get through to Caroline on the telephone and say, "Honey, it was all my fault." "Oh, no, darling, it was all my fault," Caroline responded, and then Allen said fearfully, "I have to hang up now—Helen's coming."

Meanwhile, Caroline lived a busy and, after a time, not unhappy life at the Red House in Princeton. Unlike Allen's house in Sewanee, it was full of old furniture and rugs, mementos of the past, and paintings of the Tates by Janice Biala and Stella Bowen. She always had people living with her—a succession of "gentlemen boarders" and women friends—and she entertained often. She packed guests into the little house and cooked food that was near perfection. Her dishes had traces of French and Southern influence, and there was plenty of it, in a good hearty American style, and always of the best quality—five-rib roasts, the best leg of lamb, a ham from Virginia. (Her favorite cookbook was *French Home Cooking* by Claire de Pratz.) But cooking belonged in its place. When Ashley Brown gave her a copy of a novel that included recipes, she threw it across the room. "A mixture of genres!" she said.) After his wife died, Willard Thorp came to supper every Sunday night, begged to be allowed to wash the dishes, and always got turned down. There were now four grandchildren in all, and Caroline enjoyed the two youngest, little Caroline and her little sister, Amy; she made them a playhouse in the backyard and took them to the ten-cent store to buy ropes of beads and other glamorous objects that enchant little girls. She joined Alcoholics Anonymous and, although she wrote Léonie Adams that she was "mad about it" and told Flannery O'Connor that AA was working out St. John of the Cross's mystical ascent, she did not give up drinking for long. She visited Grace Lambert's farm in Vermont, as well as Sue Jenkins's little place in Tory Valley, and bought blue jeans to wear to Howard Adams's place near Harpers Ferry. She kept up a vast correspondence with old friends like Sally Wood, Sue Jenkins, and Léonie Adams, with her brothers and Pidie, and, as always, with young writers.

The most avowed advocate of a patriarchal society, she had always maintained that everything she learned that was worth anything she had learned from a man and said many times that women lost their power when they gained the right to vote. While she was living in the Red House, she received a letter from the Mercer County Board of Elections saying that since she had not voted in any election for the past four years, they would remove her voting records from the active files. If she wished to vote, she must re-register. Caroline kept the letter among her papers, with this note in her handwriting: "Unanswered because I don't believe that women should be allowed to vote." Everything in her life indicates that she was a strong, independent woman—who wanted to be something else. She kept her maiden name, worked all her life, was anything but a stay-at-home housewife. She acted like a feminist, talked like a Southern ninny.

She continued teaching in New York and worked on her new novel.

Ashley Brown told her the title, "A Narrow Heart," must refer to Flaubert's *"Un Coeur Simple,"* but she said she was thinking of David's "I will run the way of thy commandments once thou hast enlarged my heart."

In 1960, in another application for a Guggenheim grant (which she did not get) Caroline outlined "A Narrow Heart." Like *Aleck Maury,* it would purport to be an autobiography—her own, she said. But it would really be a novel with a woman for the protagonist. On the literal level it would be a woman's life from childhood to old age, but there would be several strands of the story and each strand would appear, disappear, and reappear at intervals until all was resolved. The woman's lifelong struggle with the demonic would be one strand. Another strand would be the story of generations of the woman's family in Europe and this country, and still another would be the effect of the writings of John Locke and John Calvin upon succeeding generations of this family. A leading character would be Charles Meriwether of Virginia, Caroline's own great-great-great-grandfather, who went back to Scotland to get his medical degree and studied with his famous relatives, Dr. John Hunter and Dr. William Hunter. Dr. John Hunter had fitted Lord Byron with an orthopedic boot and had in his backyard in Earl's Court in London a huge pile of bones, the remains of animals he had dissected. Charles Meriwether's son, James, would have a similar pile of animal bones in the backyard of his home, Meriville, in Kentucky. The theme of the supernatural, introduced in the first chapter when the heroine was a small child, would reappear in the life of her great-great-greatuncle, Jesse Ferguson, the Campbellite preacher who took up spiritualism and talked to the spirit of William Ellery Channing, the New England Unitarian preacher. She would bring in other real and famous people—Sir Walter Scott, Lord Byron, and William Wordsworth—through scenes in which her distant relative, Harriet Douglas, a "lion hunter" of her day, appeared. The mythological would mingle with the supernatural, and Orpheus would appear. "I am aware that presenting Miss Douglas and Orpheus on the same stage presents considerable technical difficulties," she wrote, but she would use the same techniques she used in *The Malefactors,* in which she had placed among her characters a saint, a madman, and a dead man. The novel would go back and forth in time from 1532 to 1958. It would have a prologue, an epilogue, and twelve chapters. The prologue, she said, had appeared in the April 1959 issue of *The Transatlantic Review.* The first chapter, which was almost finished, was "A Visit to the Grove." (It was published in *The Sewanee Review* in 1972.)

Later, Caroline added Michael Servetus, René Descartes, Meriwether Lewis, and Philip Freneau to her cast of characters. Also, she decided to have a hero instead of a heroine and have him in conflict with the devil. As her interest in Greek mythology grew, she adopted Jung's thesis that the myths were as much a part of modern man's unconscious as they were of ancient man's. She read the myths to her grandchildren, and taught a class in archetypes at the New School. (When Denver Lindley, the editor of her novel *The Malefactors,* came down to visit that class she was delighted to discover he had "kept up his Greek.") She decided to introduce into her fiction the figure of Heracles, "as Christian a hero as you can find, the only one whose mortal remains are consumed and who goes to heaven," as she told Ashley. Heracles was obviously a forerunner of Christ, she said, and the mountain that was flung on Typhoeus was a sign, a symbol of the Blessed Virgin. She found a book by a "learned Jesuit," Father Hugo Rahner, *Greek Myths and Christian Mystery,* that confirmed her idea that Heracles had "plowed the same furrow that Christ plowed as a man, only further back in time." Gradually, the novel on which she worked came to be an epic about Heracles. She told Radcliffe Squires she tried to stick to primary myths for Hera and left out Queen Omphale because "the myth not only did not suit my purpose but struck me as a Hellenistic accretion. God knows there are plenty of them! . . . The 'primary myth' . . . can be identified any time it turns up by the fact that it has turned up so often before—putting the matter roughly."

She published other excerpts from the novel from time to time— "Cock-Crow," another reminiscence that metamorphosed into a narrative of Amphitryon and Heracles, in *The Southern Review* in 1965; "Cloud Nine," a short story about Heracles, in *The Sewanee Review* in 1969; "The Strangest Day in the Life of Captain Meriwether Lewis as Told to His Eighth Cousin, Once Removed," in *The Southern Review* in 1976; and "A Walk with the Accuser," about John Calvin, in *The Southern Review* in 1977.

Although Allen never succeeded in getting her into the National Institute of Arts and Letters, Caroline did enjoy a certain amount of fame and recognition as a literary figure. Editors asked her to write about Ford Madox Ford, Flannery O'Connor, Stark Young, Katherine Anne Porter, Thomas Wolfe, Maxwell Perkins, and F. Scott Fitzgerald. She continued to work with a large number of would-be writers and write twenty- and thirty-page letters of criticism about work that former students sent her.

Her religious faith became deeper—and more idiosyncratic. One of her favorite theories, purveyed at dinner parties at the Red House, was that the revelation of the Christian gospel occurred when it did so that the basic documents of Christianity could be in Latin.

She went as writer-in-residence to the University of California at

Davis for the 1962–1963 academic year, at what she termed a "fabulous salary." ("Kidy says it's a fabulous salary," said Pidie, using Caroline's old family nickname, "but she doesn't know a dime from a dollar.") Caroline spent the California money to build a new wing on the Red House that would provide her with a source of steady rental income. In California she went birdwatching, visited cousins, and renewed her old friendship with the Howard Bakers at Terra Bella and with Yvor and Janet Winters in Palo Alto.

At Purdue as writer-in-residence for the 1963–1964 school year, Caroline was "crazy about Indiana" and the English department there, which had eighty-seven people. While in Indiana, she taught seminars at St. Mary's College at Notre Dame and said, as usual, that Catholic students were far superior to Protestants. When she went to Emory University in Atlanta for the 1966 spring term, monks from the Trappist monastery in Conyers, bearing home-baked bread and artworks for the walls of her apartment, met her plane; they even made up her bed for her. (She had long been corresponding with a Brother Charles at the monastery, who had worked with Dorothy Day before he went into the order.)

She became completely disenchanted with "creative writing" courses. Such programs were not only useless, but vicious, she said. She felt that nobody should be admitted to a creative writing class who had not had a course in elementary logic, another in grammar and syntax, one in mythology, and a course that included the reading of the major plays of Aeschylus, Sophocles, and Euripides. Those plays offered examples of almost perfect form, she said, as well as the fundamentals of abnormal psychology, since the characters were "archetypes, or the first people to do the things we keep on doing."

A true conservative, she wrote her brother Morris that she disapproved of the zip code—she was convinced "that all this computerization of human beings is a step toward the gas chambers of the future." When Katherine Anne called her from Washington to say, "Darling, as you get older, it gets harder every year," Caroline replied that "it also seems to get odder."

In an effort to earn more money, she again submitted her résumé to a speakers' bureau. She was sent to lecture in Cincinnati and to Wilmington, Ohio, where she had lived when she was in her early teens. An old friend drove her around but Caroline recognized no landmarks.

She was generous until the day she died, sending money to both her brothers and to Cousin Manny. (She sent the fifty-dollar-a-month pension she received from the University of California to Manny every month.) She gave generously to Dorothy Day's causes and sent untold sums to priests and nuns around the country for prayers and Masses for Allen.

In 1966 Caroline received a grant of $10,000 from the National Council on the Arts, and in 1967 she received an advance from Doubleday of $3,000 on her novel. In the fall of 1967 she went to Europe with her current housemate, Cary Peebles, an editor at Rutgers University Press. Peebles was born in Virginia and Caroline always claimed her as her sixth cousin several times removed. Peebles said that she and Caroline got along splendidly, "except that I was a Platonist and she was an Aristotelian." Peebles bought a Volkswagen in Europe and the two women spent two months in Greece and Italy. They went to Thessaloniki, where Peebles had to see an author, and drove all over the Peloponnesus and stayed for some time at Nauplia. Caroline wanted to visit the places where Heracles performed his twelve labors. She wrote long letters that demonstrated her ability to provide that Jamesian "specificity." They went to see the spring at Argos where Hera was said to have bathed once a year in order to renew her virginity, and found a plowman watering his mules on one side of it and nuns washing their underwear on the other.

Back home, Caroline finished the novel about Heracles. "At first glance, you may not recognize this as the novel I described to you," she wrote Stewart Richardson, her editor at Doubleday, when she sent her thousand-page manuscript to him in late 1970. "I assure you it is part of that opus, the lower half. It is experimental, I suppose, in that the action takes place on the frontiers of the archetypal conscious mind—there is such a region. . . . I don't think you will complain of being short-changed in quantity." *The Glory of Hera,* which appeared in early 1972, was the story of Heracles and his labors and his loves. Caroline used her vast knowledge of myths acquired during twenty years of serious study and wrote it in a style as limpid and pure as poetry. Allen told friends that it was a masterpiece, one of the great books of the twentieth century, a much greater work than Joyce's *Ulysses,* and the finest writing Caroline had ever done. John Hall Wheelock of Scribner's wrote her that she had organized a vast body of material and the way she had given a "unifying and meaningful pattern to so huge a tapestry of myth and legend is . . . miraculous and thrilling." Robert Fitzgerald wrote her that it was truly "Homeric." In spite of all this praise from friends, *The Glory of Hera* received very few reviews and it is hard to find anyone who has read it to the end. (Ashley Brown, faithful friend that he was, read it and called it a comedy of manners with the gods for characters.) In spite of the flawless writing it moves so smoothly and so evenly that there is no shape; it flows along over many small climaxes; there is no big waterfall. There is no tension.

She had abandoned the title "A Narrow Heart" and decided that *The Glory of Hera* would be one volume in a two-volume novel called "Behold My Trembling Heart," the title coming from a phrase of St. Augustine. The other volume would be called "Joy of the Mountains" and would comprise her reminiscences, the stories of her ancestors, including Meriwether Lewis, and tales of Calvin, Locke, and Berkeley. ("The Dragon's Teeth," which appeared in *Shenandoah* in autumn 1961, showed, she said, how the two novels intertwine. "The Dragon's Teeth" is a revision of "Summer Dust," the first story Caroline ever published. In this version, she cut out many details in the story of the little girl who, on a hot summer afternoon, becomes aware of injustice and prejudice, while the little girl's father, who did not appear in the original, tells his children stories of Heracles. "The Dragon's Teeth" was renamed "One Against Thebes" when it appeared in *Old Red and Other Stories* two years later.)

Caroline had wanted to write a biography of Meriwether Lewis in 1930, and had now become almost obsessed with him. She plunged into the same enthusiastic research that she had used on Indians, the westward migration, the Civil War, and the myths. She became convinced that Lewis did not commit suicide, as mainstream historians have maintained, but was murdered at the behest of President Thomas Jefferson. She compared Lewis to Odysseus, Heracles, and Beowulf. His story, she said, was our national epic. Furthermore, when he wasn't under the influence of Jefferson's Latinate prose, he was one of the most gifted stylists this country has ever produced.

For some time, she had very much wanted to have Robert Giroux of Farrar, Straus & Giroux, for a publisher; he was not only a Catholic but also a good editor. And he wanted her for an author; he told her she was one of the most distinguished writers alive but she must first get a release from Doubleday. This was no problem. Giroux talked of a "Caroline Gordon renascence" and gave her an advance on her next novel.

She had to grapple with a nasty situation about the rights to her other books. In 1962 she had written Charles Scribner, Jr., at Scribner's, her publisher for years, asking him to return her copyrights since her books were all out of print. Scribner did not send her the copyrights, but brought up for the first time the possibility of a new collection of her short stories, which appeared in 1963 as *Old Red and Other Stories*. Caroline did not pursue the matter of the copyrights. In 1971 she found that Scribner's had sold the paperback rights of her first eight books to Cooper Square Publishers for a total of $1,600—half of which would be hers and half Scribner's. And Cooper Square would have the exclusive rights for five years. Caroline was justly furious.

Charles Scribner, Jr., conceded that she had requested her copyrights—her letter was still in his files. Now what she regarded as her life's work had been sold for a paltry sum. It was another example of the low esteem in which they held her work, she said; they had sold reprint rights to some of her short stories for as little as a dollar and a half and had even given rights to some of them for nothing. She hired—and fired—lawyers; she threatened to take the matter to the Authors Guild. Robert Giroux was wonderfully supportive and encouraging, supplying her with drafts of letters for her to copy and send to lawyers, Scribner's, and Cooper Square. But there was nothing to be done. The contracts Scribner's had signed with Cooper Square were ironclad. Scribner's did give her their share of the money from the sale so that she got the entire $1,600 instead of $800. That was all the satisfaction she got from the uproar that went on for over a year. Always afterward, she referred to Robert Giroux as the man who rescued her from penury in her old age.

She lived in terror of poverty after Allen stopped his support payments, even though a financial statement she drew up about this time showed that she was not without resources. She had sold her papers to Princeton University for $19,000. She had the rent from half her house and social security of $188 a month. She was still getting royalties from *The House of Fiction* and *How to Read a Novel.* She had had advances from Doubleday for *Hera* and another advance from Farrar, Straus & Giroux. She made money lecturing and selling chapters of novels to magazines. Still, she felt financially insecure.

It was a bad time. Her brother Bill was dying of emphysema, cirrhosis of the liver, and arteriosclerosis. "He . . . was one of the most magnificent physical specimens I ever beheld," she wrote Ashley, "and the darling of all who beheld him—white and black." When her other brother, Morris, was dying, Caroline went to St. Petersburg on the bus to help Polly nurse him. Thanks to Allen's refusal to meet his obligations to her, she said, she had discovered the pleasures of riding the bus. There was nothing like a long trip by Greyhound, she said, to keep you in touch with the vernacular. Very useful for a novelist. She went to Chattanooga on the bus to visit Pidie and to see her Uncle Paul, who was not expected to live long.

Then came an invitation from the University of Dallas to lecture in November 1972. The University of Dallas was a small Catholic college in Irving, outside Dallas, which was having its own little renascence. The president, Donald Cowan, and his wife, Louise Cowan, had earned their Ph.D.'s at Vanderbilt, he in physics, she in English. Louise, who had written a remarkable work of literary history, *The Fugitive Group*, had been impressed with all the former Fugitives—Allen Tate, John Crowe Ransom, Robert Penn Warren, and Donald Davidson. Having interviewed them, studied their work intensively, and read everything written about them, she had become convinced that training in the classics, something her generation had missed, was essential to a good education. After Louise's book on the Fugitives came out, she was asked to do an article on Caroline Gordon, and she brooded over Caroline's work—how could you explain the dark, unrelenting view of life in the early novels and the grace in the later ones? The more she read of Caroline's work, including her criticism, the more she was affected. She wrote her article, "Nature and Grace in Caroline Gordon," and won Caroline's favor. Caroline's influence, in fact, had led Louise and her husband to become Catholics in 1955. They had come to the University of Dallas from Texas Christian University in 1959, Don as chairman of the physics department and Louise as chairman of the English department. Don became president in 1962. The Cowans built up a curriculum based on the classical education the Fugitives had, with emphasis on philosophy.

When Caroline went to Dallas at Louise's invitation, she thought Texas was "a foretaste of heavenly bliss." She couldn't understand why the Meriwethers had stopped in Kentucky and not gone on to Texas. It was like the Garden of Eden, she said; the people were "unfallen." She loved the university—it was Catholic, the students had to study logic, there was that strong emphasis on the classics. When the Cowans took her to the airport after her lecture she offered to come back on a permanent basis and start a creative writing program. The Cowans accepted.

Caroline was thrilled. Princeton was stuffy, dull, and pagan. "The worship of mediocrity, the crass materialism, the bad manners!" she said. And if you didn't practice adultery there, people thought it was because you were too dull or too poor. She and Louise would start a Center for Fictional Studies that would offer creative grammar, Greek drama, the criticism of Aristotle, Baudelaire, Coleridge, Ashley Brown, and Louise Cowan. (Louise was the only woman she had ever known who had a first-rate critical mind, Caroline said again and again.) Caroline herself was going to teach the creative grammar—the students would have to diagram Milton's Sonnet "On His Blindness," which was one long compound sentence; use Herbert Read's *English Prose Style* for their textbook; and learn about Jamesian specificity. The salary would keep the wolf a comfortable distance from Caroline's door.

And so in the fall of 1973, almost seventy-eight, Caroline set out for a new career in Texas. Just as the *dottoressa* had said, there was an adventurer in Caroline that made her ready to move on. The Cowans furnished her an apartment in a development called The Old Mill Stream across the street from the campus and provided a student driver. Her apartment had a terrace and faced a small wood, mostly post oaks, but it "cast the kind of shadows on grass which make it easier for me to write—if anything can." One of her students remembers her that fall "in a wraparound skirt and a bodysuit and looking damned good." Mostly, however, the students were terrified of her. At first, she liked them and said they ranged from "Bible-educated boys and girls to types who will quote you Aristotle or St. Thomas Aquinas at a moment's notice." She began with great enthusiasm, bringing in as visitors Sean O'Faolain, Walker Percy, Wilfrid Sheed, James Farl Powers, and John Hall Wheelock. She taught the Aristotelian primal plot with its complication, peripety, and resolution. Peripety, or peripeteia, which the dictionary defines as the reversal of fortune for the protagonist, was not what they thought it was, she said; acting it out for them, she walked briskly across the room and then turned suddenly and walked the other way. She assigned passages from Solzhenitsyn's *Cancer Ward* and students passed or failed according to whether they knew where the peripety was. At one time the entire campus seemed to be talking about peripety; one could hear the word in the cafeteria, on the playing fields, and in other classes. She made each student keep a notebook and turn it in at the end of the semester, and several of her letters about the notebooks—angry, impatient, and some as long as twenty-three pages—survive. She assigned passages from Aristotle and if the students read more than she assigned, she was furious. She told the students that the Jamesian central intelligence was the greatest development in the history of the novel—but she ordered them not to use it—and told them that if they could master the periodic sentence they could do anything. She hectored her students in class and especially disliked any student who wanted to write a novel, right then. She told them, "What I'm teaching you, you won't need for eight years." ("Twenty years," said Don Cowan. "That's right, Don," Caroline said.) Some of the students complained. Enrollment dropped.

"We didn't mind the trouble she caused," Louise Cowan remembered. "We knew we were in the presence of greatness. We couldn't get the students who would have appreciated her."

Some of her students, ten years later, could not suppress their strong emotions about her class when they talked about it. "She knew so much—if she had just told us what she knew," said one. "She was irascible, angry, overbearing, mean, and cruel," said another, "and yet I always felt sorry for her—she was unhappy. I would have walked out, but I was intrigued."

"She was nice to people like the Xerox man and the housekeeper," said Mary Mumbach, a student who lived with Caroline for two years. "None of us could stand the Xerox man, but she loved him. He started writing stories and turning them in to her. She liked one student who was a security guard at the apartment complex, and she ordered him to take creative writing." She let Mary use her father's old leather fishing bag for a book bag and then bought her a bag at Neiman-Marcus that looked like it.

Caroline acquired two dogs and a cat, and managed to keep a small garden where she grew nicotiana. It was humiliating, she said, for one who came of an unbroken line of tobacco planters to have only one plant. She loved the Texas bluebonnets. She once had a funeral for her cat, with a procession and a custom-designed tombstone. "The funny thing was," Louise Cowan said, "she had had the cat put to sleep." When she had one of the dogs, Burd Ellen, blessed, Caroline invited twelve guests including two monks to a feast—a turkey with drinks before dinner, wine during dinner, and brandy afterward. Burd Ellen's behavior was said to improve for a short time.

Caroline liked the Catholic community and went to Latin Mass every morning in the chapel on campus. The university had given land to both Cistercian and Dominican friars, so one saw plenty of clerical collars around and heard plenty of Catholic talk. She was delighted when two of her grandchildren, Caroline and Allen Wood, enrolled at the University of Dallas. She went to the Cowans' dinner parties and charmed the trustees. One Dallas millionaire was enchanted when Caroline said she admired the skyscrapers of Dallas, especially one she could see from her terrace. It turned out that this millionaire owned that skyscraper. He took her on a personal tour of the building, later visited her class, and took notes while she talked about Coleridge on "fancy."

Caroline disapproved when Louise taught a graduate seminar on her work and disapproved even more when the university sponsored a conference on her writing that brought Howard Baker from California, Radcliffe Squires from Michigan, Ashley Brown from South Carolina, and William Stuckey from Purdue to speak.

Every morning she got up at four o'clock to work on her novel. ("She said she got to know the typewriter repairman because he came so often," Mary Mumbach recounted. "She wanted to give him a present, but she couldn't give him liquor because he had a drinking problem. She made him beef bourguignonne.") One night Caroline said she woke up at the sound of a great clang—the two parts of the novel coming together. She believed she was a true innovator, and her great contribution was in returning the supernatural to the novel.

In 1977 she began a cookbook. "I hate Thomas Jefferson's guts," she wrote to Sally Wood, "but he made some wonderful additions to old Virginia cuisine, especially crème brulée." She also wrote Sally a number of letters at this time explaining yet again that New England had started the Civil War out of envy at the South's broad, fertile acres.

Besides Flaubert, James, and Joyce, she admitted that *Undine, Alice in Wonderland,* and the work of Agatha Christie, Dorothy L. Sayers, P. G. Wodehouse, Joseph Heller, and Nancy Mitford had merit. They all used the primal plot—complication, peripety, and resolution. She thought that salvation and redemption were as suitable as subjects for the novel as for Greek tragedy.

After Caroline went to Georgia in the seventies for a symposium on Flannery O'Connor she began to fail noticeably. In 1975 Donald Cowan escorted her to Greensboro to receive an honorary degree from the University of North Carolina at Greensboro, where she had first taught creative writing.

In 1974 she suffered from diverticulitis and lost thirty pounds. She complained of her "arrhythmic heart." In 1976 she had a heart attack, and Nancy flew to Dallas to look after her for three weeks. In 1977 Caroline wrote to Nancy: "I am well past eighty and I am so tired I would like to get dead as soon as possible—or would if I weren't so wicked."

Donald Cowan found her ill in her apartment and personally took her to the doctor and then arranged a sabbatical for her for the 1977–1978 academic year so she could finish her novel. The Cowans, who had been generous and supportive far beyond the call of duty, were under fire from their trustees—Don's chief supporter on the board had died—and were fighting for their own survival and the life of the little college they had built. Caroline did what she could (writing letters and making telephone calls to the trustees) to help the Cowans and then, in 1978, finally decided to retire. Nancy and Percy had been insisting that she return to Princeton to live in an apartment they would build on the back of the Hodge Road house. Now they had decided that Percy would retire early and they would move to a house they had bought in Mexico at San Cristóbal de las Casas in Chiapas. Caroline must go there to live, they said, where there would be plenty of servants to look after her. Caroline, who had visited San Cristóbal earlier, was not displeased. She sold the Red House and bought the little house next door to the Woods' house in Mexico. It would require extensive renovation to make the two houses livable and to merge them into a walled compound with a paved patio between them, but everyone realized it was time for Caroline to leave the University of Dallas.

Then Nancy, still in Princeton, got a call from Allen asking her to find him a nursing home in Princeton. "Daddo, we're moving to Mexico," she told him. When Caroline heard this, she said, "The house you're fixing for me is too fine. It would be perfect for Allen." Was it possible they would be reunited? No. Allen said, "Who would I talk to in Mexico—the Indians? Who would know who I am?"

Caroline made one last romantic gesture. She took a large chunk of the money from the sale of the Red House and purchased a motor home in which she could travel and view the passing scenery while sitting comfortably in a chair or even lying down. She was afraid she was going blind and wanted to do some sightseeing. Repenting, she told Percy to sell the camper. "I have seen all the sights I need to see," she said. The plan for Nancy and Percy and Caroline to move to Mexico at the same time was thwarted when the Hodge Road house caught fire. Caroline would have to leave Dallas and be in Mexico without them. Nancy came to Dallas to fly down with her and had a dreadful time getting two dogs on the plane—the airline would fly one dog, but not two—and finding a hotel in Mexico City that would take dogs at all. Eventually, on April 26, 1978, Nancy got her mother to San Cristóbal and flew back to Princeton to see about her house, leaving Caroline in the unfinished house with her namesake granddaughter and little Caroline's husband and baby. At one point Caroline herself was alone in the house with the servants for a few weeks, she speaking no Spanish and the servants no English.

Caroline complained of the altitude, the poverty of the Indians, the difficulty of communication because of the language barrier, and boredom. Her library and papers had been delayed in Dallas. She needed, she said, to be able to telephone editors.

When some of her letters to Sally Wood were published in *The Southern Review,* she wrote to Sally somewhat wistfully, "What good times we seem to have had in those days." She continued to write to Sally, almost until the day she died, berating her for New England's insolence toward the South.

"She was a strong personality, completely lost here," said Jean de Vos, a Flemish priest and anthropologist who became her friend in San Cristóbal. "She was alone a lot. Lots of anger had built up during her life. She said exactly what she thought and would say to anyone's face, 'Get out.' She enjoyed that—seeing the reaction to her words."

Nancy and Percy were in Mexico on vacation when Allen died in Nashville on February 9, 1979. Nancy stayed in San Cristóbal with

Caroline while three of her children went to the funeral at St. Henry's Catholic Church in Nashville, where they were taken in by the Cheneys and Andrew Lytle. At a requiem Mass for Allen at the Dominican church in San Cristóbal, the priest said, "This Mass is for Allen Tate, a stranger. He was of our faith and therefore no stranger," making a play on the Spanish word *extranjero,* which means both "foreigner" and "stranger."

For a long time, Caroline tried to write, but she never really finished "Joy of the Mountains"—the jumble of manuscript is in Firestone Library at Princeton University.

Nancy hired a full-time nurse for her, a member of the third order of the Dominicans, who dressed her, bathed her, and followed two steps behind her with a portable chair. Sally Fitzgerald came down to see her, as did John Prince. Finally, Nancy and Percy Wood arrived for good. Howard Baker and his wife came down from California in the spring of 1981. Caroline had had a fairly severe stroke on March 1 and trouble with a toe that became gangrenous. Doctors decided to amputate her leg. She stayed in the hospital four days and then came home. She never spoke again after the operation. When Jean de Vos came to call, he was disturbed by her anguish.

A little later, Caroline was obviously dying. Percy went in search of Jean de Vos, who was at a dinner party but came immediately. "I spoke half an hour with her," de Vos recalled. "I told her to try and listen so she could get peace. She was agitated, breathing rapidly, she was not happy. Then there was a complete change. I told her, 'I know you can't speak anymore. I know you would like to speak. It's as good as if you make a confession.' She calmed down. There was a great change. She received the last sacraments in a complete state of calmness."

"There was a look of delight—not peace—delight," when Jean gave her the sacraments," Nancy said. She died immediately afterward. It was April 11, 1981.

The Mexican maids sat up with the body all night, singing, drinking rum, and praying. The next day they brought flowers from the market and helped a friend of Nancy's dress Caroline in a magnificent purple dress she'd worn for lectures. The coffin maker, who lived next door, delivered the coffin. While the grave was being dug, the gravediggers' little boys played leapfrog. Caroline would have enjoyed the scene. The words of Jacques Maritain are on her tombstone: "It is for Adam to interpret the voices which Eve hears."

Acknowledgments

"If you don't write a biography, you can always write a cookbook," an envious friend said to me as I recounted yet another blissful gastronomic experience from my latest research trip for this book.

No one should be surprised that the biographer of Caroline Gordon, that superb cook and generous hostess, would be entertained and dined and lunched by Caroline's relatives and friends wherever she went. I was, of course, impressed with her literary achievements, but early on, the warmth, loyalty, and generosity of her friends convinced me of the worth of the character of Caroline Gordon. For the unstinting help and cooperation, as well as openhanded hospitality, of a great many people, I am abjectly grateful.

The first person I went to see was Ashley Brown, a great friend of Caroline Gordon's in her later years and a sympathetic critic of her work. I cannot overestimate the value of his help; he pointed me in the right direction and provided me with specific advice many times, never losing his patience when I turned to him again and again. Andrew Lytle, a friend of Caroline and Allen Tate for sixty years, and Brainard and Frances Cheney, who had known the Tates almost as long, shared their memories and answered questions many, many times. Access to the letters that Caroline wrote all four of them was extremely helpful.

Nancy Tate Wood, Caroline's only child, is surely the ideal survivor of the subject of a biography: open, honest, and forthcoming. She and Percy Wood put me up and endured days, not hours, of relentless questioning with patience and never-faltering courtesy. Other relatives were also willing to aid this project: Caroline's first cousin Margaret Campbell Carden; her cousins Douglas Campbell, Paul Campbell, and Nelson Sudderth; her sister-in-law Polly Gordon; her nephew the late Meriwether Gordon; and her cousin Clyde Meriwether Littleton.

Other friends of Caroline who provided valuable information in interviews were: Léonie Adams, the late Penelope Allen, W. T. Bandy,

Ursula Beach, Dora Bernhard, Sheila Brantley, Cleanth Brooks and the late Tinkum Brooks, Virginia Brown, William Slater Brown, George Core, Donald and Louise Cowan, Malcolm and Muriel Cowley, Ward Dorrance, David and Virginia Erdman, Sally Fitzgerald, William Price Fox, Charles Goolsby, Marian Kelleher and the late Joseph Kelleher, Mary Phillips Kirby-Smith, the late Sally Wood Kohn, the late Edwy Lee, Madeleine L'Engle, Janet Lewis, Bruce Ligon, Frederick Morgan, Mary Mumbach, Cary Peebles, Walker Percy, John Prince, Thomas P. Roche, Danforth and Dorothy Ross, James Ross, Charles Scribner, Jr., Eileen Simpson, Sister Alice Smith, Peter Taylor, Willard Thorp, Leonard Unger, Dorothy Van Doren, Susannah Watson, the late Glenway Wescott, and Marcella Winslow.

I am grateful to these people who supplied information: Philip S. Agar, Carlos Baker, Howard Baker, Bette Bentley, Nelson Bentley, George Street Boone, Mrs. John R. Bridgewater, Elizabeth Brown, Harry Brown, George Buechel, Peter J. Casagrande, Mrs. Winslow Chapman, John M. Coleman, William Combs, Richard Hauer Costa, Ward H. Dennis, John M. Duggan, Ivar Lou Duncan, Leon Edel, Robert Fagles, Frances Gamblin, Brewster Ghiselin, Charlotte Goodman, Roger Grant, Thomas B. Greenslade, Mary Ann Harmon, Don Harrell, Robert B. Heilman, George Hendrick, Frank M. Hodgson, Irene Holdin, Lawrence Hughes, John R. Humphreys, Laura Riding Jackson, Mary Jarrell, Carol Johnson, Mary McIntosh Johnston, Margaret Keenan, Forrest H. Kirkpatrick, Laura Lester, Mildred Lewis, G. R. Loughead, Catherine Maccoy, Anne S. Major, Brooks Major, Annemarie Marek, Henry Martin, Mrs. Jackson Matthews, Mary McCarthy, Judy McCartin, John J. McGarraghy, William McIlwaine, David I. McWhirter, Alice Warner Milton, Mrs. C. H. Moore, Polly Moore, William H. Moore, Deane Mowrer, Herbert Norton, Dennis J. O'Brien, R. J. M. Paul, Clell T. Peterson, Jim Pfaff, Samuel B. Pierce, David Ragan, Tony Redd, Richard Rorty, F. H. Rouda, Steven Ryan, Mrs. F. J. Schweitzer, Celestine Sibley, Nancy Sloan, Monroe Spears, Elizabeth Spencer, Sondra J. Stang, G. Robert Stange, Hugh Staples, Robert O. Stephens, W. J. Stuckey, William S. Vaughan, Thomas William Waldron, Robert Penn Warren, Floyd C. Watkins, Ritchie Watmson, Manfred Weidhorn, Cora Wilson, Robert M. Wren, Alice Wood Wynd.

I am grateful to Princeton University on two counts. First, as my employer, the university was generous and compassionate during the years it took to write this book. Robert K. Durkee, vice-president for public affairs, suggested I apply for administrative leave, which was granted. Michael Beahan was extraordinarily helpful in allowing flexibility for my schedule, and George Eager and all my colleagues were models of patience and fortitude when I could talk of nothing but Caroline Gordon, instead of the matter at hand.

Second, as the repository for the papers of Caroline Gordon and Allen Tate, the university provided the motherlode for my research. Every person on the Rare Books and Special Collections staff of Firestone Library at Princeton kindly furnished assistance. Alfred Bush encouraged me from the very first and provided aid many times, as did Antoinette Branham, Earle Coleman, John Delaney, Stephen Ferguson, Margrethe Fitzell, Charles Green, Richard Ludwig, Dolly Pinelli, Jean Preston, Jane Snedeker, and Ann Van Arsdale. Mary George and Michael Montgomery of Firestone's Reference Room were of inestimable help many times.

Blanche T. Ebeling-Koning of the University of Maryland Libraries performed services far beyond the call of duty in tracking down a letter from Josephine Herbst to Katherine Anne Porter for me, and I gratefully acknowledge this valuable service. Marise Wolfe in Special Collections at the Vanderbilt University Library was extraordinarily helpful time and time again.

Unpublished manuscripts and uncollected letters were valuable and helpful, and I thank Ashley Brown, William Slater Brown, Margaret Campbell Carden, Laura Riding Jackson, John Prince, Danforth Ross, James Ross, and Marcella Winslow for letting me use the ones in their possession.

I appreciate Isabel Bayley's gracious permission to quote from Katherine Anne Porter's unpublished letters; Helen Ransom Foreman's permission to quote from an unpublished letter of John Crowe Ransom; Hilton Kramer's permission to quote from an unpublished letter of Josephine Herbst; Timothy Seldes's permission to quote from an unpublished letter of Jean Stafford; Janice Biala Brüstlein's permission to quote from Ford Madox Ford's unpublished letters; Frank Donovan's permission to quote from an unpublished letter of Dorothy Day; Dorothy Van Doren's permission to quote from Mark Van Doren's letters; and Dr. Dora Bernhard's permission to quote from her unpublished letters.

The publishers and I are grateful for permission to use excerpts from the following copyrighted material: *Sunset and Twilight: From the Diaries of 1947–1958* by Bernard Berenson. Reprinted by permission of Susanna Zevi, Agenzia Letteraria Internazionale. "Green Centuries" by John Peale Bishop from *The Collected Poems of John Peale Bishop*, edited by Allen Tate. Copyright © 1948 Charles Scribner's Sons; copyright renewed 1976 Charles Scribner's Sons. Reprinted with the permission of Charles Scribner's Sons. "Passage" by Hart Crane from *The Complete Poems and Selected Letters and Prose of Hart Crane*, edited by

Brom Weber. Copyright © 1933, 1958, 1966 by Liveright Publishing Corporation. Reprinted with the permission of Liveright Publishing Corporation. *The Literary Correspondence of Donald Davidson and Allen Tate,* edited by John Tyree Fain and Thomas Daniel Young. Copyright © 1974 the University of Georgia Press. "Old Red" and "One Against Thebes" by Caroline Gordon from *The Collected Stories of Caroline Gordon.* Copyright © 1981 by Caroline Gordon. Reprinted by permission of Farrar, Straus & Giroux, Inc. *Penhally* by Caroline Gordon. Copyright © 1931 by Caroline Gordon, renewed 1959 by Charles Scribner's Sons. Reprinted by permission of Farrar, Straus & Giroux, Inc. "The Equilibrists" by John Crowe Ransom. Copyright © 1927 by Alfred A. Knopf, Inc., renewed 1955 by John Crowe Ransom. Reprinted from *Selected Poems* (third edition, revised and enlarged) by Jonn Crowe Ransom, by permission of Alfred A. Knopf, Inc. *Poets in Their Youth: A Memoir* by Eileen Simpson. Copyright © 1982 by Eileen Simpson. Reprinted by permission of Random House, Inc. "Emblems" and "Mediterranean" by Allen Tate from *Collected Poems 1919–1979.* Copyright © 1965 by Allen Tate. Reprinted by permission of Farrar, Straus & Giroux, Inc. "The Only Poem" by Robert Penn Warren from *Being Here: Poetry 1977–1980.* Copyright © 1978, 1979, 1980 by Robert Penn Warren. Reprinted by permission of Random House, Inc.

I am particularly grateful to Landon Y. Jones, who first suggested this project to me. Friends who were good enough to read and criticize various versions of the manuscript include Robert and Mary Sherrill, Thomas William Waldron, Stephanie Shapiro, Laura and Richard O'Brien, J. W. Johnson, Ashley Brown, and Richard Ludwig. Martha Lou Stohlman not only read it all but marked innumerable corrections. Jean Friedmann helped with the notes. Stanley Cooper and Robert Nanni of the Princeton University Press provided technical assistance. Faith Sale demonstrated that she deserves her formidable reputation as an editor; Anna Jardine proved that she is, surely, the world's best copy editor; Ben McCormick, Faith Sale's assistant, was endlessly helpful.

NOTES

Listed below are the abbreviations used in the notes and the name of the library in which letters to each person are deposited.

AB   Ashley Brown, Firestone Library, Princeton University

AGW   Anne Goodwin Winslow, Mississippi Valley Collections, John Willard Brister Library, Memphis State University

AL   Andrew Lytle, Jean and Alexander Heard Library, Vanderbilt University

AT   Allen Tate, Firestone Library, Princeton University

BC   Brainard Cheney, Jean and Alexander Heard Library, Vanderbilt University

CG   Caroline Gordon, Firestone Library, Princeton University

CW   Catherine Wilds, Kentucky Library, Bowling Green

EL   Edna Lytle, Jean and Alexander Heard Library, Vanderbilt University

FC   Frances Cheney, Jean and Alexander Heard Library, Vanderbilt University

FMF   Ford Madox Ford, Cornell University

GMO   George Marion O'Donnell, Washington University, St. Louis

HAM   Henry Allen Moe, John Simon Guggenheim Foundation, New York City

JB   Janice Biala, Cornell University

JGF   John Gould Fletcher, University Libraries, University of Arkansas

JH   Josephine Herbst, Beinecke Library, Yale University

JHW   John Hall Wheelock, Scribner Deposit, Firestone Library, Princeton University

JLW   Janet Lewis Winters, Stanford University

JMG   James Morris Gordon, Princeton University

JS   Jean Stafford, McFarlin Library, University of Tulsa

KAP   Katherine Anne Porter, McKeldin Library, University of Maryland

LA	Léonie Adams, Beinecke Library, Yale University
MC	Malcolm Cowley, Newberry Library, Chicago
MMM	"Little May" Meriwether Morse, Kentucky Library, Bowling Green
MP	Maxwell Perkins, Scribner Deposit, Princeton University
MVD	Mark Van Doren, Columbia University
NMG	Nancy Meriwether Gordon, Princeton University
NTW	Nancy Tate Wood, Firestone Library, Princeton University
PP	Phelps Putnam, Beinecke Library, Yale University
RL	Robert Lowell, Houghton Library, Harvard University
RPW	Robert Penn Warren, Beinecke Library, Yale University
RS	Radcliffe Squires, Washington University, St. Louis
RWS	Robert Wooster Stallman, Alderman Library, University of Virginia
SWK	Sally Wood Kohn, Firestone Library, Princeton University
SY	Stark Young, Harry Ransom Humanities Research Center, University of Texas
UP	Una Putnam, Beinecke Library, Yale University
VLT	Virginia L. Tunstall, Alderman Library, University of Virginia
WD	Ward Dorrance, Southern Historical Collection, Wilson Library, University of North Carolina, Chapel Hill
WM	William Meredith, Firestone Library, Princeton University
YW	Yvor Winters, Stanford University

Private Collections

AW	Letters to Ann Waldron
DVD	Letters to Dorothy Van Doren
JP	Letters to John Prince
JR	Letters to James Ross
MMC	Letters to and a memoir by Margaret Meriwether Campbell, in the possession of Mrs. Frank Carden
MW	Letters of Marcella Winslow to Anne Goodwin Winslow, in the possession of Marcella Winslow
WSB	Letters to William Slater Brown

1. Benfolly, the Summer of 1937
15–25

"the most inconvenient of all houses": CG to DVD, April 6, 1937.

bombé forehead: Eileen Simpson, *Poets in their Youth: A Memoir* (New York, Vintage, 1983), p. 195.

"in a moment of maternal abandon": CG to JB, n.d.

"She loves to hang around": ibid.

"You will like her": NTW to CG, n.d.

"very indifferent cuisine": CG to JB, n.d.

"an earthly near-paradise": Ford Madox Ford, *The Great Trade Route* (New York: Oxford University Press, 1937), p. 348.

"strangest visitation": CG to SWK, n.d.

"a real writer": Ian Hamilton, *Robert Lowell: A Biography* (New York, Vintage, 1982), p. 42.

most intelligent person: ibid., p. 43.

Ford told Lowell: Steven Gould Axelrod, *Robert Lowell: Life and Art* (Princeton: Princeton University Press, 1978), p. 22.

"stately yet bohemian": Robert Lowell, "Visiting the Tates," *The Sewanee Review* 67, p. 557.

Tate quoted a stanza: ibid.

Tate . . . dismissed droves: ibid., p. 558.

"This is a recurrent shock": CG to KAP, n.d.

"I have discovered": CG to SWK, May 1937.

After a triumphant course: FMF to Dale Warren, May 29, 1937, *Letters of Ford Madox Ford,* ed. by Richard Ludwig (Princeton: Princeton University Press, 1965), p. 278.

"a pretty, modest child": CG to SWK, n.d.

Wally . . . was startled: Wally Tworkov, in *The Presence of Ford Madox Ford: A Memorial Volume of Essays, Poems, and Memoirs,* ed. by Sondra J. Stang (Philadelphia: University of Pennsylvania Press, 1981), p. 216.

Janice and Wally were sometimes appalled: Hamilton, p. 49.

"an old man mad about writing": Tworkov, p. 216.

"The grandnephew of James Russell Lowell": CG to SWK, July 10, 1937.

Nancy hated having the Fords: interview with NTW, March 25, 1984, San Cristóbal de las Casas, Chiapas, Mexico.

"She can't learn to ride": ibid.

"I moaned and groaned": CG to AGW, n.d.

"slapped her paws": CG to SWK, n.d.

Allen . . . predicted that Ford: ibid.

Caroline . . . would drop Janice: ibid.

"I won't have hogs again": interview with NTW, March 25, 1984.

"I never published": interview with BC, November 29, 1983, Nashville, Tennessee.

like living with intellectual desperadoes: FMF to Dale Warren, June 11, 1937, *Letters,* p. 278.

Allen asked Ford: Anne Goodwin Winslow, *The Dwelling Place* (New York: Knopf, 1943), p. 24.

"The household groaned": Lowell, "Visiting the Tates," p. 558.

Caroline confessed: CG to KAP, n.d.

"Vanderbilt made little effort": CG to AGW, n.d.

"called everybody by their right name": CG to KAP, n.d.

"We have just concluded": FMF to Dale Warren, June 11, 1937, *Letters,* p. 278.

"three days in sweet Alexandria": KAP to JH, August 15, 1937.

"By taking two naps a day": CG to SWK, October 16, 1937.

"big, ample, shining place": KAP to JH, August 15, 1937.

Katherine Anne did no writing: CG to AL, September 14, 1937.

"You are a kind of saint": KAP to CG, September 20, 1937.

2. The Fugitives—and One of Their Reviewers, 1921–1924
26–32

In November 1921: Radcliffe Squires, *Allen Tate: A Literary Biography* (New York: Pegasus, 1971), p. 31.

Sidney Hirsch suggested: ibid.

"The Fugitive flees": ibid., p. 35.

Merrill Moore . . . would write: ibid., p. 36.

Allen left Vanderbilt: ibid., p. 36.

"dirty little town": AT to DD, November 29, 1922, *The Literary Correspondence of Donald Davidson and Allen Tate*, ed. by John Tyree Fain and Thomas Daniel Young (Athens: University of Georgia Press, 1974), p. 53.

"a new personality": "Current Magazines," *The New York Times Book Review and Magazine*, July 16, 1922, p. 28.

Edmund Wilson . . . "expected great things": Edmund Wilson to AT, January 3, 1923.

Caroline told her friends: interview with SWK, January 16, 1984.

dressing him like Little Lord Fauntleroy: ibid.

"Had not the editors": Allen Tate, "The Fugitives 1922–1925," *Princeton University Library Chronicle* 3 (April 1942), p. 81.

"easy lesson . . . conjure up": ibid., p. 80.

Robert Graves and his wife: T. S. Matthews, *Under the Influence: Recollections of Robert Graves, Laura Riding, and Friends* (London: Cassell, 1977), p. 121.

a laudatory article: Chattanooga *News*, February 10, 1923.

Allen Tate . . . yearned for: Squires, p. 51.

Warren made an unsuccessful attempt: Jesse Wills to AT, May 22, 1924.

Red Warren . . . wrote to Allen: RPW to AT, early spring 1924.

Warren's mother wrote: Squires, p. 52.

"a peach . . . a 160-pounder": AT to DD, June 8, 1924, *Literary Correspondence*, p. 119.

"We no longer wear": interview with MC, September 30, 1984, Sherman, Connecticut.

"a very keen and refreshingly unpretentious": AT to DD, June 15, 1924, *Literary Correspondence*, p. 120.

"opposed on principle": AT to DD, June 8, 1924, ibid., p. 119.

Mrs. Warren received a telephone call: RPW to AW, August 25, 1984.

"I saw her in the driveway": Danforth Ross, "Memories of Allen Tate," unpublished memoir, p. 8.

Warren remembers: RPW to AW, August 25, 1984.

Caroline Gordon was overwhelmed: ibid.

3. Caroline and the Meriwethers, 1895–1924
33–39

old Mrs. Meriwether was fond: MMC, unpublished memoir.

"We're all crazy now": Danforth Ross, "Caroline Gordon, Uncle Rob, and My Mother," unpublished memoir, p. 14.

Woodstock, the largest: Frances Marion Williams, *The Story of Todd County, Kentucky, 1820–1970* (Nashville: Parthenon Press, 1972), p. 354.

"ridden with Forrest": CG, "When My Brother and I Were Children," unpublished memoir, CG papers, Princeton, p. 1.

he died a suicide: CG to AB, February 1, 1963.

"If I only knew!": CG, "A Narrow Heart," *The Transatlantic Review*, 3 (Spring 1960), p. 8.

his father, trained as a lawyer: Veronica Makowsky, "The Forest of the South," Ph.D. dissertation, Princeton, 1981.

her grandmother accepted her: "A Narrow Heart," p. 12.

"sifted air": interview with AL, November 30, 1983, Monteagle, Tennessee.

Nancy Gordon taught: NMG to "Miss Ella," February 9, 1902.

The Gordons were very poor: NMG to her mother, December 24, 1917.

She liked her job: interview with Virginia Brown, October 13, 1984, Chattanooga, Tennessee.

She and Jane Snodgrass: ibid.

Years later: CG to MMC, July 1954.

"slightly crooked but very attractive":

Alice Wood Wynd to AW, December 2, 1984.

they decided to room together: SWK to AW, March 3, 1984.

"Look her up": interview with SWK, December 11, 1983.

Other people . . . asked: Williams, p. 326.

Caroline's mother wrote: NMG to CG, February 8, 1925.

her father congratulated her: JMG to CG, February 8, 1925.

"We'll back you": ibid.

Caroline's mother told her: NMG to CG, February 8, 1925.

the "physique" of the city: AT to DD, June 8, 1924, *Literary Correspondence*, p. 119.

"There's nothing like": AT to DD, December 30, 1924, ibid., p. 134.

"a wispy, blond young man": Matthew Josephson, *Life Among the Surrealists: A Memoir* (New York: Holt, Rinehart & Winston, 1962), p. 252.

He refused to review: AT to DD, December 8, 1924, *Literary Correspondence*, p. 130.

He also refused: AT to DD, December 17, 1924, ibid., p. 132.

"She wasn't 'one of us' ": MC to AW, [1985].

That was when: CG to AT, [1958].

4. A Wedding—and Hart Crane, 1925–1926
40–53

Caroline complained: interview with MC, September 30, 1984.

Allen told his daughter: interview with NTW, March 25, 1984.

he was extremely reluctant: interview with MC, September 30, 1984, and with WSB, October 7, 1984, Rockport, Massachusetts.

Sue Jenkins . . . supported: interview with MC, September 30, 1984.

Caroline called Sally: interview with SWK, July 24, 1984.

Caroline wanted desperately: interview with WSB, October 7, 1984.

she told her co-workers: interview with Virginia Brown, October 13, 1984.

Caroline and Allen sent news: RPW to AW, August 25, 1984.

"We are all a little queer": NMG to CG, February 6, 1925.

"Oh, I hope I'm pregnant!": Deane Mowrer interview with CG, Tivoli, New York, May 19, 1970. Dorothy Day–Catholic Worker Collection, Marquette University Archives.

"We can't even buy": Susan Jenkins Brown, *Robber Rocks: Letters and Memoirs of Hart Crane, 1923–1932* (Middletown, Connecticut: Wesleyan University Press, 1969), p. 31.

"to make it work": Ashley Brown, "Caroline Gordon and Hart Crane: A Literary Relationship," *The Visionary Company*, Spring 1982, p. 63.

she called her friend: interview with SWK, January 16, 1984.

"stupendous novelty": AT to DD, September 30, 1925, *Literary Correspondence*, p. 158.

"Laura is great company": ibid.

To Laura, Caroline: Laura Riding, unpublished memoir.

Mrs. Graves was dressing her: CG to AB, [1960s].

"so you wouldn't freeze": CG to NTW, December 25, 1955.

"darlingest baby": CG to SWK, n.d.

"afraid Allen would break down": ibid.

"I'll never name another child": NMG to "Miss Ella," February 9, 1902.

Caroline shuddered: CG to SWK, n.d.

They were ecstatic: AT to DD, March 3, 1926, *Literary Correspondence*, p. 158.

Allen . . . boasted that his right arm: AT to DD, January 3, 1926, ibid., p. 156.

Caroline's parents sent: CG to SWK, February 5, 1926.

"ranging over the hills": Hart Crane to Charlotte and Richard Rychtarck, December 31, 1925.

Eliot . . . asked Allen to write: AT to MC, March 30, 1926.

"a little ole brown thing": interview with WD, April 15, 1985, Washington, D.C.

Allen . . . said he was living: AT to CG, n.d.

"Of course we drank": CG to SWK, May 15, 1926.

"moderately kind heart": Malcolm Cowley, *A Second Flowering: Works and Days of the Lost Generation* (New York: Viking, 1973), p. 203.

"Eugene O'Neill situation": CG to SWK, May 15, 1926.

"skipping right over seven-foot drifts": CG to SWK, February 5, 1926.

The Tates . . . were more annoyed: John Unterecker, *Voyager: The Life of Hart Crane* (New York: Farrar, Straus & Giroux, 1969), p. 432.

"constricted his imagination": ibid., p. 433.

"If you've got a criticism": Hart Crane to his mother, April 18, 1926, *Letters of Hart Crane and His Family*, ed. by Thomas

S. W. Lewis (New York: Columbia University Press, 1974), p. 478.

"perfect amazement": ibid.

"While I could bury my pride": Unterecker, p. 434.

"And my poem was progressing": ibid., p. 444.

"a darling little white room": CG to SWK, n.d.

"a young gentleman is in love": CG to SWK, May 15, 1926.

"fecund period": ibid.

"I wish I could offer": ibid.

his "thoughts would have turned": CG to SWK, n.d.

"from one freelance check": CG to MC, n.d.

Irita Van Doren . . . offered: CG to WD, 1941.

"a perfect frenzy": CG to SWK, May 15, 1926.

Caroline . . . could only: CG to SWK, n.d.

"However we have our troubles": ibid.

Mrs. Gordon . . . told her daughter: interview with WSB, October 7, 1984.

"harried" and "hectic": CG to SWK, n.d.

"I suppose I try": ibid.

"Allen has the strangest attitude": CG to SWK, n.d.

5. New York, 1926–1928
54–62

Allen . . . could not face: AT to VLT, January 3, 1927.

Allen, outraged: Josephson, p. 306.

Allen was astonished: AT to DD, January 19, 1927, *Literary Correspondence*, p. 183.

"Art is all important": Frank MacShane, *The Life and Work of Ford Madox Ford* (New York: Horizon Press, 1965), p. 18.

"a man and a half": Janice Biala, in *The Presence of Ford Madox Ford*, p. 197.

"far and away the finest book": MacShane, p. 197.

"rambling, old, gloomy apartments":

Ford Madox Ford, *It Was the Nightingale* (Philadelphia: Lippincott, 1933), p. 359.

"and I love to see": CG to SWK, n.d.

Ford decided . . . tea party: Ford, *It Was the Nightingale*, p. 359.

"a nice fellow and a good poet": Arthur Mizener, *The Saddest Story: A Biography of Ford Madox Ford* (New York: World, 1971), p. 359.

Josephine Herbst wrote: Josephine Herbst, "A Year of Disgrace," *Noble Savage* 3, p. 139.

"rather snooty": CG to SWK, n.d.

"mostly in tourist camps": CG to SWK, November 20, 1927.

"putting powder, blood, dirt": AT to DD, May 13, 1927, *Literary Correspondence,* p. 203.

"little princess of the aryan race": JMG to CG, January 25, 1927.

"she would make two . . . Dander": JMG to CG, March 2, 1927.

"I know you are counting": JMG to CG, August 4, 1927.

She offered to send Caroline: JMG to CG, March 2, 1927.

"fine pre-Revolutionary tenement": CG to SWK, n.d.

"The ladies of the house": Squires, p. 58.

Caroline said they stayed: CG to SWK, November 20, 1927.

word came from Kentucky: MMC to CG, August 16, 1927.

"the worst spoiled child": CG to SWK, n.d.

"We did manage . . . to establish": ibid.

"I was afraid if you and Allen": JMG to CG, January 17, 1928.

"happy, happy to breathe": KAP to JH, May 5, 1928.

"Go on, Daddy": CG to SWK, n.d.

"everybody was drunk": KAP to JH, May 5, 1928.

Allen exulted: AT to DD, March 16, 1928, *Literary Correspondence,* p. 208.

"I have gotten . . . bitter": CG to SWK, n.d.

"My God! There's Mama": interview with AL, December 1, 1983, Monteagle, Tennessee.

Caroline hated to leave: CG to SWK, August 17, 1928.

the *Tribune* announced it: CG to SWK, n.d.

Caroline . . . lamented: ibid.

"I don't see how I did it": ibid.

"I am sort of suspended": CG to SWK, September 1928.

"We already know the place": CG to SWK, September 1928.

6. Europe, 1928–1929
63–77

"Where's the captain?": CG to VLT, September 28, 1928.

"mostly dark, wistful-looking Jews": CG to SWK, October 8, 1928.

it looked . . . as though the whole range: AT to VLT, September 30, 1928.

"quite morbid": CG to SWK, October 8, 1928.

eulogy . . . written by Allen: ibid.

"I could afford a nurse": ibid.

"London would be hellish": CG to AL, n.d.

would gladly eat curried rice: ibid.

"Caroline had thought of herself": interview with LA, July 17, 1984, New Milford, Connecticut.

A friend of Warren's: CG to AL, October 27, 1928.

"a grand place to work": CG to SWK, December 3, 1928.

Red, "always an angel": CG to SWK, n.d.

railroad fare . . . was quite an item: CG to SWK, December 2, 1928.

"the Dôme and Rotonde": CG to SWK, December 2, 1928.

"a handsome face, a Southern face": interview with William Bandy, December 1, 1983, Nashville, Tennessee.

"people who make a cult": CG to SWK, December 2, 1928.

"You can get the powders": CG to NMG, n.d.

Caroline . . . "too southern": Elizabeth Carroll Spindler, *John Peale Bishop: A Biography* (Morgantown, West Virginia:

West Virginia University Library, 1980), p. 47.

"It's none of your damned business": James Mellow, *Invented Lives* (Boston: Houghton Mifflin, 1984), p. 84.

Zelda . . . a victim: AT to JPB, December 12, 1930, *The Republic of Letters in America: The Literary Correspondence of John Peale Bishop and Allen Tate*, ed. by Thomas Daniel Young and John J. Hirdle. (Lexington: University Press of Kentucky, 1981), p. 16.

talked to her imaginary family: CG to SWK, July 9, 1929.

"It upsets me": ibid.

"There's Monsieur Stonewall Jackson": ibid.

"I've been nibbling": CG to JH, n.d.

doctor in pin-striped trousers: interview with NTW, March 25, 1984.

"Great God, it's snowing": CG to KAP, n.d.

"his goings on at the Coupole": CG to JH, n.d.

postcard to Mrs. Turner: CG to JH, March 22, 1929.

everyone was tired of Allen: AT to MC, April 15, 1929.

"This is the man": ibid.

"Allen and I held together": CG to SWK, July 9, 1929.

"Nancy's head": ibid.

"pitched in and helped him": CG to MMM, n.d.

"They are . . . too beautiful": ibid.

"a slip of a thing": Leon Edel to AW, June 25, 1986.

"Allen was young and lithe": ibid.

"doing something about the South": DD to AT, February 5, 1929, *Literary Correspondence*, p. 218.

he was heading . . . toward Catholicism: AT to DD, February 18, 1929, *Literary Correspondence*, p. 222.

"It seems strange": CG to MMM, n.d.

The story had been turned down: CG to SWK, July 9, 1929.

"That is real masterly": Flannery O'Connor to A., December 11, 1956, *The*

Habit of Being: Letters, ed. by Sally Fitzgerald (New York: Vintage, 1979), p. 187.

"I was with him for an hour": Leon Edel to AW, June 25, 1986.

"at her happiest": Howard Baker to AW, March 26, 1985.

"Voici Madame Gau": interview with NTW, March 25, 1984.

Bandy . . . announced: William Bandy, "Memories of Montparnasse: Ford Madox Ford's Sonnet Parties," unpublished article, p. 2.

"Ford's a friend of yours": AT to Carlos Baker, April 2, 1963.

"He is trying to persuade us": CG to JH, n.d.

"a place in the country": ibid.

"not that he has any great love": ibid.

he thought it was a masterpiece: AT to Carlos Baker, April 2, 1963.

the only novelist Hemingway liked: ibid.

Hemingway . . . asked them: AT to Carlos Baker, April 19, 1963.

"Is he still married to that girl?": interview with Peter Taylor, May 24, 1985, Athens, Georgia.

"We ate and drank steadily": CG to KAP, n.d.

"swell" novel: CG to JH, October 6, 1929.

Caroline said she didn't have: ibid.

Nancy had acquired: CG to SWK, January 21, 1930.

"beautiful writing": ibid.

Ford flew into a great rage: ibid.

"You have no passion": ibid.

"You are right about Allen": CG to JH, n.d.

"to protect his reputation": CG to KAP, n.d.

"I could stay in Paris": CG to MMM, n.d.

"Bring a lot of unattached young men": CG to JH, n.d.

"Come and let us have": ibid.

"I hated leaving Paris": CG to SWK, January 5, 1930.

7. Benfolly, 1930–1932
78–89

"I didn't want to come": CG to LA, n.d.

"You can't finish your novel": ibid.

"I have *never* in all the course": FMF to CG, February 4, 1930.

"If you don't bring": CG to JH, n.d.

"I took two stories": ibid.

"The trouble with you Southerners": CG to MMM, n.d.

"What a splendid woman": CG to JH, n.d.

"Why, pray, can you not": CG to MMM, n.d.

Allen could use his fourth-best: CG to JH, n.d.

"That's the house": CG to JH, n.d.

it was a telegram: CG to KAP, March 11, 1930.

"Our hill": CG to SWK, July 31, 1930.

"Here comes the *charbonnier*": CG to KAP, March 11, 1930.

"nothing special": CG to JH, n.d.

"We send a little Negro": CG to MP, April 28, 1930.

"even broker than usual": CG to JH, n.d.

razzle-dazzle: ibid.

"Stark Young suggested": SY to AT, August 5, 1930, *Stark Young: A Life in the Arts: Letters, 1900–1962*, ed. by John Pilkington. (Baton Rouge: Louisiana State University Press, 1974), p. 345.

"The doctor, in his ignorance": CG to LA, n.d.

"Some of the objects": ibid.

"Let's go visit the Tates": interview with AL, December 1, 1983.

"with one eye on going to New York": CG to KAP, n.d.

"I swear that is how": ibid.

"My lovely tomatoes": CG to LA, n.d.

"Mr. Perry's two mules": CG to SWK, September 10, 1930.

Stark Young sent a recipe: SY to AT, November 18, 1931, *Stark Young*, p. 376.

"the one piece of ground": Mark Van Doren, *The Autobiography of Mark Van Doren* (New York: Harcourt, Brace, 1958), p. 186.

"a very nice person": CG to SWK, October 20, 1930.

"It was harder the second time": SWK to AW, December 12, 1983.

"fairly good fiddler": CG to JLW, n.d.

"the lack of money": Anthony Curtis, *New Statesman and Nation* 44 (November 8, 1952), p. 552.

"We were becoming artists": Andrew Lytle in speech to Hometown Symposium on Evelyn Scott and Caroline Gordon, Austin Peay State University, Clarksville, Tennessee, November 7–9, 1985.

they should be wagging: CG to MVD, November 14, 1930.

"damned old manuscript": CG to KAP, n.d.

"None of the townsfolk called": CG to DD, n.d.

"A fine game": CG to Cinina Warren and RPW, n.d.

"We all expressed ourselves": ibid.

"These debauches are very weakening": CG to KAP, n.d.

"*Teeth!*": interview with NTW, March 25, 1984.

"who several years ago, nursed me": CG to FMF, n.d.

"He is an oldfashioned drunkard": CG to Cinina Warren and RPW, n.d.

"He patted my fierce grandmother": CG to KAP, n.d.

"Such a pleasant gentleman": ibid.

"It was very strenuous": CG to SWK, January 8, 1931.

"We go straight to our typewriters": CG to SWK, July 31, 1930.

black-eyed and black-haired: Ross, "Caroline Gordon, Uncle Rob, and My Mother," p. 1.

poem for specialized readers: Danforth Ross, "Remembering Allen Tate," unpublished memoir, p. 5.

8. Writing, 1930–1932
90–99

"I am glad you are wallowing": CG to KAP, n.d.

"I know now, from experience": CG to JH, n.d.

"dealing with murder": CG to SWK, October 20, 1930.

"tragic and gruesome": MP to CG, January 5, 1931.

"I'm sure Perkins couldn't": CG to RPW, n.d.

"When I say": CG to SWK, February 21, 1931.

"I am sure you are": CG to Lincoln Kirstein, n.d.

"a beautifully conceived description": CG to KAP, n.d.

"the loveliest spot": CG to SWK, January 1931.

"all sorts of fancy things": ibid.

"Aw, Miz Tate, we can't": CG to SWK, May 4, 1931.

"If you're going to do": ibid.

"Then he can't put him": ibid.

"Two families, white and poor white": ibid.

"My progress is so slow": CG to MP, n.d.

She told Sally Wood: CG to SWK, May 30, 1931.

"The stage has been swept": CG to KAP, n.d.

"I really don't know": ibid.

Perkins sent the manuscript: MP to CG, June 8, 1931.

"I hope nothing will divert": MP to CG, July 28, 1931.

"It is certainly much harder": CG to MP, August 1, 1931.

"such rough writing": CG to KAP, n.d.

"but if you don't *have* to": CG to SWK, August 21, 1931.

"the sweetest chest of drawers": ibid. CG to KAP, n.d.

"Marion Sadler, the son of the druggist": CG to SWK, August 21, 1931.

much nicer, Caroline thought: CG to SWK, fall 1931.

"Is that the lady": ibid.

"Don't you know that lightning": CG to FMF, n.d.

Cousin Armistead Gordon . . . wrote: Armistead Gordon to CG, September 15, 1931.

Stark Young wrote: SY to AT, September 12, 1931; SY to CG, December 18, 1931, *Stark Young*, pp. 364, 382.

"I think of a novel": CG to JLW, November 12, 1931.

"and God knows": CG to FMF, n.d.

"The young man went out": ibid.

"a triumphant tragedy": Ford Madox Ford, "Stage in American Literature," *The Bookman*, December 1931, p. 371.

"to have golden opinions": CG to FMF, n.d.

She told Ford: CG to FMF, n.d.

"I am thirty-seven years old": CG to SWK, November 2, 1931.

"I feel sorry about the Indians": CG to LA, n.d.

"It is the story": CG to JLW, n.d.

She was so furious: CG to RPW, n.d.

"My treatment of this story": CG to MP, n.d.

9. Agrarians and the Agrarian Life, 1930–1932
100–109

"wholly obscure": YW to KAP, November 16, 1930.

"a fine turnip sallet patch": CG to SWK, October 1930.

she could farm Nancy out: CG to VLT, n.d.

Allen said that Barr lost: AT to MC, December 19, 1930.

Davidson made mincemeat: CG to SWK, May 30, 1931.

"God knows when we'll get": CG to RPW, n.d.

"quite as well as 'Prime Leaf' ": CG to RPW, n.d.

she actually looked forward: CG to SWK, August 20, 1931.

"I can't hand Cinina much": ibid.

"the night Mrs. Warren got loose": telephone interview with NTW, February 7, 1987.

"poor devil": CG to LA, n.d.

"never saw his feet": CG to JH, n.d.

"the most gorgeous thing": CG to SWK, August 20, 1931.

"magnificent": CG to LA, n.d.

"God knows when he'll get": CG to KAP, n.d.

"Perkins really is nice": ibid.

"It's just Mr. Balch": CG to SWK, n.d.

"a sort of Southern Ouida": CG to FMF, n.d.

"It was really like a gathering": ibid.

"He was trying to say": CG to LA, n.d.

"What do you think, Mr. Faulkner?": CG to LA, n.d.

Allen had written to Donald Davidson: AT to DD, December 12, 1929, *Literary Correspondence*, p. 243.

10. Europe Again, 1932–1933
110–121

Caroline wrote to Ford: CG to FMF, n.d.

She wrote to Sally Wood: CG to SWK, March 12, 1932.

she always thought Allen: SWK to AW, April 17, 1984.

"To have even one person": CG to SWK, March 12, 1932.

"work like hell": CG to SWK, n.d.

"The family doctor": CG to KAP, August 7, 1932.

"with heartfelt thanks": CG to SWK, April 14, 1932.

"unbelievably green": CG to SWK, April 28, 1932.

"the tide of reminiscence": CG to KAP, n.d.

"Cousin Molly Ferguson": CG to FMF, June 18, 1932.

he couldn't write a poem: CG to SWK, June 15, 1932.

it was strange how anybody: CG to SWK, May 3, 1932.

"The honoree": ibid.

Pidie was trying to persuade: CG to KAP, n.d.

They learned of Hart Crane's suicide: CG to KAP, n.d.

Allen said that he felt: CG to HAM, March 3, 1932.

she would be glad: CG to FMF, June 18, 1932.

"I wanted to go to Europe": interview with NWT, March 25, 1984.

"Nancy was delighted": CG to RPW, n.d.

Villa Paul was doubtless: CG to LA, n.d.

"She is a Russian Jew": ibid.

"tiny *plage*": CG to KAP, n.d.

"embowered in mulberries and roses": CG to LA, n.d.

"properly respectful to a poet": CG to CW, November 17, 1932.

"cauliflower and celery growing": CG to KAP, n.d.

"so that it should click": CG to JB, n.d.

"Madame, your relative": *The Southern Mandarins: Letters of Caroline Gordon to Sally Wood, 1924–1937*, ed. by Sally Wood (Baton Rouge: Louisiana State University Press, 1984), p. 121.

It was perfect: CG to KAP, n.d.

Caroline wrote to ask the Guggenheim: CG to HAM, November 2, 1932.

Allen said he had: CG to JLW, n.d.

But it was really very pleasant: CG to FMF, n.d.

"You get used to it": CG to SWK, November 1932.

"We are both working": CG to SWK, November 23, 1932.

There was not one soul: ibid.

"Thank God": CG to SWK, December 1, 1932.

"horrid dark little rooms": ibid.

"It's Gertrude Stein": ibid.

"Miss Toklas says": CG to JB, n.d.

Finally she broke down: ibid.

"I certainly have been lucky": CG to SWK, January 1933.

She wrote Maxwell Perkins: CG to MP, January 15, 1933.

Katherine Anne kept saying: CG to SWK, January 13, 1933.

"Monsieur Tate is so conservative": Allen Tate, *Memoirs and Opinions 1926–1974* (Chicago: Swallow Press, 1975), p. 67.

"Allen turns out to be": CG to SWK, January 13, 1933.

"You mean this is the first time": CG, afterword to *Aleck Maury, Sportsman* (Carbondale: Southern Illinois University Press, 1980), p. 294.

"I don't know how": CG to SWK, January 1933.

"lack of cohesion": AL to AT and CG, n.d.

"I was really more interested": CG to SWK, February 10, 1933.

"He wrote five pages": CG to SWK, January 1933.

"fine, red-blooded ampoules": CG to SWK, February 10, 1933.

Jess Staton . . . wrote to say: CG to SWK, February 1933.

"The Tates came": KAP to JLW, March 31, 1934.

11. The Summer of 1933
122–130

"You missed the strangest sight": CG to SWK, May 20, 1933.

Caroline immediately wrote to Perkins: CG to MP, March 4, 1933.

Perkins obligingly sent her the money: MP to CG, March 7, 1933.

"Thank you very much": CG to "Miss McAfee" of *The Yale Review*, n.d.

"I nearly fainted": CG to JB, March 11, 1933.

"grateful indeed": CG to HAM, March 23, 1933.

"except for not having cash": CG to JB, March 15, 1933.

"Red Warren says": CG to Muriel Cowley, n.d.

"I'm saving every cent": CG to MP, March 7, 1933.

"This place produces": CG to MP, March 10, 1933.

They didn't even have to buy: CG to JB, March 15, 1933.

"We were a strange sight": CG to SWK, May 20, 1933.

Caroline said she'd have to think: CG to Muriel Cowley, n.d.

Caroline wrote to Perkins: CG to MP, March 10, 1933.

"Then I had to poison": CG to JH, n.d.

she horrified them: CG to LA, n.d.

"Allen is still following": CG to FMF, n.d.

"radical conservative": CG to JB, March 15, 1933.

"He would have said": CG to JB, n.d.

"waste and ruin of New York": SY to AT, April 14, 1933, *Stark Young*, p. 461.

"he would be gaping": CG to Muriel Cowley, n.d.

"expected niggers to work": interview with MC, September 30, 1984.

"We're planning a big picnic": CG to MC, n.d.

Allen told Malcolm: AL to MC, April 22, 1933.

"They had no money": interview with MC, September 30, 1984.

"very dark and very nervous": interview with NTW, March 25, 1984.

She told Malcolm: interview with MC, September 30, 1984.

"But they're all *dead* Yankees": ibid.

"Mama would show him": interview with NTW.

"Caroline didn't confide": interview with MC, September 30, 1984.

"She always made it plain": interview

with Clyde Meriwether, October 20, 1984.

"You go out too much": CG to SWK, June 6, 1933.

"I've been in love": interview with MC, September 30, 1984.

"There was a scene": ibid.

Danforth Ross . . . said he never: Ross, "Caroline Gordon, Uncle Rob, and My Mother," p. 12.

"nervous collapse": CG to SWK, June 6, 1933.

"who are humble": ibid.

"I am in no shape": ibid.

12. Aleck Maury and Robert E. Lee, 1933–1934
131–136

"hand to mouth, meal to meal": CG to FMF, n.d.

"We worked all morning": CG to SWK, October 1933.

"I wrote the book": CG to KAP, n.d.

"He is, however, penitent": CG to SWK, October 1933.

She offered him: CG to AB, April 10, 1972.

"It seems to me": CG to SWK, October 22, 1933.

"written most of a long-planned life": "After the Big Wind," *Time*, March 1, 1937, p. 70.

"my father's autobiography": CG to FMF, n.d.

"our whole thoughts were bent": CG to SWK, n.d.

"Reviewing isn't as hard": ibid.

"Allen . . . said there would have to

be": Robert Buffington, "Allen Tate: Society, Vocation, and Communion," *The Southern Review* 18 (Fall 1979), p. 67.

"Allen and I slept": CG to SWK, January 9, 1934.

"I have got to get": CG to KAP, n.d.

"I always thought it was": CG to SWK, January 1934.

"lesson in construction": CG to SWK, January 9, 1934.

"a regular book factory": CG to AL, n.d.

"Fortunately, it was raining": CG to KAP, n.d.

"I think the inmates": CG to AL, n.d.

"It could have been": ibid.

"they make the most delicious jam": CG to AL, n.d.

"Scribner's salesmen have titled it": CG to KAP, n.d.

13. Memphis, 1934
137–145

chiefly for the benefit: CG to LA, n.d.

"damn car wreck": CG to RPW, n.d.

To fellow Agrarian: CG to FMF, n.d.

"acres and acres of . . . woods": CG to LA, n.d.

It was sad: CG to SWK, October 1, 1934.

"the most wonderful niggers": ibid.

"Not being able to understand": CG to LA, n.d.

"so lonely and bored": CG to SWK, October 1, 1934.

"one of those peculiarly offensive": CG to SWK, March 6, 1935.

like an apple twirling on her toes: CG to LA, n.d.

"I went to Snowden School": interview with NTW, March 25, 1984.

"the chill of the grave": CG to SWK, November 27, 1934.

"Let no one say": CG to MVD, November 15, 1934.

"honoring" the Tates: CG to DD, n.d.

"But he says he can't teach": CG to LA, n.d.

"two yards long": CG to RPW, n.d.

"As we were leaving": ibid.

"I knew a poet": Nathan Asch, *The Road in Search of America* (New York: Norton, 1937), p. 55.

they thought Fletcher: CG to RPW, n.d.

When he wrote that the Agrarians: CG to JGF, n.d.

"None of the others will listen": ibid.

Caroline thought living in Cincinnati: CG to RPW, n.d.

"My book is dedicated to you": CG to FMF, n.d.

"as if a gentleman of the Old South": KAP to CG, spring 1934.

Howard Baker . . . wrote: Howard Baker to CG, January 12, 1935.

Red Warren suggested: CG to LA, n.d.

Malcolm Cowley said: ibid.

she thought of getting: ibid.

"As I never seem to get above 2,500": CG to FMF, n.d.

She was dismayed: CG to LA, n.d.

"As it discussed no burning problem": CG to LA, n.d.

"as a sort of literary spree": CG to RPW, n.d.

"I have just been sitting here": CG to FMF, n.d.

Caroline had written to Lincoln Kirstein: CG to Lincoln Kirstein, n.d.

"plunged today into the Civil War": CG to RPW, n.d.

she wrote to Maxwell Perkins: CG to MP, December 13, 1934.

"I was in the Bloody Tinth": Caroline Gordon, "When My Brother and I Were Children," unpublished manuscript, p. 2.

"a mere skirmish": CG to SWK, late October 1934.

It would be mad: CG to RPW, n.d.

"all the in-laws absent": CG to MVD, n.d.

"made a fine oration": ibid.

"Dry martinis and oysters": CG to LA, n.d.

"We got up at nine": interview with AL, December 1, 1983.

"lovely cottage": CG to DD, n.d.

"I drank so much": interview with AL, December 1, 1983.

Caroline wrote Warren: CG to RPW, n.d.

14. Memphis, 1935–1936
146–159

"I am still trying": CG to AL, n.d.

"I wonder if Caroline's success": *Republic of Letters*, p. 112.

"I enjoyed hearing from you": MVD to "John," March 18, 1935.

"horrible, awful": CG to KAP, n.d.

"Allen at last is working": CG to SWK, n.d.

"the poetess": CG to SWK, n.d.

"lesser literary people": SY to AT, April 23, 1935, *Stark Young*, p. 606.

he would like a ride: CG to SWK, n.d.

"mild as milk": ibid.

"It was divided quite neatly": CG to SWK, n.d.

the Northern journalists came: CG to LA, n.d.

"I went out driving with James": CG to AL, n.d.

"He's a *baaad* niggah!": Richard Rorty to AW, May 21, 1985.

"Well, it was awful": CG to AL, n.d.

Rorty always said: Richard Rorty to AW, May 21, 1985.

"He was awfully decent": CG to AL, n.d.

"I don't think the chief knows": CG to LA, n.d.

"Neither Allen nor I": CG to SWK, n.d.

"The poor white man": CG to AL, n.d.

"communists": Deane Mowrer interview with CG, May 19, 1970.

"fellow travelers": CG to AL, n.d.

"I think Dorothy began praying": Deane Mowrer interview with CG, May 19, 1970.

Rosy, the Memphis sophisticate: interview with NTW, March 25, 1984.

"that we could ill afford": CG to SWK, July 1935.

"could come to the heart": interview with AL, December 1, 1983.

"something marvelous for dinner": CG to SWK, July 1935.

"Why, that man": ibid.

She produced, she said: ibid.

"We see plainly": MP to D. W. Hiltman, April 19, 1938.

Perkins had hinted: CG to SWK, July 1935.

"the leafy end": CG to SWK, July 1935.

"Now, Nancy, can't you": CG to LA, n.d.

"With me . . . it is September": CG to SWK, October 27, 1935.

"Mama, I don't care": ibid.

"I wrote *Aleck Maury*": CG to JH, November 1, 1935.

she promptly asked him: CG to MP, January 1936.

Allen replied that he could not: AT to JH, November 1, 1935.

"It's strange the way": CG to JH, November 1, 1935.

a very confusing holiday: CG to "Mister Bob" Lytle, January 13, 1936.

"My idea of a good Christmas": CG to SWK, January 8, 1936.

"It seemed a good plan": ibid.

Andrew could see strains: interview with AL, December 1, 1983.

"It is certainly splendid": CG to RPW, n.d.

"He is like Abraham Lincoln": CG to SWK, January 8, 1937.

"Speak not to me": interview with Peter Taylor, May 24, 1985.

"I had had a very conventional life": ibid.

"When I went to Vanderbilt": ibid.

"Allen Tate, Confederate bred": Buffington, p. 67.

15. *Monteagle and* None Shall Look Back, *1936–1937*
160–170

"a Civil War Becky Sharp": CG to FMF, n.d.

"very pleasant elm-shaded village": CG to FMF, n.d.

"Don't come near me": CG to SWK, September 10, 1936.

"What infantry was that?": CG to DVD, July 30, 1936.

"very respectable old colored women": CG to FMF, n.d.

"ate too much, drank too much": CG to SWK, September 10, 1936.

"just what he was doing six years ago": CG to FMF, n.d.

Caroline talked to Maxwell Perkins: CG to SWK, September 10, 1936.

"It fascinates me": CG to LA, n.d.

"only long enough to say hello": CG to FMF, n.d.

"They begged to have her": ibid.

"quite hideous cottages": CG to DVD, August 26, 1936.

"The dominant dowagers": CG to FMF, n.d.

"It was quite effective": CG to "Mister Bob" Lytle, n.d.

"one only passes through": CG to FMF, n.d.

"I do not expect": CG to FMF, n.d.

"I can't help it": CG to MP, n.d.

"I got the reviews": interview with AL, December 1, 1983.

"handsome Cimabuean blue": CG to FMF, n.d.

"enraged the brethren": CG to AGW, n.d.

she could not swallow: CG to MP, n.d.

"Don't worry your head": CG to AGW, n.d.

"Mama, don't tell them": CG to LA, n.d.

"My grandmother is in high feather": CG to SWK, January 8, 1937.

"got through nicely": ibid.

"It was just the kind": CG to DVD, February 8, 1937.

"drunk and dumb": CG to SWK, January 8, 1937.

"And it had plenty of minks": MW to AGW, January 4, 1937.

"Next year": CG to SWK, n.d.

"He fought hard": CG to DVD, February 8, 1937.

"I have no heart for it": CG to KAP, n.d.

"another novel to write": ibid.

She urged him: CG to BC, n.d.

One guest was reminded: CG to DVD, February 8, 1937.

"I wanted Forrest": CG to BC, n.d.

Katherine Anne Porter wrote: "Dulce et Decorum Est," *The New Republic*, March 31, 1937, pp. 244–245.

"It is not a review": CG to KAP, n.d.

"It feels strange": John Crowe Ransom to CG, April 6, 1937.

"tall, dark, and efficient": CG to RPW, n.d.

Scribner's was really pushing: CG to FMF, n.d.

"It went dead": CG to FC, March 29, 1937.

she told Perkins: CG to MP, n.d.

"Three illicit love affairs": CG to DVD, April 6, 1937.

"Thank God for being": ibid.

"absolutely blue": ibid.

"We are going to stay": ibid.

"The Nelson ladies": CG to FMF, n.d.

16. *Benfolly and Greensboro, 1937–1938*
171–179

"a sort of super feeling": CG to KAP, n.d.

"histrionic pervert": CG to KAP, n.d.

"with those Hutchinsons": ibid.

"demon child": CG to KAP, n.d.

a book about Merry Mont: CG to MP, August 1937.

"for practical reasons": MP to CG, August 1937.

"Really you have to struggle": CG to KAP, n.d.

"Mr. Norman took Minnie": ibid.

"that October haze": CG to SWK, October 16, 1937.

"You'll regret this": CG to AL, November 11, 1937.

"half a dozen of the best plots": CG to MP, [1936].

"The death has cast": CG to AGW, January 1938.

Allen "doesn't think": CG to MP, October 1937.

Maxwell Perkins wrote her: MP to CG, December 21, 1937.

"It would be swell pay": CG to MP, December 8, 1937.

"the first literary hotel": CG to AGW, January 1938.

"It is one of the most romantic": ibid.

"frightful": CG to MP, n.d.

"Allen's work": CG to AL, April 26, 1938.

"haughty blankness": CG to KAP, n.d.

lie in bed at night: CG to MP, n.d.

brought her bouquets: CG to DVD, March 18, 1938.

One of the students: interview with Sue Watkins, November 20, 1986, Greensboro, North Carolina.

It was his ironic smile: interview with Sheila Brantley, Princeton, New Jersey, 1984.

One day Eleanor Ross: interview with James Ross, November 20, 1986, Greensboro, North Carolina.

"They had to pay": interview with James Ross, November 20, 1986.

"Everybody (except me)": CG to KAP, n.d.

"as though they had been skinned": CG to MP, n.d.

She always remembered: CG to MVD, n.d.

her Kingsport friend: Paul A. Counce to CG, December 18, 1939.

A Chattanooga lawyer: J. P. Brown to CG, May 3, 1940.

good dose of mountain laurel: CG to DVD, March 10, 1938.

Caroline was delighted: CG to DVD, May 12, 1938.

Allen told Caroline: ibid.

until he started his own: ibid.

Allen said he was no Flaubert: AT to MVD, June 2, 1938, Squires, p. 126.

As for Caroline: ibid.

Andrew wrote that he was sorry: AL to AT, June 14, 1938.

"I can't take it in": CG to KAP, n.d.

Red Warren wrote from Italy: CG to KAP, n.d.

17. Connecticut and Greensboro, 1938–1939
180–187

Benfolly . . . had never looked so nice: CG to JB, n.d.

The cottage in West Cornwall: CG to JB, n.d.

which . . . made up: CG to KAP, n.d.

Dot was madly in love: interview with NTW, March 25, 1984.

Allen began getting up: CG to KAP, n.d.

"the first time we've been free": CG to KAP, n.d.

"However, when you're in a hole": CG to JB, n.d.

"most awful fink": interview with NTW, March 25, 1984.

"I wish you wouldn't": ibid.

"None of the guests": CG to KAP, n.d.

"large, expensive, gloomy": ibid.

"Edmund, who is no longer": ibid.

"incredible confusion": ibid.

"a horrible evening": CG to PP and UP, September 14, 1938.

"swallowed three-fourths": CG to GMO, n.d.

"After all, we don't need": ibid.

"the brutes": CG to EL, May 23, 1939.

"Clique!": CG to KAP, n.d.

"He feels that he has exhausted": ibid.

"We are all rather bewildered": ibid.

"The writer came": ibid.

"He lives up to all": ibid.

"not wanting to give up": ibid.

Caroline "has imperceptibly": AT to Frank Graham, May 1, 1939. University of North Carolina, Chapel Hill.

"And I just planted": CG to KAP, n.d.

Caroline wrote to Allen's biographer: CG to RS, n.d.

she was glad to get out: CG to EL, May 23, 1939.

"Pretty stuffy": CG to UP, n.d.

It would be easier: CG to KAP, n.d.

She was the best cook: CG to KAP, n.d.

"I am too upset": CG to JB, June 1939.

"and there at the bottom": CG to KAP, n.d.

only one meal alone: CG to WD, n.d.

18. Princeton, 1939–1941
188–196

Allen was struck: AT to Paul Green, September 18, 1939. University of North Carolina, Chapel Hill.

"The bigwigs": CG to BC, October 31, 1939.

"The contrast between the two": CG to EL, September 16, 1939.

"quaint and ceremonious": Russell Fraser, *A Mingled Yarn: The Life of R. P. Blackmur* (New York: Harcourt Brace Jovanovich, 1981), p. 187.

Caroline saw Einstein: CG to DVD, November 15, 1939.

"amazingly competent": AT to Paul Green, January 2, 1940. University of North Carolina, Chapel Hill.

"gentlemanly, courteous": interview with Frederick Morgan, January 15, 1986, New York City.

She would say: ibid.

"If they know who": CG to Muriel Cowley, n.d.

Willard Thorp said: interview with Willard Thorp, June 28, 1986.

"Young Poets by Appointment": CG to AL and EL, April 14, 1941.

"and not even put coal on": ibid.

She wrote Andrew: CG to AL, n.d.

"He is what Ma used to call": CG to MMM, n.d.

"I had always been": telephone interview with NTW, February 7, 1987.

best critic in America: interview with NTW, March 25, 1984.

"powerful . . . unusually integrated": *Columbia Review,* April 1936.

John Peale Bishop wrote: John Peale Bishop to CG, February 10, 1940, *Republic of Letters,* p. 162.

"I will do it": CG to EL, April 27, 1940.

"Mama *made* him stop drinking": interview with NTW, March 25, 1984.

"He is working steadily": CG to WD, n.d.

"I don't think": interview with NTW, March 25, 1984.

Caroline wrote to Andrew: CG to AL, February 1940.

"Do you reckon": CG to EL, April 27, 1940.

She then asked Edna: ibid.

"This library": CG to BC, July 5, 1941.

"She spent less than Caroline": interview with AL, December 1, 1983.

"I never expected": CG to DVD, October 17, 1940.

He told her for once: CG to KAP, n.d.

"Just one novel after another": ibid.

Caroline said she missed: ibid.

When Bill inherited: interview with JP, April 15, 1985, Washington, D.C.

Bill began to drink: CG to PP and UP, n.d.

19. Princeton, 1941–1942
197–206

"Ordinary people": SY to Ellen Glasgow, September 7, 1932, *Stark Young,* p. 419.

"was up to all sorts": ibid.

"All but four": CG to KAP, n.d.

the trouble was circulatory: CG to EL, June 17, 1941.

"he ran at a trot": CG to EL, July 26, 1941.

it was mostly insomnia: CG to AL and EL, n.d.

"I have germs": CG to DVD, April 29, 1942.

"It is in the nature": CG to JS, n.d.

"It was awkward": CG to EL, May 4, 1941.

"the queerest fish": CG to MMM, n.d.

"I hurt Cleanth's feelings": CG to AL and EL, n.d.

"Yes, it's like John Ransom": CG to KAP, n.d.

"Allen helped manfully": CG to EL, June 17, 1941.

"We are simply mad": CG to MC, n.d.

another Princeton winter: CG to PP and UP, n.d.

"My conscience hurt": ibid.

"very cultivated": ibid.

"They grow out of trees": ibid.

necessary spice of danger: CG to WD, n.d.

"People always seem": CG to PP and UP, n.d.

"the indefatigable McIlvaine": ibid.

"thirty-five howling young demons": CG to EL, November 22, 1941.

"Isn't it fun?": CG to PP and UP, n.d.

"The life of a person who is not": CG to MMM, n.d.

"The life of a person who isn't": CG to BC, November 22, 1941.

"Hack work": CG to AL, October 15, 1941.

"He was in the hospital twice": CG to PP and UP, n.d.

All her heroes had been: CG to KAP, n.d.

It looked, she said: CG to MMM, February 1942.

"a knockout": KAP to CG, December 19, 1941.

She wrote Andrew: CG to AL, n.d.

"I can't live through": interview with Tom Roche, May 7, 1984, Princeton, New Jersey.

"I feel as if some horrible Grendel": CG to WD, n.d.

"Red gave a good one": CG to AL, May 19, 1942.

"Meanwhile he goes to New York": CG to UP, September 23, 1941.

"He is a high class . . . writer": ibid.

"Dick's perfidious tales": CG to AT, n.d.

"light and popular": CG to DVD, April 29, 1942.

nothing commercial about her: CG to KAP, January 16, 1942.

"with what I owe": CG to EL, n.d.

"the coonskin cap group": CG to KAP, n.d.

"unsettled as a jaybird": CG to DVD, April 29, 1942.

"but they were so insulting": CG to MVD, n.d.

"With our combined": CG to MVD, n.d.

"We will just hole up": CG to MC, n.d.

20. Monteagle with the Lowells, 1942–1943
207–215

Caroline often described: CG to KAP, n.d.

the stairs were easier: ibid.

"cramping" themselves: CG to LA, n.d.

"I haven't seen you": AT to VLT, January 19, 1943.

"We always start working": CG to LA, n.d.

"having [her] novel torn to pieces": CG to JS, n.d.

it would not be like: CG to WM, January 19, 1943.

"Like 'broken colours' ": ibid.

"little mountain maid": CG to KAP, n.d.

"amiable venom": Simpson, p. 136.

"I haven't come to that": CG to KAP, n.d.

"They had lots": interview with Willard Thorp, June 6, 1986.

"It has been so long": CG to WM, January 19, 1943.
"darling Dr. Wolf": CG to LA, n.d.
"the only mycologist in the state": CG to JS, n.d.
"The first morning": CG to FC, n.d.
Caroline wrote Fannie Cheney: ibid.
"We washed, dusted, and polished": CG to KAP, n.d.
"He regarded me": interview with AL, December 1, 1983.
"ravishing": interview with NTW, March 25, 1984.
"I was impressed": CG to AL, March 15, 1943.
"I never answered it": interview with AL, December 1, 1983.
"these novels": CG to MVD, n.d.

"My father couldn't stand": interview with Peter Taylor, May 24, 1985.
"Jean wanted Peter": interview with NWT, March 25, 1984.
"I fell in love with Caligula": Simpson, p. 144.
"inside the vast welter": CG to KAP, n.d.
"The worst thing about Princeton": ibid.
There was hardly an unoccupied cranny: ibid.
"It was the worst thing": ibid.
"Look at Mama": CG to MVD, n.d.
Allen said she could have: CG to KAP, n.d.
"The woodland scene": ibid.

21. Washington, D.C., 1943–1944
216–224

"I tried to make it": CG to JS, n.d.
"Whenever Allen has sent anybody": CG to JS, n.d.
"What about Mrs. Cheney?": CG to JS, n.d.
"The Tates set the tone": interview with BC, November 30, 1983.
"A doorman has lots of time": CG to JS, n.d.
"This is my friend": interview with JP, April 15, 1985.
"She insists on . . . shopping": CG to JS, n.d.
"Caroline had done": interview with FC, November 29, 1983, Nashville, Tennessee.
"When Caroline invited me": MW to AGW, October 20, 1943.
"To have such good reviews": MW to AW, February 1987.
"But God, I got worn": CG to JS, n.d.
"If you could see": CG to AT, n.d.
"Daddo agreed to the wedding": interview with NTW, March 25, 1984.
"So far as I know": CG to AT, n.d.
"Now, Zov": CG to AT, n.d.

"His long study": CG to JS, n.d.
"Last night he wanted": CG to AT, n.d.
"The Phillips people": CG to JS, n.d.
"He totters": CG to JS, n.d.
"He got a bad cold": ibid.
"And we may have brought": interview with BC, November 30, 1983.
"She would walk miles": CG to JS, n.d.
"Get up, get up": interview with FC, November 30, 1983.
Allen told Katherine Anne's biographer: Joan Givner, Katherine Anne Porter: A Life (New York: Simon & Schuster, 1982), p. 331.
"cryptic and peculiar novel": Orville Prescott, "Books of the Times," The New York Times, May 11, 1944, p. 17.
"I was trying": CG to Edmund Wilson, May 17, 1944.
"None of my books": CG to SWK, August 3, 1944.
"writing very lucidly": CG to JS, n.d.
a black Guggenheim fellow: CG to SWK, August 3, 1944.
"Willard Thorp and Mark Van Doren": CG to JS, n.d.

22. Sewanee, 1944–1945
225–234

"Isn't it awful": MMC to Cousin Mag, July 22, 1944.

"We dyed them red": CG to JS, n.d.

"rustic ease": CG to KAP, [1944].

"laughing out of the wrong sides": ibid.

"twang the right chords": ibid.

"I hope to do better": CG to JS, n.d.

Pidie wrote to Caroline: interview with JP, April 15, 1984.

"Allen said he made him": CG to JS, n.d.

"The house was a wreck": ibid.

Forty years later: interview with JP, April 15, 1984.

"living room": CG to Percy Wood, October 6, 1944.

"People talk a lot of nonsense": ibid.

"Allen got his first copy": CG to FC, n.d.

When Katherine Anne wrote: CG to FC, n.d.

"I was gorged on babies": ibid.

"God, that James!": CG to JS, n.d.

"had gone to school to him": CG to David Ragan, answering written questions for an interview, autumn 1945.

"the kind of thing Bram Stoker": CG to FC, n.d.

the damnedest trip: CG to FC, n.d.

Caroline said she had heard: ibid.

"a long, sharp pin": CG to JS, n.d.

"exactly like that fat man": CG to JS, n.d.

They could have a bedroom: CG to JS, n.d.

"quite a Madonna aspect": ibid.

"bolly-wolly time": CG to JS, n.d.

"having flu": CG to JS, n.d.

"which, of course . . . brought": CG to JS, n.d.

"Who in hell": CG to JS, n.d.

"went completely Meriwether": MW to AGW, April 1945.

"He will gladly do it": CG to KAP, September 1945.

"That family": ibid.

"many a rousing talk": CG to JS, n.d.

"It was her only fault": telephone interview with Mary Phillips Kirby-Smith, November 27, 1984.

"The church bell rang like mad": CG to KAP, September 1945.

"thick with figures hurrying": CG to KAP, October 6, 1945.

23. Divorce, September 1945–April 1946
235–248

Willard Thorp remembered: interview with Willard Thorp, June 28, 1986.

Some years later: CG to Robert Barnett, June 8, 1959. Copy in CG papers, Princeton.

"I'm going to New York": interview with NTW, March 25, 1984.

"They got me into a third rate": CG to Robert Barnett, June 8, 1959.

"One usually looks": CG to MC, n.d.

"Your mother's been so cruel": interview with NTW, March 25, 1984.

"Baby neglected": ibid.

"Nancy and Allen got tired": CG to JS and RL, n.d.

"ten hideous, expensive days": CG to JS and RL, n.d.

"We are getting a divorce": CG to JS, n.d.

"Allen and I are getting": CG to KAP, [October 6, 1945].

"Evidently we gave the impression": ibid.

"What am I going to do now?": CG to SWK, n.d.

"I, of course, am like": CG to KAP, [October 6, 1945].

Catherine "in herself": CG to SWK, n.d.

Allen worried, too: AT to SWK, October 27, 1945.

"Allen, really, seemed": CG to KAP, n.d.

Peter Taylor tells: telephone interview with Peter Taylor, December 21, 1984.

"I would let the fires": CG to JS and RL, n.d.

"Thank God for that winter": CG to KAP, n.d.

"break everything": JS to her sister, Mary Lee Frichtel, n.d. University of Colorado, Boulder.

"to talk things over": CG to WD, December 7, 1945.

"You don't call the sheriff": telephone interview with Peter Taylor, December 21, 1984.

"I do not think": CG to RL, n.d.

"The issue between us": CG to WD, December 7, 1945.

"worst idea I ever had": CG to WD, December 18, 1945.

"Allen was such a liar": telephone interview with Mary Phillips Kirby-Smith, November 27, 1984.

"he was marvellous": CG to WD, December 18, 1945.

"I have bad news": interview with Meriwether Gordon, November 8, 1985, Clarksville, Tennessee.

Meriwether . . . recalls that Caroline: ibid.

"I don't mind wrestling": CG to WD, December 31, 1945.

"It is such a relief": CG to WD, January 8, 1946.

"fair draw the heart": CG to WD, n.d.

"When we got there": telephone interview with Peter Taylor, November 5, 1984.

"I am convinced": CG to AT, n.d.

"Or we could spend a few days": CG to AT, March 1946.

"From the beginning": CG to SWK, n.d.

"excited as a new bridegroom": MW to AGW, April 12, 1946.

"We want to come in!": interview with DVD, July 17, 1984.

"Allen and I just remarried": William A. Owens to AW, February 7, 1985.

"This is a wonderful day": interview with Danforth Ross, December 1, 1983.

24. New York, 1946–1947
249–256

front-page review: "Mr. Faulkner's Southern Saga," *The New York Times Book Review*, May 5, 1946, p. 1.

"literally one of the most charming": CG to WD, n.d.

"as ignorant as catfish": CG to WSB, n.d.

"You can't say": Danforth Ross, "Caroline Gordon's Golden Ball," *Critique* 1, 1 (Winter 1952), p. 7.

"If I didn't have respect": interview with JP, April 15, 1985.

"We started out": telephone interview with Madeleine L'Engle, July 25, 1985.

"the most stimulating . . . teacher": Bette Bentley to AW, February 24, 1985.

"You're a natural": telephone interview with William Price Fox, July 8, 1985.

"It has made me do": CG to BC and FC, July 26, [1947].

"so much more charming": CG to WD, n.d.

"I had been married": interview with NWT, March 25, 1984.

"Allen's face was scratched": interview with WSB, October 7, 1984.

an imbalance of the glands: CG to WD, n.d.

"whether he might not be": ibid.

"I was worried about Caroline": SWK to Robert Barnett, June 14, 1959.

"She never gets the woman": interview with NWT, March 25, 1984.

"I think he ought": CG to MVD, n.d.

"Allen and I have been": CG to BC and FC, April 21, 1947.

"He has given us some advice": ibid.

when Allen "can't write": CG to WD, n.d.

"That's all right": CG to LA, June 24, 1947.

"I simply cannot realize": CG to WD, n.d.

"classical": CG to BC and FC, July 26, [1947].

"use a scythe, plow a field": interview with JP, April 15, 1985.

25. The Catholic Church, 1947–1948
257–261

her faith, revealed to her: CG to WSB, n.d.

She told Andrew: CG to AL, January 11, 1955.

Sigrid Undset's books: CG to NTW, [fall 1953].

"gripped her by the soul": interview with DVD, July 17, 1984.

An important incident: Caroline Gordon, "The Art and Mystery of Faith," *Newman Annual*, December 1955, p. 59.

"Everything they did": ibid., p. 60.

"forlorn girl": CG to NTW, St. Martin's Day, 1950.

"I am a Catholic": CG to BC, [1951].

"who are muddled in their heads": ibid.

She wrote to Andrew: CG to AL, January 11, 1955.

"I am an artist": CG to BC, November 20, 1952.

"Sam, you take this": interview with Leonard Unger, December 3, 1985, Minneapolis, Minnesota.

Protestantism "not only": CG to NTW, [1951?].

"What a psychologist!" CG to WD, May 21, 1948.

"Yet Robert Graves in his *White Goddess*": CG to KAP, September 7, 1948.

"It is simply wonderful": CG to WSB, n.d.

"It's the last": CG to FC, December 17, 1947.

26. New York and Chicago, 1948–1949
262–268

"Don't kill him off": CG to WD, n.d.

"Mr. Tate and I cook": CG to WD, n.d.

"People are always saying": CG to BC and FC, [June 25, 1948].

"he had turned into": ibid.

"Looks something like a gym strap": ibid.

"Kansas is not at all": CG to WSB, n.d.

"We must have a drawing card": KAP to JLW, August 18, 1948.

the "gabbling" nuns: CG to WSB, n.d.

"Might as well get": ibid.

"along with everything else": ibid.

"enough forsythia roots": CG to KAP, August 27, 1948.

"One thing I have learned": CG to WD, August 30, 1948.

"A central intelligence": CG to WD, n.d.

"fabulous salary": CG to WD, October 28, 1948.

"almost too good to be true": CG to WD, n.d.

Notes

"swing in a balloon": ibid.
"the usual objections": CG to WD, n.d.
"utter simplicity and great learning": CG to RL, n.d.

"So maybe we're not so unlucky": CG to WD, n.d.
she wrote a "brilliant": CG to RL, n.d.
"The constant yelling": CG to RL, July 4, 1949.

27. Princeton Again, 1949–1950
269–277

"touches of Benfolly": CG to FC, n.d.
"The last few weeks": CG to SY, n.d.
"It ought to be fine": CG to NWT, n.d.
"run literally off my feet": CG to FC, n.d.
"worked wonders in the pagan breast": CG to WD, [1950].
"was struck by the size": Simpson, p. 195.
That fall: Andrew Lytle, "Caroline Gordon and the Historic Image," *The Sewanee Review* 57 (Autumn 1949), pp. 565–586.
"could not appear": CG to AL, December 3, 1962.
Edmund Wilson: CG to WD, n.d.
"Bunny Wilson is here": Simpson, p. 198.
"Allen was utterly charming": interview with Louise Cowan, October 6, 1984, Nashua, New Hampshire.
"white and wan": CG to WD, August 8, 1950.
"I use Lucy's eye": CG to WD, Octave Day of All Saints, 1950.
"So I used it": CG to RL, [1951].
"a thing to sift soil": CG to WD, n.d.
"Cranesbill, Jack-in-the-pulpit": ibid.
conversation piece: CG to WD, n.d.
"Are you *sure*": CG to WD, March 1, 1950.
"This sentence could not": CG to JB, n.d.
"The last two months": CG to FC, November 13, 1950.
"It really is the cutest": ibid.
"She is quite a sight": CG to NTW, St. Martin's Day, 1950.

28. Princeton, 1950–1951
278–286

Allen had prepared for his baptism: CG to WD, [1950].
"a careful Jesuit": CG to RWS, Feast of the Annunciation, 1951.
"As a Catholic of many weeks": Randall Jarrell to RL, *Randall Jarrell's Letters*, ed. by Mary Jarrell (Boston: Houghton Mifflin, 1985), p. 248.
"but he might as well": ibid.
"It seems that entering": CG to RWS, February 9, 1951.
"I have decided": CG to NTW, n.d.
"Right now this seems": ibid.
"or, rather subordinated themselves": CG to BC, March [18], 1950.
"the tremendous implications": Sister Bernetta to CG, December 6, 1950.
"I wanted more range": CG to SY, St. Scholastica's Day, 1951.
"unholy prejudice against Holy Rollers": CG to BC, February 23, 1951.
"I want to show people": ibid.
Caroline made a bargain: interview with NTW, March 25, 1984.
"The truth is": CG to LA, n.d.
"You are getting a letter": CG to WD, July 27, 1951.
"We suddenly began": CG to NWT, [1951].
some pharaoh had started and quit: CG to WD, July 27, 1951.
"Could you and your Sexual Partner":

CG to SY, Feast of St. Stephen, 1951. "the wildest party": interview with BC, November 29, 1983.

"He's been going about": CG to SY, n.d.

"the sly irony springing": Curtis, p. 552.

"She was the only literary person": telephone interview with Walker Percy, 1984.

"had sort of disappeared": CG to BC, December 31, 1951.

"This girl is a real novelist": CG to Robert Fitzgerald, [May 1951], quoted by Sally Fitzgerald, "A Master Class: From the Correspondence of Caroline Gordon and Flannery O'Connor," *Georgia Review* 33 (Winter 1979), p. 832.

"and she certainly increased": Flannery O'Connor to Robert and Sally Fitzgerald, n.d., ibid., p. 830.

"who knows anything": Flannery O'Connor to CG, n.d., ibid., p. 845.

"It is no accident": CG to BC, December 31, 1951.

29. Minneapolis, 1951–1952
287–294

placed on the lot: CG to JS, Feast of St. Thecla, [1951].

The earth was rich: CG to BC, September 28, 1951.

"a fountainhead of artificial insemination": CG to JHW, n.d.

"an ingenious quality": interview with Virginia Erdman, July 15, 1985, Stony Brook, New York.

she had gone into a church: interview with Leonard Unger, December 3, 1985.

"Of course, you must admit": G. Robert Stange to AW, September 30, 1986.

who thought all Southerners: Danforth Ross, unpublished paper read at Hometown Symposium on Evelyn Scott and Caroline Gordon, Austin Peay State University, Clarksville, Tennessee, November 7–9, 1985.

"I keep my breviary there": CG to NTW, October 10, 1951.

"I must have some wildlife": CG to NTW The Vigil of All Saints, 1951.

"and a few other things": CG to NTW, Feast of Sts. Faustina and Jovita, 1951.

"It was so badly needed": ibid.

Caroline wrote Lon: CG to BC, n.d.

"We're too fine": interview with Leonard Unger, December 3, 1985.

"I cooked this duck": ibid.

"They were always rushing": CG to RL, n.d.

"if she had espoused Jesus": CG to BC, September 28, 1951.

But Caroline's high standards: interview with Sister Alice Smith (formerly Sister Maris Stella), December 3, 1985, Minneapolis, Minnesota.

"what man can create": *The New York Times*, March 30, 1952.

"a caricature of culture": *The New York Times*, May 1, 1952.

"few writers talk well": Genêt, "Letter from Paris," *The New Yorker* 28, (June 14, 1952), p. 108.

The New York Times revealed: *The New York Times*, May 5, 1966.

"three perfect days": AT to KAP, June 13, 1952.

Caroline had promised God: CG to NTW, n.d.

"Gpa had a marvelous time": ibid.

"Just one ice cube": telephone interview with Edwy Lee, 1983.

Edwy Lee recalled: ibid.

Percy must get her: CG to NTW, n.d.

She predicted that little Caroline: CG to JS, June 1953.

living "in a balloon": CG to BC and FC, October 28, 1952.

"I have never stuck": ibid.

"the finest experience": CG to AT, n.d.

"I know quite well": CG to AT, n.d.

The walls were paneled: CG to AT, St. Dominic's Day, 1952.

"Imagine not owing": CG to AT, St. Cajetan's Day, 1952.

She almost wished: CG to NTW, Birthday of the Blessed Virgin, 1952.

30. St. Paul, 1952–1953
295–302

Caroline liked St. Paul: CG to NTW, n.d.

nicest one she had ever lived in: ibid.

the only man in American politics: CG to BC and FC, October 28, 1952.

It was going to be: CG to NTW, n.d.

He loved Italy: CG to JHW and Phyllis Wheelock.

"I am convinced that": CG to Elizabeth Hardwick and RL, n.d.

Later Caroline would tell her friends: CG to FC, n.d.

"Catullus' lake seems": CG to BC and FC, October 3, 1952.

the greatest poetic seizure: CG to BC and FC, October 28, 1952.

She promised to send: CG to NTW, n.d.

The quotation had the whole school: CG to NTW, St. Polycarp's Day, 1953.

"Not one word": CG to BC and FC, March 9, 1953.

"He went to sleep one night": CG to BC, November 20, 1952.

"What's wrong with you?": CG to BC, November 20, 1952.

In January 1953 she wrote: CG to JHW, January 8, 1953.

This would not be possible: CG to NTW, March 1953.

"I miss you so": CG to AT, n.d., 1953.

he told her he was at the top: AT to MW, April 28, 1953.

Caroline wrote to him: CG to AT, St. Philip and [James's] Day, 1953.

"The trouble with us": CG to AT, n.d.

"Darling . . . there is": ibid.

not to worry about her: CG to AT, n.d.

The poor mountain hardly got out: CG to BC and FC, St. Fidelis of Sigmaringen's Day, [1953].

"I go to Mass by way of": CG to NTW, n.d.

she might read something: CG to AT, Maundy Thursday, 1953.

"humanly fascinating": CG to NTW, n.d.

Wheelock replied that Caroline: JHW to AT, December 19, 1952.

In February, thanks to royalties: JHW to AT, February 10, 1953; February 14, 1953.

she hoped to be able: CG to BC and FC, St. Fidelis of Sigmaringen's Day, [1953].

she told Nancy she stuck: CG to NTW, July 1953.

"It is divine": CG to AT, n.d.

retreat, conducted this year: CG to AT, July 21, 1953.

"I pray for you": ibid.

"DON'T YOU DARE FIRE HER": CG to NTW, July 17, 1953.

31. Rome, 1953–1954
303–315

"good meals with . . . wine": CG to NTW, July 30, 1953.

"envy reared its head": CG to NTW, August 19, 1953.

"But she is an ardent Catholic": ibid.

"It gave me the most vivid impression": ibid.

"If you ever have a tooth out": CG to NTW, August 16, 1933.

"all the old haunts around the

Odéon": CG to NTW, September 3, 1953.

"the holiest church in Paris": ibid.

"cling to the skirts": CG to "Dear Children," n.d.

"I wish I could have met": CG to NTW, n.d.

"walking down the street": CG to "Dear Children," n.d.

where "St. Peter . . . You are also": ibid.

"Grandpa and I have decided": CG to NTW, n.d.

"The first time I went": CG to NTW, n.d.

"It is great fun": CG to WD, Station of the Four Holy Crowned Martyrs, 1954.

"like something you'd find": CG to NTW, October 3, 1953.

They were having such a heavenly time: CG to "Dear Children," n.d.

"The whole restaurant": ibid.

Allen had a sty: CG to Percy Wood, St. Paul's Day, 1953, Princeton.

She admired Berenson: ibid.

"The Allen Tates are staying": Bernard Berenson, *Sunset and Twilight: From the Diaries of 1947–1958.* (New York: Harcourt, Brace, 1963), p. 334.

"the most wonderful garden": CG to WD, Station of the Four Holy Crowned Martyrs, 1954.

"a darling little . . . pig": ibid.

She was in despair: CG to MMC, July 1954.

"too much of a confection": CG to NTW, Feast of the Immaculate Conception, 1953.

"It was the most beautiful rite": CG to MW, n.d.

Nancy had a particular devotion: CG to BC, n.d.

Caroline brooded that it marked: CG to WD, February 15, 1954.

"The day is so long": CG to "Dear Children," n.d.

she had written to Sam Monk: CG to NTW, n.d.

She asked their doctor: CG to WD, February 19, 1954.

"one of the most powerful": ibid.

"But my husband has wonderful dreams": ibid.

"The idea is that the human psyche": ibid.

"We have got a whole series": ibid.

She described one dream: CG to Percy Wood, St. Paul's Day, 1953, Princeton.

"My! It certainly is fascinating": CG to WD, February 19, 1954.

"When she got to questioning": CG to NTW, n.d.

She explained to the *dottoressa:* typed notes in Caroline Gordon papers, Princeton, p. 2.

"If I had identified myself": ibid., p. 4.

" 'I'd rather see you in your grave' ": ibid., p. 5.

"identic:" ibid., p. 6.

"You are firmly established": ibid., p. 2.

Allen . . . had quit drinking: CG to LA, February 1, 1954.

Dr. Bernhard remembers: interview with Dora Bernhard, December 23, 1986.

"a psychotic episode": interview with NTW, March 25, 1984.

32. Princeton and Minnesota, 1954–1955
316–325

"torture chamber": CG to MMC, July 1954.

"Excessive fatigue": ibid.

"It was more than fatigue": telephone interview with NTW, February 7, 1987.

"Nancy's spending sprees": CG to AT, April 26, 1954.

Allen, meanwhile, wrote: AT to CG, April 21, 1954.

"we sort of walk around": CG to MMC, July 1954.

maybe she should buy: ibid.

The first person who saw: CG to FC, May 4, 1954.

The architects were the Charles Addams brothers: CG to WSB, St. Catherine of Siena's Day, 1954.

so hopelessly out of date: CG to MMC, July 1954.

"It is a nice test": ibid.

"architectural marvels": ibid.

"bandstand at a county fair": ibid.

"which bristles with closets": ibid.

"He started out": ibid.

"If any boy ever sets foot": ibid.

"It stands rather high": CG to AT, Pentecost, 1954.

The books were as prolific: CG to JHW and Phyllis Wheelock, n.d.

"wonderful" star magnolia: CG to MMC, July 1954.

"At first I was thought": CG to MMC, July 1954.

When Nancy and Percy were invited: interview with NTW, March 25, 1984.

Nancy cried, and Caroline called: CG to AT, Pentecost, 1954.

"Allen has not yet been allowed": CG to MMC, July 1954.

"an enchanting child": ibid.

"Whar you, Omma?": ibid.

Caroline wrote back: CG to Elizabeth Hardwick, n.d. Houghton Library, Harvard.

In another letter to Elizabeth: CG to Elizabeth Hardwick, n.d. Houghton Library, Harvard.

Caroline regretted very much: CG to SY, n.d.

dire calamity: ibid.

Drinking was such a problem: AT to CG, January 2, 1955.

Allen could work better: CG to SY, November 5, 1954.

"It seems to me": ibid.

Conditions for work were ideal: CG to AT, March 28, 1955.

Caroline embroidered: CG to SY, Feast of St. Peter's Chair in Rome, 1955.

She wrote to the Lytles: CG to AL and EL, June 15, 1955.

"dear old Malcolm Cowley and . . . Brooks": Flannery O'Connor to Sally and Robert Fitzgerald, June 10, 1955, *The Habit of Being*, p. 85.

"It was interesting to see": CG to FC, n.d.

Brooks said later: CG to AL and EL, June 15, 1955.

Allen's biographer states: Squires, pp. 54–55.

"My husband would not": CG to Robert Barnett, June 8, 1959. Copy in Caroline Gordon papers, Princeton.

Caroline, edgy and bitter: CG to AT, August 11, 1955.

she let her infantilism: CG to AT, St. Stephen's Day, 1955.

she had not done a lick: CG to AT, August 17, 1955.

"one of the most profound things": ibid.

"All that information": CG to AT, August 21, 1955.

"It is, I suspect": CG to AT, St. Stephen's Day, 1955.

"I have been thinking": ibid.

Their house was twice the size: CG to AT, September 10, 1955.

"The house has got something": ibid.

"My father tried it": ibid.

"Uncle Doc was there disguised": ibid.

33. Rome and Kansas, 1955–1956
326–338

With no car: CG to BC and FC, n.d.

"such a splendid place": ibid. "The Barnabiti," the letter continues, "are next to [the convent] (founded by St. Anthony M. Zaccaria, who after he got his degree of Doctor of Medicine from the University of Padua, learned in a vision that his task was to be to cure spiritual ills rather than physical. Makes a splendid place to pray for a psychiatrist son-in-law!)."

"I just nip around two corners": CG to AT, October 12, 1955.

"the little daisy-like plants": CG to AT, October 14, 1955.

She asked Allen to become: CG to AT, October 12, 1955.

"catacombian sort of fish": ibid.

"Remember that I am a paintress": CG to AT, September 26, 1955.

Life, she said, was just so: CG to SY, n.d.

The "work" . . . was going better: Dora Bernhard to AT, October 13, 1955.

Dr. Bernhard said years later: interview with Dora Bernhard, December 23, 1986, Rome.

"other women found this out": ibid.

"More and more I feel handicapped": CG to AT, November 3, 1955.

Lon said he had always considered: BC to Flannery O'Connor, March 22, 1953, *The Correspondence of Flannery O'Connor and the Brainard Cheneys*, ed. Ralph Stephens (Jackson: University Press of Mississippi, 1986), p. 5.

One owed as much to one's godchildren: CG to NTW, November 12, 1955.

Besides, it might be: CG to AT, November 3, 1955.

"The dottoressa says": CG to AT, October 27, 1955.

wrote Allen that Caroline: ibid.

"You are right in what you say": CG to AT, November 9, 1955.

"pretty far underground": ibid.

"Once, when you were very upset": CG to AT, November 13, 1955.

"Our situation is like": CG to AT, November 25, 1955.

telling him it was Caroline's: ibid.

Mother Immaculata sent word: ibid.

an offer came from the University of Kansas: CG to AT, October 14, 1955.

it would be falling: CG to AT, December 5, 1955.

"A pressure under which": ibid.

"I want to say one more thing": CG to AT, November 9, 1955.

Miss Day said that did a lot: Dorothy Day to Denver Lindley, January 30, 1956. Dorothy Day–Catholic Worker Col-

lection, Marquette University Archives.

"such a relief after all": CG to RL, n.d.

He told her they had to face: AT to CG, January 5, 1956.

"wonderful commentary": CG to AT, January 7, 1956.

"hideous" place where she was: CG to AT, January 24, 1956.

"I tell myself": CG to NWT, February 20, 1956.

She told Allen she was glad: CG to AT, January 24, 1956.

"We were born . . . in a jungle": ibid.

"I am a little vain": CG to SY, May 17, 1956.

Maritain wrote that few books: Jacques Maritain to CG, March 28, 1956.

"The poet is nourished": John Simons, "A Cunning and Curious Dramatization, *Commonweal*, April 13, 1956, pp. 54–55, quoted by CG to Jacques Maritain, April 19, 1956.

Her *Commedia*: Ashley Brown, "The Novel as Christian Comedy," in *Reality and Myth: Essays in American Literature in Honor of Richmond Croom Beatty*, ed. by William E. Walker and Robert L. Welker (Nashville: Vanderbilt University Press, 1964), p. 161.

"You are right": CG to AT, Septuagesima Sunday, 1956.

"time when we were sure": CG to AT, Quinquagesima Sunday, 1956.

It was "at Benfolly": ibid. There are those who think that Allen had an affair with Sally Wood, just as there are those who believe he also had one with Caroline's cousin Marion "Manny" Meriwether. If he did and if Caroline knew about it, she simply ignored it—and that does not seem to have been her style.

"They were mad for each other": interview with Marian Kelleher, March 19, 1984, Princeton, New Jersey.

"I am sorry if I seemed": CG to AT, April 11, 1956.

"marvelous food seemed to leap": CG to NTW, [May 1956].

"all but stuffed": CG to SY, May 17, 1956.

"I keep your letter": CG to AT, n.d.

34. Ground Beneath Her Feet, 1956–1959
339–354

"One would not have to spend": St. Ephrem's Day, 1956.

Virginia Erdman called Caroline: CG to AT, n.d.

"none of them split": CG to BC and FC, July 1956.

"ancient lilacs and syringas": CG to Flannery O'Connor, n.d.

"after another poet": CG to AB, n.d.

"a magic enclosure": CG to BC, n.d.

Sue, according to Caroline: ibid.

Allen would drive her: CG to Robert Barnett, June 8, 1959. Copy in Caroline Gordon papers, Princeton.

Allen wrote from the Princeton Club: AT to CG, August 30, [1956].

"Allen and I are separated": CG to Philip Rahv, n.d. *Partisan Review* papers, Boston University.

"He wants to go back": MW to AGW, December 17, 1956.

"I imagine you have put": CG to AT, [January 1957].

Caroline often said that they had: CG to AT, January 11, 1957.

"Man is supposed to lead": ibid.

"but I stick to one drink": CG to AT, n.d.

"the finest Catholic psychiatrist": CG to LA, n.d.

she offered to turn the house: CG to AT, n.d.

"little outburst the other night": CG to AT, January 27, 1957.

She asked Allen to return: CG to AT, [early June 1957].

"lilacs, apple trees, peach trees": ibid.

"I find that the best way to prepare": CG to FC, St. Teresa's Day, 1957.

she looked forward: ibid.

"It is barely possible": Louis D. Rubin, Jr., "A Novelist Discusses the Craft of Novel Writing," Baltimore *Sun*, November 6, 1957.

"I see my own life now": CG to AT, November 13, 1957.

Allen told Nancy: interview with NTW, March 25, 1984.

Fannie Cheney remembers: telephone interview with FC, February 2, 1987.

"I am sorry I marred": CG to BC, n.d.

"In my long and misspent life": CG to FC, n.d.

To Allen she wrote: CG to AT, Saturday after the Assumption, [1958].

"The postulancy lasts a year": CG to AT, St. George's Day, 1958.

Again she asked Allen: CG to AT, n.d.

"It was stupid of me about the bills": ibid.

"get organized and live at Sabine Close": January 11, 1958.

"the young men have the same expression": CG to AT, Holy Thursday, 1958.

"so much like me": ibid.

"You *have* emerged": CG to AT, March, [1958].

"He went up to Assumption": CG to BC, Feast of St. Francis Caracciolo, 1958.

She said her hold: CG to AT, Feast of St. Paul of the Cross, 1958.

"Allen has been through": CG to MVD, May 9, 1958.

"Oh, no!" screamed Caroline: interview with WD, April 15, 1985; SWK to Robert Barnett, June 14, 1959.

"Your discourtesy in failing": CG to AT, August 13, 1958.

Allen told her: AT to CG, August 19, 1958.

"My opinion of Allen": CG to FC, n.d.

"The letter from Caroline": Flannery O'Connor to BC and FC, December 2, 1958, *Correspondence of O'Connor and the Cheneys*, p. 80.

"We had our first quarrel": CG to AT, first Sunday in Advent, [1958].

She told her lawyer: CG to Robert Barnett, December 5, 1958. Copy in Caroline Gordon papers, Princeton.

"I have consulted several priests": CG to AT, First Sunday in Advent, [1958].

"I am hanging on to my job": ibid.

"had to do all of Allen's": CG to FC, n.d.

"a Dane with eyes like blue marbles": ibid.

She wrote Allen: CG to AT, December 12, 1958.

"I feel as if I could": CG to Marion (Manny) Meriwether, March 30, 1959. Caroline Gordon papers, Princeton.

"I said to myself": BC to Flannery O'Connor, May 24, 1959, *Correspondence of O'Connor and the Cheneys*, p. 87.

"I have finally found": CG to Father Lynch, n.d. Draft in Caroline Gordon papers, Princeton.

Lowell reported that Allen fancied: CG to Dr. Lolli, n.d. Draft in Caroline Gordon papers, Princeton.

"eight pages of 'The Narrow Heart' ": CG referred to her novel-in-progress sometimes as "The Narrow Heart," more often as "A Narrow Heart." It is this latter title that appears on the unfinished novel manuscript in her papers at the Princeton University Library. This was also the title of her autobiographical essay that appeared in *The Transatlantic Review* in 1960.

"helped to create evil": CG to Robert Barnett, May 23, 1959. Copy in Caroline Gordon papers, Princeton.

He agreed with Father McCoy: CG to Robert Barnett, May 23, 1959. Copy in Caroline Gordon papers, Princeton.

She told Allen that the minute: CG to AT, n.d.

"The gossip is that you": ibid.

Ashley Brown, who: Flannery O'Connor to BC and FC, August 5, 1959, *Correspondence of O'Connor and the Cheneys*, p. 94.

Allen told Léonie: AT to LA, May 29, 1959.

"Allen will not like": CG to Robert Barnett, June 10, 1959. Copy in Caroline Gordon papers, Princeton.

"This sounds bold": CG to HAM, May 12, 1959.

"Cream of sorrel soup": CG to FC, St. Bruno's Day, 1959.

"The divorce was the tragedy": interview with Walker Percy, 1985.

35. Princeton, Dallas, San Cristóbal, 1959–1981
355–369

"She always does better": RS to CG, February 6, 1972.

He told her he was saving: AT to CG, February 1, 1964.

In 1965 he wrote her: AT to CG, October 21, 1965.

"You are the only editor": CG to AT, June 18, 1970.

"Honey, it was all my fault": interview with Sally Fitzgerald, July 23, 1984.

When Ashley Brown: interview with AB, November 28, 1983.

"mad about it": CG to LA, June 27, 1961.

and told Flannery: Flannery O'Connor to BC and FC, July 23, 1961, *Correspondence of O'Connor and the Cheneys*, p. 138.

"Unanswered because I don't": Caroline Gordon papers, Princeton.

Ashley Brown told her: CG to AB, June 7, 1961.

In 1960, in another application: application to John Simon Guggenheim Foundation, October 17, 1960. Foundation files.

"kept up his Greek": CG to AB, May 22, 1962.

"as Christian a hero": CG to AB, September 15, 1961.

She told Radcliffe Squires: CG to RS, n.d.

One of her favorite theories: Dennis O'Brien to AW, January 2, 1985.

"crazy about Indiana": CG to AB, November 5, 1963.

Catholic students were far superior: CG to AB, April 30, 1964.

Such programs were not only: ibid.

"that all this computerization": CG to Morris Gordon, June 12, 1967. Princeton.

"Darling, as you get older": CG to MMC, December 7, 1964.

"except that I was a Platonist": interview with Cary Peebles, October 18, 1983.

"At first glance": CG to Stewart Richardson, September 23, 1970. Princeton.

"unifying and meaningful": JHW to CG, March 26, 1972.

She became convinced: CG to Donald Jackson, August 23, 1977.

For some time: Letters between Caroline and Robert Giroux are in the Caroline Gordon papers at Princeton, and letters between Caroline and Scribner's are in the Scribner Deposit at Princeton.

"He . . . was one": CG to AB, October 15, 1972.

Thanks to Allen's refusal: CG to NWT, January 18, 1971.

"a foretaste of heavenly bliss": CG to Chauncey Stillman, January 29, 1971. Princeton.

"The worship of mediocrity": CG to Robert Giroux, January 24, 1974. Copy in Caroline Gordon papers, Princeton.

"cast the kind of shadows": CG to Deane Mowrer, June 21, 1973.

"in a wraparound skirt": Jim Pfaff to AW, April 24, 1985.

"Bible-educated boys": CG to David McDowell, December 23, 1974.

At one time the entire campus: interview with Louise Cowan, October 6, 1984.

"What I'm teaching you": ibid.

"We didn't mind the trouble": ibid.

"She knew so much": telephone interview with Bruce Ligon, October 27, 1984.

"She was irascible": ibid.

"She was nice": interview with Mary Mumbach, October 6, 1984, Nashua, New Hampshire.

"The funny thing": interview with Louise Cowan, October 6, 1984.

One Dallas millionaire: CG to NTW, December 10, 1973.

"She said she got to know": interview with Mary Mumbach, October 6, 1984.

"I hate Thomas Jefferson's guts": CG to SWK, February 19, 1976.

"I am well past eighty": CG to NTW, April 29, 1977.

"What good times": CG to SWK, July 25, 1980.

"She was a strong personality": interview with Jean de Vos, March 27, 1984, San Cristóbal de las Casas, Mexico.

"This mass is for": NTW to FC, March 31, 1979.

"I spoke half an hour": interview with Jean de Vos, March 27, 1984.

"There was a look of delight": interview with NTW, March 25, 1984.

Published Works
by Caroline Gordon

NOVELS
Penhally (1931)
Aleck Maury, Sportsman (1934)
 Reissued with an afterword in 1980. Published in Great Britain
 as *The Pastimes of Aleck Maury: The Life of a True Sportsman.*
None Shall Look Back (1937)
The Garden of Adonis (1937)
Green Centuries (1941)
The Women on the Porch (1944)
The Strange Children (1951)
The Malefactors (1956)
The Glory of Hera (1972)

SHORT STORY COLLECTIONS
The Forest of the South (1945)
Old Red and Other Stories (1963)
The Collected Stories of Caroline Gordon (1981)

OTHER BOOKS
The House of Fiction: An Anthology of the Short Story (1950)
 With Allen Tate. Revised edition, 1960.
How to Read a Novel (1957)
A Good Soldier: A Key to the Novels of Ford Madox Ford (1957)

INDEX

Kenyon College, 23, 24, 264, 267, 268, 273, 282
Kenyon Review, The, 199, 213, 302
Kirby-Smith, Betty, 228, 231
Kirby-Smith, General Edmund, 226
Kirby-Smith, Henry, 231, 234
Kirby-Smith, Mary Phillips, 234, 243
Kirkland, James H., 23, 24
Kirstein, Lincoln, 92, 96, 143
Knath, Karl, 220
Knepes, Gyorgy, 288
Knickerbocker, W. S., 102
Koch, Vivienne, 244, 245, 263, 335
Kubie, Lawrence, 252–54
Ku Klux Klan, 168

Lafayette, Marquis de, 82
Lambert, Grace, 191, 214, 274, 331, 350, 357
Lambert, Jerry, 191, 214, 331, 343
Lanier, Chink, 102, 113, 114, 134
Lanier, Lyle, 18, 101, 102, 113, 114, 134
Lanngjkear, Erik, 350, 353
"Last Day in the Field, The" (Gordon), 142
Lee, Edwy, 289, 291, 292
Lee, Robert E., 71, 85, 95, 100, 102–4, 106, 107, 115, 116, 132–33, 181, 280
Leger, Alexis [pseud. St.-John Perse], 224, 227
L'Engle, Madeleine, 251
Levi, Julian, 346
Lewis, Janet (Mrs. Yvor Winters), 71, 96, 360
Lewis, Meriwether, 75
Lewis, R. W. B., 317
Lewis, Sinclair, 149, 239
Lewis, Wyndham, 55, 227
Library of Congress, 121, 214, 217, 219, 221, 224
Lindbergh, Charles A., 191
Lindley, Denver, 300, 323, 333, 359
Loeb, Harold, 56, 84
Lolli, Giorgio, 343, 345, 346
"Long Day, The" (Gordon), 71, 80, 91
Louisiana State University, 25, 193, 205

Lovat Dickson, 141
Lowell, James Russell, 19, 21
Lowell, Robert, 18–21, 23, 24, 27, 171, 190, 192–93, 204, 206–9, 213, 214, 216, 217, 227, 230, 232–34, 237, 240–42, 250, 253, 263, 267–68, 273, 284, 293, 296, 320, 347, 351, 352, 355
Lubbock, Percy, 251, 344
Luce, Claire Boothe, 257
Lyric, The, 27
Lytle, Andrew, 16–19, 24, 56, 61, 64, 85, 86, 93, 100–102, 107–9, 114, 120, 124, 129–30, 134, 135, 144–47, 149, 150, 152–55, 157, 158, 161–63, 166, 168, 170, 175, 179, 183, 185, 186, 191, 194–95, 199–201, 203, 205, 207, 211–12, 240, 258, 260, 271, 273, 275, 284, 321, 322, 342, 353, 369
Lytle, Edna Barker, 179, 185, 186, 194, 198–201, 207, 211, 212, 260
Lytle, Polly, 157, 162

Mabry, Tommy, 248, 257, 272, 283, 295, 297, 301, 348
MacLaren, Mrs. Malcolm, 237
MacLeish, Archibald, 214
MacNeice, Louis, 290, 291
Malefactors, The (Gordon), 280, 321, 323, 333, 335–36, 358, 359
Mann, Thomas, 188
Mariano, Nicky, 308
Maritain, Jacques, 227, 260, 270–71, 278, 293, 297, 335–36, 343, 353, 369
Maritain, Raissa, 270, 274, 278
Mathews, Jackson, 298, 305
Mathews, Marthiel, 298, 305
Mauriac, François, 297
Maurin, Peter, 333, 336
Maxfield, Mary, 37, 41
Mayo, Alida, 236, 239, 246
McCarthy, Abigail, 290, 295
McCarthy, Eugene, 290, 295
McCarthy, Mary, 181, 182, 202, 204, 308
McCormick, Isabella Gardner, 351–53, 356
McCoy, Horace, 351, 352